Olympic Track & Field

Complete men's
and women's Olympic
track and field,
results, 1896-1976,
plus a wealth of
other Olympic
esoterica.

From the Editors of Track & Field News

Published by Tafnews Press
Book Division of Track & Field News, Inc.
Box 296, Los Altos, California 94022 USA

ISBN 0-911520-82-1

Printed in the United States of America

This book was prepared by the Senior Editors of *Track & Field News,* under the guidance of Bert Nelson. The bulk of the historical material was prepared by European Editor Roberto L. Quercetani and Editor Emeritus Don Potts and originally saw print in their 1952-1968 editions of *The ATFS Olympic Handbook.* This material has been rewritten in places where new data has come to light.

Managing Editor Garry Hill and Features Editor Jon Hendershott provided the coverage of the last three Games, while Nelson is the calculating figure behind the wealth of statistical analysis which closes the book.

Editor-In-Chief: Bert Nelson
Production Coordinator: Garry Hill
Production Staff: Grace Light, Debra Sims, Alicia Phillips.

Contents

The Founding Father

On Wednesday, April 6, 1896, King George of Greece addressed the capacity crowd of 45,000 which jammed the Stadium of Herodis in Athens and blackened the surrounding hills: "I hereby proclaim the opening of the First International Olympic Games."

With that royal proclamation, the dream of a little French nobleman had come true.

Pierre de Coubertin was born the first day of 1863 and was always destined for a military career. But army life did not appeal to him and he chose instead to work for the betterment of youth—specifically French youth, which had been badly defeated as soldiers in the Franco-Prussian War of 1870.

One way to do this, he felt, would be to restage the glorious athletic and cultural festivals of ancient Greece—and specifically the Olympic Games. He first proposed the idea in late 1892 and got a cool reception from his countrymen. So he took his idea to friends in other nations and received enthusiastic support. Two years later, an Olympic Congress met in Paris and decided to stage the first modern Olympics in 1896 in Athens, the capital of the homeland of the ancient Games.

Enthusiasm after the first Games ran high and de Coubertin nursed the early Games through being sideshows of World's Fairs, national bickering and international indifference. At Stockholm in 1912, the Games reached maturity and achieved the worldwide importance they enjoy today.

De Coubertin worked tirelessly to forward the Olympic movement and its ideals, serving as International Olympic Committee President from its inception in 1894 until 1925. He advised Olympic leaders until his death in 1939. He was buried in Lausanne, Switzerland, present site of IOC headquarters.

De Coubertin's philosophy of the Olympic Games, and of life itself, is perhaps best presented in his statement which eventually became the Olympic Creed:

"The important thing in the Olympic Games is not winning, but in taking part. The essential thing in life is not conquering, but in fighting well."

The Games In Brief

IN THE BEGINNING—No one knows for certain when the ancient Olympic Games were first held. The first recorded Games occurred in 776 B.C., but there is evidence the Games took place more than 10 centuries earlier. How the Games began is also unknown. Some Greek legends say the gods of the sky and the gods of the earth wrestled for supremacy of the land and the victorious gods of the earth began the Olympics to celebrate their triumph. Regardless of how they really did start, the Games were always religiously oriented. Warring factions in Greece laid down their arms and declared a truce at the time of the Games so everyone could travel to the Games in safety. The Games were held every four years in the city of Olympia and the four-year period which culminated with the celebration of the Games was called an "Olympiad," as it is today. The only event on the program for centuries was a one-stade race (about 200 yards). The first known champion was a young cook, Coroebus of Elis, and the ancient Games are dated from his victory. Gradually longer races and such sports as wrestling, boxing, chariot-racing and a pentathlon were added. The Games became so popular and prestigious that cheating eventually became common, professionalism flourished and events were fixed. In 394 A.D., Roman emperor Theodosius, a Christian opposed to pagan spectacles, ordered the Games abolished. By the middle of the fourth century the Games were dead. They stayed that way for 1502 years.

ATHENS 1896—Through the efforts of young French nobleman Baron Pierre de Coubertin the Olympics were reborn, fittingly in the home of the ancient Games. Many ancient venues were utilized, including the Stadium of Herodis. The stadium was refurbished for the Games with a 333.333 meter track, but the turns were very sharp and held back times. Races were also run counterclockwise. Most foreign athletes came to Athens on their own and in no way was it a true world championship. American club athletes dominated in track, double victories going to Thomas Burke (100, 400), Ellery Clark (HJ, LJ) and Robert Garrett (SP, DT). Australian Edwin Flack won the 800 and 1500. American James B. Connolly became the first champion of the modern Olympics when he won the triple jump on opening day. Glory for Greece was saved in the last event, the marathon, when shepherd Spiridon Louis loped to an emotional victory.

PARIS 1900—This edition became "Olympic" only at the last minute. The athletic program originally was advertised merely as another international aspect of the World's Fair. But when French officials turned for technical advice to Baron Pierre de Coubertin, he agreed to help only if the Games would be "Olympic." Some athletes learned this only after reading the notation on the back of their medals. The quality of entrants was far superior to the previous Games, but the facilities were poor at best—the "track" was a 500-meter oval laid out on a horse race track. American Alvin Kraenzlein gained Olympic immortality by winning four gold medals: the 60 meters, 110 meter high and 200 meter low

hurdles and long jump. Ray Ewry won the first two of 10 gold medals in the standing jumps and John J. Flanagan won the first of three consecutive hammer titles. Between them, the US and Great Britain won 20 of 22 events.

ST. LOUIS 1904—Like Paris, these Games were held in conjunction with a World's Fair. And like Paris, they played distinct second fiddle. They did not, in fact, even approximate a world championship as few top-flight foreign entrants made the trip to America. The Games could best be called an American club championship. Americans won 21 of 22 events staged, the lone foreign victor being Canadian Etienne Desmarteau in the 56-lb. weight throw. Triple winners were the stars, including Archie Hahn (60, 100, 200), Harry Hillman (400, 200 lows, 400 hurdles) and spring-legged Ray Ewry (standing HJ, LJ, TJ).

LONDON 1908—The bickering between the US and Britain made almost as many headlines as the athletics at this first truly representative Olympics. More than 1500 athletes from 19 nations competed, but the Games almost became a replay of the Revolutionary War as the British and Americans seemingly argued about everything. Things came to a head in the 400 when American winner J.C. Carpenter was disqualified and the other Americans withdrew in protest. That left Briton Wyndham Halswell to "win" a walk-over for his gold medal. The weather was often wet, but during the marathon the heat and humidity helped make history. Italian candymaker Dorando Pietri entered the Olympic stadium first but made a wrong turn, staggered and collapsed. Officials debated whether to help him, as that would disqualify him. Pietri finally wobbled across the finish as American Johnny Hayes entered the stadium. The Italian was eventually disqualified and Hayes declared the winner. Mel Shepperd won the 800 and 1500, Ray Ewry won standing jump golds 9 and 10, Martin Sheridan won the regular and "classic" discus throws and Erik Lemming took both styles in the javelin.

STOCKHOLM 1912—Those critics who thought the Games should be ended after the squabble-plagued London festival were quieted by the highly-successful Stockholm Olympics, which cemented international friendship through sports stronger than ever. Technical innovations included running the 400 in lanes all the way, timing most, if not all, non-winning places and timing in tenths. A pair of champions were the heroes of Stockholm: American Indian Jim Thorpe won both the decathlon and pentathlon, and Hannes Kolehmainen won the 5000, 10,000 and cross country titles. That was the beginning of the domination of the distances by tiny Finland. Thorpe, of course, was later forced to return his medals when it was revealed he played semi-professional baseball one summer. One of the classic Olympics stories is his reply to the compliment of the Swedish king that Thorpe was the greatest athlete in the world: "Thanks, king." American teenager Ted Meredith set a world record in winning the 800 and Ralph Craig won both sprints.

BERLIN 1916—Games canceled due to World War I.

ANTWERP 1920—The United States, which had been the preeminent nation in the Olympics, received a shock at Antwerp as Sweden and Finland asserted their running strength. Charley Paddock (100), Allen Woodring (200) and Frank Loomis

(400 hurdles) were the only US track victors. Finland flexed her muscles on the field (winning the TJ, SP, DT, JT and pentathlon) as well as the track. The newly-laid 400 meter track wasn't fast, and heavy rains didn't help, but neither stopped a young Finn named Paavo Nurmi, who chugged to wins in the 10,000 and cross country. Double distance champ Hannes Kolehmainen returned to win the marathon. Briton Albert Hill won both the 800 and 1500. The Games themselves were plagued by confusion in war-torn Belgium. The stadium, capacity 30,000, was never full until officials opened the gates to school-children—and eventually the general public—free of charge.

PARIS 1924—These should have been named the "Nurmi Games." Originally scheduled for Amsterdam, they were switched to Paris, where they were held in near-chaos in 1900. But this time, the Games were well-run and crowds of 60,000 per day in *Stade Colombes* were common. And what a show they saw from the expressionless Nurmi, the running machine in the blue of Finland. His greatest feat was in winning the 1500 in Olympic record time and coming back less than an hour later to do the same in the 5000. He also won the individual 10,000-meter cross country and 3000-meter team runs, and was a member of Finland's victorious teams. Until 1972, no athlete in any sport won more gold medals in one Games than Nurmi's six. Save for Jackson Scholz's 200 win, the US was shut out in the flat track races. Dan Kinsey and Morgan Taylor won respective hurdle victories. Bud Houser won the shot and discus, while Harold Osborn won a historic double of the open high jump and decathlon. No athlete since has won an open event and the decathlon in the same Games.

AMSTERDAM 1928—The domination of the Games built by the US during the 30-plus years of their existence came crashing down in Amsterdam. The US claimed just one of 10 individual running and hurdling events, that being the 400 by Ray Barbuti. Otherwise, it was upsets and more upsets. Unheralded Canadian schoolboy Percy Williams took both sprints, veteran Douglas Lowe of Britain won the 800 and Finland won every distance race longer than two laps. The US saved some face by winning both relays, equaling the world 400 record and setting a new one in the 1600. Things went a bit better on the field, as John Kuck won the shot in a world record and second-placer Herm Brix also bettered the former mark. Bud Houser retained his discus title and Sabin Carr (PV), Bob King (HJ), and Ed Hamm (LJ) were other winners. Women appeared in the Games for the first time (any woman even caught at the site of the ancient Games was put to death!) and the US got its first Olympic winner in 100 champ Elizabeth Robinson. The track was 400 meters in length, which became the standard size for the Games.

LOS ANGELES 1932—The world was in the grip of the biggest economic depression in history in 1932. That, and the great distance of California from Europe, held Olympic participation down somewhat. But the 1427 athletes from 37 countries were treated to the finest weather and some of the best facilities yet. The track was probably the best so far in the Games and the Coliseum had 86,443 on one day of track and crowds averaged over 60,000. The fast track was partly responsible for the toppling of Olympic records in all but three of 22 events with seven global standards being set. Italian Luigi Beccali (1500), Pole Janusz

Kusocinski (10,000) and Argentinian Juan Carlos Zabala (marathon) broke the Finnish distance stranglehold and scored first-ever wins for their nations. Finn Lauri Lehtinen edged American Ralph Hill in a tight 5000 finish marred by charges, later rejected, of interference. Eddie Tolan took both sprints, as the US won 11 events to three for Finland. The heroine of the Games was US schoolgirl Babe Didrikson, who won the 80 meter hurdles and javelin and high jumped to second.

BERLIN 1936—The Olympics, and world track, had a new hero after Berlin: Jesse Owens. The young American joined Paavo Nurmi as one of the immortals of the Olympics with four victories (100, 200, LJ, 400 relay). Nazi overtones marred the atmosphere of the Games, but Owens went a long way toward combatting prejudicial feelings both with his friendly, outgoing personality and his stunning performance. These Games were the most competitive and best-organized yet. The Germans spent $30 million to build a stadium to seat 100,000. A record-breaking 49 nations sent 3741 male athletes, who were housed in a handsome 134-acre Olympic Village. The carrying of the Olympic Torch from Greece was introduced, as was recording of every result for every athlete. And there was plenty to record as Jack Lovelock of New Zealand outdueled American Glenn Cunningham in a world record 1500, the Finns returned to distance dominance. Americans won three of four jumps, but Germans took three of four throws.

TOKYO and HELSINKI 1940 and LONDON 1944—Canceled due to World War II.

LONDON 1948—London did a hurry-up job of staging the '48 Games amid the ravages of war. For the most part, the British utilized existing facilities, including 83,000-seat Wembley Stadium. A total of 59 countries responded to the return of peace and entered 4030 men (who were quartered in an army camp) and 438 women (housed in college dormitories). Ten different nations, more than ever before, contributed winners with the US winning 11 and Sweden five as Finland was shut out of the distances. The wet weather during the Games couldn't hold back Holland's "Marvellous Mama," housewife Fanny Blankers-Koen, who won an unprecedented four gold medals (100, 200, 80 hurdles, 400R). Young American Bob Mathias (age 17) became the youngest Olympic champion in history with his decathlon victory. Upsets were the order of the Games, as hurdler Harrison Dillard won the 100, Jamaica produced her first stars in Arthur Wint and Herb McKenley and Emil Zatopek of Czechoslovakia won the 10,000 in his agonized style, beginning his domination of the distances which lasted for nearly the next decade.

HELSINKI 1952—Tiny Finland, which contributed so much luster to the rolls of Olympic championships, got its chance to stage the Games and proved to the world that size isn't necessary to stage an Olympics of the first order. Everyone was thrilled as Paavo Nurmi carried the torch into the stadium and passed it to Hannes Kolehmainen, who lit the torch. Technical conduct of the Games was virtually perfect and the track remained fast despite intermittent rains. Nearly 5000 athletes from 69 countries competed and the Iron Curtain countries established their own Olympic Village as the USSR competed for the first time. This was the Olympics of the Zatopeks—Emil won a stunning distance triple of the 5000, 10,000 and marathon and wife Dana won the women's javelin. Bob Mathias, now a mature 21,

retained his decathlon title with a world record 7887 total. Horace Ashenfelter won a shocking victory with a world record run in the steeplechase. Mal Whitfield took his second 800 title, Harrison Dillard finally won the highs and Cy Young became the only American ever to win the javelin as the US won 14 gold medals. Australian Marjorie Jackson won both women's sprints.

MELBOURNE 1956—The first -ever Games held in the Southern Hemisphere had to be staged in December for the best weather. Still, 67 nations sent 3174 athletes. Political tension was evident following trouble in Hungary and the Suez. Three double champions vied for center stage: American Bobby Morrow took both sprints and anchored the US 400 relay team to a world record, Soviet Vladimir Kuts heralded the arrival of the USSR as a major power with machine-like victories in the 5000 and 10,000 and Betty Cuthbert became Australia's heroine with a sprint double and relay victory. Second-time winners included Bob Richards (PV), Parry O'Brien (SP) and Adhemar da Silva (TJ), while young Al Oerter won his first discus title and Lee Calhoun his first in the highs. Egil Danielsen of Norway won the javelin with a world record and American Hal Connolly won the hammer—and the heart of women's discus champ Olga Fikotova whom he married after the Games. Emil Zatopek ran sixth in the marathon as long-time rival Alain Mimoun finally won one from the great Czech.

ROME 1960—The ancient wonders of Rome provided a glittering background as 5396 athletes from 84 nations competed in venues ranging from basketball in the ultramodern *Palazetto de Pier Luigi Nervi* to wrestling in the ancient and crumbling *Basilica de Maxentius.* Track was held in a glittering marble stadium, which was rivaled by the brightness of US sprinter Wilma Rudolph. Wondrous Wilma (so named because she was crippled until age six) won both sprints and anchored the winning US 400 relay team. The US men suffered upsets in the sprints and high jump, but Lee Calhoun and Glenn Davis defended their hurdles titles and Al Oerter took discus gold No. 2. Unheralded Peter Snell won the 800 and masterful Herb Elliott took the 1500 with a world record. Unknown Abebe Bikila trod through the marathon in bare feet to victory, while American Rafer Johnson won a tense decathlon battle with close friend C.K. Yang. US veteran Otis Davis edged Carl Kaufmann in a world record 400, while Ralph Boston took the long jump.

TOKYO 1964—Japan spent lavishly and organized meticulously for the first Games to be held in Asia. The world's largest city welcomed 5558 athletes from 94 nations. The US regained a large measure of the prestige it lost in Rome as only peerless Peter Snell with a superb 800-1500 double, and Belgian steepler Gaston Roelants could dent American domination on the track. The US even won the 5000 and 10,000. The emotional highlight of track was Billy Mills's frenzied sprint to a stunning 10,000 upset. Both US relay teams set world records. Al Oerter kept rolling along with his third discus win, while Jozef Schmidt made it a pair in the triple jump. Abebe Bikila won his second marathon, this time wearing shoes. Betty Cuthbert made a triumphant return as she won the 400, Iolanda Balas defended her high jump title and Tamara Press won both the shot and discus while sister Irina took the pentathlon.

MEXICO CITY 1968—African distance runners exploded into prominence in the first Games held in Latin America and at altitude (more than 7300 feet). Competition was staged in architecturally-sparkling facilities and amid a fiesta atmosphere. The outstanding single performance was Bob Beamon's mind-boggling 29-2½ long jump, track's greatest performance ever. Close behind were Viktor Saneyev's last-jump win in the triple, Dave Hemery's shocking intermediates win and swift sprints by Tommie Smith, Jim Hines and Lee Evans. No less superb were the African distance runners. Kenyans Kip Keino, Naftali Temu and unknown Amos Biwott won golds (Keino and Temu also won a silver and bronze), and Mohamed Gamoudi (Tunisia) and Mamo Wolde (Ethiopia) each won a gold and one other. Of 12 medals available in the steeple through the marathon, Africans won nine. Al Oerter turned in an unprecedented fourth discus victory, more than any other champion. Wyomia Tyus became the first person to successfully defend a 100 crown while Maureen Caird, only 17, won the 80 meter hurdles.

MUNICH 1972—The Games returned to Germany after a 36-year absence and the hosts staged the most lavish, technically-competent festival yet, featuring fully automatic timing and measuring, superb facilities and an ultramodern Olympic Park. A trio of double-champions starred: Soviet Valeriy Borzov and East Germany's Renate Stecher in the sprints and Finnish distance runner Lasse Viren. The latter set a world record in winning the 10,000 despite a jarring mid-race fall. Rod Milburn (110H), John Akii-Bua (400H), Nikolay Avilov (decathlon), Lyudmila Bragina (1500) and Mary Peters (pentathlon) all struck gold with world records, as did relay teams from the US (men's 400), West Germany (women's 400) and East Germany (women's 1600). Frank Shorter became the first American to win the marathon in 64 years, Czech Ludvik Danek completed a set of discus medals with a gold and Heide Rosendahl was a heroine to her countrymen with a LJ victory, pentathlon 2nd and a victorious 400 relay anchor ahead of Stecher. Off the track, the Games were terribly affected by the murder of 11 Israeli athletes and coaches by Arab terrorists.

MONTREAL 1976—The first Olympics held in the North America in 44 years were a Games of "records"—most expensive ever (more than $1 billion), 5 men's world marks and 4 women's plus an unofficial best in the walk, 5 men's Olympic records (plus one tie) and 6 women's. The big stars were three doublers who turned in first-ever feats: Alberto Juantorena, first to win the 400 and 800 (world record); Lasse Viren, first to successfully defend titles at 5000 and 10,000; and Tatyana Kazankina, first woman ever to win both the 800 (world record) and 1500. East Germany's powerful women's team won all the field events but the shot, both relays, and the 200 and hurdles. The US won the most golds with 6 (4 individual and 2 relay), while the Soviet hammer throwers scored the first 1-2-3 sweep since '68. East Germany's pentathletes took all three medals, only the second women's sweep in Olympic history. Besides Juantorena and Kazankina, world marks fell to Anders Garderud (steeple), Edwin Moses (400H), Miklos Nemeth (JT), Bruce Jenner (decathlon), Annegret Richter (100), Irena Szewinska (400—her 7th medal in 5 events spanning 4 Olympics) and the East German 1600 relayers.

The Greatest

T&FN's selectors were unable to name the single most outstanding athlete of the Olympics. The voting resulted in a tie between Paavo Nurmi (right) and Al Oerter. Nurmi was a star in the Olympics of 1920, 1924 and 1928. He won six golds in individual events (1500, 5000, 10,000 and cross country), three in team events and three silvers. Oerter is the only four-time winner of an event, capturing the discus title in 1956, 1960, 1964 and 1968.

The No. 1s By Games

1896   *Robert Garrett* (US), first of the double winners. SP 36-9¾; DT 95-7.

1900   *Alvin Kraenzlein* (US), winner of 60, 7.0; 110H, 15.4; 200H, 25.4; LJ, 23-7.

1904   *James Lightbody* (US) winner of 800 in OR 1:56.0 and 1500 in WR 4:05.4. Also won 2500m steeplechase.

1908   *Mel Sheppard* (US), Olympic record in 1500 (4:03.4) and WR in 800 (1:52.8).

1912   *Jim Thorpe* (US), winner of decathlon and pentathlon, =4th in HJ (6-1¾).

1920   *Albert Hill* (GB), third winner of the popular 800-1500 double, 1:53.4 4:01.8.

1924   *Paavo Nurmi* (Finland), with one of the top performances ever. Five gold medals—1500 (3:53.6), 5000 (14:31.2), cross country and two teams.

1928   *Paavo Nurmi* (Finland), OR in 10,000 (30:18.8), 2nd in 5000 and steeple.

1932   *Eddie Tolan* (US), firsts in both sprints, 10.3 WR and 21.2 OR.

1936   *Jesse Owens* (US), four golds. 100 in 10.3w, 200 in 20.7 OR, long jump in 26-5¼w, and 400 relay (leadoff) in 39.8 WR.

1948   *Mal Whitfield* (US), first 800 (1:49.2 OR), 3rd 400 (46.9), 1st 1600 relay.

1952   *Emil Zatopek* (Czechoslovakia), first long-distance doubler and he made it a triple: 5k (14:06.6 OR), 10k (29:17.0 OR) marathon (2:23:03 OR).

1956   *Vladimir Kuts* (USSR), 5000 in 13:39.6 OR and 10,000 in 28:45.6 OR.

1960   *Herb Elliott* (Australia), winner of 1500 in WR 3:35.6.

1964   *Peter Snell* (New Zealand), double winner (1:45.1 OR, 3:38.1).

1968   *Bob Beamon* (US), with perhaps the greatest performance ever—29-2½ LJ.

1972   *Lasse Viren* (Finland), two wins, 5000 in 13:26.4 OR and 10,000 in 27:38.4 WR.

1976   *Alberto Juantorena* (Cuba), the first 400/800 double (44.26/1:43.5 WR).

1928   *Elizabeth Robinson* (US), first in 100 in WR 12.2, second in relay.

1932   *Babe Didrikson* (US) won 80H (11.7 WR); JT (153-5 OR); 2nd HJ (5-5 WR).

1936   *Helen Stephens* (US), 100 in 11.5w, first in relay.

1948   *Fanny Blankers-Koen* (Holland), the only four-event winner: 100 in 11.9, 200 in 24.4, 80H in 11.2 OR, and anchor leg in relay, 47.5.

1952   *Marjorie Jackson* (Australia), first in 100 in 11.5 WR, 200 in 23.7.

1956   *Betty Cuthbert* (Australia), winner of 100 in 11.5, 200 in 23.4, 400R.

1960   *Wilma Rudolph* (US), winner of 100 in 11.0w, 200 in 24.0, 400R.

1964   *Mary Rand* (GB), WR in LJ, 22-2¼; 2nd in pentathlon; 3rd in 400R.

1968   *Wyomia Tyus* (US), 100 in WR 11.0; 400R.

1972   *Heide Rosendahl* (WG), won LJ (22-3), 2nd pentathlon, 1st 400R.

1976   *Tatyana Kazankina* (SU), 800/1500 double in 1:54.9 WR/4:05.5.

Olympic Participation

| | ALL SPORTS | | | | TRACK & FIELD | | | | | | |
| | Nations | Athletes | | | Nations | | | | Athletes | | |
		M	W	Tot	M	W	Tot		M	W	Tot
1896	13	311	--	311	10	—	10		59	--	59
1900	22	1319	11	1330	16	—	16		127	--	127
1904	12	617	8	625	9	—	9		132	--	132
1908	22	1999	36	2035	20	—	20		455	--	455
1912	28	2490	57	2547	26	--	26		556	--	556
1920	29	2543	64	2607	25	--	25		564	--	564
1924	44	2956	136	3092	40	--	40		652	--	652
1928	46	2724	290	3014	40	18	58		625	101	726
1932	37	1281	127	1408	34	11	45		330	55	385
1936	49	3738	328	4066	43	20	63		675	98	773
1948	59	3714	385	4099	53	27	80		600	140	740
1952	69	4407	518	4925	57	37	94		773	184	957
1956	67	2813	371	3184	59	27	86		570	148	718
1960	84	4738	610	5348	73	33	106		808	204	1012
1964	94	4457	683	5140	80	41	121		779	237	1016
1968	112	4750	781	5531	92	41	133		780	239	1019
1972	122	6068	1063	7131	104	56	160		1184	415	1599
1976	93	4915	1274	6189	78	48	126		713	326	1039
Totals		55,838		62,580					12,530		10,383
			6742							2147	

WOMEN'S TRACK & FIELD EVENTS

	100 / 200	400 / 800	1500 / H	4x100 / 4x400	HJ	LJ	SP	DT	JT	Pent	Total
1928	X	X (800)		X (4x100)	X			X			5
1932	X		X (H)	X (4x100)	X			X	X		6
1936	X		X (H)	X (4x100)	X			X	X		6
1948	X X		X (H)	X (4x100)	X	X	X	X	X		9
1952	X X		X (H)	X (4x100)	X	X	X	X	X		9
1956	X X		X (H)	X (4x100)	X	X	X	X	X		9
1960	X X	X (800)	X (H)	X (4x100)	X	X	X	X	X		10
1964	X X	X X	X (H)	X (4x100)	X	X	X	X	X	X	12
1968	X X	X X	X (H)	X (4x100)	X	X	X	X	X	X	12
1972	X X	X X	X X	X X	X	X	X	X	X	X	14
1976	X X	X X	X X	X X	X	X	X	X	X	X	14
1980*	X X	X X	X X	X X	X	X	X	X	X	X	14

The hurdles switched from 80m to 100m in 1972. No women's events have been discontinued.

*At this writing, there is strong sentiment in many quarters for the addition of the 3000m and 400H (plus less general support for the addition of a marathon).

MEN'S TRACK & FIELD EVENTS

Year	100	200	400	800	1500	St	5K	10K	Mar	Walks	HH	IH	4x100	4x400	HJ	PV	LJ	TJ	SP	DT	HT	JT	Dec	Other	Total
1896	X		X	X	X				X		X				X	X	X	X	X	X					12
1900	X	X	X	X	X	1,2			X		X	X			X	X	X	X	X	X	X			8,10,18,22,23,24	23
1904	X	X	X	X	X	1			X		X				X	X	X	X	X	X	X		32	8,10,14,22,23,24,25	24
1908	X	X	X	X	X	3			X	4,5	X	X	31		X	X	X	X	X	X	X	X		9,19,22,23,26,27	26
1912	X	X	X	X	X		X	X	X	6	X		X	X	X	X	X	X	X	X	X	X	X	11,15,20,21,22,23,28,29,30	30
1920	X	X	X	X	X	X	X	X	X	6,7	X	X	X	X	X	X	X	X	X	X	X	X	X	12,16,20,21,25	29
1924	X	X	X	X	X	X	X	X	X	6	X	X	X	X	X	X	X	X	X	X	X	X	X	13,17,20,21	27
1928	X	X	X	X	X	X	X	X	X		X	X	X	X	X	X	X	X	X	X	X	X	X		22
1932	X	X	X	X	X	X	X	X	X	50K	X	X	X	X	X	X	X	X	X	X	X	X	X		23
1936	X	X	X	X	X	X	X	X	X	50K	X	X	X	X	X	X	X	X	X	X	X	X	X		23
1948	X	X	X	X	X	X	X	X	X	6 50K	X	X	X	X	X	X	X	X	X	X	X	X	X		24
1952	X	X	X	X	X	X	X	X	X	6 50K	X	X	X	X	X	X	X	X	X	X	X	X	X		24
1956	X	X	X	X	X	X	X	X	X	20K 50K	X	X	X	X	X	X	X	X	X	X	X	X	X		24
1960	X	X	X	X	X	X	X	X	X	20K 50K	X	X	X	X	X	X	X	X	X	X	X	X	X		24
1964	X	X	X	X	X	X	X	X	X	20K 50K	X	X	X	X	X	X	X	X	X	X	X	X	X		24
1968	X	X	X	X	X	X	X	X	X	20K 50K	X	X	X	X	X	X	X	X	X	X	X	X	X		24
1972	X	X	X	X	X	X	X	X	X	20K 50K	X	X	X	X	X	X	X	X	X	X	X	X	X		24
1976	X	X	X	X	X	X	X	X	X	20K	X	X	X	X	X	X	X	X	X	X	X	X	X		23
1980	X	X	X	X	X	X	X	X	X	20K 50K	X	X	X	X	X	X	X	X	X	X	X	X	X		24

OTHER (DISCONTINUED) EVENTS

(1) 2500m steeple; (2) 4000m steeple; (3) 3200 steeple; (4) 3500m walk; (5) 10M walk; (6) 10,000m walk; (7) 3000m walk; (8) 60m; (9) 5M; (10) 200m hurdles; (11) 12,000m cross country individual; (12) 8000m cross country individual; (13) 10,000m cross country individual; (14) 4M cross country team; (15) 12,000m cross country team; (16) 8000m cross country team; (17) 10,000m cross country team; (18) 5000m cross country team; (19) 3M team; (20) 3000m team; (21) pentathlon; (22) standing HJ; (23) standing LJ; (24) standing TJ; (25) 56lb weight; (26) ancient-style DT; (27) classical-style javelin; (28) SP both hands; (29) DT both hands; (30) JT both hands; (31) sprint medley relay: 200, 200, 400, 800; (32) All-around: 100y, mile, 880y walk, HJ, PV, LJ, SP, HT, 561lbWt.

Note: The tug-of-war was contested as part of the track & field program in 1900-04-08-12-20, but is not considered as a track & field event in this book.

NATIONS IN TRACK & FIELD

All countries competing in Olympic track and field athletics, with first year of competition and total number of Olympics participated in. * = won medal(s).

135 nations in men's track, 88 in women's track; including 85 in both. 54 nations earned medals in men's track, 27 in women's.

	Men		Women	
Afghanistan	36	2		
Algeria	72	1		
Antigua	76	1		
Argentina*	24	12	48	6
Australia*	96	18	28	11
Austria	00	16	28	10
Bahamas	56	6	72	2
Barbados	68	3	72	2
Belgium*	00	15	28	6
Belize	68	12		
Bermuda	48	3	48	3
Bohemia*	00	4		
Bolivia	72	2		
Brazil*	24	10	48	5
Bulgaria*	24	6	52	6
Burma	48	6		
Cambodia	72	1	72	1
Cameroon	64	3		
Canada*	00	17	28	11
C.Afr.R.	68	1		
Chad	64	3		
Chile*	96	14	36	7
China	32	3	36	1
Colombia	32	8	72	2
Congo	64	2		
Costa Rica	68	2	68	1
Cuba*	04	10	56	6
Czech.*	20	12	36	9
Dahomey	72	1		
Denmark*	96	17	48	6
Dominican R	64	3	76	1
E.Germany*	56	6	56	6
Ecuador	24	2		
Egypt	20	7		
Eire*	24	11	56	4
El Salvador	68	1	68	1
Estonia*	20	5		
Ethiopia*	56	5		
Fiji	56	5	76	1

	Men		Women	
Finland*	08	15	36	8
France*	96	17	28	10
Germany*	96	8	28	3
Ghana	52	5	64	3
Great Britain*	96	18	32	10
Greece*	96	18	36	3
Guatemala	52	3	52	1
Guyana	48	4	56	2
Haiti*	24	5	72	2
Holland*	08	14	28	10
Honduras	68	2		
Hong Kong	64	1		
Hungary*	96	17	28	10
Iceland*	36	9	6	1
India*	00	14	52	5
Indonesia	56	3	72	2
Iran	52	7	64	1
Iraq	48	3		
Israel	52	6	52	6
Italy*	00	16	28	10
Ivory Coast	64	4	76	1
Jamaica*	48	8	48	6
Japan*	12	13	28	9
Kenya*	56	5	68	2
Korea	48	6	48	5
Kuwait	68	3		
Latvia*	24	4	28	1
Lebanon	60	1	72	1
Lesotho	72	1		
Liberia	56	4		
Libya	68	2		
Liechtenstein	36	5	76	1
Lithuania	28	1		
Luxembourg*	12	13	48	1
Malagasy Rep	64	3		
Malawi	72	2	72	1
Malaysia	56	5	56	2
Mali	64	3	72	1
Malta	36	2		
Mexico*	24	12	32	4

Country				
Monaco	20	3		
Mongolia	64	2	68	1
Morocco*	60	4	72	1
Nepal	64	3		
Neth. Antilles	76	1		
New Guinea	76	1		
New Zealand*	20	13	28	9
Nicaragua	68	3	72	1
Nigeria	52	6	64	3
North Borneo	56	1		
North Korea	72	2		
Norway*	00	16	48	6
Pakistan	48	7		
Panama*	48	3	60	2
Paraguay	72	2		
Peru	36	4	72	2
Philippines*	24	12	56	5
Poland*	24	12	28	11
Portugal*	12	12		
Puerto Rico	48	7	76	1
Rhodesia	60	2		
Rumania*	28	9	28	8
Russia	08	2		
Saar	52	1	52	1
San Marino			76	1
Saudi Arabia	72	2		
Senegal	64	4	76	1
Sierra Leone	68	1		
Singapore	48	4	52	2
Somalia	72	1		
South Africa*	04	12	28	5
South Korea			72	1
Spain	20	9	76	1
Sri Lanka*	48	8		
Sudan	60	3		
Surinam	68	4		
Swaziland	72	1		
Sweden*	96	17	28	9
Switzerland*	08	14	52	3
Syria			72	1
Taiwan*	56	5	60	4
Tanzania	64	3		
Thailand	52	5	64	1
Togo	72	1		
Trinidad	48	7	72	1
Tunisia*	60	4		
Turkey*	12	10	48	2
Uganda*	56	5	60	4
United States*	96	18	28	11
Upper Volta	72	1		
Uruguay	48	6	48	5
U.S.S.R.*	52	7	52	7
Venezuela*	52	7	72	2
Viet Nam	52	3		
Virgin Islands	68	3	76	1
W. Germany*	52	7	52	7
West Indies*	60	1		
Yugoslavia*	12	13	36	9
Zambia	64	3	72	1

Event-By-Event Results

This section lists the results of each final (preliminaries are not carried) for every event still contested on the Olympic program, men and women. We have made these results as complete as possible, although holes do still exist. All results will not exactly jibe with those given in the official Olympic results, or with those in any other book. They represent, however, the best information available to our compilers from years of study of old books, films and photos, which have revealed errors in the original results. We feel these are the most accurate results available anywhere.

Other than in the events which have at times had "unlimited" entries (10,000, marathon, walks, decathlon/pentathlon) we have listed all known finalists.

Explanation of the introduction of each event, which will appear in a format such as this: (36. H-QF 16 July; SF 17 July; F 18 July). That means 36 people started the event; the heats and quarterfinals were on July 16, the semifinals the 17th and the final the 18th. For field events, the qualifying round is indicated by "Q."

Listed with each event are any World Records (WR) or Olympic Records (OR) altered. Records made in preliminary rounds (or in a series of a field event) are listed after the summaries for the year.

All marks are presented in "modern" notation. This means that current measurement rules (i.e., no odd centimeters in long throws) are employed. Decimals in old decathlon scores have been dropped. In 1976, odd 10ths were allowed in times for distance races.

A thorny problem still confronting all Olympic scholars is that of automatic timing. In keeping with international rules, we only list the 100ths figures for automatic timing in events through the 400. In years when automatic timing was used, we have rounded times in longer races to 10ths. This rounding was done in accordance with the rules in effect through 1978, which permitted the rounding of times through x.04 back down.

The problem arises in finding out just what was automatic, and what the specific time was. A brief history of Olympic timing: from 1896 through 1960, the Olympics were officially hand timed, but various phototiming devices also took times. In 1964 and 1968 automatic timing devices became the rule, although they had an inherent 0.05 delay (to make them "equal" to hand timing) and the results were converted and announced in 10ths. In 1972 and 1976, automatic (100th)

timing was used and announced as such.

British timing expert Bob Sparks was able to resurrect many of the old photos, thus we have been able to provide the 100th-second timing (in addition to the official 10ths) for virtually all the finals in the 1952-56-60 Games. The 1964 Games still have many holes, and 1968 also has a few omissions in the lower places.

More problems arise with 1964 and 1968, where the "hand" (10th) times no longer jibe with the 100th timing because of the 0.05 delay (e.g., Bob Hayes's 10.05 of '64 is a 10.0 instead of a 10.1; or, Ralph Doubell's 1:44.3 WR has now been re-read and found to be a 1:44.40).

Through 1968, any references we make to sprint records (WR or OR) are to the 10th-second timing then in force.

In the field events we have given the measurements in both English and metric for the first 6. The remaining places, plus all series marks, are given in meters only.

Names of countries: we have listed all countries with their current names (Sri Lanka is the old Ceylon); countries which no longer exist (Bohemia, now a part of Czechoslovakia) are listed as separate entities in the results, and in medal compilations.

Germany presents us with a different case. Germany competed as a nation from 1896 through 1936 (but not at all in 1920 and 1924). The country split politically in 1945 and did not compete in the 1948 Games. The team for 1952 came entirely from the Western sector, and we list it as such. In 1956-60-64 the "Germany" team consisted of members of both blocs. We have listed these as either West or East, and distributed the medals accordingly. A few of the relay teams in these years are mixed (in which case they are credited to Germany), although most are solely West.

In 1908 and 1912, Australia and New Zealand entered a combined team under the name "Australasia." We have separated these athletes back into their native countries.

Due to ties, disqualifications and the like, 3 medals haven't always been awarded. The differences: 400—1st only in 08 and two 3rds in 56; 110H, 1st and 2nd only in 96; 400R—1st and 2nd only in 12; HJ, two 2nds in 96 (no 3rd); PV—two 1sts, no 2nd, three 3rds in 08 and two 2nds and no 3rd in 12. In discontinued events: 5000 team—1st and 2nd only in 00; cross country team—1st and 2nd only in 04. The womens' medals have been regular.

In this book, we use the terms gold, silver and bronze interchangably with places 1-2-3, which is technically incorrect. The medals awarded in the 1896 Games were of silver and bronze.

This book does not concern itself with the Games held in Athens in 1906, which were not a part of the regular 4-year cycle, and hence are not considered as an official Olympics.

100 METERS

1896 (21. H 6 April; F 10 April): Burke ran the third heat in 11.8 (OR). Thomas Curtis (USA), winner of the second heat, withdrew from the final.

1. Thomas Burke (US)	12.0	4. Francis Lane (US)	12.6
2. Fritz Hofmann (Ger)	12.2	5. Alexandros Chalkokondilis (Gr)	12.6
3. Alajos Szokolyi (Hun)	12.2		
(Burke 11.8 OR, H))			

1900 (19. H-SF-F 14 July): Jarvis ran the third heat in 10.8 (OR), which time was equaled by Tewksbury in the second semi-final. The favorite was Duffey, the "World's Fastest Human," who had just won the British AAA 100-yard title from Jarvis and Tewksbury. In the final, he went into the lead early but at 50 meters he suddenly dropped to the ground with a strained tendon. Jarvis crossed the line first, closely pursued by Tewksbury, who edged Rowley for 2nd.

1. Frank Jarvis (US)	11.0	3. Stanley Rowley (GB)	11.2
2. Walter Tewksbury (US)	11.1	— Arthur Duffey (US)	inj, dnf
(Jarvis 10.8 OR =WR, H; Tewksbury 10.8 =OR =WR, SF)			

1904 (15. H-F 3 Sept): The only non-US entrant in this event was Bela de Mezo of Hungary. Hahn was away at the gun and was never headed. Cartmell, a slow starter, closed a bit in the last 25 meters but to no avail. A strong adverse wind prevented the winner from matching the Olympic record.

1. Archie Hahn (US)	11.0	4. Fay Moulton (US)	
2. Nate Cartmell (US)	11.2	5. Fred Heckwolf (US)	
3. William Hogenson (GB)	11.2	6. Lawson Robertson (US)	

1908 (57. H 20 July; SF 21 July; F 22 July): Rector tied the Olympic record (10.8) in his heat and again in the semi. Walker also did 10.8 in his semi. In the decisive race, Walker was the early leader, while Kerr got off badly. At 50 meters Rector just passed Walker, the others being close. Then Walker spurted magnificently, got level with Rector, and shot ahead near the end to win by the better part of a meter. Rector was only centimeters ahead of Kerr, while Cartmell trailed by about 2 meters.

1. Reggie Walker (S Afr)	10.8=OR	3. Bob Kerr (US)	11.0
2. James Rector (US)	10.9	4. Nate Cartmell (US)	11.2
(Rector 10.8 =OR, H & SF; Walker 10.8 =OR, SF)			

1912 (68. H-SF 6 July; F 7 July): In the 16th heat, Lippincott set a new world record of 10.6. In the next round, Craig caused the elimination of Europe's top man, Richard Rau of Germany, while Lippincott did likewise to the British champion, William Applegarth. Meyer, Craig and Lippincott all did 10.7 in their semis. Howard Drew (US) strained a tendon in winning the first semi-final in 11.0 and did not run the final. There were eight false starts. At the right one, Patching soon forged ahead and had a half-meter lead at 40 meters. Then Craig began to close, caught Patching at 60 meters, and was a fraction ahead at 75 meters. Meyer was then practically even with Patching, while the other two were a half meter back. Craig pulled away in the closing stage to win by 60 centimeters. Lippincott just caught Patching at the line and finished 15 centimeters behind Meyer.

1. Ralph Craig (US)	10.8	4. George Patching (S Afr)	11.0
2. Alvah Meyer (US)	10.9	5. Frank Beloit (US)	
3. Donald Lippincott (US)	10.9		
(Lippincott 10.6 OR WR, H)			

1920 (59. H-QF 15 Aug; SF-F 16 Aug): In the qualifying rounds, 10.8s were returned by Paddock (three times), Scholz and Edward (each twice) and Murchison (once). In the final, the clerk of the course cautioned Paddock not to put his hands over the mark just as the men were about to start. Murchison, accustomed to the methods of American starters in similar instances,

expected an order to "stand up" and proceeded to arise just as the others were off. Naturally, he was never in the race and finished a distant last. At 50 meters, Scholz led Edward by 60 centimeters, with Kirksey and Paddock close. All four came fast, Paddock using his characteristic "jump" finish to beat Kirksey by 30 centimeters. At first, Scholz was placed 5th behind Ali Khan. Later, however, the judges placed Scholz 4th. And some observers at the finish were convinced that he had actually finished 3rd.

1. Charley Paddock (US)	10.8	4. Jackson Scholz (US)	11.0
2. Morris Kirksey (US)	10.8	5. Emile Ali Khan (Fr)	11.1
3. Harry Edward (GB)	11.0	6. Loren Murchison (US)	

1924 (82. H-QF 6 July; SF-F 7 July): In the second round, Abrahams equaled the Olympic record (10.6). He repeated this time the next day in his semi-final, despite a very poor start. The starter dispatched the finalists to a magnificent start on the first attempt. At 25 meters they were all together, but at 50 meters Abrahams was clear of Scholz and Bowman. The English champion held his lead and won by 60 centimeters. Porritt finished with an astounding burst to nip Bowman for 3rd place.

1. Harold Abrahams (GB)	10.6=OR	4. Chester Bowman (US)	10.9
2. Jackson Scholz (US)	10.7	5. Charley Paddock (US)	10.9
3. Arthur Porritt (NZ)	10.8	6. Loren Murchison (US)	11.0
(Abrahams 10.6 = OR, H & SF)			

1928 (74. H-QF 29 July; SF-F 30 July): In the second round, Williams clocked 10.6 (=OR). McAllister won the first semi in 10.6 from Williams, while London took the second, also in 10.6. At the first attempt to get the runners off, Legg broke, and on the second Wykoff was the offender. The third time the men were away together, with Williams immediately going into the lead. He stayed in front all the way and won by 60 centimeters. Perhaps 30 centimeters separated 2nd from 5th. McAllister strained a tendon and finished last.

1. Percy Williams (Can)	10.8	4. Frank Wykoff (US)	11.0
2. Jack London (GB)	10.9	5. Wilfred Legg (S Afr)	11.0
3. Georg Lammers (Ger)	10.9	6. Bob McAllister (US)	11.0
(Williams 10.6 = OR, H; London 10.6 = OR, SF; McAllister 10.6 = OR, SF)			

1932 (32. H-QF 31 July; SF-F 1 Aug): In the second round, Tolan set a new Olympic record of 10.4 The semi-finals were won by Tolan (10.7) and Metcalfe (10.6). In the final Joubert broke on the first attempt, but the field was off well on the next try. Yoshioka, perhaps the world's fastest starter, was off in front, but even Tolan and Metcalfe, usually indifferent starters, were off well for once. At 40 meters the Japanese was clearly in front, but Tolan soon pulled even. The others were a meter back, almost abreast. Then Metcalfe shot forward. At 60 meters, Yoshioka faded, and Tolan still had 30 centimeters on Metcalfe. The latter pulled even at 80 meters and the two struggled mightily over the final 20 meters and hit the tape virtually even. Finally it was announced that Tolan was the winner. Movies later showed the margin of victory to be only an inch. Jonath finished about one meter back, nipping Simpson for 3rd.

1. Eddie Tolan (US)	10.3 =WR	4. George Simpson (US)	10.5
2. Ralph Metcalfe (US)	10.3 =WR	5. Daniel Joubert (S Afr)	10.6
3. Arthur Jonath (Ger)	10.4	6. Takayoshi Yoshioka (Japan)	10.8
(Tolan 10.4 OR, H)			

1936 (63. H-QF 2 Aug; SF-F 3 Aug): Owens won the 12th heat in 10.3 (=OR), aided by a legal wind of 1.7 mps. In the second round he improved to 10.2, with an illegal assisting wind of 2.3. The following day he won the first semi-final in 10.4, while Metcalfe took the second in 10.5. Owens was off with the gun and had a lead of nearly 2 meters at the final's halfway mark. In the last 25 meters Metcalfe, who started poorly, closed the gap to some extent, but was still a meter 25 at the finish, although a meter and a half in front of Osendarp. Strandberg strained a tendon at 80 meters and came home last. During the semi-finals and final, the wind was said to be 2.7 mps., diagonal from behind.

1. Jesse Owens (US)	10.3	4. Frank Wykoff (US)	10.6
2. Ralph Metcalfe (US)	10.4	5. Erich Borchmeyer (Ger)	10.7
3. Martinus Osendarp (Hol)	10.5	6. Lennart Strandberg (Swe)	10.9

(Owens 10.3 =OR, H; Owens 10.2w QF)

1948 (68. H-QF 30 July; SF-F 31 July): The fastest time in the heats was Dillard's 10.4, which he duplicated in the second round. The other quarter-finals were won by the three pre-meet favorites: Ewell (10.5), Patton (10.4) and LaBeach (10.5). The semis were won by Dillard (10.5) and Patton (10.4). There was one break in the final and then the field was off together. Patton and McDonald Bailey lost ground in the early running and were never in the race. Dillard grabbed an early lead and held it. Ewell never saw Dillard and thought he had won in beating out LaBeach and Patton, who were on either side of him. But the photo finish showed Dillard clearly out in front. The official place times were obviously in error and the hand times used are based on the phototimer.

1. Harrison Dillard (US)	10.3=OR	4. Alistair McCorquodale (GB)	10.4
2. Barney Ewell (US)	10.4	5. Mel Patton (US)	10.5
3. Lloyd LaBeach (Pan)	10.4	6. E. McDonald Bailey (GB)	10.6

1952 (71. H-QF 20 July; SF-F 21 July): McDonald Bailey and Remigino both ran 10.4 in their heats. That time was duplicated in the second round by Smith and Remigino. The semi-finals were won by McDonald Bailey (10.5) and McKenley (10.4). The finals field came out of the blocks well, with Smith slightly ahead. But Remigino quickly moved to the front and had a good lead at 50 meters. Smith and McDonald Bailey were in close pursuit. McKenley got into stride and rushed past those two and Remigino just as the four went into the tape. But Remigino had made a last-ditch lunge at the finish that gave him the victory by about an inch, as was revealed by the phototimer.

1. Lindy Remigino (US)	10.4 (10.79)	4. Dean Smith (US)	10.4 (10.84)
2. Herb McKenley (Jam)	10.4 (10.79)	5. Vladimir Sukharyev (SU)	10.5 (10.88)
3. Emmnl McD. Bailey (GB)	10.4 (10.83)	6. John Treloar (Aus)	10.5 (10.91)

1956 (65. H-QF 23 Nov; SF-F 24 Nov): The fastest time in the heats was Morrow's 10.4 (no wind). In the second round he improved to 10.3 (adverse wind: 1.4 m/s), a time duplicated by Murchison (no wind). The semi-finals were won by Murchison (10.5) and Morrow, who again equaled the Olympic record, 10.3 (adverse wind: 1.1 m/s). There was a cold, adverse wind of 5 mps during the final, run two hours later. Hogan got off in front of the rest and steamed away from the field. Morrow set out in hot pursuit, his powerful strides steadily closing the gap. He passed Hogan at 50 meters and strode away with no one else getting close. Murchison and Baker ran hard in an effort to catch Hogan and were second and third with 25 meters to go, but in the final stages Hogan rallied and Murchison faded. Baker just saved 2nd by a frantic forward lean.

1. Bobby Morrow (US)	10.5 (10.62)	4. Ira Murchison (US)	10.6 (10.80)
2. Thane Baker (US)	10.5 (10.77)	5. Manfred Germar (WG)	10.7 (10.86)
3. Hector Hogan (Aus)	10.6 (10.77)	6. Mike Agostini (Trin)	10.7 (10.88)

(Morrow 10.3 =OR, H & SF; Murchison 10.3 =OR, H)

1960 (61. H-QF 31 Aug; SF-F 1 Sept): In the second quarter-final, Hary lowered the Olympic record to 10.2 in winning from Sime's 10.3 (adverse wind 0.32 m/s). In the first of the semi-finals one of the favorites, Harry Jerome of Canada, co-holder with Hary of the world record of 10.0, was eliminated. He was in front when he pulled a muscle and had to give up at 50 meters. In the second semi, Hary led all the way and won in 10.3. At the first start both Sime and Hary appeared to jump, but the gun was not fired. At the next attempt, Hary broke and the recall gun was fired. Finally, the German ace was off fairly and had a meter lead in the first five meters. Sime was a hopeless last in the early part of the race, but came like the wind, closing tremendously. Still, he couldn't quite catch Hary, who won by almost half a meter. Radford displayed a tremendous closing burst to edge Figuerola for the bronze. No wind.

1. Armin Hary (WG)	10.2 (10.32)=OR	4. Enrique Figuerola (Cuba)	10.3 (10.44)
2. Dave Sime (US)	10.2 (10.35)=OR	5. Frank Budd (US)	10.3 (10.46)
3. Peter Radford (GB)	10.3 (10.42)	6. Ray Norton (US)	10.4 (10.50)

1964 (72. H-QF 14 Oct; SF-F 15 Oct): Hayes won the first semi, riding a 5.28 tailwind to a 9.94 clocking and an easy win over Maniak, Robinson, and Schumann. The wind shifted during the second race, which was won by Jerome in 10.3. He was followed by Kone, Figuerola, and Pender. The latter also sustained a muscle pull in the second round, in the ribs, and finished in considerable pain. The start was almost perfectly even, with Figuerola, as expected, and Hayes, surprisingly, off slightly better than the rest. By 10 meters, the quick pickups of the favorites, Hayes, Figuerola, and Jerome, gave them a 2-foot lead over the rest. Hayes simply exploded to gain a full meter lead at the 40-meter mark, kept powering ahead, and was never threatened. He won by a still-growing margin of seven feet—an edge almost insulting to an Olympic final field. Figuerola stood off Jerome's closing rush and took the silver by less than a foot. The wind was a legal 1.03.

1.	Bob Hayes (US)	10.0 (10.05)=WR	5.	Heinz Schumann (WG)	10.4 (10.46)
2.	Enrique Figuerola (Cuba)	10.2 (10.24)	6.	Gaoussou Kone (IC)	10.4 (10.47)
3.	Harry Jerome (Can)	10.2 (10.26)		Mel Pender (US)	10.4 (10.47)
4.	Wieslaw Maniak (Pol)	10.4 (10.41)	8.	Tom Robinson (Bah)	10.5 (10.56)

1968 (67. H-QF 13 Oct; SF-F 14 Oct): The first two rounds saw the favorites coming through except for injured Soviet star Vladislav Sapeya. Hines won the first semi coming from behind to nip Bambuck. Eliminated were Cubans Figuerola and Ramirez. Greene took the second semi ahead of Miller. The three Americans were off best in the final (wind 0.3 mps) with Miller not far behind, Pender quickly accelerating to a lead at 30 meters. But then Hines began a sustained drive, moving to a lead which he held to the tape. Greene attempted to close but felt a cramp at 70 meters and had to ease up, losing second to Miller. Montes and Bambuck charged up to pass Pender in the final 20 meters to get 4th and 5th.

1.	Jim Hines (US)	9.9 (9.95) =WR	4.	Pablo Montes (Cuba)	10.1 (10.14)
2.	Lennox Miller (Jam)	10.0 (10.04)	5.	Roger Bambuck (Fr)	10.1 (10.15)
3.	Charles Greene (US)	10.0 (10.07)	6.	Mel Pender (US)	10.1 (10.17)

7. Harry Jerome (Can) 10.1 (10.20); 8. Jean-Louis Ravelomanantsoa (Mad) 10.2 (10.27). (Greene 10.0 =OR, QF; Ramirez [Cuba] 10.0 =OR QF; Hines 10.0 =OR, SF)

1972 (85. H-QF 31 Aug; SF-F 1 Sept): The primary incident of the first two rounds was the failure of Americans Eddie Hart and Rey Robinson (both had equaled the world record of 9.9 in the U.S. Trials) to show up in time for the second round. So these two almost-certain finalists were out. In winning his quarter-final Borzov set a European record of 10.07. He won the first of the semis the next day over Crawford, who finished second despite suffering a hamstring pull in the closing stages. Taylor won the second semi. Kornelyuk, as expected, was out fastest in the final, run into a minor breeze (0.3 mps). Crawford started despite his injury of the previous day but had to give up after a few strides. Borzov, off well, accelerated rapidly and was in front by 30 meters with Taylor in close attendance. Borzov continued to pull away and won easily by a meter, while Taylor hung on for second against Miller. The latter was fifth at the halfway mark but came up strongly to get the bronze.

1.	Valeriy Borzov (SU)	10.14	4.	Aleksandr Kornelyuk (SU)	10.36
2.	Robert Taylor (US)	10.24	5.	Mike Fray (Jam)	10.40
3.	Lennox Miller (Jam)	10.33	6.	Jobst Hirscht (WG)	10.40

7. Zenon Nowosz (Pol) 10.46;. . . dnf—Hasely Crawford (Trin).

1976 (63. H-QF 23 July; SF-F 24 July): The first round produced nothing unexpected, but some highly-touted sprinters failed to survive round 2. The most notable was Silvio Leonard of Cuba, running with a cut foot. Glance won the first semi followed by Borzov and Kurrat. Crawford won the second over Quarrie and Jones. Casualty of this round was Steve Riddick (US), expected to be in the medal hunt. At the gun, Glance was out in front with Borzov close behind. Quarrie began to move up at 50 meters and went ahead in the next 20 meters. But in the closing stages Crawford came up to nip him at the finish. Borzov passed the fading Glance to get the bronze. Wind (-0.1 mps) was not a factor.

1.	Hasely Crawford (Trin)	10.06	4.	Harvey Glance (US)	10.19
2.	Don Quarrie (Jam)	10.07	5.	Guy Abrahams (Pan)	10.25
3.	Valeriy Borzov (SU)	10.14	6.	Johnny Jones (US)	10.27

7. Klaus-Dieter Kurrat (EG) 10.31; 8. Petar Petrov (Bul) 10.35.

1896 (not contested).

200 METERS

1900 (15. F 22 July): One preliminary round (21 July). In the final, Tewksbury won by 5 meters, with Pritchard edging Rowley for second by a meter.

1. Walter Tewksbury (US)	22.2	3. Stan Rowley (Aus)	22.9
2. Norman Pritchard (India)	22.8		

1904 (7. F 31 Aug): 2 heats on a straight course. At the gun Hahn was off "like a shell out of a coast gun" and soon had a substantial lead. At 20 meters Cartmell was 6 meters behind Hahn. At 70 meters Cartmell really began to move and passed Hogenson and Moulton. Hahn, sensing the challenge, put on a delayed burst to win by 2 meters.

1. Archie Hahn (US)	21.6 OR	3. William Hogenson (US)
2. Nate Cartmell (US)	21.9	4. Fay Moulton (US)

1908 (43. H 21 July; SF 22 July; F 23 July): Kerr, a 5-7½ (1.71 m) Irish-born Canadian, ran the fastest heat with 22.2. The semi-finals were hotly contested. In the final Kerr led at the start, but entering the straight Cloughen and Cartmell began to close on him. Yet Kerr managed to stay in front and won by no more than 20 centimeters, with Cloughen edging Cartmell for second by 30 centimeters.

1. Bob Kerr (Can)	22.6	3. Nate Cartmell (US)	22.7
2. Robert Cloughen (US)	22.6	4. George Hawkins (GB)	

1912 (60. H-SF 10 July; F 11 July): Among those who were eliminated in the hotly contested semi-finals was the American champion, Alvah Meyer. Rau was off a shade behind the others. Coming out of the curve Applegarth had a slight lead, but Craig and Lippincott soon came abreast of the British champion. With 80 meters to go Craig had taken the lead, with Lippincott close behind. Craig was a safe winner 40 meters from the finish, although hard pressed by Lippincott in the final stages. The struggle between Applegarth and Rau for 3rd-place was hot, but the Briton finally proved the stronger of the two.

1. Ralph Craig (US)	21.7	4. Richard Rau (Ger)	22.2
2. Donald Lippincott (US)	21.8	5. Charlie Reidpath (US)	22.3
3. Willie Applegarth (GB)	22.0	6. Donnell Young (US)	22.3

1920 (45. H-QF 19 Aug; SF-F 20 Aug): The fastest time in the quarter-finals was Edward's 22.0. He suffered a muscle injury in the next round yet managed to qualify for the final. In the decisive race Paddock was off in front and led entering the straight, with Woodring close. As they neared the tape Paddock gathered for his characteristic "jump" but Woodring shot past him to take the race. Edward, starting poorly, surprisingly held off Murchison for 3rd.

1. Allen Woodring (US)	22.0	4. Loren Murchison (US)	
2. Charley Paddock (US)	22.1	5. George Davidson (NZ)	
3. Harry Edward (GB)	22.2	6. Jack Oosterlaak (S Afr)	

1924 (62. H-QF 8 July; SF-F 9 July): The fastest time in the preliminary rounds was 21.8 by Kinsman (South Africa) and Norton (US) in the heats; Carr (Australia), Scholz and Hill in the quarter-finals; and Scholz and Paddock in the semis. Abrahams had to fight hard to qualify for the final and eventually caused the elimination of Carr. The runners were off to a fine start at the first shot. As they entered the straight they were level, save Abrahams, who trailed by about half a meter. After a tremendous struggle, Scholz won by a half meter, with Paddock 1½ meters ahead of Liddell. The next two were very close while Abrahams, the 100-meter champion, was never in the hunt.

1. Jackson Scholz (US)	21.6=OR	4. George Hill (US)	22.0
2. Charley Paddock (US)	21.7	5. Bayes Norton (US)	22.0
3. Eric Liddell (GB)	21.9	6. Harold Abrahams (GB)	22.3

1928 (62. H-QF 31 July; SF-F 1 Aug): In the second round Kornig equaled the Olympic record of 21.6. The next round saw the elimination of two leading contenders from the U.S., Charley Paddock and H.S. Henry Cumming, thus leaving only the defending champion, Scholz, in the final of this traditionally "American" event. Kornig entered the straight in front, with Scholz close. With 50 meters to go Williams and Rangeley went past the German champion. In the closing meters Williams (20) pulled away to win by 60 centimeters. The judges could not separate Kornig and Scholz and bracketed them for third place. Later they decided on a run-off, but Scholz declined and third was given to Kornig. A photo of the finish shows that Kornig was clearly third anyway.

1. Percy Williams (Can)	21.8	4. Jackson Scholz (US)	21.9
2. Walter Rangeley (GB)	21.9	5. John Fitzpatrick (Can)	22.1
3. Helmut Kornig (Ger)	21.9	6. Jakob Schuller (Ger)	22.2

(Kornig 21.6 =OR, H)

1932 (25. H-QF 2 Aug; SF-F 3 Aug): In the second round, Metcalfe and Tolan beat the Olympic record, both with 21.5, only to have Bianchi Lutti and Jonath improve the mark to 21.4. The semi-finals were won by Metcalfe and Jonath (both 21.5). In the final, Bianchi Luti was first off the mark, but when the field entered the straight Simpson led by 60 centimeters, with Tolan second. The two Americans battled down the straight for 50 meters, then Tolan went ahead to win by 2 meters. Metcalfe came up near the end to nip Jonath for third. Later, it was learned that Metcalfe had been given a handicap of about a meter because of a deplorable error in the measurement of his lane. Yet he refused to ask for a rerun, since he did not wish to jeopardize Uncle Sam's medal monopoly.

1. Eddie Tolan (US)	21.2 OR	4. Arthur Jonath (Ger)	21.6
2. George Simpson (US)	21.4	5. Carlos Bianchi Lutti (Arg)	21.7
3. Ralph Metcalfe (US)	21.5	6. William Walters (S Afr)	21.9

(Metcalfe 21.5 OR, QF; Tolan 21.5 =OR, QF; Bianchi Lutti 21.4 OR, QF; Jonath 21.4 OR, QF)

1936 (44. H-QF 4 Aug; SF-F 5 Aug): Owens beat the Olympic record in the first round with 21.1. He equaled this time in the second round, assisted by a 3.7 mps wind. The semi-finals were won by Robinson (21.1, wind 3.0) and Owens, who coasted to an easy 21.3. The final was held with a drizzle coming down as the runners approached the starting line. The wind had dropped a bit, shifting to a diagonal direction from behind in the straight. Owens soon drew level with Robinson and led by about 1½ meters entering the straight. In his seemingly effortless style he increased his lead further and won easily. Hanni closed fast near the end but could not catch Osendarp.

1. Jesse Owens (US)	20.7 OR	4. Paul Hanni (Switz)	21.6
2. Mack Robinson (US)	21.1	5. Lee Orr (Can)	21.6
3. Martinus Osendarp (Hol)	21.3	6. Wijnand van Beveren (Hol)	21.9

(Owens 21.1 OR, H)

1948 (53. H-QF 2 Aug; SF-F 3 Aug): McKenley and Bourland returned 21.3 in the first round and again in the second. These two were also the winners of the semi-finals. But in the final neither could beat any of the pre-meet favorites: Patton, Ewell & LaBeach. Patton pulled away from McKenley, entering the straight with nearly 2 meters lead. But Ewell and LaBeach set out in hot pursuit. Ewell crept up as they flew down the stretch. Just as he was about to catch Patton the latter rallied with a closing burst to win by 60 centimeters.

1. Mel Patton (US)	21.1	4. Herb McKenley (Jam)	21.2
2. Barney Ewell (US)	21.1	5. Cliff Bourland (US)	21.3
3. Lloyd LaBeach (Pan)	21.2	6. Les Laing (Jam)	21.6

1952 (71. H-QF 22 July; SF-F 23 July): McDonald Bailey ran 21.0 in the third quarter-final, and Stanfield did 20.9 in the fifth. These two were the semi-final winners. McDonald Bailey got a good start while Laing was off poorly. Stanfield led as they entered the straight, with Baker almost even with him and Gathers fourth just behind McDonald Bailey, who lost form in the

stretch and was soon out of contention. Stanfield, smooth and steady, won comfortably from Baker, who finished well clear of Gathers in spite of the official hand times. McDonald Bailey was a close 4th.

1.	Andy Stanfield (US)	20.7 (20.81)=OR	4.	Emmanuel McD. Bailey	21.0 (21.14)
2.	Thane Baker (US)	20.8 (20.97)	5.	Les Laing (Jam)	21.2 (21.45)
3.	Jim Gathers (US)	20.8 (21.08)	6.	Gerardo Bonnhoff (Arg)	21.3 (21.59)

1956 (67. H & QF 26 Nov; SF & F 27 Nov): The main item of note in the first round was Morrow's bandaged thigh, due to a slight groin pull sustained in the 100 final. In the first semi Baker (21.1) beat Morrow (21.3) while Stanfield took the other in 21.2. In the final Morrow got the break in the lane assignment, being placed in lane 3 where he could watch chief rivals Stanfield (4) and Baker (6). All were off well and no one was coasting the turn. Into the straight, the three Americans were in front. Then Morrow shot away from the others and soon had a big lead. Stanfield strained mightily but futilely to close the gap, while Baker had no trouble nailing the third spot.

1.	Bobby Morrow (US)	20.6 (20.75) OR	4.	Mike Agostini (Trin)	21.1 (21.34)
2.	Andy Stanfield (US)	20.7 (20.97)	5.	Boris Tokaryev (SU)	21.2 (21.41)
3.	Thane Baker (US)	20.9 (21.04)	6.	J.T. da Conceicao (Brz)	21.3 (21.56)

1960 (62. H-QF 2 Sept; SF-F 3 Sept): Seye did 20.8 in the first semi-final to win easily from Foik (21.0) and Carney (21.1). The second semi featured some bad seeding, pitting the three world record holders (Norton, Johnson, Radford) against another leading candidate, Berruti. The Italian tore around the turn to lead at the straight and went on to win easily in the world record equaling time of 20.5. In the final there was one jump with both Johnson and Berruti getting away but neither were charged. At the next start, Berruti blazed the turn to lead into the straight. He continued to run strongly and was never headed. Norton also ran the turn hard and was second with 80 meters to go. However, he had nothing left. Johnson came off the turn fourth yet he failed to show the stretch drive expected of him (it was later learned that he ran with a temperature). Carney, running in his favorite outside lane, was third into the straight, passed Norton and closed slightly on Berruti in the final part of the race. Seye, who made the mistake of running too easily on the turn, moved up into the straight to get the third spot and just managed to stay in front of the fast-closing Foik in the final stages.

1.	Livio Berruti (It)	20.5 (20.62)=WR	4.	Marian Foik (Pol)	20.8 (20.90)
2.	Les Carney (US)	20.6 (20.69)	5.	Stone Johnson (US)	20.8 (20.93)
3.	Abdoulaye Saye (Fr)	20.7 (20.82)	6.	Ray Norton (US)	20.9 (21.09)
(Berruti 20.5 OR =WR, SF)					

1964 (57. H-QF 16 Oct; SF-F 17 Oct): The first round saw no upsets, with Drayton's 20.7 the fastest clocking. Drayton continued to look best, winning the first semi-final in 20.5 to equal the Olympic record. Carr showed better than he had the previous day by coming from behind to win the second semi-final in 20.6. Everyone started well in the final but it soon became obvious that Stebbins was running poorly and Carr had nothing wrong with him. Into the stretch he was a full yard ahead and he increased his lead by another foot or so. Drayton, second into the straight, had to battle Roberts all the way to gain the silver medal. The two Italians ran the turn hard and Berruti was a strong fourth entering the straight, but Jerome fought his way past to place 4th while Ottolina faded to last. Stebbins, a poor last into the straight, gained a little, almost catching Foik and Berruti. Wind: adverse 0.78.

1.	Henry Carr (US)	20.3 OR (20.38)	4.	Harry Jerome (Can)	20.7
2.	Paul Drayton (US)	20.5	5.	Livio Berruti (It)	20.8
3.	Edwin Roberts (Trin)	20.6	6.	Marian Foik (Pol)	20.8

7. Richard Stebbins (US) 20.8; 8. Sergio Ottolina (It) 20.9.
(Carr 20.5 =OR, QF)

1968 (49. H-QF 15 Oct; SF-F 16 Oct): The first round produced fast times with Smith doing 20.37 and then Norman ran 20.23 for a new Olympic record. Casualties of the second round were veterans Berruti and Jerome. Carlos took the first semi in 20.11 running in lane one.

Norman came up for second ahead of Fray and Bambuck. Smith came from behind to win the second in 20.13 ahead of Roberts. But he limped off the track with an obvious cramp and his chances in the final looked dim. Carlos blasted away at the gun, attacked the turn and led by over a meter going into the straight. Smith, showing no sign of his injury, was also off quickly and entered the straight in second place. He shifted into overdrive, caught Carlos at 140 meters, and went on to win in a world record 19.83. Norman came off the bend in sixth, charged down the straight gaining on everyone, and nailed Carlos in the last few meters. The rest were never in the medal hunt. Wind: 0.9 mps.

1.	Tommie Smith (US)	19.8 (19.83) WR	4.	Edwin Roberts (Trin)	20.3 (20.34)
2.	Peter Norman (Aus)	20.0 (20.06)	5.	Roger Bambuck (Fr)	20.5 (20.51)
3.	John Carlos (US)	20.0 (20.10)	6.	Larry Questad (US)	20.6 (20.62)

7. Mike Fray (Jam) 20.6 (20.63); 8. Jochen Eigenherr (WG) 20.6 (20.66).
(Smith 20.3 =OR, H; Norman 20.2 OR, H; Smith 20.2 =OR, QF; Carlos 20.1 OR, SF; Smith 20.1 =OR, SF)

1972 (57. H-QF 3 Sept; SF-F 4 Sept): The major result of the semis was the elimination of Don Quarrie, the Jamaican who had ranked first in '71. He fell to the track just before coming out of the turn with a muscle pull in his left leg. The two semis were won by the now-established favorites, Borzov and Black. The lanes for the final were: 1. Black, 2. Mennea, 3. Smith, 4. Jellinghaus, 5. Borzov, 6. Burton, 7. Zenk, 8. Schenke. Black, one of the world's best on the turn, was off fast but Borzov was also off exceptionally well. They hit the straight virtually even, then Borzov gradually pulled away. His lead continued to increase until he eased off in the final 10 meters as he won with 2 meters to spare. Burton held down 3rd until he succumbed to Mennea's strong stretch run in the last 25 meters. The winning time was the best ever for automatic timing at low altitudes. No wind.

1. Valeriy Borzov (SU)	20.00	4. Larry Burton (US)	20.37
2. Larry Black (US)	20.19	5. Chuck Smith (US)	20.55
3. Pietro Mennea (It)	20.30	6. Siegfried Schenke (EG)	20.56

7. Martin Jellinghaus (WG) 20.65; 8. Hans-Joachim Zenk (EG) 21.05.

1976 (45. H-QF 25 July; SF-F 26 July): Entered but absent from the first round were Borzov and Leonard. The only first-round casualty was injured Mark Lutz (US), as the other favorites made it to the final. Mennea won the first semi over Hampton and Crawford while Quarrie took the second over Evans, as prelim times were generally unspectacular. These five figured to be in the hunt for the medals. The draw put Mennea on the inside. Quarrie and Evans were off in front. Entering the straight, Hampton came up to challenge Quarrie. These two gradually pulled away. But Hampton made no dent on Quarrie's lead. Evans hung on for third despite another strong stretch run by Mennea. Crawford suffered a cramp at 60 meters and pulled up. +0.72 m/s.

1. Don Quarrie (Jam)	20.23	4. Pietro Mennea (It)	20.54
2. Millard Hampton (US)	20.29	5. Ruy Da Silva (Braz)	20.84
3. Dwayne Evans (US)	20.43	6. Bogdan Grzejszczak (Pol)	20.91

7. Colin Bradford (Jam) 21.17; 8. Hasely Crawford (Trin) 1:19.6.

400 METERS

1896 (16. H 6 April; F 7 April): Jamison was the fastest qualifier with a time of 56.8. In the final Hofmann was the early leader, but as they entered the straight Burke easily ran away from the others to win by a comfortable margin.

1. Thomas Burke (US)	54.2	3. Fritz Hofmann (Ger)	
2. Herbert Jamison (US)		4. Charles Gmelin (GB)	

1900 (15. H 14 July; F 15 July): Long was the fastest qualifier with a time of 50.4 (OR). Three of the US entrants, Dixon Boardman, William Moloney and H.G. Lee, withdrew from the final on religious grounds when they heard that the race would be run on a Sunday. Holland led for

the greater part of the race but Long caught him in the closing stages and won by a scant meter. Schultz finished third, some 15 meters behind.

1. Maxie Long (US)	49.4 OR	3. Ernst Schultz (Den)	
2. William Holland (US)	49.6		
(Long 50.4 OR, H)			

1904 (13. F 29 Aug): Groman took the lead at 70 meters and opened a gap. Poage was a good second, running wide, and Hillman was third. As the field swung around the turn after 195 meters, Poage fell behind. Hillman went into the lead, with Waller and Fleming coming up for a determined challenge. Hillman crossed the finish line about 5 meters in front of Waller, with Groman less than a meter further back. Fleming just edged Prinstein for fourth in a hard contest. Among the also-rans were George Poage (US) and Percival Molson (Canada).

1. Harry Hillman (US)	49.2 OR	4. Joseph Fleming (US)	
2. Frank Waller (US)	49.9	5. Myer Prinstein (US)	
3. Herman Groman (US)	50.0	6. George Poage (US)	

1908 (36. H 21 July; SF 22 July; F 23 & 25 July): Semi winners were J.C. Carpenter 49.4, Halswell 48.4 OR, J.B. Taylor 49.8, and W.C. Robbins 49.0, all Americans save Halswell. As the runners turned into the homestretch Halswell and Carpenter swung to the outside in an effort to pass Robbins. Carpenter succeeded but also began to run a diagonal course, giving Halswell little or no chance to pass. The crowd raised an immediate uproar and officials on the turn signaled "foul" to those at the finish. They immediately broke the tape and attempted to flag down the runners. But Carpenter kept on and finished the race. There are two versions of the unofficial winning time for Carpenter. American sources give 47.8 while British sources gave 48.6. The race was declared no contest and Carpenter was disqualified. A runover was ordered for 25 July. None of the Americans appeared for the race. Halswell "walked over" in 50 seconds flat. Pictures taken of the finish and the footprints of the runners clearly indicate that Carpenter did run wide in an attempt to discourage Halswell from passing.

1. Wyndham Halswell (GB)   50.0
(Halswell 48.4 OR, SF)

1912 (49. H-SF 12 July; F 13 July): In the third semi, Meredith eliminated Mel Sheppard. In the fifth Donnell Young (US), who finished first, fouled Braun on the initial turn and was disqualified, allowing Braun to advance to the final. The runners were placed in lanes. Meredith set a hot pace, catching Braun by the middle of the first straight. However, Braun increased his pace at the halfway mark and was soon in the lead. In the middle of the last curve Reidpath (who had run the fastest semi, 48.7) began his hard spurt and managed to press past Braun in the last 15 meters.

1. Charlie Reidpath (US)	48.2 OR	4. Ted Meredith (US)	49.2
2. Hanns Braun (Ger)	48.3	5. Carroll Haff (US)	49.5
3. Edward Lindberg (US)	48.4		

1920 (37. H-QF 19 Aug; SF-F 20 Aug): Nobody bettered 50 seconds in the first two rounds. The semis were won by Engdahl (49.4) and Shea (50 flat). Meredith, the world record holder (47.4y), was eliminated in the second semi. In the decisive race Engdahl and Shea, a 47.6 quarter-miler, were the early leaders. Going into the homestretch, these two and Rudd were closely bunched. Rudd ran away from the others and Butler came up fast to take 2nd.

1. Bevil Rudd (S Afr)	49.6	4. Frank Shea (US)	
2. Guy Butler (GB)	49.9	5. E. John Ainsworth-Davis (GB)	
3. Nils Engdahl (Swe)	50.0	6. Harry Dafel (S Afr)	

1924 (60. H-QF 10 July; SF-F 11 July): In the second round, Imbach set a new Olympic record of 48.0 in winning the sixth quarter-final from Engdahl, 48.2. In the first semi-final, Fitch lowered the record to 47.8 while Liddell took the second semi in 48.2. Liddell led all the way in the final and ran 22.2 at the halfway mark. Yet Butler was still in contention, while Fitch and Taylor appeared to be closing up. Johnston and Imbach were no longer in the money.

Imbach tripped over a marking line and fell so heavily that he had to be taken to the hospital. Liddell had a big lead coming off the turn and won by about 3 meters. Fitch overtook Butler in the last few meters. Taylor sensed a pain in his ankle a few meters from the finish, fell, then crawled over the line and collapsed. Imbach did not finish but inasmuch as he was the only other finalist, the French Committee decided he would be awarded 6th.

1. Eric Liddell (GB)	47.6 OR	4. David Johnston (Can)	48.8
2. Horatio Fitch (US)	48.4	5. Coard Taylor (US)	
3. Guy Butler (GB)	48.6	6. Joseph Imbach (Switz)	

(Imbach 48.0 OR, QF; Fitch 47.8 OR, SF)

1928 (51. H-QF 2 Aug; SF-F 3 Aug): The fastest time in the preliminary rounds was 48.6 by Buchner, twice, and Ball. Barbuti ran all out from the start in the final, with only Phillips and Buchner managing to stay in contention. With 100 meters to go, Barbuti was well clear and seemed to have the race won, but Ball unleashed a killing sprint and began to close the gap. With 10 meters to go, Barbuti's lead was cut to no more than a half meter. Going into the tape, Ball glanced sideways over his left shoulder, while Barbuti flung himself over the tape and won by a scant margin, probably a half meter. Buchner edged Rinkel for 3rd after a desperate battle.

1. Ray Barbuti (US)	47.8	4. John Rinkel (GB)	48.4
2. Jim Ball (Can)	48.0	5. Harry Storz (Ger)	48.8
3. Joachim Buchner (Ger)	48.2	6. Hermon Phillips (US)	49.0

1932 (27. H-QF 4 Aug; SF-F 5 Aug): The fastest time in the first two rounds was Carr's 48.4. He won the first semi in 47.2, while Eastman took the second in 47.6. In the final, Carr and Eastman ran a race by themselves. Eastman (lane 2) was in the lead for the major part of the distance, but Carr (4) drew even with 80 meters to go. Step by step they fought down the homestretch but Carr had more steam left and finally won by almost 2 meters in world record time. The 100 meter fractions: Carr 10.9, 11.2 (22.1), 11.7 (33.8) and 12.4 (46.2); Eastman 10.8, 10.9 (21.7), 12.0 (33.7) and 12.7 (46.4).

1. Bill Carr (US)	46.2 WR	4. William Walters (S Afr)	48.2
2. Ben Eastman (US)	46.4	5. James Gordon (US)	48.2
3. Alex Wilson (Can)	47.4	6. George Golding (Aus)	48.8

(Carr 47.2 OR, SF)

1936 (42. H-QF 6 Aug; SF-F 7 Aug): Semi-final results: I. Williams 47.2, Roberts 48.0, Loaring 48.1, Mario Lanzi (Italy) 48.2; II. LuValle 47.1, Brown 47.3, Fritz 47.4, Godfrey Rampling (GB) 47.5. In the final, Williams (22.0) and LuValle ran hard early, while Roberts and Brown lost ground. The two Britons started their bid in the last curve, but going into the homestretch Williams still had a big lead. Brown collared LuValle with 40 meters to go, then put on a devastating burst which brought him within centimeters at the tape. Roberts came up fast and just failed to catch LuValle. The official times were obviously in error, as was shown by the photo-finish camera, which gave 46.66 for Williams, 46.68 for Brown, 46.84 for LuValle and 46.87 for Roberts.

1. Archie Williams (US)	46.5	4. William Roberts (GB)	46.8
2. Godfrey Brown (GB)	46.7	5. William Fritz (Can)	47.8
3. Jimmy LuValle (US)	46.8	6. John Loaring (Can)	48.2

1948 (53. H-QF 4 Aug; SF-F 5 Aug): Wint won the first semi in 46.3 from Curotta (47.2), Whitfield (47.4) and George Rhoden of Jamaica (47.6). McKenley won the second semi-final in 47.3, with Bolen and Guida shunting Denis Shore of South Africa to fourth. In the final McKenley met his one-time school rival Wint. McKenley started like a bullet and hit halfway in 21.4, well ahead of Wint (22.2). But when Wint, with his enormous strides, started his bid, McKenley gradually faded. The two Jamaicans were level with 20 meters to go, then Wint drew away and won by a good 2 meters. Whitfield was never in the hunt yet he finished a fairly close third. Given the condition of the track and the humid and smoky London atmosphere, the initial pace was probably too fast even for the world record holder.

1. Arthur Wint (Jam)	46.2=OR	4. Dave Bolen (US)	47.2
2. Herb McKenley (Jam)	46.4	5. Morris Curotta (Aus)	47.9
3. Mal Whitfield (US)	46.9	6. George Guida (US)	50.2

Wint surprised countryman McKenley for the '48 400 title. Whitfield trails.

1952 (71. H-QF 24 July; SF-F 25 July): Wint won the first semi in 46.3—same as four years earlier in London—from Haas (46.4), Whitfield (46.4), and Gene Cole of the US (46.8). McKenley won the second in 46.4 from Rhoden (46.5), Matson (46.7), and Hans Geister of Germany (46.7). Wint was off fast and though not a sprinter he led at the 200 with a startling 21.7. Rhoden (22.2) and particularly McKenley (22.7) were ostensibly biding their time—wise tactics, especially after the gruelling semis earlier in the afternoon. As the runners turned into the homestretch, Wint began to fade. Losing ground rapidly, he was soon out of contention. Rhoden shot into the lead, with McKenley about 4 meters back. But the latter produced his best-ever finish, gradually closed the gap and just failed to catch Rhoden.

1.	George Rhoden (Jam)	45.9 (46.09) OR	4.	Karl-Friedrich Haas (WG)	47.0 (47.22)
2.	Herb McKenley (Jam)	45.9 (46.20)	5.	Arthur Wint (Jam)	47.0 (47.24)
3.	Ollie Matson (US)	46.8 (46.94)	6.	Mal Whitfield (US)	47.1 (47.30)

1956 (42. H-QF 28 Nov; SF-F 29 Nov): Ignatyev won the first semi in 46.8 from Mal Spence (47.2), Jones (47.3) and Mal Spence of Jamaica (47.5). In the second, Kevin Gosper of Australia lowered his personal best to 46.2 yet placed no higher than 4th behind Jenkins (46.1), Hellsten (46.1) and Haas (46.2). World Record holder Jones led the way in the final, and with 100 meters to go, was still leading (33.4). Ignatyev was by then very close, while Jenkins and

Haas were gathering momentum. Jones suddenly tied up and Ignatyev shot to the front, with Hellsten and Jenkins in hot pursuit. In the closing stages Jenkins impressively drew away from the rest and won in fine style. Haas, dead last with 100 meters to go, came strongly, gained on all and eventually moved to 2nd. Hellsten and Ignatyev were involved in an unusual dead heat for 3rd.

1.	Charlie Jenkins (US)	46.7 (46.86)		Ardalion Ignatyev (SU)	47.0 (47.15)
2.	Karl-Friedrich Haas (WG)	46.8 (47.12)	5.	Lou Jones (US)	48.1 (48.35)
3.	Voitto Hellsten (Fin)	47.0 (47.15)	6.	Mal Spence (S Afr)	48.3 (48.40)

1960 (54. H-QF 3 Sept; SF 5 Sept; F 6 Sept): The first semi was won by Davis in a sizzling 45.5 (OR) from Singh (45.9), Kinder (46.0) and Robbie Brightwell of Britain (46.1). Kaufmann won the second in 45.7 from Spence (45.8), Young (46.1) and Abdul Amu of Nigeria (46.6). For the first time since 1912, the final came on the following day. This new scheduling did much to improve the quality. Spence went out the quickest and hit the half in 21.2 with Kaufmann, Singh and Davis running evenly at 21.8, Kinder and Young being behind. Davis and Young made their move in the middle of the final turn and Davis entered the homestretch with a commanding lead. He passed 300 meters in 32.6, which means that his time for the third 100 meters was 10.8. Kaufmann was fourth (33.3) and gained on Davis all the way to the tape. He almost made it but in the last few meters Davis rallied and won by a very narrow margin, as both were caught in the world record time of 44.9. Automatic times were 45.07 and 45.08. Spence, who ran with a temperature, just edged Singh for 3rd.

1.	Otis Davis (US)	44.9 (45.07) WR	4.	Milka Singh (Ind)	45.6 (45.73)
2.	Carl Kaufmann (WG)	44.9 (45.08)=WR	5.	Manfred Kinder (WG)	45.9 (46.04)
3.	Mal Spence (S Afr)	45.5 (45.60)	6.	Earl Young (US)	45.9 (46.07)
(Davis 45.5 OR, SF)					

1964 (50. H-QF 17 Oct; SF 18 Oct; F 19 Oct): The two semis were run in heavy rain. Brightwell won the first in 45.7 followed by Mottley, Williams, and Vassella. The second went to Larrabee in 46.0 who came up in the final straight to beat early leader Badenski. Skinner came from way back to get 3rd ahead of Graham and shunted Ollan Cassell of the US to a non-qualifying 5th. The weather was clear again for the final. Mottley, Badenski, Williams and Brightwell were out fast. They were in that order at 200m with Mottley clocking 21.6. Larrabee, off slowly, was 6th. He moved up to 5th around the turn and then proceeded to mow down all those in front of him. He finally caught Mottley about 10 meters from the tape and won going away. Mottley held off every one else, while Badenski just edged Brightwell for the bronze medal.

1.	Mike Larrabee (US)	45.1 (45.15)	4.	Robbie Brightwell (GB)	45.7 (45.75)
2.	Wendell Mottley (Trin)	45.2 (45.24)	5.	Ulis Williams (US)	46.0 (46.01)
3.	Andrzej Badenski (Pol)	45.6 (45.64)	6.	Tim Graham (GB)	46.0 (46.08)

7. Peter Vassella (Aus) 46.3 (46.32); 8. Ed Skinner (Trin) 46.8 (46.86).

1968 (54. H 16 Oct; QF-SF 17 Oct; F 18 Oct): The first round produced no less than 15 under 46 seconds as the rarefied atmosphere produced its expected aid to fast times. In round 2 Britain's Martin Winbolt-Lewis ran 45.9 and failed to advance. Gakou, a surprise from Senegal, won the first semi in 45.17 ahead of Freeman and Badenski and looked like a strong threat for a medal. Evans, the pre-meet favorite, won the second in 44.82, a new Olympic record, with James and Jellinghaus in close attendance. Evans, whose usual strategy was to lay back and come from behind, ran hard from the gun. He powered through the 100 meters and held form down the straight to finish ahead of a slowly-closing James. Freeman ran away from the rest to get the bronze well ahead of Gakou. Evans: 10.7, 21.1 (10.4), 32.2 (11.1), 43.8 (11.6).

1.	Lee Evans (US)	43.8 (43.86) WR	4.	Amadou Gakou (Sen)	45.0 (45.01)
2.	Larry James (US)	43.9 (43.97)	5.	Martin Jellinghaus (WG)	45.3 (45.32)
3.	Ron Freeman (US)	44.4 (44.41)	6.	Tegegne Bezabeh (Eth)	45.4 (45.42)

7. Andrzej Badenski (Pol) 45.4 (45.42); 8. Amos Omolo (Uga) 47.6.
(Evans 44.8 OR, QF)

1972 (64. H 3 Sept; QF-SF 4 Sept; F 7 Sept): Amadou Gakou, fourth in 1968, was eliminated in the quarterfinals and Dave Jenkins, European champion in 1971, was eliminated in the heavily stacked first semi. Smith, who had been ailing from a sore muscle in his upper left leg, pulled up early in the race and dropped out. Matthews led down the back straight with the rest more or less even. In the third 100 Collett closed a bit on him, and Sang moved ahead of the rest. Matthews entered the straight with about a 2-meter lead over Collett, which he held to the tape. Collett hung on for 2nd against faster-finishing Kenyans Sang and Asati.

1. Vince Matthews (US)	44.66	4. Charles Asati (Ken)	45.13
2. Wayne Collett (US)	44.80	5. Horst-Rudiger Schloske (WG)	45.31
3. Julius Sang (Ken)	44.92	6. Markku Kukkoaho (Fin)	45.49

7. Karl Honz (WG) 45.68;. . . dnf—John Smith (US).

1976 (44. H-QF 26 July; SF 28 July; F 29 July): The first two rounds accomplished their task of paring the field down to 16, with no surprise eliminations. Juantorena took the first semi over Brydenbach and Parks while Newhouse won the second over Jenkins and Frazier. Newhouse and Frazier went out hard with Juantorena moving just fast enough to keep them from getting away. Newhouse led at 200 meters (21.5) with Frazier and Juantorena not far behind. Brydenbach and Parks on the outside, were way back. Halfway through the turn Juantorena made his move. He passed Frazier and reached the 300 in 32.3 just 0.2 back of Newhouse. It became a two-man race until the Cuban's pressure became inexorable. He went into the lead with 20 meters to go and won going away. Frazier, struggling to hold form, managed to save the bronze from Brydenbach's late rush.

1. Alberto Juantorena (Cuba)	44.26	4. Fons Brydenbach (Bel)	45.04
2. Fred Newhouse (US)	44.40	5. Maxie Parks (US)	45.24
3. Herman Frazier (US)	44.95	6. Richard Mitchell (Aus)	45.40

7. Dave Jenkins (GB) 45.57; 8. Jan Werner (Pol) 45.63.

800 METERS

1896 (14. H 6 April; F 9 April): Flack was the fastest qualifier with 2:10.0 (OR). The winner of the second heat, Albin Lermusiaux of France, withdrew from the final.

1. Edwin Flack (Aus)	2:11.0	3. Dimitrios Golemis (Gr)
2. Nandor Dani (Hun)	2:11.8	
(Flack 2:10.0 OR, H)		

1900 (15. H 14 July; F 16 July): Hall was the fastest qualifier with 1:59.0 (OR). The final was a three-man struggle involving Cregan, Tysoe and Deloge until the Frenchman faded and lost third to the fast-closing Hall.

1. Alfred Tysoe (GB)	2:01.2	4. Henri Deloge (Fr)
2. John Cregan (US)	2:03.0	5. Zoltan Speidl (Hun)
3. David Hall (US)		6. John Bray (US)
(Hall 1:59.0 OR, H)		

1904 (14. F 1 Sept): The large field had to negotiate 1½ laps of the oval-shaped track. Cohn and Breitkreutz were the early leaders. At the halfway mark Runge was in the lead, then Verner, Breitkreutz and Valentine took command. All this time Lightbody had been watching the field "like a hawk does a chicken." Then he began to pass his opponents, running wide, a practice that was then rather unusual. He closed steadily and with about 30 meters to go shot into the lead. He won by about 2 meters, with Valentine clearly ahead of the next three, who literally ran themselves into exhaustion.

1. James Lightbody (US)	1:56.0 OR	4. George Underwood (US)
2. Howard Valentine (US)	1:56.3	5. Johannes Runge (Ger)
3. Emil Breitkreutz (US)	1:56.4	6. Frank Verner (US)

Also competed: George Bonhag, Harvey Cohn, L.E. Hearn, John Joyce, Harry Pilgrim (all US); Peter Deer, John Peck (both Canada).

1908 (39. H 20 July; F 21 July): Fairbairn-Crawford set a hot pace in the early stages and was a dozen meters ahead at 200 meters. Shortly afterwards he began to fade and soon disappeared from the picture. Sheppard then took the lead, with Lunghi and Just trailing. Just dropped back after a while, but Lunghi chased the leader all the way. Sheppard won by about 8 meters after covering the first half in a sensational 53-flat. He eased up after breaking the 800-meter tape and was clocked in no better than 1:54.0 for 880 yards.

1. Mel Sheppard (US)	1:52.8 WR	4. Odon Bodor (Hun)	1:55.4
2. Emilio Lunghi (It)	1:54.2	5. Theodore Just (GB)	
3. Hanns Braun (Ger)	1:55.2	6. John Halstead (US)	

dnf—C. B. Beard (US), I. F. Fairbairn-Crawford (GB).

1912 (48. H 6 July; SF 7 July; F 8 July): Meredith won the first semi in 1:54.4 from Braun (1:54.6) and Sheppard (1:54.8). Brock took the second in 1:55.7. In the final Sheppard set a very fast pace, timed in 52.4, with Meredith close. Braun, Davenport and Edmundson followed, closely bunched. Sheppard still lay first as the men entered the homestretch, but Meredith came with a devastating spurt. For a moment it looked as though Braun would join the two Americans in the battle for first, but the pace was too hot. Davenport came up fast in the closing stages, but Meredith had enough steam to draw away from Sheppard. He won by a half meter from Sheppard, who was only a hand's breadth ahead of Davenport. Meredith went on to break another tape, at 880 yards, in 1:52.5, thus getting two world records and an Olympic gold medal with a single stroke! He was not yet 20. Official results for the next three places were, 4. Braun 1:52.2; 5. Caldwell 1:52.3; 6. Brock no time. However, these places and times do not stand up under close scrutiny of available photographs and reports from various sources. We here list "revised" results.

1. Ted Meredith (US)	1:51.9 WR	4. Melville Brock (Can)	1:52.7
2. Mel Sheppard (US)	1:52.0	5. Daniel Caldwell (US)	1:52.8
3. Ira Davenport (US)	1:52.0	6. Hanns Braun (Ger)	1:53.1

7. Clarence Edmundson (US); 8. Herbert Putnam (US).

1920 (39. H 15 Aug; SF 16 Aug; F 17 Aug): The fastest time in the early rounds was Rudd's 1:55.0. In the final Campbell set the pace for a good part of the distance, with Mountain taking over in the second lap. As they went round the last curve, Rudd surged and shot into and lead—only to drop back again in the stretch. In the closing stages the race was a two-man battle between Hill and Eby, with the Briton winning by about a meter.

1. Albert Hill (GB)	1:53.4	4. Edgar Mountain (GB)	
2. Earl Eby (US)	1:53.6	5. Donald Scott (US)	
3. Bevil Rudd (S Afr)	1:54.0	6. Albert Sprott (US)	

7. Esparbes (Fr); 8. Adriaan Paulen (Hol) 1:56.4; . . . dnf—Tom Campbell (US).

1924 (41. H 6 July; SF 7 July; F 8 July): Stallard had the fastest time in the prelims—1:54.2. In the final he was reportedly bothered by an injured foot, yet he led the field for the greater part of the distance with times of 54.0 and 1:21.4. At the end of the first lap he had a big lead on the field, which was closely bunched. Lowe and Martin started their bid with 200 meters to go, sprinting past Stallard 100 meters from home. In a hectic finish, Lowe just edged Martin, with Enck rallying to beat Stallard for the last medal at the post as the Briton collapsed after crossing the line.

1. Douglas Lowe (GB)	1:52.4	4. Henry Stallard (GB)	1:53.0
2. Paul Martin (Switz)	1:52.6	5. William Richardson (US)	1:53.8
3. Schuyler Enck (US)	1:53.0	6. Ray Dodge (US)	1:54.2

7. John Watters (US); 8. Charles Hoff (Nor); 9. H. Houghton (GB).

1928 (54. H 29 July; SF 30 July; F 31 July): In the third semi, Hahn hit the halfway mark level with Edwards (54.0) and went on to win in 1:52.6 from the Canadian and world record holder Martin. The other semis were won by Fuller and Bylehn. Otto Peltzer of Germany, holder of the 880 world record, was an undistinguished 5th in the semi won by Fuller and failed to advance. Defending champion Lowe qualified easily: in the final he started on the pole and held the lead to the first turn, where Hahn rushed to the front, with Edwards in his wake. At 400

meters Hahn was still leading (55.2), with Lowe, Edwards, Martin, Engelhardt and Bylehn following. Lowe launched his attack in the backstretch of the final lap and ran away from the field. Hahn and Martin faded badly towards the end, while Bylehn, coming up fast, nipped Engelhardt for 2nd.

1. Douglas Lowe (GB)	1:51.8 OR	4. Phil Edwards (Can)	1:54.0
2. Erik Bylehn (Swe)	1:52.8	5. Lloyd Hahn (US)	1:54.2
3. Hermann Engelhardt (Ger)	1:53.2	6. Sera Martin (Fr)	1:54.6

7. Earl Fuller (US) 1:55.0; 8. Jean Keller (Fr); 9. Ray Watson (US).

1932 (19. H 31 July; F 2 Aug): The fastest time in the heats was Hornbostel's 1:52.4. In the final Edwards lost no time in taking the lead. His pace caused Peltzer and Martin to drop back almost immediately. At the bell the Canadian had a big lead (52.3). Genung was leading the pursuers several meters behind, with Hampson at fifth in 54.8. Early in the second lap Wilson and Hampson began to chase Edwards and collared him down the backstretch. Going into the last curve, Wilson was in the lead, with Hampson trailing. In a desperate fight down the homestretch, Wilson staved off Hampson's attacks—all but the last—a few meters from home the Briton drew away and won by a scant meter. For the first time, 1:50 was broken, and by two men in the same race. For official purposes, times were rounded to 5ths, and Hampson's record went into the books as 1:49.8.

1. Tom Hampson (GB)	1:49.7 WR	4. Eddie Genung (US)	1:51.7
2. Alex Wilson (Can)	1:49.9	5. Edwin Turner (US)	1:52.5
3. Phil Edwards (Can)	1:51.5	6. Chuck Hornbostel (US)	1:52.7

7. Jack Powell (GB) 1:53.0; 8. Sera Martin (Fr) 1:53.6; 9. Otto Peltzer (Ger).

1936 (43. H 2 Aug, SF 3 Aug, F 4 Aug): Edwards posted the fastest heat (1:53.7) in just beating Hornbostel, same clocking. Woodruff won the fastest semi in 1:52.7, after 400 in 52.0. The final was run in mild temperature with hindering winds. Edwards, by now an old Olympic campaigner, went into the lead at the gun and stayed there for the greater part of the first lap. Woodruff, after fluctuating back and forth in the early stages, emerged just before the bell and was in the lead at 400 meters, with Edwards and Kucharski trailing. The pace until then was funereal (57.4). Lanzi, a distant 8th at that stage, and apparently locked in, really began to move in the second lap. He was 4th with 200 meters to go, when Edwards was back in the lead, with Woodruff on his heels and Kucharski third. Edwards began to fade in the last curve and Woodruff easily drew away from him. Lanzi, still closing fast, passed Kucharski, then shot past Edwards in the short homestretch. By then, however, long-legged Woodruff had the race won, and the best Lanzi could do was to end up a good 2 meters behind the American.

1. John Woodruff (US)	1:52.9	4. Kazimierz Kucharski (Pol)	1:53.8
2. Mario Lanzi (It)	1:53.3	5. Chuck Hornbostel (US)	1:54.6
3. Phil Edwards (Can)	1:53.6	6. Harry Williamson (US)	1:55.8

Other finishers: J. C. Anderson (Arg), G. Backhouse (Aus), B. McCabe (GB).

1948 (41. H 30 July; SF 31 July; F 2 Aug): The fastest time in the heats was Whitfield's 1:52.8. The first semi was easily the fastest of the three, with Hansenne winning in 1:50.5 from Whitfield (1:50.7) and Parlett (1:50.9). The others were won by Bengtsson (1:51.2) and Barten (1:51.7). Doug Harris of New Zealand, a 1:49.4 half-miler, snapped the Achilles tendon of his left leg in the second semi and was carried off the track. In the final, Chefd'hotel went into the lead early, but Hansenne, starting on the outside, was unable to follow in his countryman's wake. Whitfield, always in good position, took the lead at the bell (54.2), with the gigantic Wint at his heels. In the backstretch Whitfield put in a fine turn of speed and soon spreadeagled the field. Wint appeared to be in trouble for a while but came charging back in the last curve and down the homestretch. Whitfield, however, was not to be taken, winning by about 2 meters. Hansenne closed fast in the final stages but had to be content with 3rd.

1. Mal Whitfield (US)	1:49.2 OR	4. Herbert Barten (US)	1:50.1
2. Arthur Wint (Jam)	1:49.5	5. Ingvar Bengtsson (Swe)	1:50.5
3. Marcel Hansenne (Fr)	1:49.8	6. Robert Chambers (US)	1:52.1

7. Robert Chefd'hotel (Fr) 1:53.0; 8. Niels Holst-Sorensen (Den) 1:53.4; 9. John Parlett (GB) 1:54.0.

1952 (50. H 20 July; SF 21 July; F 22 July): Ulzheimer's 1:51.4 led the heats. Nielsen won the first semi in a fast 1:50.0, from Whitfield (1:50.1) and Webster (1:50.1), who shut out Audun Boysen of Norway (1:50.4). The others were won by Wint (1:52.7) and Ulzheimer (1:51.9). In the final, Whitfield was drawn in one of the outside lanes but lost no time in securing a good position. Wint was in the lead at 54.0, with Whitfield in his shadow (54.2). Once again, Whitfield made his main effort in the backstretch, passed Wint and went into the last curve as the leader, with Wint, Ulzheimer, Steines, Nielsen and Webster bunched closely. In the homestretch, Wint nearly managed to pull to Whitfield's shoulder, but the latter had enough steam left to put on a strong finishing burst, which eventually won the race for him. Whitfield's winning time and his 400 fractions were identical to his London clockings four years earlier. Wint was a fairly close 2nd, while Ulzheimer just saved 3rd from the wildly charging Nielsen.

1. Mal Whitfield (US)	1:49.2 =OR	4. Gunnar Nielsen (Den)		1:49.7
2. Arthur Wint (Jam)	1:49.4	5. Albert Webster (GB)		1:50.2
3. Heinz Ulzheimer (Ger)	1:49.7	6. Gunther Steines (Ger)		1:50.6

7. Reggie Pearman (US) 1:52.1; 8. Lars-Erik Wolfbrandt (Swe) 1:52.1; 9. Hans Ring (Swe) 1:54.0.

1956 (38. H 23 Nov; SF 24 Nov; F 26 Nov): The fastest time in the heats was Johnson's 1:50.8. Courtney won the first semi in 1:53.6, with European champion Lajos Szentgali of Hungary a close yet non-qualifying 5th in 1:53.9. The second was much faster and Sowell won in 1:50.0 from Boysen (1:50.0), Johnson (1:50.2) and Leva (1:50.4), while Mike Rawson of Britain, 5th in 1:50.4, just failed to survive for the final. The start was on a curved line near the initial turn. Courtney, second from the pole, quickly jumped into the lead, with Sowell, Boysen, Johnson trailing in that order. Then Sowell moved into the lead, hitting 25.1, 52.8, 1:20.4. At the 600, Courtney came alongside his countryman, while Johnson moved to 3rd. As they entered the straight, Johnson saw a gap between the two Americans and immediately found his way through it. While Sowell began to fade, Johnson and Courtney staged an epic battle, running into a stiff wind. For a seemingly long time they were never more than a few centimeters apart, until Courtney finally built up a narrow lead.

1. Tom Courtney (US)	1:47.7 OR	4. Arnie Sowell (US)		1:48.3
2. Derek Johnson (GB)	1:47.8	5. Mike Farrell (GB)		1:49.2
3. Audun Boysen (Nor)	1:48.1	6. Lon Spurrier (US)		1:49.3

7. Emil Leva (Bel) 1:51.8; 8. Bill Butchart (Aus).

1960 (51. H-QF 31 Aug; SF 1 Sept; F 2 Sept): Snell, an unheralded neophyte who came to Rome with a PR of 1:49.2y, began by posting the fastest time of round 1—1:48.1. Tom Murphy (US) won the first quarterfinal in 1:48.0, as Don Smith of NZ was eliminated while running 1:48.4. Moens took the last QF in 1:48.5, with Snell an easy runner-up in 1:48.6. In the semis, 6 of the 12 competitors beat Courtney's Olympic record and one of these did not even qualify. Kerr won the first in 1:47.1 from Waegli (1:47.3), Matuschewski (1:47.4), Jorg Balke of Germany (1:47.5). Snell won the second in 1:47.2 from Moens (1:47.4) and Schmidt (1:47.8). The Swiss, a strong front runner, led in 25.4 and 51.9 with Schmidt, Kerr, Snell and Moens next. Waegli was still first at 600m (1:19.1) but began to fade with 100m to go and WR holder Moens took over. In the homestretch the Belgian looked around three times, but Snell came charging up on the inside. It was only in the last three seconds of the race that Snell drew away to win by less than a meter. Kerr earned the bronze, while Waegli faded to 5th behind Schmidt.

1. Peter Snell (NZ)	1:46.3 OR	4. Paul Schmidt (WG)		1:47.6
2. Roger Moens (Bel)	1:46.5	5. Christian Wagli (Switz)		1:48.1
3. George Kerr (W Indies)	1:47.1	6. Manfred Matuschewski (EG)		1:52.0
(Kerr 1:47.1 OR, SF)				

1964 (47. H 14 Oct; SF 15 Oct; F 16 Oct): As in Rome, the races were in staggered lanes around the first curve. Most notable casualty in round 1 was Morgan Groth (US), who had the fastest pre-Games time (1:46.4y) but was out of training because of an injury. The fastest time was 1:47.8 by Kiprugut. Snell won the first semi in 1:46.9 from Siebert (1:47.0) and Pennewaert (1:47.0), while European champion Manfred Matuschewski (1:47.3), was eliminated. Kerr won the second in 1:46.1 (OR) from Kiprugut (1:46.1), Bogatzki (1:46.9) and

John Boulter of GB (1:47.1). The only qualifiers in the last semi were Crothers (1:47.3) and Farrell (1:47.8). In the final, the sturdily built Kiprugut led through 24.9 and 52.0, from a tightly packed field. Coming off the penultimate turn, Snell worked his way out of a dangerous box: at 600m (1:19.4) he was the leader and from then on he was practically unchallenged. He ran the second half (52.2) faster than the first (52.9). Crothers went past Kerr and Kiprugut in the homestretch.

1. Peter Snell (NZ)	1:45.1 OR	4. George Kerr (Jam)	1:45.9
2. Bill Crothers (Can)	1:45.6	5. Tom Farrell (US)	1:46.6
3. Wilson Kiprugut (Ken)	1:45.9	6. Jerry Siebert (US)	1:47.0

7. Dieter Bogatzki (WG) 1:47.2; 8. Jacques Pennewaert (Bel) 1:50.5.
(Kerr 1:46.1OR SF)

1968 (44. H 13 Oct; SF 14 Oct; F 15 Oct): In the first round, the most prominent casualty was Wade Bell, a 1:45.0 performer from the U.S.—a victim of "Montezuma's revenge." Fastest time (1:46.1) was by Kiprugut, a solid front runner. Adams won the first semi in 1:46.4 and Ralph Doubell the second in 1:45.7, after catching Kiprugut (1:45.8) near the end. Chief victim here was Franz-Josef Kemper of West Germany, holder of the ER (1:44.9). The final too was shaped by the tireless Kiprugut, who led the field through 24.1, 51.0 and 1:17.8, at which stage his closest pursuer was Doubell (1:18.5). The Aussie started his bid around the final turn and drew away with less than 50m to go. Kiprugut was a close second, well ahead of the fast finishing Farrell. The possibly harmful effects of altitude were seemingly belied by results: the winner equalled the WR, the next three also ran faster than they had ever done, and the fifth man, 19-year-old Plachy, tied his EJrR of the day before.

1. Ralph Doubell (Aus)	1:44.3=WR	4. Walter Adams (WG)	1:45.8
2. Wilson Kiprugut (Ken)	1:44.5	5. Jozef Plachy (Czech)	1:45.9
3. Tom Farrell (US)	1:45.4	6. Dieter Fromm (EG)	1:46.2

7. Thomas Saisi (Ken) 1:47.5; 8. Benedict Cayenne (Trin) 1:54.3.

1972 (61. H 31 Aug; SF 1 Sept; F 2 Sept): In heat 1, Rick Wohlhuter of the U.S., a leading pre-Games performer (1:45.0), fell after 150m while fourth ("tripped over a sunbeam best describes it," he said later). Despite a gallant recovery, he missed the vital third place by a tantalizing 0.05. Fastest time in round 1—which saw other notable casualties in Walter Adams of WG and Thomas Saisi of Kenya—was Dieter Fromm's 1:46.9. Fastest time in the semis was Boit's 1:45.9. The two Kenyans, Boit and Ouko, led the field in the first lap and hit 400m almost abreast in 52.3, while Wottle, known for his tendency to lag behind and kick near the end, closed up the rear in 53.3. European champion Arzhanov made his move with 300m to go and led a tightly bunched field at 600m (1:19.2). But Wottle was by then in full swing: in the last 200 he passed one man after the other, collared Arzhanov 2m from the tape and won by 0.03 while the Russian fell across the line in a desperate lunge for the finish. Boit had enough left to finish a close 3rd, while Ouko was nipped for 4th by a fast-finishing Kemper. The winner ran the second half (52.6) considerably faster than the first (53.3).

1. Dave Wottle (US)	1:45.9	4. Franz-Josef Kemper (WG)	1:46.5
2. Yevgeniy Arzhanov (SU)	1:45.9	5. Robert Ouko (Ken)	1:46.5
3. Mike Boit (Ken)	1:46.0	6. Andy Carter (GB)	1:46.6

7. Andrzej Kupczyk (Pol) 1:47.1; 8. Dieter Fromm (EG) 1:48.0.

1976 (42. H 23 July; SF 24 July; F 25 July): Wohlhuter's 1:45.7 was the fastest time in Round 1, which had as notable victims John Walker of New Zealand, holder of the world mile record, and Mark Enyeart, the '75 American champion. Juantorena, a well-known quantity as a 400 man but a novice at this distance (although credited with 1:44.9 shortly before the Games), won the first semi in 1:45.9 from Van Damme (1:46.0), Ovett (1:46.1) and Ram Singh (1:46.4), who nosed out late-coming James Robinson (1:46.4). The second was a rough affair: Wohlhuter, the winner in 1:46.7, was first disqualified, then reinstated. The Cuban was off slowly in the final, but down the backstretch his long strides began to eat the field. At 200m he was still led by Wohlhuter (25.5 to 25.7) but shot ahead after the second turn, as the runners left their lanes. He hit the bell in 50.85, at which point he was briefly challenged by the surprising Singh, whose best pre-Games effort was only 1:47.0. At 600m it looked like a

three-man battle, with Juantorena (1:17.0) leading Wohlhuter and Van Damme. The American tried to pass as they entered the homestretch, but Juantorena's superior height and stamina eventually won the day in world record time. A wildly charging Van Damme finally nipped Wohlhuter for 2nd. Five of the eight finalists improved on their previous bests.

1. Alberto Juantorena (Cuba)   1:43.5 WR   4. Willi Wulbeck (WG)   1:45.3
2. Ivo Van Damme (Bel)   1:43.9   5. Steve Ovett (GB)   1:45.4
3. Rick Wohlhuter (US)   1:44.1   6. Luciano Susanj (Yug)   1:45.8
    7. Sri Ram Singh (Ind) 1:45.8; 8. Carlo Grippo (It) 1:48.4.

1500 METERS

1896 (8. F 7 April): Lermusiaux acted as pacesetter for the greater part of the distance but was overtaken near the end by Flack and Blake.

1. Edwin Flack (Aus)   4:33.2   4. Karl Galle (Ger)   4:39.0
2. Arthur Blake (US)   4:34.0   5. Angelos Fetsis (Gr)
3. Albin Lermusiaux (Fr)   4:36.0   6. Dimitrios Golemis (Gr)

1900 (9. F 15 July): Alexander Grant and John Cregan, the leading US contenders withdrew, presumably because the event was held on a Sunday. The race was a two-man fight between Bennett and Deloge, who drew away from the rest of the field and finished about 2 meters apart.

1. Charles Bennett (GB)   4:06.2 WR   4. Christian Christensen (Den)
2. Henri Deloge (Fr)   4:06.6   5. David Hall (US)
3. John Bray (US)   4:07.2   6. Hermann Wraschtil (Aut)

1904 (9. F 3 Sept): Lightbody, Verner and Hearn, all members of the Chicago AA, had the race well under control. They drew away from the others and finished in that order. Runge (the only European in the field), though unaccustomed to the particular conditions, gave a good account of himself.

1. James Lightbody (US)   4:05.4 WR   4. D. C. Munson (US)
2. Frank Verner (US)   4:06.8   5. Johannes Runge (Ger)
3. Lacey Hearn (US)   6. Peter Deer (Can)
    7. Howard Valentine (US); 8. Harvey Cohn (US); 9. Bacon (US).

1908 (43. H 13 July; F 14 July): Hallows ran the fastest heat, 4:03.4 (OR), in just beating Emilio Lunghi of Italy (4:03.8), who failed to qualify although he ran faster than any of the winners in the other heats. Others who failed to survive were defending champion James Lightbody, J.P. Halstead (US), Hanns Braun (Germany) and Jean Bouin (France). In the final, Fairbairn-Crawford set a fast pace in the first half of the race, and at 450 meters Loney unsuccessfully tried to take the job. As a result, the pace slackened considerably. Wilson, who was barely 5-4 (1.62) tall, started his bid 270 meters from home. He went into the straight as the leader, with Hallows trailing, but Sheppard, still full of running, came closing fast and decisively outpaced his British rivals to win by almost 2 meters.

1. Mel Sheppard (US)   4:03.4=OR   4. John Tait (Can)
2. Harold Wilson (GB)   4:03.6   5. Ian Fairbairn-Crawford (GB)
3. Norman Hallows (GB)   4:04.0   6. Joe Deakin (GB)
    Also competed: James Sullivan (US), E. V. Loney (GB)
(Sheppard 4:05.0OR H; Hallows 4:03.4OR H)

1912 (46. H 9 July; F 10 July): Fastest time in the heats was Kiviat's 4:04.4. In the final, Arnaud led for the first two laps, the field keeping well together. At the bell, Kiviat took the lead, with Taber and Jones close behind. In the backstretch, Jackson joined the leading group, to which Wide was now getting closer. In the last curve Kiviat was still leading, with Taber,

Jackson, Jones, Sheppard next, closely bunched, then Wide somewhat behind. The homestretch battle was one of extraordinary severity, "each man doing all he knew." In the last 30m Kiviat drew away from Taber and Jones and seemed to have the race won when Jackson, coming up fast, passed the tiring American trio with his giant strides and won by a safe margin. Kiviat took second from Taber on a photofinish decision, and Jones was a close 4th. Wide was probably the fastest of all in the closing stages but had to be content with 5th.

1. Arnold Jackson (GB)	3:56.8 OR	4. John Paul Jones (US)	3:57.2
2. Abel Kiviat (US)	3:56.9	5. Ernst Wide (Swe)	3:57.6
3. Norman Taber (US)	3:56.9	6. Philip Baker (GB)	4:01.0e

7. John Zander (Swe) 4:02.0e. Also competed: Mel Sheppard (US), H. Arnaud (Fr), Oscar Hedlund (US), Walt McClure (US), L. Madeira (US), E. Bjorn (Swe), E. von Sigel (Ger).

1920 (26. H 18 Aug; F 19 Aug): The fastest time in the heats was 4:02.4 by Vohralik. World record holder Zander, attempting a comeback after his retirement in 1918, qualified for the final, in which he dropped out with about halfway to go. Ray led for the greater part of the distance, with Vohralik trailing. The British duo Hill-Baker went into the lead at the bell. In the backstretch Baker ran alongside his countryman "to protect him from attacks." Then Hill drew away and won the race. Ray, reportedly handicapped by a bad tendon, was overtaken by several others on the final lap.

1. Albert Hill (GB)	4:01.8	4. Vaclav Vohralik (Czech)	
2. Philip Baker (GB)	4:02.4	5. Sven Lundgren (Swe)	
3. Lawrence Shields (US)	4:03.1	6. Andre Audinet (Fr)	

7. A. Porro (It); 8. Joie Ray (US). Also competed: D. McPhee (GB), James Connolly (US), L. Fourneau (Bel);... dnf—John Zander (Swe).

1924 (40. H 9 July; F 10 July): Scherrer had the fastest heat (4:06.6). Nurmi, who was to compete in the 5000 75 minutes later, set a final pace that suited himself (500m in 1:13.2, 1000m in 2:32.0), and the field was strung out behind him. The Finn wound up an easy winner, apparently as fresh as when he started. Stallard made a great effort in order to pass Scherrer, but the Swiss had enough left to come up again in the last few meters and nailed 2nd.

1. Paavo Nurmi (Fin)	3:53.6 OR	4. Douglas Lowe (GB)	3:57.0
2. Willy Scherrer (Switz)	3:55.0	5. Ray Buker (US)	3:58.6
3. Henry Stallard (GB)	3:55.6	6. Lloyd Hahn (US)	3:59.0

7. Ray Watson (US) 4:00.0;... (Fin) 4:00.4;... (Fin) 4:00.6;... (Fr) 4:02.4;... (Fin) 4:04.0.

1928 (54. H 1 Aug; F 2 Aug): Bocher had the fastest heat (3:59.6). In the final, Larva and Purje showed excellent teamwork and always appeared to have the race under control. Ladoumegue, trapped during the early stages, came to the fore in the backstretch of the final lap to wrest the lead from Purje. But Larva, after biding his time, launched his attack in the homestretch, collared Ladoumegue and drew away 20 meters from the finish to win by a comfortable margin. Wichmann closed fast to take 4th.

1. Harri Larva (Fin)	3:53.2 OR	4. Hans Wichmann (Ger)	3:56.8
2. Jules Ladoumegue (Fr)	3:53.8	5. Cyril Ellis (GB)	3:57.6
3. Eino Purje (Fin)	3:56.4	6. Paul Martin (Switz)	3:58.4

7. H. Kraus (Ger) 3:59.0;... 8. W. Whyte (Aus) 4:00.0; 9. Paul Kittel (Czech) 4:04.4; 10. Ray Conger (US); 11. Jean Keller (Fr);... dnf—H. Bocher (Ger).

1932 (27. H 3 Aug; F 4 Aug): Fastest time in the heats was Cunningham's 3:55.8. Cunningham and Lovelock set the pace in the first lap, with Beccali 3rd. Then Ny went into the lead for a while. Going into the third lap Edwards shot out of the bunched field, with Cunningham in his wake. These two soon opened up a gap. At the bell, Beccali and the others were a good 20 meters behind the leaders. With 300 meters to go Cornes began to chase the fugitives, and Beccali was in his wake. On the last curve Edwards and Cunningham still lay in the lead but seemed to have given all they had. Beccali ran away from Cornes, then collared Cunningham at the entrance to the homestretch, and finally overtook Edwards. The Italian won by a sizable

margin, breaking the twine with his hands, as was his custom. Cornes too, drew away from Edwards and Cunningham and finished a good 2nd. The Finns (including defending champ Larva), were apparently in trouble because of the hot pace and warm California climate, and were never in contention.

1. Luigi Beccali (It)	3:51.2 OR	4. Glenn Cunningham (US)	3:53.4
2. John Cornes (GB)	3:52.6	5. Eric Ny (Swe)	3:54.6
3. Phil Edwards (Can)	3:52.8	6. Norwood Hallowell (US)	3:55.0

7. Jack Lovelock (NZ) 3:57.8; 8. Frank Crowley (US); 9. Martti Luomanen (Fin); 10. Harri Larva (Fin);. . . dnf—Eino Purje (Fin).

1936 (44. H 5 Aug; F 6 Aug): Fastest time in the heats was Goix's 3:54.0. In the final, Beccali was on the pole, while Cunningham and Lovelock were in the outer lanes. Cunningham led at 61.5, with Ny, Schaumburg, Lovelock and Beccali trailing. Ny was in front at 2:05.0, followed by Lovelock, Cunningham and Beccali. On the 3rd lap Cunningham tried to run away from the field, but Lovelock was quick to follow in his wake. At 1000 meters (2:35.0) the two seemed to have things under control. Lovelock started his bid at 1100 meters (2:51.0) and almost flew away from his American rival. From then on the New Zealander was never threatened. Cunningham fought hard but was unable to make any impression on his fast closing opponent. Beccali, reportedly spiked while in the middle of the field, was a gallant 3rd, ahead of young San Romani, while the veteran Edwards, appearing in an individual Olympic final for the *fifth* time, achieved his best-ever performance in this event by finishing 5th. Lovelock covered the last 300 in 42.8 and the last 200 in 28.8.

1. Jack Lovelock (NZ)	3:47.8 WR	4. Archie San Romani (US)	3:50.0
2. Glenn Cunningham (US)	3:48.4	5. Phil Edwards (Can)	3:50.4
3. Luigi Beccali (It)	3:49.2	6. John Cornes (GB)	3:51.4

7. Miklos Szabo I (Hun) 3:53.0; 8. Robert Goix (France) 3:53.8; 9. Gene Venzke (US) 3:55.0; 10. Friedrich Schaumburg (Ger) 3:56.2; 11. Eric Ny (Swe) 3:57.6; 12. Werner Bottcher (Ger) 4:04.2.

1948 (36. H 4 Aug; F 6 Aug): The fastest time in the heats was Bergkvist's 3:51.8. The final was run on a sodden track and in a downpour. Hansenne set the pace for a sizable part of the distance (58.3, 2:02.6) but disappeared from the picture in the third lap. The Swedish trio, Eriksson-Strand-Bergkvist, forged ahead and led the field at 3:05.0. Eriksson, a strongly-built runner who had previously run in Strand's shadow, for once proved stronger than his rival in braving fatigue and the adverse elements. The talented Strand almost gave up the struggle in the homestretch and just got up again in the last few meters to save 2nd from the assault of fast-closing Slykhuis. Bergkvist dropped back to 5th in the closing stages.

1. Henry Eriksson (Swe)	3:49.8	4. Vaclav Cevona (Czech)	3:51.2
2. Lennart Strand (Swe)	3:50.4	5. Gosta Bergkvist (Swe)	3:52.2
3. Willem Slykhuis (Hol)	3:50.4	6. Bill Nankeville (GB)	3:52.6

7. Sandor Garay (Hun) 3:52.8; 8. Erik Jorgensen (Den); 9. Josy Barthel (Lux); 10. Don Gehrmann (US); 11. Marcel Hansenne (Fr); 12. Denis Johansson (Fin).

1952 (52. H 24 July; SF 25 July; F 26 July): The fastest time in the first round was Aberg's 3:51.0. The two semis were won by Johansson (3:49.4) and Barthel (3:50.4). Stanislav Jungwirth (Czechoslovakia) was the fastest non-qualifier (3:51.0). In the final Lamers took the lead soon after the start, presumably to pave the way for the last-minute appearance of his countryman Lueg, co-holder of the world record. Lamers passed the 400 in 57.8 and 800 in 2:01.4, leading from Lueg, Boysen, El Mabrouk and Bannister. On the third lap Lueg took the lead, passing 1000 meters in 2:32.8 and 1200 meters in 3:03.0. He went into the last curve with a 3-meter lead, but Barthel, running close to the curb, was beginning to exploit his reserves. At the same time McMillen, after staying with the rear guard for the greater part of the race, came up fast. Lamers was by then fading, while El Mabrouk and Bannister were desperately trying to emerge from the outer lanes. Barthel kept moving fast down the straight, collared Lueg 50 meters from home and drew away. McMillen was the fastest finisher and just failed to catch Barthel, who won by half a meter. Bannister barely held off El Mabrouk for 4th. Six of the

twelve finalists beat their personal records, by margins ranging from 0.6 (Lamers) to 4.1 (McMillen).

1. Josef Barthel (Lux)	3:45.1 OR	4. Roger Bannister (GB)	3:46.0
2. Bob McMillen (US)	3:45.2	5. Patrick El Mabrouk (Fr)	3:46.0
3. Werner Lueg (Ger)	3:45.4	6. Rolf Lamers (Ger)	3:46.8

7. Olle Aberg (Swe) 3:47.0; 8. Ingvar Ericsson (Swe) 3:47.6; 9. Don Macmillan (Aus) 3:49.6; 10. Denis Johansson (Fin) 3:49.8; 11. Audun Boysen (Nor) 3:51.4; 12. Warren Druetzler (US) 3:56.0.

1956 (37. H 29 Nov; F 1 Dec): The heats were murder and saw the untimely death of such men as defending champion Josy Barthel, Istvan Rozsavolgyi of Hungary, Ingvar Ericsson and Dan Waern, both of Sweden. The winners were Richtzenhain (3:46.6), Lincoln (3:45.4) and Scott (3:48.0). In the final, Halberg was the early leader (58.4, 1:29.3). Then Lincoln went to, the fore (2:00.1), with Boyd second. At 1100m (2:46.6), Lincoln and Hewson were running abreast, while Landy was in the middle of the field, and Delany was tenth. Lincoln, sensing a pain in his leg, had to give up, and so Hewson was first at 1200m (3:01.3), with Richtzenhain and Boyd trailing, while Landy and Delany began to move up. The Irishman caught Richtzenhain and Boyd in the last curve, then passed Hewson and flew to the tape. Landy produced the greatest finishing kick of his career and just failed to catch Richtzenhain. Delany had "jogged" the first three laps in 60.0, 61.4, 61.0, then capped his effort with a superlative 38.8 for the last 300. His last lap was 53.8.

1. Ron Delany (Eire)	3:41.2 OR	4. Laszlo Tabori (Hun)	3:42.4
2. Klaus Richtzenhain (Ger)	3:42.0	5. Brian Hewson (GB)	3:42.6
3. John Landy (Aus)	3:42.0	6. Stanislav Jungwirth (Czech)	3:42.6

7. Neville Scott (NZ) 3:42.8; 8. Ian Boyd (GB) 3:43.0; 9. Ken Wood (GB) 3:44.8; 10. Gunnar Nielsen (Den) 3:45.7; 11. Murray Halbert (NZ) 3:45.9; 12. Merv Lincoln (Aus) 3:51.9.

1960 (39. H 3 Sept; F 6 Sept): Elliott won the first heat in a fast 3:41.4 from Rozsavolgyi (3:42.0) and Burleson (3:42.2), while Terence Sullivan of Rhodesia (3:42.8) was the fastest non-qualifier. The second heat, won by Bernard in 3:42.2, saw the elimination of East Germany's Siegfried Valentin, who had done 3:38.7 only seven days earlier. Waern won the third heat in 3:43.9. In the final, Bernard led for over half the distance (58.2, 1:57.8), with Waern and Vamos trailing. With 700m to go, Elliott was fourth, followed by Jazy and Rozsavolgyi. At this stage, the holder of the world mile record made his move and in no time he was in the lead. He hit 1000m in 2:25.4 and 1200m in 2:54.0, by which time he was beginning to draw away from Rozsavolgyi, Jazy and Vamos. From then on he was never challenged and won in 3:35.6, a new WR. He ran his last 800 in 1:52.8, 400 in 55.6, 300 in 41.6 and 200 in 28.0. Jazy moved to second with 200m to go and finished 2.8 behind the winner, improving his PR by 3.8. Rozsavolgyi was a solid third, while Waern came from behind and moved from 6th to 4th in the closing stages.

1. Herb Elliott (Aus)	3:35.6 WR	4. Dan Waern (Swe)	3:40.0
2. Michel Jazy (Fr)	3:38.4	5. Zoltan Vamos (Rum)	3:40.8
3. Istvan Rozsavolgyi (Hun)	3:39.2	6. Dyrol Burleson (US)	3:40.9

7. Michel Bernard (Fr) 3:41.5; 8. Jim Grelle (US) 3:45.0; 9. Arne Hamarsland (Nor) 3:45.0.

1964 (43. H 17 Oct; SF 19 Oct; F 21 Oct): Siegfried Valentin of East Germany was again the most illustrious casualty in the first round. Simpson had the fastest time: 3:42.8. Snell won the first semi in a sizzling 3:38.8 from Baran (3:38.9), Odlozil (3:39.3), Bernard (3:39.7) and Whetton (3:39.9). The latter qualified as the fastest loser, since the second semi was won in 3:41.5 by Burleson. Among those who failed to make it were 17-year-old Jim Ryun, Kipchoge Keino of Kenya (who had run the 5000 in rainy weather the day before), and Tom O'Hara, one of the pre-meet favorites. The final was to be Snell's sixth race in six days. Just as in Rome, Bernard was the early pace setter (400m in 58.0). Davies took over in the second lap and led through 2:00.5 and 2:59.3, followed by Baran, Snell and Burleson. Snell made his move in the backstretch and quickly moved up front. Once again, nobody was able to challenge him effectively and he went home an easy winner in 3:38.1, thus completing the first 800/1500

double since 1920. He ran the last 400 in 52.7.

1. Peter Snell (NZ)	3:38.1
2. Josef Odlozil (Czech)	3:39.6
3. John Davies (NZ)	3:39.6
4. Alan Simpson (GB)	3:39.7
5. Dyrol Burleson (US)	3:40.0
6. Witold Baran (Pol)	3:40.3

7. Michel Bernard (Fr) 3:41.2; 8. John Whetton (GB) 3:42.4; 9. Jean Wadoux (Fr) 3:45.4.

1968 (54. H 18 Oct; SF 19 Oct; F 20 Oct): Fastest time in the heats was 3:45.7 by WR holder Ryun. Caution was the keyword in the semis with competition flaring up only in the last 300 or so. Ryun was again the fastest qualifier (3:51.2). Keino, a "child of altitude" who had previously competed in the 5000 and 10,000, went into the final with a bold, well-defined plan: take the sting out of Ryun with a hot pace from the start. He was aided by unheralded countryman Jipcho, who led in a punishing 56.0, with Norpoth and Keino a few meters behind and Ryun hidden in the middle of the pack. Keino then took over and reached 800 in 1:55.3, with 10m to spare on Tummler, while Ryun still lagged far behind. Trying as he did from then on, Ryun could only move to second, ahead of Tummler, while Keino won in his fastest ever time, 3:34.9 (OR). Splits—Keino 56.6, 58.7, 58.1, last 300m in 41.5; Ryun 58.5, 60.0, 57.5, last 300 in 41.8 (easing up). Incredible as it may sound, both men had been hampered by serious ailments in previous weeks: gall bladder trouble for Keino, mononucleosis for Ryun.

1. Kip Keino (Ken)	3:34.9 OR
2. Jim Ryun (US)	3:37.8
3. Bodo Tummler (WG)	3:39.0
4. Harald Norpoth (WG)	3:42.5
5. John Whetton (GB)	3:43.8
6. Jacques Boxberger (Fr)	3:46.6

7. Henryk Szordykowski (Pol) 3:46.6; 8. Josef Odlozil (Czech) 3:48.6; 9. Tom Von Ruden (US) 3:49.2; 10. Ben Jipcho (Ken) 3:51.2; 11. Andre de Hertoghe (Bel) 3:53.6; 12. Marty Liquori (US) 4:18.2.

Running his first-ever 1500 final, Pete Snell capped his Tokyo double with a 3:38.1. John Davies (l) was 3a Alan Simpson (r) was 4th.

1972 (66. H 8 Sept; SF 9 Sept; F 10 Sept): Top casualty in Round 1 was WR holder Jim Ryun. Ryun fell while trying to pass between two runners with 550m to go and tried to recover but to no avail. Keino won in 3:40.0, the fastest time in Round 1. The semis were nail-biting affairs. 800 winner Dave Wottle, running his fifth race in 10 days, failed to make the final by an infinitesimal margin (his time was identical to that of the third man down to 1/100th of a second!). The last semi—which saw the elimination of European champion Francesco Arese of Italy—was the fastest of the three as Dixon just won from Vasala (3:37.9 for both), Foster

(3:38.2) and Wellmann (3:38.4). In the final, Keino lagged behind initially, as Foster led to a 61.4 400. The Kenyan forged ahead in the second lap (2:01.4), then applied the pressure with a third lap in 55.1, but Vasala was still in his wake, with Boit and Dixon close. The bearded Finn passed Keino in the homestretch to complete his last 400 in 53.4 (his last 800 was a sensational 1:49.0). Dixon closed fast to clinch third.

1. Pekka Vasala (Fin)	3:36.3		4. Mike Boit (Ken)	3:38.4
2. Kip Keino (Ken)	3:36.8		5. Brendan Foster (GB)	3:39.0
3. Rod Dixon (NZ)	3:37.5		6. Herman Mignon (Bel)	3:39.1

7. Paul-Heinz Wellmann (WG) 3:40.1; 8. Vladimir Pantyeley (SU) 3:40.2; 9. Tony Polhill (NZ) 3:41.8; 10. Tom B. Hansen (Den) 3:46.6.

1976 (42. H 29 July; SF 30 July; F 31 July): Walker, still affected by his failure in the first round of the 800, drove hard to win his heat in 3:36.9—which was to remain the fastest time of the Montreal series. He went on to win the first semi in 3:39.7, as Thomas Wessinghage of West Germany, supposedly Europe's best, ran 3:40.1 for 5th and failed to advance to the final. Coghlan showed a fast finish to win the second semi in 3:38.6. The two qualifying rounds produced an unprecedented mass of sub-3:40 performances (25): not surprisingly, the final was featured by a "walking" pace for two laps—62.5, 2:03.2. Coghlan was leading at the 1200 (3:01.2), with Walker on his shoulder. Then the New Zealander launched his attack and ran the last three 100m sections in 12.5, 12.2 and 13.2. Van Damme came from behind to close even faster but failed to catch Walker by 0.10. Wellmann also produced a strong finish to beat Coghlan for 3rd. The final times were unimpressive by 1976 standards, yet the first five finishers all negotiated the last 800 in times ranging from 1:50.8 (Van Damme) to 1:51.5.

1. John Walker (NZ)	3:39.2		4. Eamonn Coghlan (Eire)	3:39.5
2. Ivo Van Damme (Bel)	3:39.3		5. Frank Clement (GB)	3:39.7
3. Paul-Heinz Wellmann (WG)	3:39.3		6. Rick Wohlhuter (US)	3:40.6

7. Dave Moorcroft (GB) 3:40.9; 8. Graham Crouch (Aus) 3:41.8; 9. Janos Zemen (Hun) 3:43.0.

3000 METER STEEPLECHASE

1896 (not contested).

1900 Two steeplechase events were contested, a 2500m (11. F 15 July) and a 4000m (14. F 16 July). Many of the leaders were the same in both races, although Robinson was the only one to come away with 2 medals. Bennett, a close runner-up in the longer race, had set a WR in the 1500 the previous day.

2500m		4000m	
1. George Orton (Can)	7:34.4	1. John Rimmer (GB)	12:58.4
2. Sidney Robinson (GB)	7:38.0	2. Charles Bennett (GB)	12:58.6
3. Jacques Chastanie (Fr)		3. Sidney Robinson (GB)	12:58.8
4. Arthur Newton (US)		4. Jacques Chastanie (Fr)	
5. Hermann Wraschtil (Aut)		5. George Orton (Can)	
6. Franz Duhne (Ger)		6. Franz Duhne (Ger)	

1904 (10. F 29 Aug—2500m): Lightbody began the 3-victory string which made him the outstanding performer of the Games with a 1-second win over Daly in a time 5.2 seconds slower than the 1900 winner.

1. James Lightbody (US)	7:39.6	4. Frank Verner (US)	
2. John Daly (GB-Eire)	7:40.6	5. George Bonhag (US)	
3. Arthur Newton (US)		6. Harvey Cohn (US)	

1908 (24. F 18 July—3200m): Russell and Robertson gave the locals something to cheer about with a close 1-2 as Eisele finished 20m back.

1. Arthur Russell (GB)	10:47.8	4. Guy Holdaway (GB)	
2. Archie Robertson (GB)	10:48.4	5. H. Sewell (GB)	
3. John Lincoln Eisele (US)		6. William Galbraith (Can)	

1912 (not contested).

1920 (18. H 16 Aug; F 20 Aug): The race was run on the grass just inside the cinder track. The fastest time in the heats was Hodge's 10:17.4. In the final Ambrosini was the early leader but on the second lap Hodge moved up. From then on the Englishman, regarded as an expert in the steeplechase department, was never threatened. He won easily, by a margin which was estimated at nearly 100 meters. There was less than half that distance between 2nd and 3rd. Mattsson was a close 4th.

1. Percy Hodge (GB)	10:00.4 OR	4. Gustaf Mattsson (Swe)
2. Patrick Flynn (US)		5. Michael Devaney (US)
3. Ernesto Ambrosini (It)		6. Albert Hulsebosch (US)

7. L. Hedvall (Swe); 8. Ray Watson (US).
(Devaney 10:23.0 OR, H; Hodge 10:17.4 OR, H)

1924 (21. H 7 July; F 9 July): The fastest time in the heats was Katz's 9:43.8 (OR). Ritola, the class of the field in spite of his relatively poor technique, soon built up a long lead in the final and was never headed. Montague injured a knee in attempting to clear the water jump when in 3rd, and subsequently dropped back irreparably. Katz tripped over a hurdle in the closing stages and had to fight in order to save 2nd.

1. Ville Ritola (Fin)	9:33.6 OR	4. Marvin Rick (US)		9:56.4
2. Elias Katz (Fin)	9:44.0	5. Karl Ebb (Fin)		9:57.6
3. Paul Bontemps (Fr)	9:45.2	6. Evelyn Montague (GB)		

7. Mike Devaney (US); 8. A. Isola (Fr) 10:14.9; 9. S. A. Newey (GB).
(Katz 9:43.8 OR, H)

1928 (22. H 1 Aug; F 4 Aug): One day after their duel in the 5000, Nurmi and Ritola returned to the track for the steeplechase final. Their countryman Loukola had posted the fastest time in the heats, 9:37.6. In the decisive race, Ritola lost contact with the leaders rather early and eventually dropped out. Nurmi, who had fallen headlong into the water in a heat, looked better than his arch-rival in the final but still lacked the proper hurdling technique. Loukola, always in good position, alternated in the lead with Andersen, Dalton and Duquesne and on the fifth lap he went out on his own. Nurmi and Andersen made it a clean sweep for Finland.

1. Toivo Loukola (Fin)	9:21.8 OR	4. Nils Eklof (Swe)		9:38.0
2. Paavo Nurmi (Fin)	9:31.2	5. Henri Dartigues (Fr)		9:40.0
3. Ove Andersen (Fin)	9:35.6	6. Lucien Duquesne (Fr)		9:40.6

7. Mel Dalton (US); 8. W. O. Spencer (US);. . . dnf—Ville Ritola (Fin).

1932 (15. H 1 Aug; F 6 Aug): Evenson beat the Olympic record in the first heat with 9:18.8. In the second Iso-Hollo lowered the record to 9:14.6. In the final the runners negotiated an extra lap due to an official error. In fact the official scheduled to count the laps was taken ill and his substitute failed to hold up the numbers the first time the athletes came past. Iso-Hollo won the race handily, and none of his opponents asked for a rerun. *=3450m

1. Volmari Iso-Hollo (Fin)	10:33.4*	4. Martti Matilainen (Fin)		10:52.4
2. Thomas Evenson (GB)	10:46.0	5. George Bailey (GB)		10:53.2
3. Joe McCluskey (US)	10:46.2	6. Glen Dawson (US)		

7. G. Lippi (It); 8. Walter Pritchard (US); 9. V. Toivonen (Fin); 10. N. Bartolini (It).
(Evenson 9:18.8 OR, H; Iso-Hollo 9:14.6 OR, H)

1936 (28. H 3 Aug; F 8 Aug): The fastest time in the heats was Dompert's 9:27.2. In the final, Heyn was the early leader. Defending champion Iso-Hollo forged ahead on the third lap and set

a hot pace. Matilainen managed to stay with him for a while, but in the next lap "Iso" drew away from his countryman. Increasing his lead gradually, Iso-Hollo finally won in world record time (unofficial, since world records were not accepted for this event in those days). Matilainen dropped to 4th in the closing stages, while Tuominen held off Dompert in a grand fight for 2nd.

1. Volmari Iso-Hollo (Fin)	9:03.8 OR	4. Martti Matilainen (Fin)	9:09.0
2. Kaarlo Tuominen (Fin)	9:06.8	5. Harold Manning (US)	9:11.2
3. Alfred Dompert (Ger)	9:07.2	6. Lars Larsson (Swe)	9:16.6

7. W. Wihtols (Lat) 9:18.8; 8. Glen Dawson (US) 9:21.2; 9. W. Heyn (Ger) 9:26.4; 10. Joe McCluskey (US) 9:29.4; 11. R. Rerolle (Fr) 9:40.8;... dnf—H. Holmqvist (Swe).

1948 (26. H 3 Aug; F 5 Aug): The fastest time in the heats was Elmsater's 9:15.0. In the final the Swedish trio Sjostrand-Elmsater-Hagstrom ran a masterful race. Their most serious rival, European champion Pujazon, was assailed by stomach trouble near the halfway mark and had to retire. At that stage, Elmsater was in the lead, with Sjostrand and Siltaloppi of Finland trailing, while Hagstrom was lagging behind. The two Swedes alternated in the lead and dropped Siltaloppi in the last lap. Then Sjostrand drew away from Elmsater, who was until then history's only sub-9:00 performer. In the closing stages, Hagstrom produced an electrifying burst of speed and moved from 5th to 3rd, while Guyodo beat the tiring Siltaloppi for 4th.

1. Thore Sjostrand (Swe)	9:04.6	4. Alex Guyodo (Fr)	9:13.6
2. Erik Elmsater (Swe)	9:08.2	5. Pentti Siltaloppi (Fin)	9:19.6
3. Gote Hagstrom (Swe)	9:11.8	6. Petar Segedin (Yug)	9:20.4

7. Browning Ross (US) 9:23.2; 8. C. Miranda (Sp) 9:25.0; 9. R. Everaert (Bel) 9:28.2; 10. Aarne Kainlauri (Fin) 9:29.0; 11. R. Chesneau (Fr) 9:30.2;... dnf—Raphael Pujazon (Fr).

1952 (35. H 25 July; F 27 July): No less than eight beat Iso-Hollo's Olympic record in the qualifying round. Kazantsev won the first heat in 8:58.0, Disley just beat Rinteenpaa in the second as both ran 8:59.4, and Ashenfelter took the third heat in a surprising 8:51.0—improving on his PR by 15.4 seconds!—from Saltikov, 8:55.8. In the final, Saltikov led the field in the first kilometer, but on the third lap Ashenfelter moved up front with Kazantsev in his wake. After another lap these two had a 5-meter lead on their nearest pursuer, Rinteenpaa. At the bell, Ashenfelter and Kazantsev were still running abreast, while Disley began to emerge from behind. Just before they entered the last curve, Kazantsev made a big effort and wrested the lead from his American rival. But the last water jump saw Kazantsev (holder of the world record, 8:48.6) in trouble. Ashenfelter regained his front position and opened up a decisive gap, which widened steadily to the end. Disley had a great finish and barely failed to catch Kazantsev on the post. The winner was rewarded with a new world record. Intermediate times: 2:49.8 (Saltikov), 5:47.4 (Ashenfelter). Last lap 68.6 (Ashenfelter).

1. Horace Ashenfelter (US)	8:45.4 WR	4. Olavi Rinteenpaa (Fin)	8:55.2
2. Vladimir Kazantsev (SU)	8:51.6	5. Curt Soderberg (Swe)	8:55.6
3. John Disley (GB)	8:51.8	6. Gunther Hesselmann (WG)	8:55.8

7. Mikhail Saltikov (SU) 8:56.2; 8. Helmut Gude (WG) 9:01.4; 9. Jozsef Apro (Hun) 9:04.2; 10. Cahit Onel (Tur) 9:04.4; 11. Chris Brasher (GB) 9:14.0; 12. Gunnar Karlsson (Swe) 10:26.4.
(Kazantsev 8:58.0 OR, H; Ashenfelter 8:51.0 OR, H)

1956 (23. H 27 Nov; F 29 Nov): Defending champion Horace Ashenfelter duplicated his qualifying time of '52 in Helsinki (8:51.0) only to find that such a mark no longer sufficed to make the final! His heat was won by Rozsnyoi from Disley (8:46.6 for both). Krzyszkowiak withdrew from the final because of an injury. Larsen immediately shot into the lead; after 3 laps he had 8m on Rozsnyoi and Rzhishchin. The last-named duo caught Larsen in the second kilometer, while Brasher moved up to fourth. In the penultimate curve Larsen swung out a little and Brasher went through the gap immediately, not without pushing Larsen aside. The Briton went on to win, while Rozsnyoi barely held off Larsen for second. At first, Brasher was disqualified for hindering an opponent (Larsen), but was later reinstated by the Jury of Appeal who came to the conclusion that the foul had been unintentional and not determinant on the outcome of the race. Intermediate times: 2:52.4, 5:53.8 (Larsen).

1. Chris Brasher (GB)	8:41.2 OR	4. Heinz Laufer (WG)		8:44.4
2. Sandor Rozsnyoi (Hun)	8:43.6	5. Semyon Rzhishchin (SU)		8:44.6
3. Ernst Larsen (Nor)	8:44.0	6. John Disley (GB)		8:44.6

7. Neil Robbins (Aus) 8:50.0; 8. Eric Shirley (GB) 8:57.0; 9. Deacon Jones (US) 9:13.0;...
dnc—Zdzislaw Krzyszkowiak (Pol).

1960 (32. H 1 Sept; F 3 Sept): Sokolov won the first heat in 8:43.2 from Tjornebo (8:48.6), Huneke (8:50.4) and Georgios Papavasiliou of Greece (8:51.2). European champion and world record holder Krzyszkowiak took the second heat in 8:49.6 from Muller (8:49.6), Konov (8:50.0) and George Young (US) (8:50.8). Rzhishchin won the third heat in 8:48.0 from Jones (8:49.2), Roelants (8:49.4), with Hermann Buhl of Germany the fastest non-qualifier at 8:49.6. In the final, two days later, the weather was hot (30° C). Konov led the pack in the first kilometer, with Roelants and Sokolov in close attendance, while Krzyszkowiak lay quietly in the middle of the field. In the second Konov dropped back and Sokolov took the lead. Krzyszkowiak had by then moved up to third, behind Roelants. In the backstretch of the last lap, the Pole forced the pace, and none of his rivals was able to respond. The two Soviet veterans, Sokolov and Rzhishchin, took 2nd and 3rd while Roelants—who bettered 9:00 for the first time in 1959—was a good 4th. Intermediate times: 2:45.0 (Konov), 5:45.8 (Sokolov).

1. Zdzislaw Krzyszkowiak (Pol)	8:34.2 OR	4. Gaston Roelants (Bel)	8:47.6
2. Nikolay Sokolov (SU)	8:36.4	5. Gunnar Tjornebo (Swe)	8:58.6
3. Semyon Rzhishchin (SU)	8:42.2	6. Ludwig Muller (Ger)	9:01.6

7. Deacon Jones (US) 9:18.2; 8. Aleksey Konov (SU) 9:18.2;... dnf—Hans Huneke (WG)..

1964 (29. H 15 Oct; F 17 Oct): Herriott won the second heat in 8:33.0 (OR) from Gustafsson and Young (8:34.2 both), while Texereau (8:34.6) made the final as the fastest loser. Aleksiejunas won the third heat in 8:31.8 (OR) from Roelants (8:33.8). The last two were the leaders in the early stages of the final (1000m 2:52.0), then the Belgian, holder of the world record, built up a sizeable lead. At 2000m (5:38.6) he was way ahead of Texereau (5:40.4), Young and Aleksiejunas. With a lap and a half to go, Roelants had a huge lead and Young was trying to pull away from the others. But strongest of them all in the closing stage was Herriott, who came from behind to pass all but the leader, whose margin at the end was however cut to 10m or so. Belyayev and de Oliveira closed strongly to shunt Young to 5th. Roelants had kilometer fractions of 2:52.0, 2:46.6 and 2:52.2, while Herriott's were 2:53.2, 2:50.8 and 2:48.4.

1. Gaston Roelants (Bel)	8:30.8 OR	4. Manuel de Oliveira (Por)	8:36.2
2. Maurice Herriott (GB)	8:32.4	5. George Young (US)	8:38.2
3. Ivan Belyayev (SU)	8:33.8	6. Guy Texereau (Fr)	8:38.6

7. Adolfas Aleksiejunas (SU) 8:39.0; 8. Lars-Erik Gustafsson (Swe) 8:41.8; 9. Ben Azouz El Ghazi (Mor) 8:43.6; 10. Ernie Pomfret (GB) 8:43.8.
(Herriott 8:33.0 OR, H; Aleksiejunas 8:31.8 OR, H)

1968 (40. H 14 Oct; F 15 Oct): Only two men ducked under 9:00 in the heats: Kenyans Kogo and Biwott. The latter, an unheralded runner with a pre-Games best of 8:44.8, chalked up the fastest time (8:49.4), winning with over 11 seconds to spare. His giant strides and his safety-first form over the water-jump (which he leaped as if he thought crocodiles were swimming in it) proved very popular with both experts and laymen. He and Kogo (the pre-race favorite of some) led the field cautiously in the early stages of the final. In the second kilometer, European champion Viktor Kudinskiy fell badly and sustained a hip injury which forced him to drop out. Former world record holder Gaston Roelants took up the running in the fifth lap and led until the end of the seventh, when the front group was reduced to five—Kogo, Roelants, Young, O'Brien and Morozov. In the backstretch of the last lap, Young and O'Brien tried to break away but they couldn't shake Kogo and Biwott. The two Kenyans surged from behind to reverse positions. Victory finally went to the "wrong" Kenyan, Biwott. Intermediate times: 3:04.2 (Kogo), 6:03.2 (Roelants).

1. Amos Biwott (Ken)	8:51.0	4. Kerry O'Brien (Aus)	8:52.0
2. Ben Kogo (Ken)	8:51.6	5. Aleksandr Morozov (SU)	8:55.8
3. George Young (US)	8:51.8	6. Mikhail Zhelev (Bul)	8:58.4

7. Gaston Roelants (Bel) 8:59.4; 8. Arne Risa (Nor) 9:09.0; 9. Jean-Paul Villain (Fr) 9:16.2;
10. Bengt Persson (Swe) 9:20.6; 11. Javier Alvarez (Sp) 9:24.6;. . . dnf—Viktor Kudinskiy (SU).

1972 (49. H 1 Sept; F 4 Sept): The heats were murder, the chief casualty being world record
holder Kerry O'Brien of Australia, who lost a shoe with 200m to go, failed to clear the next
hurdle and limped off the track. Others who failed to qualify were Anders Garderud of Sweden
and Kazimierz Maranda of Poland, who fell and injured a leg. Kantanen won the first heat in
8:24.8 (OR) from Keino (8:27.6) and Koyama (8:29.8). Sub-8:30 performances were also
achieved by Paivarinta (8:29.0) in heat 3, defending champion Biwott (8:23.8, OR) and
Malinowski (8:28.2) in heat 4. The final was not the hyperfast affair many had anticipated.
European champion Villain led at 1000m in 2:54.4. Malinowski increased the pace somewhat in
the second kilometer (5:44.8), but the three Kenyans, plus Kantanen, Bite and Moravcik were
still in contention at the penultimate water-jump. A while later, Keino launched his attack:
only Jipcho and Kantanen managed to hang on. Positions did not change in the last lap and
Keino strode home a comfortable winner (last lap 59.2). Jipcho barely held off the Finn for
2nd. The winner, a novice to the barrier event, shaved 0.2 off the newly set OR.

1. Kip Keino (Ken)	8:23.6 OR	4. Bronislaw Malinowski (Pol)	8:28.0
2. Ben Jipcho (Ken)	8:24.6	5. Dusan Moravcik (Czech)	8:29.2
3. Tapio Kantanen (Fin)	8:24.8	6. Amos Biwott (Ken)	8:33.6

7. Romualdas Bite (SU) 8:34.6; 8. Pekka Paivarinta (Fin) 8:37.2; 9. Takaharu Koyama
(Japan) 8:37.8; 10. Mikko Ala-Leppilampi (Fin) 8:41.0; 11. Jean-Paul Villain (Fr) 8:46.8; 12.
Mikhail Zhelev (Bul) 9:02.6.
(Kantanen 8:24.8 OR H;. . . 8:23.8 OR H)

1976 (24. H 25 July; F 28 July): The heats were torrid affairs, with five men bettering the OR.
Malinowski won the first in 8:18.6 from Baumgartl (8:21.3) and Garderud (8:21.4), while
Coates surpassed himself in taking the second in 8:19.0 from Kantanen (8:20.8). In the final
they were off to a fast start thanks to Campos, who led in 2:43.6. When he began to fade,
Malinowski took over, with Baumgartl, Garderud and Kantanen in his wake. At 2000m
(Malinowski 5:29.1), the four-man group was very close to WR pace. With 300m to go,
Garderud flew by Malinowski, only 21-year-old Baumgartl giving chase. The German made a
great effort as they approached the last hurdle, but reaching a little too much he had to chop
his stride, hit the hurdle with his trail leg and fell onto the track. Garderud went on toward an
uninhibited victory, while Malinowski cool-headedly hurdled over Baumgartl and nabbed
second place. The Swede and the Pole both knocked the world record. Baumgartl rose to his
feet and bravely spurted to the finish for the bronze—still beating his previous best by more
than 7 seconds.

1. Anders Garderud (Swe)	8:08.0 WR	4. Tapio Kantanen (Fin)	8:12.6
2. Bronislaw Malinowski (Pol)	8:09.2	5. Michael Karst (WG)	8:20.1
3. Frank Baumgartl (EG)	8:10.4	6. Euan Robertson (NZ)	8:21.1

7. Dan Glans (Swe) 8:21.5; 8. Antonio Campos (Sp) 8:22.7; 9. Dennis Coates (GB) 8:23.0;
10. Henry Marsh (US) 8:24.0; 11. Tony Staynings (GB) 8:33.7; 12. Ismo Toukonen (Fin)
8:42.7.
(Malinowski 8:18.6 OR, H)

5000 METERS

1896—1908 (not contested).

1912 (32. H 9 July; F 10 July): Bouin won his heat in a fast 15:05.0, while Kolehmainen
qualified with 15:38.9 in another. In the final, only 11 started. Kolehmainen took an early
lead. After futile attempts to interfere by Bonhag, Scott and Hutson, Kolehmainen and Bouin
drew away from the rest of the field. Bouin led for the greater part of the distance, with
Kolehmainen always in close attendance, while Bonhag was leading the group far behind. The

last lap was a titanic battle, both men trying to run each other into the ground, with no success. Only with 20m to go did the tide finally turn: Kolehmainen drew level with Bouin, then, gradually and inexorably, he inched his way ahead to win by a scant meter in world record time. Hutson just beat Bonhag for third. The times of the first two were sensational, with no one ever having broken 15:00 before.

1. Hannes Kolehmainen (Fin)	14:36.6 WR	4. George Bonhag (US)		15:09.8
2. Jean Bouin (Fr)	14:36.7	5. Tell Berna (US)		15:10.0
3. George Hutson (GB)	15:07.6	6. Mauritz Karlsson (Swe)		15:18.6

Also competed: Henry Scott (US), A. Decoteau (Can), J. Keeper (Can), F. N. Hibbins (GB), C. H. A. Porter (GB).
(Bouin 15:05.0 OR, H)

1912 (37. H 16 Aug; F 17 Aug): The fastest time in the heats was 15:17.8 by Falk. In the final, Nurmi took over on the third lap, carrying little Guillemot with him. They quickly opened a gap. Guillemot started his bid as they went round the last curve but Nurmi was unable to respond as the Frenchman increased his lead steadily and won by a safe margin. Backman stayed with Koskenniemi and Falk for the greater part of the race. With two laps to go, Falk dropped out and Backman went on to take 3rd. Guillemot and Nurmi both achieved PRs.

1. Joseph Guillemot (Fr)	14:55.6	4. Teodor Koskenniemi (Fin)	15:17.0
2. Paavo Nurmi (Fin)	15:00.0	5. Charles Blewitt (GB)	
3. Erik Backman (Swe)	15:13.0	6. William Seagrove (GB)	

7. C. Speroni (It); 8. A. H. Nichols (GB); 9. J. van Campenhout (Bel); 10. N. Bergstrom (Swe). Other finalists: H. C. Irwin (GB), E. Lundstrom (Swe), Horace Brown, Ivan Dresser, C. Furnas (all US), R. Falk (Swe).

1924 (39. H 8 July; F 10 July): Nurmi went to the starting line 75 minutes after winning the 1500. He and Ritola stayed with arch-rival Wide for the major part of the race and only pulled away from the Swede when they thought the time was ripe for decision. In the closing stages Nurmi staved off Ritola's attack and won rather comfortably. Wide was a lone 3rd, while Romig (who led the heats with 15:14.6) had a hard fight with Seppala for 4th. Kilometers: 2:46.4, 5:43.6 (Wide), 8:42.6, 11:38.8 (Nurmi). Last lap (500m): Nurmi 1:23.0.

1. Paavo Nurmo (Fin)	14:31.2 OR	4. John Romig (US)	15:12.4
2. Ville Ritola (Fin)	14:31.4	5. Eino Seppala (Fin)	15:18.4
3. Edvin Wide (Swe)	15:01.8	6. Charles Clibbon (GB)	15:29.0

7. L. Dolques (Fr) 15:33.0; 8. A. Eriksson (Swe) 15:38.0; 9. L. Mascaux (Fr) 15:39.0; 10. F. C. Saunders (GB) 15:54.0. Other finalists: E. P. Rastas (Fin), Katsuo Okazaki (Japan).

1928 (36. H 31 July; F 3 Aug): The fastest heat time was Lermond's 15:02.6. In the final Ritola took the lead just after the first kilometer, with Nurmi, Lermond and Wide trailing. They stayed together till the penultimate lap, when first Lermond, then Wide, dropped back. Ritola ran away from Nurmi on the last curve. Nurmi did not seem to exert himself too much and was content to save 2nd from Wide's counterattack.

1. Ville Ritola (Fin)	14:38.0	4. Leo Lermond (US)	14:50.0
2. Paavo Nurmi (Fin)	14:40.0	5. Ragnar Magnusson (Swe)	14:59.6
3. Edvin Wide (Swe)	14:41.2	6. Armas Kinnunen (Fin)	15:02.0

Also competed: S. Petkevics (Lat), N. Eklof (Swe), B. C. V. Oddie (GB), Macauley Smith (US), H. A. Johnston (GB); . . . dnc—E. Purje (Fin).

1932 (19. H 2 Aug; F 5 Aug): Virtanen and Lehtinen soon took the lead, while Hill (the heat leader at 14:59.6) stayed in the rear guard. At the halfway mark only Lindgren, Savidan and Hill were still with the two Finnish leaders. Soon afterwards Lehtinen, Virtanen and Hill were out in front by themselves. In the closing stages Virtanen lost contact. The last lap was a drawn-out (69.2) yet torrid affair, in which Lehtinen and Hill ran themselves to exhaustion in trying to kill each other. As they entered the homestretch, Lehtinen was still in the lead. Hill challenged, but Lehtinen closed in again, forcing Hill to cut his stride. In a desperate race for the tape, Hill got up again for a final challenge. Lehtinen lost a little ground but still managed

to win by a scant margin, apparently less than half a meter. Some of the officials voted for the disqualification of Lehtinen but were overruled by Chief Judge Gustavus T. Kirby. Spectators were on the point of rioting, but announcer Bill Henry quieted them down with the words: "Remember, please, these people are our guests." Kilometer fractions for the leaders: 2:46, 2:59, 2:54, 2:57, 2:54.

1. Lauri Lehtinen (Fin)	14:30.0 OR	4. John Savidan (NZ)	14:49.6
2. Ralph Hill (US)	14:30.0	5. Jean-Gunnar Lindgren (Swe)	14:54.8
3. Lauri Virtanen (Fin)	14:44.0	6. Max Syring (Ger)	14:59.0

7. J. Burns (GB); 8. E. Pettersson (Swe) 15:13.4; 9. Daniel Dean (US); 10. J. A. Hillhouse (Aus); 11. Robert Rankine (Can). Other finalists: S. Takenaka (Japan), Roger Rochard (Fr), Paul Rekers (US).

1936 (41. H 4 Aug; F 7 Aug): The fastest time in the heats was Jonsson's 14:54.6. In the final Salminen took an early lead, closely followed by Lehtinen and the rest of the pack. In the second kilometer Lash, holder of the world 2-mile record, attempted to forge ahead but his moment was short-lived. Midway in the race, Murakoso took over, with Hockert, Lehtinen, Salminen, Jonsson and Noji, while Lash dropped back. The 6-man group continued to lead the race till the last kilometer. Then Hockert launched his attack, while Salminen collided with Lehtinen and fell. Hockert easily forged ahead and went home a brilliant victor, apparently without giving all he had. Lehtinen had little trouble in beating Jonsson and Murakoso. Salminen gamely got up and regained some of the ground he had lost because of his fall.

1. Gunnar Hockert (Fin)	14:22.2 OR	4. Kohei Murakoso (Japan)	14:30.0
2. Lauri Lehtinen (Fin)	14:25.8	5. Jozef Noji (Pol)	14:33.4
3. Henry Jonsson (Swe)	14:29.0	6. Ilmari Salminen (Fin)	14:39.8

7. U. Cerati (It) 14:44.4; 8. Lou Zamperini (US) 14:46.8; 9. R. Hansen (Nor) 14:48.0; 10. H. Siefert (Den) 14:48.4; 11. P. Ward (GB) 14:57.2; 12. F. Close (GB); 13. Don Lash (US); 14. B. Hellstrom (Swe);. . . dnf—A. Reeve (GB).

1948 (32. H 31 July; F 2 Aug): Ahlden's 14:34.2 led the heats. The final was run on a rain-sodden track. Zatopek set a hot pace, and very soon the only ones who could stay with him were Slykhuis, Reiff and Ahlden. In the fourth kilometer Reiff put on a devastating burst and opened up a gap. Going into the last lap the Belgian had 20 meters on Slykhuis and twice as many on Zatopek. By then, however, the Czech had passed his crisis and was charging back. He soon collared Slykhuis; then he began to cut Reiff's lead at a threatening rate. In the homestretch it looked as if he would forge ahead, but Reiff, sensing the danger, rallied his last resources and came home a scant meter ahead of his great rival. Slykhuis was a distant but safe 3rd. Nyberg dropped out with a little more than a lap to go while 6th. The leaders: 2:48, 5:38, 8:33, 11:25. Reiff's last lap was 69.6.

1. Gaston Reiff (Bel)	14:17.6 OR	4. Erik Ahlden (Swe)	14:28.6
2. Emil Zatopek (Czech)	14:17.8	5. Bertil Albertsson (Swe)	14:39.0
3. Willem Slykhuis (Hol)	14:26.8	6. Curt Stone (US)	14:39.4

7. Vaino Koskela (Fin) 14:41.0; 8. Vaino Makela (Fin) 14:43.0; 9. Marcel Vandewattyne (Bel); 10. Martin Stokken (Nor); 11. Helge Perala (Fin);. . . dnf—Evert Nyberg (Swe).

1952 (43. H 22 July; F 24 July): The heats were hotly contested and produced many fast clockings. In the second Schade broke the Olympic record, winning in 14:15.4 from Parker (14:18.2) and Beres (14:19.6). The other heats were won by Mimoun (14:19.0) and Anufriyev (14:23.6). In the final the pre-meet favorites took command after the first kilometer, with Schade leading Chataway, Reiff, Mimoun and Zatopek. In the next two kilometers Pirie joined the group and stayed in the lead for a while. In the last kilometer Reiff suddenly lost contact and disappeared from the picture, while Pirie dropped back just before the bell. Zatopek was the leader of the 4-man group as the last lap saw a titanic struggle. In the backstretch Chataway wrested the lead from Zatopek, but on the last curve the young Briton visibly began to tire. By then Zatopek was starting his final bid, charging wildly. As they approached the homestretch, he began to look like a sure winner, while Chataway, probably brushed by someone, hit the curb and fell. In the straight, Mimoun and Schade desperately tried to hang on to Zatopek but had to surrender. Pirie came from behind to nip the gallant Chataway for 4th. Intermediate

times: 2:47, 5:37.4, 8:30.4, 11:24.8 (Schade). Zatopek finished in 58.1 and 28.3.

1. Emil Zatopek (Czech)	14:06.6 OR	4. Gordon Pirie (GB)	14:18.0
2. Alain Mimoun (Fr)	14:07.4	5. Chris Chataway (GB)	14:18.0
3. Herbert Schade (WG)	14:08.6	6. Les Perry (Aus)	14:23.6

7. Ernö Beres (Hun) 14:24.8; 8. Ake Andersson (Swe) 14:26.0; 9. Bertil Albertsson (Swe) 14:27.8; 10. Aleksandr Anufriyev (SU) 14:31.4; 11. Alan Parker (GB) 14:37.0; 12. Ilmari Taipale (Fin) 14:40.0; 13. Erno Tuomaala (Fin) 14:54.2; 14. Lucien Theys (Bel) 14:59.0;...
dnf—Gaston Reiff (Bel).
(Schade 14:15.4 OR, H)

1956 (23. H 26 Nov; F 28 Nov): The heats were won by Pirie (14:25.6), Lawrence (14:14.6, with Kuts second in 14:15.4) and Thomas (14:14.2). In the final, Kuts went into the lead very early. At 1000 meters he was still followed by a closely bunched group, but in the next kilo the hot pace began to tell and only Pirie and Ibbotson stayed with him, while little Thomas led the second division a few meters behind the leaders. In the third kilometer Chataway joined the front group. At 3000 meters Kuts was thus followed by three Britons. Shortly afterwards, Chataway had a crisis and soon disappeared from the picture. At 4000 meters Kuts had burned off Pirie (the world record holder) and Ibbotson. The Soviet built up a substantial lead and went home an easy, impressive winner. Pirie outsprinted Ibbotson in the straight. Intermediate times: 2:40.1, 5:26.2, 8:11.2, 10:57.4. Kuts' last lap: 62.8.

1. Vladimir Kuts (SU)	13:39.6 OR	4. Miklos Szabo II (Hun)	14:03.4
2. Gordon Pirie (GB)	13:50.6	5. Albie Thomas (Aus)	14:04.6
3. Derek Ibbotson (GB)	13:54.4	6. Laszlo Tabori (Hun)	14:09.8

7. Nyandika Maiyoro (Ken) 14:19.0; 8. Thyge Thogersen (Den) 14:21.0; 9. Pyotr Bolotnikov (SU) 14:22.4; 10. Ivan Chernyavskiy (SU) 14:22.4; 11. Chris Chataway (GB) 14:28.8; 12. Herbert Schade (WG) 14:31.8;... dnf—Bill Dellinger (US), Velisa Mugosa (Yug);... dnc—Al Lawrence (Aus).

1960 (48. H 31 Aug; F 2 Sept): The first heat was the fastest, mostly because Conti forced the pace on his way to a national record 14:01.6, though he finished second to Grodotzki (14:01.2). The other heats were won by Flosbach (14:08.4), Janke (14:04.4) and Power (14:03.0). The final, two days later, was relatively quiet for over half the race. The field remained bunched for more than seven laps, at which point Conti was the first to lose contact. Up to that time, Zimny had led the field for most of the way. Halberg was in the rear guard and only began to move up during the seventh lap. After a short-lived attempt to run away by Power, Halberg struck with sudden boldness in the tenth lap and soon opened up a gap. While the others, led by Grodotzki, were churning along in full but futile pursuit, Halberg increased his lead to nearly 20 meters. In the last lap Grodotzki closed part of the gap, while Janke and Zimny came from behind to challenge for second place. Halberg understandably faded a bit in the closing stages but managed to earn a hard-won victory, as Zimny nearly caught Grodotzki for 2nd. Intermediate times: 2:41.1 (Zimny), 5:28.2 (Thomas), 8:19.3 (Zimny), 11:01.7 (Halberg). Halberg ran the last 2000 in 5:23.6.

1. Murray Halberg (NZ)	13:43.4	4. Friedrich Janke (Ger)	13:46.8
2. Hans Grodotzki (EG)	13:44.6	5. Dave Power (Aus)	13:51.8
3. Kazimierz Zimny (Pol)	13:44.8	6. Nyandika Maiyoro (Ken)	13:52.8

7. Michel Bernard (Fr) 14:04.2; 8. Horst Flosbach (WG) 14:06.6; 9. Aleksandr Artinyuk (SU) 14:08.0; 10. Sandor Iharos (Hun) 14:11.4; 11. Albie Thomas (Aus) 14:20.4; 12. Luigi Conti (It) 14:34.0.

1964 (48. H 16 Oct; F 18 Oct): In the heats no less than 11 ducked under 14:00, against only 9 in the whole of the previous history of the Games! Clarke posted the fastest time, 13:48.4. Defending champion Murray Halberg of New Zealand was eliminated in the third heat. The final was run on a rainy day with the stadium lights on. Mohamed Gammoudi, a silver medalist in the 10,000 two days earlier, scratched. Clarke led for the greater part of the race at a relatively slow pace, as 9 runners were still together with a lap and a half to go. Then Dellinger, a veteran of the '56 Games, surged ahead to lead at the bell. Jazy charged back around the penultimate turn and began to draw away from the rest. At one time he had up to ten meters on his closest pursuer, Schul. With 50m to go Jazy suddenly tied up and Schul, who had been closing the gap gradually, shot ahead to finish a mud-spattered but glorious 1st. He ran the last

lap in 54.8, and the last 300 in 38.7. Norpoth (55.6) and Dellinger also nosed out Jazy in the closing stage. Intermediate times: 2:50.2, 5:39.4, 8:22.2 (Clarke always the leader), 11:15.6 (Jazy).

1. Bob Schul (US)	13:48.8	4. Michel Jazy (Fr)	13:49.8
2. Harald Norpoth (WG)	13:49.6	5. Kip Keino (Ken)	13:50.4
3. Bill Dellinger (US)	13:49.8	6. Bill Baillie (NZ)	13:51.0

7. Nikolay Dutov (SU) 13:53.8; 8. Thor Helland (Nor) 13:57.0; 9. Ron Clarke (Aus) 13:58.0; 10. Styepan Baidyuk (SU) 14:11.2; 11. Mike Wiggs (GB) 14:20.8;. . . dnc—Mohamed Gammoudi (Tun).

1968 (39. H 15 Oct; F 17 Oct): Altitude dictated a slow pace, yet several top ranking men failed to survive the heats, where the fastest time was 14:19.8 by Wadoux. In the final, world record holder Clarke led the 13-man field at 1000m (2:53.6) and let Keino move ahead just before the end of the second kilometer (5:44.0). Then the Aussie just found himself unable to exert the kind of forcing he was used to in races run at sea level. The pace slackened a bit toward the middle of the race, when Sviridov was usually in the lead (3000 in 8:38.8). Clarke again moved up front for another spell (4000 in 11:30.8), then had to give way to Gammoudi. At the bell only 5 appeared to be still in contention: Gammoudi, Temu, Keino, Martinez and Clarke. The last lap was an all-African affair, as first Temu then Keino tried to pass Gammoudi. The stubborn Tunisian (altitude trained, but not an altitude native, as were the Kenyans) held on desperately and finally won from Keino by a good meter. His last lap took 54.8, fantastic running under the circumstances.

1. Mohamed Gammoudi (Tun)	14:05.0	4. Juan Martinez (Mex)	14:10.8
2. Kip Keino (Ken)	14:05.2	5. Ron Clarke (Aus)	14:12.4
3. Naftali Temu (Ken)	14:06.4	6. Wohib Masresha (Eth)	14:17.6

7. Nikolay Sviridov (SU) 14:18.4; 8. Fikru Degefu (Eth) 14:19.0; 9. Jean Wadoux (Fr) 14:20.8; 10. Rex Maddaford (NZ) 14:39.8; 11. Bob Finlay (Can) 14:45.0; 12. Emiel Puttemans (Bel) 14:59.6;. . . dnf—Harald Norpoth (WG);. . . dnc—Jack Bacheler (US), Mamo Wolde (Eth).

1972 (61. H 7 Sept; F 10 Sept): The heats, held 4 days after the 10,000 final, were torrid affairs. Among those who failed to survive the heats was Ben Jipcho of Kenya, who had won silver in the steeplechase 3 days before. Miruts Yifter, third in the 10,000, failed to start: he mistook the entry gate and could not get into the arena in time. Puttemans lowered the OR to 13:31.8 in winning heat 2 from Prefontaine (13:32.6) and Norpoth (13:33.4), while European champion Vaatainen won heat 4 in 13:32.8 from Stewart (13:33.0). Sviridov, best European in both the 5 and 10 at Mexico City, led at 1000m (2:46.4), then was relieved by Viren (2000 5:32.6) and Bedford. Alvarez was in the lead at 3000 (8:20.2). With 4 laps to go, Prefontaine made his move and gradually opened up (4000 in 11:00.0): only Viren, Puttemans, defending champion Gammoudi and Stewart were able to hang on. Viren took over just before the bell, with Pre and Gammoudi close on his heels. The Finn repulsed a challenge by Gammoudi in the backstretch, then covered the last 200 in 28.0 to win by a safe margin. Stewart closed faster than anyone else, nipped Pre for 3rd and just failed to catch Gammoudi. The winner covered his last 2000 in 5:06.0 (faster than the Finnish record), 1000 in 2:26.2, 800 in 1:56.0, last lap in 56.0.

1. Lasse Viren (Fin)	13:26.4 OR	4. Steve Prefontaine (US)	13:28.4
2. Mohamed Gammoudi (Tun)	13:27.4	5. Emiel Puttemans (Bel)	13:30.8
3. Ian Stewart (GB)	13:27.6	6. Harald Norpoth (WG)	13:32.6

7. Per Halle (Nor) 13:35.5; 8. Nikolay Sviridov (SU) 13:39.4; 9. Frank Eisenberg (EG) 13:40.8; 10. Javier Alvarez (Sp) 13:41.8; 11. Ian McCafferty (GB) 13:43.2; 12. Dave Bedford (GB) 13:43.2; 13. Juha Vaatainen (Fin) 13:53.8;. . . dns—Mariano Haro (Sp). (Puttemans 13:31.8 OR H)

1976 (36. H 28 July; F 30 July): The heats were won by Quax (13:30.9), Polleunis (13:45.2) and Foster (13:20.3, OR) as heat 3 produced a set of times which remained unsurpassed in the final. Under the pressure applied by European champion Foster, the first nine finishers all bettered 13:30—and three of them failed to qualify! In the final, two days later, the early pace was relatively slow (2:41.3, 5:26.4, 8:16.2), as Foster and Viren alternated in the lead without really putting on the pressure. The Finn began to look serious with 2½ laps to go (4000m

10:55.4): From then on his sustained, relentless drive took the sting out of a bunch of men all with supposedly superior basic speed. Quax made up for his poor show in the 10,000 heats a week earlier (when he was ill) and finished a close second, while Hildenbrand wrested the bronze medal from Dixon with a desperate dive over the finish line. Viren ran the last kilometer in 2:29.4, the last 400 in 55.0. Ultimately, he was 1.6 seconds faster than in Munich 4 years earlier.

1. Lasse Viren (Fin)	13:24.8	4. Rod Dixon (NZ)	13:25.5
2. Dick Quax (NZ)	13:25.2	5. Brendan Foster (GB)	13:26.2
3. Klaus-Peter Hildenbrand (WG)	13:25.4	6. Willy Polleunis (Bel)	13:27.0

7. Ian Stewart (GB) 13:27.7; 8. Aniceto Simoes (Port) 13:29.4; 9. Knut Kvalheim (Nor) 13:30.3; 10. Detlef Uhlemann (WG) 13:31.1; 11. Enn Sellik (SU) 13:36.7; 12. Paul Geis (US) 13:42.5; 13. Pekka Paivarinta (Fin) 13:46.6;... dnf—Boris Kuznyetsov (SU) (fell).
(Foster 13:20.3 OR, H)

10,000 METERS

1896—1908 (not contested).

1912 (30. H 7 July; F 8 July): The fastest time in the heats was Richardson's 32:30.8. Only 11 of the 15 qualifiers showed up for the final. Kolehmainen took the lead in the second lap and set a hot pace. Karlsson and Scott managed to stay with the Finn for five laps, then Scott dropped back and a little later Karlsson too was forced to give up. The Swede eventually dropped out at the halfway mark, which Kolehmainen reached in 15:11.4. By then Tewanima had moved to 2nd, with Stenroos on his heels. Tatu Kolehmainen, Hannes' elder brother, retired at 6000 meters while 5th. The sun and the pace began to tell and the field was narrowed to 5. Kolehmainen covered the second half of the race in 16:09.4 but reportedly finished in good condition—in fact, four other Olympic races awaited him in the next seven days! Tewanima ran away from Stenroos in the closing stages.

1. Hannes Kolehmainen (Fin)	31:20.8	4. Joseph Keeper (Can)	32:36.2
2. Louis Tewanima (US)	32:06.6	5. Alfonso Orlando (It)	33:31.2
3. Albin Stenroos (Fin)	32:21.8		

dnf— M. Karlsson (Swe), Tatu Kolehmainen (Fin), Henry L. Scott (US), W. Scott (GB), H. F. Maguire (US), Len Richardson (S Afr).
(H. Kolehmainen 33:49.0 OR, H; Richardson 32:30.8 OR, H)

1920 (37. H 19 Aug; F 20 Aug): The fastest time in the heats was 32:08.2 by Liimatainen. In the early stages of the final Wilson, Guillemot and Nurmi alternated in the lead, but after 4 laps the Finn was some 20 meters behind. Then the pace slackened, and Nurmi, then little Maccario, were able to join the leaders. Guillemot forced the pace with five laps to go and Maccario dropped back. At the bell Nurmi took over, while Wilson lost contact. Guillemot trailed Nurmi and even managed to regain the lead for a while. But when Nurmi spurted again, down the homestretch, the Frenchman could not respond.

1. Paavo Nurmi (Fin)	31:45.8	4. Augusto Maccario (It)	
2. Joseph Guillemot (Fr)	31:47.2	5. James Hatton (GB)	
3. James Wilson (GB)	31:50.8	6. Jean Manhes (Fr)	

7. Heikki Liimatainen (Fin); 8. Frederick Faller (US). Other finalists: Charles Clibbon (GB) G. Heuet (Fr), O. Garin (Switz).

1924 (43. F 6 July): For the first time, there were no heats, and the field was a large one. After two laps Wide and Ritola ran away from the pack and soon built up a big lead, steadily gaining ground as the race progressed. Ritola outpaced Wide toward the end to win easily in world record time, an amazing achievement in the warm weather. Kilometers: 2:47.8, 5:45.2, 8:47.4 (Wide), 11:52.6, 15:00.2, 18:05.6, 21:05.6, 24:14.2, 27:19.6 (Ritola).

1. Ville Ritola (Fin)	30:23.2 WR	4. Vaino Sipila (Fin)	31:50.2
2. Edvin Wide (Swe)	30:55.2	5. Ernest Harper (GB)	
3. Eero Berg (Fin)	31:43.0	6. Halland Britton (GB)	

7. G. Tell (Fr) 32:12.0; 8. Earl Johnson (US); 9. R. Marchal (Fr) 32:33.0; 10. A. Motmillers (Lat).

1928 (24. F 29 July): Beavers and Ray were the early leaders, but after four laps Ritola and Nurmi moved up, followed by Wide and Ray. On the ninth lap, Beavers was again in the lead but for only a moment. He dropped back irreparably just before the halfway. By then the famous Scandinavian trio of Ritola-Nurmi-Wide had decisively run away from the rest. The two Finns dropped their Swedish rival in the 18th lap, then ran together till the last lap, when Nurmi managed to build up a narrow but safe margin with a long, sustained spurt. The second half of the race was faster than the first (15:07.8 vs. 15:11.0).

1. Paavo Nurmi (Fin)	30:18.8 OR	4. Jean-Gunnar Lindgren (Swe)	31:26.0
2. Ville Ritola (Fin)	30:19.4	5. Anthony Muggridge (GB)	31:31.8
3. Edvin Wide (Swe)	31:00.8	6. Ragnar Magnusson (Swe)	31:37.2

7. Toivo Loukola (Fin); 8. K. Matilainen (Fin); 9. W. Beavers (GB); 10. J. S. Smith (GB); 11. R. Marchal (Fr); 12. G. C. Constable (GB); 20 finished.

1932 (16. F 31 July): Kusocinski went into the lead at the start and negotiated the first 1500 meters in 4:17.0. By then only Iso-Hollo, Virtanen, Syring, Lindgren and Savidan were still with him. The Pole went on at relentless speed, occasionally receiving some help from Iso-Hollo. At 5000 meters (14:56.6), the front group consisted of only four: Kusocinski, Iso-Hollo, Virtanen, Savidan. Soon afterwards Kusocinski and Iso-Hollo were out in front alone. The decision came about in the last 200 meters, when Kusocinski gradually ran away from the Finn. After running wildly for a while, the Pole dropped to a dog trot in the last few meters but managed to cross the line well ahead. The winner's time was the second best on record up to that time, only Nurmi having run faster (30:06.1 in 1924). Kusocinski ran the last lap in 62 seconds.

1. Janusz Kusocinski (Pol)	30:11.4 OR	4. John Savidan (NZ)	31:09.0
2. Volmari Iso-Hollo (Fin)	30:12.6	5. Max Syring (Ger)	31:35.0
3. Lauri Virtanen (Fin)	30:35.0	6. Jean-Gunnar Lindgren (Swe)	31:37.0

Also competed: M. Kitamoto (Japan), S. Takenaka (Japan), F. Cicarelli (Arg), A. Cardoso (Braz), J. M. Rodriguez (Mex), J. Ribas (Arg), Thomas Ottey (US), Louis Gregory (US), Eino Pentti (US), Calvin Bricker (Can).

1936 (30. F 2 Aug): The stocky Murakoso went into the lead soon after the start and led for more than half the race. Potts and Eaton, both of Britain, Gebhardt of Germany, Salminen, Iso-Hollo, Askola and Noji were the others in the front group. Soon after the halfway mark, the Japanese and the three Finns ran away from the rest. In the seventh kilometer the Finnish trio forged ahead, while Murakoso grimly hung on. It was only after the bell that he finally lost contact. When Salminen started his bid, Iso-Hollo too dropped back. Askola, known as Salminen's perennial underdog, ran the race of his lifetime but ultimately succumbed to his tall compatriot by a narrow margin. Kilometers: 2:46, 5:45, 8:53, 11:56, 15:01, 18:06 (Murakoso), 21:12 (Askola), 24:19 (Iso-Hollo), 27:29 (Askola).

1. Ilmari Salminen (Fin)	30:15.4	4. Kohei Murakoso (Japan)	30:25.0
2. Arvo Askola (Fin)	30:15.6	5. James Burns (GB)	30:58.2
3. Volmari Iso-Hollo (Fin)	30:20.2	6. Juan Carlos Zabala (Arg)	31:22.0

7. M. Gebhardt (Ger) 31:29.6; 8. Don Lash (US) 31:39.4; 9. O. Rasdal (Nor) 31:40.4; 10. H. Seifert (Den) 31:52.6; 11. Giuseppe Beviacqua (It) 31:57.0; 12. Janos Kelen (Hun) 32:01.0; 29 finished.

1948 (27. F 30 July): World record holder Heino took the lead in the first lap, with Heinstrom trailing and Zatopek lagging behind. It was only after nine laps that Zatopek moved up and took the lead. Soon after the half-way mark these two were left alone to battle for victory. With 10 laps to go, the Czech made an all-out effort and Heino dropped back immediately. Zatopek's spurts and the warm weather had apparently taken too much out of the Finn, and in

the seventh kilometer he ran off the track. Zatopek went on and on to win by a huge margin over Mimoun, who ran a steady race throughout and came up fast near the end to take 2nd from Albertsson. The latter thought he had lapped the Frenchman and when he realized his mistake he could do nothing to remedy the situation. Sixth was first awarded to Robert Evaraert of Belgium, who had in fact retired after 8000 meters. The time for the first 5000 was 14:54 (Heino). Zatopek ran the last lap in 66.6.

1. Emil Zatopek (Czech)	29:59.6 OR	4. Martin Stokken (Nor)	30:58.6
2. Alain Mimoun (Fr)	30:47.4	5. Severt Dennolf (Swe)	31:05.0
3. Bertil Albertsson (Swe)	30:53.6	6. Abdallah ben Said (Fr)	31:07.8

7. Stan Cox (GB) 31:07; 8. Jim Peters (GB) 31:16; 9. Salomon Kononen (Fin).

1952 (32. F 20 July): Perry was the leader for the first two laps, then Anufriyev took over. Zatopek, after lagging behind in the early stages, moved up in the third kilometer and jumped into the lead. At the half-way point he was followed by Mimoun, Pirie, Anufriyev, Sando and Posti, with the rest of the field spread-eagled. In the sixth kilometer, Zatopek's recurrent spurts caused all but Mimoun to drop back—in the eighth, even Mimoun was dropped. Zatopek had the race won, yet he exerted himself in a gallant but vain effort to beat his own world record (29:02.6). Anufriyev had a crisis midway but recovered well enough to take 3rd ahead of Posti, who ran a well-paced race. Kilometers: 2:52, 5:51 (Anufriyev), 8:48, 11:45.6, 14:43.4, 17:39.2, 20:34, 23:31, 26:28 (Zatopek). Zatopek ran the last lap in 64.0.

1. Emil Zatopek (Czech)	29:17.0 OR	4. Hannu Posti (Fin)	29:51.4
2. Alain Mimoun (Fr)	29:32.8	5. Frank Sando (GB)	29:51.8
3. Aleksandr Anufriyev (SU)	29:48.2	6. Valter Nystrom (Swe)	29:54.8

7. Gordon Pirie (GB) 30:09.5; 8. Fred Norris (GB) 30:09.8; 9. Ivan Pozhidayev (SU) 30:13.4; 10. Martin Stokken (Nor) 30:22.2; 11. Nikifor Popov (SU) 30:24.2; 12. Bertil Albertsson (Swe) 30:34.6. 32 finished.

1956 (25. F 23 Nov): Kuts disclosed his plot at the start by excoriating the field with a 61.2 opening lap. Pirie was the only one who managed to stay with him for the greater part of the race. At the halfway mark, Kut's time (14:07) was just a shade slower than Zatopek's Olympic record for the 5000! In the fifth kilometer Pirie lost contact for a while but a quick recovery again brought him in the wake of his great rival. Kuts occasionally weaved out to the second, even third lane, offering Pirie room to pass, but the Briton constantly declined the invitation. It was only in the 20th lap that Pirie somehow found himself in the lead, while Kuts used his back seat position to relax from pressure and plan a new attack. Before the lap was over, the Soviet again took the lead and gradually drew away from Pirie, who finally collapsed and disappeared from the hunt. Kovacs, who was at one time 18 seconds behind the leaders, came closing fast in the final stages and took second place from Allan Lawrence of Australia with a 61.7 last lap. Kuts did not exert himself too much in the closing stages and his last lap took 66.7 seconds. Kilometers (Kuts): 2:43, 5:31, 8:26, 11:16, 14:07, 17:02, 20:01, 23:01, 25:53.

1. Vladimir Kuts (SU)	28:45.6 OR	4. Zdzislaw Krzyszkowiak (Pol)	29:05.0
2. Jozsef Kovacs (Hun)	28:52.4	5. Ken Norris (GB)	29:21.6
3. Al Lawrence (Aus)	28:53.6	6. Ivan Chernyavskiy (SU)	29:31.6

7. David Power (Aus) 29:49.2; 8. Gordon Pirie (GB) 29:49.6; 9. Herbert Schade (WG) 30:00.6; 10. Frank Sando (GB) 30:05.0; 11. Pavel Kantorek (Czech); 12. Alain Mimoun (Fr). 23 finished.

1960 (32. 8 Sept): Little or nothing happened during the first half of the race, if we except a short-lived attempt to run away by Bolotnikov and Rhadi. The front group usually comprised 20 or so, but was reduced to 14 at 7000m. With 7 laps to go Power tried to run away from the rest, and only Bolotnikov, Grodotzki and Desyatchikov managed to stay with him. When Bolotnikov started his final bid, with 700m to go, the other three had to give up. His last lap was 57.4. Grodotzki was a good second, while Power outkicked Desyatchikov for third. It should be noticed that Bolotnikov had finished only 16th at Melbourne in '56 when a supposedly mature runner of 26. Nine of the first ten finishers improved on their PRs by margins ranging from 2.0 (Pirie) to 53.8 (Power). Intermediate times: 2:48.2, 5:37.4, 8:29.8, 11:24.6, 14:22.2, 17:18.6, 20:11.8, 23:01.8 and 25:53.6.

1. Pyotr Bolotnikov (SU)	28:32.2 OR	4. Aleksey Desyatchikov (SU)	28:39.6
2. Hans Grodotzki (EG)	28:37.0	5. Murray Halberg (NZ)	28:48.6
3. Dave Power (Aus)	28:38.2	6. Max Truex (US)	28:50.2

7. Zdzislaw Krzyszkowiak (Pol) 28:52.4; 8. John Merriman (GB) 28:52.6; 9. Martin Hyman (GB) 29:04.8; 10. Gordon Pirie (GB) 29:15.2; 11. Sandor Iharos (Hun) 29:15.8; 12. Gerhard Honicke (EG) 29:20.4; 15. Jozsef Kovacs (Hun) 29:42.2. 20 finished.

1964 (29. 14 Oct): The track was wet from the morning rain but there were no puddles. World record holder Clarke was at or near the front all the way. At the halfway point the leading group consisted of 5 men: Mills (14:04.6), Clarke, Wolde, Gammoudi and Tsuburaya. That was clearly a world record pace. The Japanese was first to lose contact in the second half, when the pace inevitably slackened. With one lap to go, it was a three-man affair involving Clarke, Gammoudi and Mills. Around the last curve, Gammoudi tried to steal the race by rushing through Clarke and Mills. But his lead was short-lived, as was Clarke's when the Aussie star took over. Mills surged from behind, caught his rivals with 50m to go and went through the tape as the No. 1 upset of the Games in 28:24.4, at a comparative value about 35 seconds faster than his pre-Games best for 6 miles (27:56.2). Gammoudi, as a close second, improved on his PR by an even greater margin. Intermediate times: 2:42.0 (Lindgren), 5:29.6 (Clarke), 8:20.0 (Lindgren), 11:13.0 (Clarke), 14:04.6 (Mills), 16:57.8, 19:52.6, 22:47.0, 25:42.8 (all Clarke).

1. Billy Mills (US)	28:24.4 OR	4. Mamo Wolde (Eth)	28:31.8
2. Mohamed Gammoudi (Tun)	28:24.8	5. Leonid Ivanov (SU)	28:53.2
3..Ron Clarke (Aus)	28:25.8	6. Kokichi Tsuburaya (Japan)	28:59.4

7. Murray Halberg (NZ) 29:10.8; 8. Tony Cook (Aus) 29:15.8; 9. Gerry Lindgren (US) 29:20.6; 10. Franc Cervan (Yug) 29:21.0; 11. Siegfried Herrmann (EG) 29:27.0; 12. Henri Clerckx (Bel) 29:29.6; 13. Jean Fayolle (Fr) 29:30.8; 14. Teruo Funai (Japan) 29:33.2; 15. Jean Vaillant (Fr) 29:33.6. 29 finished.

1968 (37. 13 Oct): As the first final of the "altitude Games," this race set the style for things to come in the distance events. As top ranking runners from the "plains" dropped from contention one by one, Africans (mostly "mountaineers") surged ahead to score the first of their five victories (1500 through marathon). The race unfolded at a cautious pace: except for the first lap (69.0), all subsequent ones were in the 70-74 range, until the 22nd lap, when Wolde began to apply the pressure (67.2). The leading group had by then narrowed to 7: Wolde, Clarke, Temu, Gammoudi, Martinez, Keino and Sviridov. It was at that stage that Keino staggered off the track and lay for a while, only to resume racing as an also-ran when a stretcher party was about to relieve him. At the bell it looked like a 3-man battle involving Wolde, Temu and Gammoudi. The Ethiopian held on till 50m to go, then Temu proved the stronger and completed a 57.2 last lap to win by a couple of strides. Intermediate times: 2:58.6 (Szerenyi), 5:57.4 (Sviridov), 8:56.2 (Sviridov), 11:54.8 (Sviridov), 15:00.6 (Masresha), 17:58.6 (Martinez), 20:57.2 (Martinez), 23:57.8 (Hill), 26:51.2 (Wolde).

1. Naftali Temu (Ken)	29:27.4	4. Juan Martinez (Mex)	29:35.0
2. Mamo Wolde (Eth)	29:28.0	5. Nikolay Sviridov (SU)	29:43.2
3. Mohamed Gammoudi (Tun)	29:34.2	6. Ron Clarke (Aus)	29:44.8

7. Ron Hill (GB) 29:53.2; 8. Wohib Masresha (Eth) 29:57.0; 9. Nedo Farcic (Yug) 30:01.2; 10. Alvaro Mejia (Col) 30:10.6; 11. Tracy Smith (US) 30:14.6; 12. Rex Maddaford (NZ) 30:17.2. 31 finishers.

1972 (52. H 31 Aug; F 3 Sept): For the first time since 1920, qualifying heats were held. Among those who failed to survive were defending champion Naftali Temu of Kenya and sub-28:00 man Rashid Sharafyetdinov of the USSR. Puttemans and Bedford made the first heat a very fast one, the Belgian winning by 0.2 in 27:53.4 (OR). Gammoudi won heat 2 in 27:54.8 from Haro (27:56.0) and Shorter (27:58.2). In the final, Bedford set the stage in his unmistakable style, running the first lap in 60.0 and hitting 800m in 2:04.6. He continued to lead at a good but steadily diminishing pace, and many of his opponents were able to hang on. In the 12th lap, Viren, while lying 5th, suddenly fell and caused Gammoudi to sprawl across the track. The Finn was back on his feet almost immediately and regained contact with the leaders, while Gammoudi, more seriously shaken, dropped out after a belated, half-hearted effort. The

lead changed several times until 600m to go, when Viren made a decisive move and began to drop his pursuers. At the bell, he led Puttemans by a couple of strides, with Yifter 10m behind. Viren increased his lead further in the last lap to finally clip an even second from Clarke's WR. He sped the last kilometer in 2:29.0, the last 800 in 1:56.6, the last lap in 56.6. Intermediate times: 2:37.0, 5:18.8, 8:06.4, 10:55.6, 13:44.0 (Bedford always), 16:35.8 (Viren), 19:27.8 (Yifter), 22:17.8 (Viren), 25:09.2 (Yifter).

1. Lasse Viren (Fin)	27:38.4 WR	4. Mariano Haro (Sp)	27:48.2
2. Emiel Puttemans (Bel)	27:39.6	5. Frank Shorter (US)	27:51.4
3. Miruts Yifter (Eth)	27:41.0	6. Dave Bedford (GB)	28:05.4

7. Dane Korica (Yug) 28:15.2; 8. Abdelkader Zaddem (Tun) 28:18.2; 9. Josef Jansky (Czech) 28:23.6; 10. Juan Martinez (Mex) 28:44.2; 11. Pavel Andreyev (SU) 28:46.4; 12. Javier Alvarez (Sp) 28:56.4; 13. Paul Mose (Ken) 29:03.0; 14. Willy Polleunis (Bel) 29:10.2; ... dnf—Mohamed Gammoudi (Tun).

(Puttemans 27:53.4 OR, H)

1976 (41. H 23 July; F 26 July): Unlike 4 years earlier in Munich, there were no sub-28:00 efforts in the heats, which nonetheless provided some fierce battles. Winners were Lopes (28:04.5), Smet (28:22.1) and Simmons (28:01.8). Among those who lost out were sub-28 men like Dick Quax of New Zealand, bogged down with an illness, and Victor Mora of Colombia, nursing a bad tendon. In the final the early kilometers (2:53.0, 5:44.1, 8:33.4) were slower than in the heats. Then Lopes took over and the pace livened up (11:22.8). After passing the halfway mark in 14:08.9, Lopes continued his constant acceleration (16:52.3). At 7000m, reached in 19:36.3, only Viren and Foster were still with the little Portuguese. After 8000m (22:20.2), Foster began to lose contact. Lopes reached 9000m in 25:02.9, with Viren in his wake. The Finn proved much the stronger in the decisive stage: he shot ahead of Lopes just before the bell and quickly built up an imposing lead. He finally missed his Munich time by 2 seconds, yet he ran the last 800 in 2:05.4 and the last 400 in 61.3. More significantly, his *second* 5000 was a fantastic 13:31.3. Lopes, an easy 2nd, developed severe blisters.

1. Lasse Viren (Fin)	27:40.4	4. Tony Simmons (GB)	27:56.3
2. Carlos Lopes (Port)	27:45.2	5. Ilie Floroiu (Rum)	27:59.9
3. Brendan Foster (GB)	27:54.9	6. Mariano Haro (Sp)	28:00.3

7. Marc Smet (Bel) 28:02.8; 8. Bernie Ford (GB) 28:17.8; 9. Jean-Paul Gomez (Fr) 28:24.1; 10. Jos Hermens (Hol) 28:25.0; 11. Karel Lismont (Bel) 28:26.5; 12. Chris Wardlaw (Aus) 28:29.9; 13. Garry Bjorklund (US) 28:38.1; 14. Dave Fitzsimons (Aus) 29:17.7; ... dnf—Emiel Puttemans (Bel) & Knut Boro (Nor).

MARATHON

42.195 km unless indicated otherwise.

1896 (25. F 10 April; 40km): The race was on a one-way course, from Marathon Bridge to Athens Stadium. Albin Lermusiaux, a very slim French middle distance ace, was the pacesetter for a good part of the distance. At Pikermi, near the halfway point, he was still in the lead, well ahead of Edwin Flack, the 800/1500 champion, Arthur Blake, Kellner and three Greeks. Soon afterwards Blake gave up the struggle and Vasilakos moved to third. At Karvati, Lermusiaux was still in the lead, but on a steep hill right after that he began to tire and a little later dropped out. Flack then took over the lead. Louis, a Greek from Maroussi who had been lagging behind in the early stages, began to draw nearer and nearer, passing one rival after the other. By the 32nd kilometer he overtook Flack, then ran just a few meters ahead of the Australian for the next 4 kilometers. The two were then followed by Kellner, Vasilakos and Velokas.. Just before the village of Ampelokipi, outside Athens, Louis ran away from Flack, who was completely exhausted and was picked up by an ambulance.

1. Spyridon Louis (Gr)	2:58:50	4. Ioannis Vretos (Gr)	
2. Charilaos Vasilakos (Gr)	3:06:03	5. Dimitrios Deliyannis (Gr)	
3. Gyula Kellner (Hun)	3:06:35	6. Eleftherlos Papasimeon (Gr)	

7. H. Geracakes (Gr); 8. S. Masoures (Gr); 9. S. Lagondakes (Gr).

Velokas (Gr) 3rd in 3:06:30 but disqualified.

1900 (19. F 19 July; 40.260km): The race was started on the track, then continued through the *Bois de Boulogne* and all around the old city walls, circling Paris, to end where it was started. The course, approximately oval shaped, was not sufficiently well patrolled. It was a blistering-hot day and only eight finished. Three were Frenchmen, including the winner.

1. Michel Theato (Fr)   2:59:45   4. Eugene Resse (Fr)
2. Emile Champion (Fr)   3:04:17   5. Arthur Newton (US)
3. Ernst Fast (Swe)   3:37:14   6. John Cregan (US)
    7. Richard Grant (US); 8. Ronald McDonald (US);...dnf—J.F. Nystrom (Swe).

1904 (31. F 30 Aug. 40km): The one-way course was laid out over roads many centimeters deep in dust and over seven hills varying from 30 to 100 meters in height. The day was warm and on the road the runners were choked by the dust, partly stirred up by the accompanying autos. At about 15 kilometers, three Americans, Mellor, Carr and Newton were bunched in the lead, with Spring and Fred Lorz about 200 meters back, and Hicks and Kneeland another ¾ mile back. But Lorz was forced to retire there because of cramps. He rode in an auto, later alighted and ran the last 8 kilometers and entered the stadium, where he was hailed a winner. Apparently he did it as a joke, but the officials took it more seriously and he was suspended by the AAU. (However, he won the Boston Marathon in 1905.) At 23 kilometers Mellor still led with Newton second, and Hicks, much closer up now, in third place. The sun and dust then began to tell, and several runners dropped out. Hicks tired badly, but was administered strychnine, raw eggs and brandy over the final 11 kilometers and managed to finish 6 minutes in front of 2nd. Carvajal, a novice in this type of grind, looked like a possible winner until he stopped to eat a couple of green apples gathered from a nearby tree. Soon afterwards he had cramps and could finish no better than 4th.

1. Thomas Hicks (US)   3:28:53   4. Felix Carvajal (Cuba)
2. Albert Corey (US)   3:34:52   5. Demeter Velouis (Gr)
3. Arthur Newton (US)   3:47:33   6. David Kneeland (US)
    7. H. A. Brawley (US); 8. Sidney Hatch (US); 9. Lentauw (S Afr); 10. C. D. Zehuritis (Gr).
14 finishers.

1908 (56. F 24 July): The race was from Windsor Castle to London's White City Stadium. The start was at 2:30 on a sweltering hot day. Price and Lord (both GB) were leading after 10 miles, with Hefferon and Pietri (Italy) 50 meters behind. Then Hefferon moved up front and by 15 miles (24 km) he had a two-minute lead on Lord, who was just ahead of Pietri. At 20 miles (32 km) Hefferon had increased his lead to nearly 4 minutes, and Pietri had moved to second. Then the Italian began to close the gap and just before the 25-mile mark (41 km) he passed the South African. This effort apparently took much out of the tiring Pietri. Hayes, who had run a wise race, was by then closing fast on the leader. Pietri entered the stadium first, but being almost unconscious he turned to the right instead of the left, then collapsed on the track. Doctors and officials rushed to his assistance. He fell several more times and was finally assisted across the finish line. Of course he was disqualified and victory went to Hayes.

1. Johnny Hayes (US)   2:55:19 OR 4. Alton Welton (US)   2:59:45
2. Charles Hefferon (S Afr)   2:56:06   5. William Wood (Can)   3:01:44
3. Joseph Forshaw (US)   2:57:11   6. Frederick Simpson (Can) 3:04:29
    7. H. Lawson (Can) 3:06:48; 8. J. Svanberg (Swe) 3:07:51. 9. Louis Tewanima (US) 3:09:15; 10. K. Nieminen (Fin) 3:09:51;... disq—Dorando Pietri (It) 2:54:47 [1].

1912 (68. F 14 July; 40.2 km): The race was run on a country road with start and finish in the stadium, in oppressively warm weather. At the first control station Tatu Kolehmainen of Finland, Ahlgren of Sweden, and Speroni passed together in 29:20. At the second control station Kolehmainen still led in 54:19 followed by the two South Africans, Gitsham and MacArthur, in 54:32. Gitsham passed the turning point first (1:12:40), followed by Kolehmainen (1:12:55) and MacArthur (1:13:15). On the return journey the order of the five leaders remained. MacArthur drew away from his countryman to win by nearly a minute.

1. Kenneth MacArthur (S Afr)   2:36:55   3. Gaston Strobino (US)   2:38:43
2. Christopher Gitsham (S Afr) 2:37:52   4. Andrew Sockalexis (US)   2:42:08

5. James Duffy (Can)   2:42:19   6. Sigge Jacobsson (Swe)   2:43:25
   7. John Gallagher (US) 2:44:20; 8. Joseph Erxleben (US) 2:45:48; 9. Dick Piggott (US)
2:46:41; 10. Joseph Forshaw (US) 2:49:50.

1920 (42. F 22 Aug: 42.750km): The Weather was almost perfect for marathon running. At the
turning point Kolehmainen and Gitsham were leading in 1:13:10, followed by Broos and Blasi
(1:13:58). Lossman moved up to 3rd soon afterwards, passing the tiring Blasi and Broos.
Gitsham too was visibly tired in the closing stages and a crisis forced him to give up with about
3 kilometers to go. Kolehmainen had to give all he had to stave off Lossman's final assault. In a
very close finish the Finn managed to be crowned marathon victor, eight years after his track
saga at Stockholm. His countrymen wrapped him in a huge Finnish flag. Lossman finished less
than 70 meters back. Arri, after lying 7th to 9th for three-quarters of the way, finished strongly
to take 3rd.

1. Hannes Kolehmainen (Fin)   2:32:36 OR 4. August Broos (Bel)   2:39:26
2. Juri Lossman (Estonia)   2:32:49   5. Juho Tuomikoski (Fin)   2:40:11
3. Valerio Arri (It)   2:36:33   6. Sofus Rose (Den)   2:41:18
   7. Joe Organ (US) 2:41:30; 8. R. Hansen (Den) 2:41:40; 9. U. Tallgren (Fin) 2:42:40; 10.
Tatu Kolehmainen (Fin) 2:44:04. 35 finishers.

1924 (58. F 13 July). The day was relatively cool with a slight breeze. At 8 kilometers Kranis
(Greece) was well ahead of Cuthbert (Canada), Alavoine (France), Broos (Belgium) and Jansen
(Denmark). At 14 kilometers Verger (France) was the leader. Then Stenroos began to move up
and while Verger dropped back, the Finn shot into the lead at the halfway point followed by
DeMar, Bertini and Mellor. With 8 kilometers to go Stenroos had a 3-minute lead, while Bertini,
DeMar, Halonen and Lossman were following closely bunched. Stenroos eventually increased
his lead to nearly 6 minutes. Bertini and DeMar drew away from the others.

1. Albin Stenroos (Fin)   2:41:23   4. Lauri Halonen (Fin)   2:49:48
2. Romeo Bertini (It)   2:47:20   5. Sam Ferris (GB)   2:52:26
3. Clarence DeMar (US)   2:48:14   6. Miguel Plaza (Chile)   2:52:54
   7 Boughera El Ouafi (Fr) 2:54:20; 8. G. Kinn (Swe) 2:54:34; 9. D. Carreras Salvador (Sp)
2:57:19; 10. Juri Lossman (Est) 2:57:55.

1928 (68. F 5 Aug): At 20 kilometers the leaders were Ray, Marttelin, Laaksonen, Yamada,
Tsuda. At the turning point El Ouafi was in 15th. At 28 kilometers the two Japanese runners
pulled away from their opponents. But Ray came back and after 31 kilometers he was second,
behind Yamada. At 35 kilometers Yamada still lay first followed by Ray, Marttelin, Tsuda and
El Ouafi. This last came up strongly near the end. He was second at 39 kilometers and a little
later he forged ahead, wresting the lead from Yamada. Meanwhile, Plaza had been running in
the wake of the Frenchman from Algeria. So Plaza moved up to second, and at the end of the
race the two were clearly ahead of the others. Marttelin took 3rd after a steady race, ahead of
the fading Yamada and Ray.

1. Boughera El Ouafi (Fr)   2:32:57   4. Kanematsu Yamada (Japan)   2:35:29
2. Miguel Plaza (Chile)   2:33:23   5. Joie Ray (US)   2:36:04
3. Martti Marttelin (Fin)   2:35:02   6. Seiichiro Tsuda (Japan)   2:36:20
   7. Y. Korholin-Koski (Fin) 2:36:40; 8. Sam Ferris (GB) 2:37:41; 9. Albert Michelsen (US)
2:38:56; 10. Calvin Bricker (Can) 2:39:24.

1932 (29. F 7 Aug): Zabala was the leader for the greater part of the race. He reached the turn
in 1:20:00, followed by Virtanen, Toivonen, Tsuda and Kin (1:22:00). Virtanen, fastest man in
the field but with no experience over the full marathon course, took the lead on the return
journey and was timed in 1:50:00 at 31 kilometers. Zabala followed 300 meters back, with
Toivonen 3rd. Virtanen began to fade and dropped out with 7 kilometers to go. At that stage
Wright made a big effort and at 35 kilometers he led the field with Zabala 2nd and Toivonen
3rd. Ferris, a great English marathoner at his third Games, then began to move up after playing
the waiting game. He was 4th with 7 kilometers to go. While Wright gradually lost ground,
Zabala went into the lead again at 37 kilometers and held it to the end, even though Ferris kept

closing in on him in the final stages. Toivonen also passed Wright to take 3rd. Zabala's winning margin was one of the narrowest in Olympic history.

1. Juan Carlos Zabala (Arg)	2:31:36 OR	4. Duncan McLeod Wright (GB)	2:32:41
2. Sam Ferris (GB)	2:31:55	5. Seiichiro Tsuda (Japan)	2:35:42
3. Armas Toivonen (Fin)	2:32:12	6. Onbai Kin (Japan)	2:37:28

7. Albert Michelsen (US) 2:39:38; 8. O. Heks (Czech) 2:41:35; 9. T. Gon (Japan) 2:42:52; 10. A. Hartington-Andersen (Den) 2:44:38; 11. Hans Oldag (US) 2:47:26; 12. Clifford Bricker (Can) 2:47:58. 20 finishers.

1936 (56. F 9 Aug): The field left the Olympic Stadium with defending champion Zabala in the lead. The Argentinean, who two months earlier had lowered his 10,000 best to 30:56.2, soon built up a substantial lead: 30 seconds at 4 kilometers, 45 seconds at 8 kilometers, 1:20 at 15 kilometers (49:55). At this stage he was followed by Dias (Portugal), Harper and Son, but he began to fade near halfway (1:11:29). Son and Harper (1:12:19) were closing in on the leader by 21 kilos, while Dias was 4th, just ahead of Enochsson. At 28 kilometers, Son and Harper overtook the tired Zabala who collapsed, then got up again and continued until the 32nd kilometer, at which stage he had a major crisis and dropped out. Son drew away from Harper, and with 10 kilometers to go, had a 30-second lead on the Englishman. Another Japanese, Nan, was closing in. At 35 kilometers Son appeared to have the race won. In fact he entered the stadium in good condition and finished with a sprint in the homestretch. His time was the fastest ever recorded.

1. Kitei Son (Japan)	2:29:20 OR	4. Erkki Tamila (Fin)	2:32:45
2. Ernest Harper (GB)	2:31:24	5. Vaino Muinonen (Fin)	2:33:46
3. Shoryu Nan (Japan)	2:31:42	6. Johannes Coleman (S Afr)	2:36:17

7. D. McN. Robertson (GB) 2:37:07; 8. H. A. Gibson (S Afr) 2:38:04; 9. M. Tarkiainen (Fin) 2:39:33; 10. T. Enochsson (Swe) 2:43:12; 11. S. Kyriakides (Gr) 2:43:21; 12. Khaled (Fr) 2:45:34. 42 finishers.

1948 (41. F 7 Aug): The race was over hard, hilly roads. At 6 miles, Gailly was out in front on his own (34:34). At this stage Cabrera was about 70 seconds behind the leader, and Richards lagged even further back. At 20 kilometers Gailly was still leading (1:09:29), with Lou (1:09:53), Guinez, Josset (1:10:35), Ostling (1:10:40) following in that order. Cabrera had moved up to sixth (1:10:51), while Richards was further back, in the company of Viljo Heino, the holder of the world 10,000 record. Except for the retirement of Lou, there weren't many changes at 30 kilometers: Gailly (1:47:01), Guinez (1:47:33), Choi (1:47:53), Cabrera (1:47:54), Ostling (1:48:25). Yun Chil Choi of Korea was by then producing his big effort. At 35 kilometers he shot into the lead (2:06:02), followed by Cabrera (2:06:30), Gailly (2:06:33), Guinez (2:06:37) and Richards (2:06:54). These five were well clear of the others. With less than 2 kilometers to go, Cabrera was in the lead with Gailly five seconds back and Richards third. As the leaders approached Wembley Stadium, Gailly wrested the lead from Cabrera. But that spurt cost him too much; though first in the stadium, the Belgian had nothing left. Cabrera, then Richards, both full of running, overtook him in the final lap. This was the greatest mass finish in marathon history, with three men closely bunched down to the end.

1. Delfo Cabrera (Arg)	2:34:52	4. Johannes Coleman (S Afr)	2:36:06
2. Tom Richards (GB)	2:35:08	5. Eusebio Guinez (Arg)	2:36:36
3. Etienne Gailly (Bel)	2:35:34	6. Thomas Sidney Luyt (S Afr)	2:38:11

7. G. Ostling (Swe) 2:38:41; 8. J. Systad (Nor) 2:38:41; 9. A. P. Sensini (Arg) 2:39:30; 10. K. Larsen (Den) 2:41:22; 11. Viljo Heino (Fin) 2:41:32; 12. A. Melin (Swe) 2:42:20. 30 finishers.

1952 (66. F 27 July): Zatopek, running his first marathon only 3 days after his second triumph on the track, proved head and shoulders above the opposition. In the early stages he kept close to the leaders at what was for him a funereal pace, and finished remarkably fresh, two and a half minutes ahead of Gorno, who ran a wise race throughout. At 10 kilometers Britain's Jim Peters was first in 31:55, followed by Jansson (32:11), Zatopek (32:12), Cox of Britain (32:41), Gorno (32:57) and defending champion Cabrera (33:13). At 20 kilometers Zatopek and Jansson were in the lead (1:04:27), closely followed by Peters (1:04:37). Cabrera was

passed by Choi and Karvonen in the closing stages, and though running about 8 minutes faster than he had done in London (on a more difficult course, it is true) he had to be content with 6th. Zatopek thus won his third gold medal in a week. His triple (5000, 10,000, marathon) is commonly rated as the greatest feat in Olympic history. Seven beat the Olympic record.

1. Emil Zatopek (Czech)	2:23:04 OR	4. Yoon Chil Choi (Kor)	2:26:36
2. Reinaldo Gorno (Arg)	2:25:35	5. Veikko Karvonen (Fin)	2:26:42
3. Gustaf Jansson (Swe)	2:26:07	6. Delfo Cabrera (Arg)	2:26:43

7. J. Dobronyi (Hun) 2:28:05; 8. E. Puolakka (Fin) 2:29:35; 9. G. Iden (GB) 2:30:42; 10. W. Hayward (S Afr) 2:31:51; 11. T. Luyt (S Afr) 2:32:41; 12. G. Ostling (Swe) 2:32:49; 13. Vic Dyrgall (US) 2:32:53; 14. L. Celedon (Chile) 2:33:46; 15. A. van de Zande (Hol) 2:33:50. 53 finishers.

This 1952 marathon win gave Emil Zatopek the finest Olympic triple ever. It was also the fastest marathon ever run on an out-and-back course—and it came in his first race.

1956 (46. F 1 Dec): The race was run on a hot day. Mimoun, a converted track specialist who had placed 2nd to Zatopek in five major championship races 1948-1952, turned his first marathon into a successful one, thus continuing the postwar tradition of Cabrera and Zatopek. Zatopek was not at his best, being short on condition due to a recent illness. Another track veteran, Mihalic took 2nd from Karvonen, one of the "purest" marathoners in the field. A detailed story of the race in figures:

10 kilometers—Kotila, Filin, Ivanov (USSR), Mimoun 33:30; F. Norris, Karvonen, Kanuti (Kenya) 33:34; Oksanen, Perry (Australia), Mihalic 33:35; Zatopek, Lee 33:37;

20 kilometers—Clark (GB), Mimoun, Ivanov, Filin, Karvonen, Mihalic 1:08:03; Nyberg (Sweden) 1:08:16; Kotila 1:08:17;. . . Zatopek 10th (1:08:26);

30 kilometers—Mimoun 1:41:47; Karvonen, Mihalic, Kawashima 1:42:59; Zatopek 1:43:50; Filin 1:44:08; Nyberg 1:44:24; Lee 1:45:12;

40 kilometers—Mimoun 2:17:30; Mihalic 2:18:44; Karvonen 2:19:37; Kawashima 2:20:35; Lee 2:20:56; Zatopek 2:21:15; Filin 2:22:35.

1. Alain Mimoun (Fr)	2:25:00	4. Chang-Hoon Lee (Kor)	2:28:45
2. Franjo Mihalic (Yug)	2:26:32	5. Yoshiaki Kawashima (Japan)	2:29:19
3. Veikko Karvonen (Fin)	2:27:47	6. Emil Zatopek (Czech)	2:29:34

7. Ivan Filin (SU) 2:30:37; 8. E. Nyberg (Swe) 2:31:12; 9. Thomas Nilsson (Swe) 2:33:33; 10. Eino Oksanen (Fin) 2:36:10; 11. Arnold Waide (Swe) 2:36:21; 12. Choon Sik Choi (Kor) 2:36:53; 13. Paavo Kotila (Fin) 2:38:59; 14. Mercer Davies (S Afr) 2:39:48; 15. Henry Hicks (GB) 2:39:55. 33 finishers.

1960 (69. F 10 Sept): For the first third of the race, a group of four—Arthur Keily (GB), Aurele Vandendriessche (Bel), Rhadi and Bikila—set the pace. They passed the 5 km point in 15:35, 10 km in 31:07, and reached 15 km in 48:02. Considering that the first 10M of the race was uphill, this was a foolhardy pace. The experienced marathoners knew this and that turned out to be their mistake. Rhadi and Bikila soon began to draw away. They passed 20 km in 1:02:39 and at the half-way point had a 35-second lead on Vandendriessche and 48 seconds on the rapidly fading Keily. Another 32 seconds back was one of the favorites, Popov. Most observers expected Bikila and Rhadi to fade, but such was not the case. They passed 40 km in 2:08:33. In the next kilometer Bikila, running barefoot, built up a lead of 50 meters and extended it to nearly 200 meters by the time he crossed the finish line. Rhadi was an easy second, while Magee, who was nearly a full minute back in the first 5 km, outlasted the rest to get the bronze medal. The winning time was easily an Olympic record. In fact, the first 15 were inside Zatopek's 1952 time. Moreover, 62 finished and only the last failed to beat 3:00:00.

1. Abebe Bikila (Eth)	2:15:17 OR	4. Konstantin Vorbyov (SU)	2:19:10
2. Rhadi Ben Abdesselem (Mor)	2:15:42	5. Sergey Popov (SU)	2:19:19
3. Barry Magee (NZ)	2:17:19	6. Thyge Togersen (Den)	2:21:04

7. Abebe Wakgira (Eth) 2:21:10; 8. Benaissa Bakir (Mor) 2:21:22; 9. Osvaldo Suarez (Arg) 2:21:27; 10. Franjo Skrinjar (Yug) 2:21:41; 11. Nikolay Rumyantsev (SU) 2:21:50; 12. Franjo Mihalic (Yug) 2:21:53; 13. Keith James (S Afr) 2:22:58; 14. Pavel Kantorek (Cze) 2:23:00; 15. Gumersindo Gomez (Arg) 2:23:00.

1964 (68. F 21 Oct): Bikila, the 32-year-old Ethiopian, achieved what had long been considered an unthinkable feat—that of duplicating an Olympic victory in the marathon. And he did it in the revered mecca of the classic event—Japan. He stayed near the lead for the entire race and finally won by a margin of more than 4:00, the largest since 1924. Clarke, desperately seeking a resounding success after his disappointing show in the track events, was the early leader, with 15:06 (5000), 30:14 (10,000), 45:35 (15,000). But Jim Hogan and Bikila were close on his feet and eventually passed him before the half-way mark. The Ethiopian led by a scanty margin at 20,000 (1:00:58). From that point on, he kept increasing his lead. He was timed in 1:16:40 at 25,000, 1:32:50 at 30,000, 1:49:01 at 35,000 and 2:05:10 at 40,000. He finished at a slower pace than in Rome, but then his victory here never was in doubt as he recorded the fastest time ever. Clarke dropped back continually in the second half of the race, and Hogan, still second with less than 7 kilometers to go, paid the price by failing to finish. Heatley and Tsuburaya finished strongly to nail 2nd and 3rd. Fifty-eight finished—all of them in less than 3:00:00.

1. Abebe Bikila (Eth)	2:12:12 WR	4. Brian Kilby (GB)	2:17:03
2. Basil Heatley (GB)	2:16:20	5. Jozsef Suto (Hun)	2:17:56
3. Kokichi Tsuburaya (Japan)	2:16:23	6. Buddy Edelen (US)	2:18:13

7. Aurele Vandendriessche (Bel) 2:18:43; 8. Kenji Kimihara (Japan) 2:19:49; 9. Ron Clarke (Aus) 2:20:27; 10. Demissie Wolde (Eth) 2:21:26; 11. Sang-Hoon Lee (S Kor) 2:22:03; 12. Benaissa Bakir (Mor) 2:22:27; 13. Eino Oksanen (Fin) 2:22:36; 14. Billy Mills (US) 2:22:56; 15. Toru Terasawa (Japan) 2:23:09.

1968 (72. 20 Oct): For the third consecutive Olympics, an Ethiopian won the marathon. Two-time winner Bikila was in this race, trying for an unprecedented third title, but was forced out after 17-kilos by a broken ankle. But 36-year-old countryman Wolde, bronze medalist earlier in the 10,000, picked up the colors and cruised to victory by a wide 3:04. The altitude-reared Wolde wasn't in the leading 10 at 15 kilos, but by 20 he was third. He took the lead before 30 kilos and ran away from his pursuers. Low-landers Kimihara and Ryan took the other medals, giving the finish the same racial representation as '64: a black African, an Oriental and a Caucasian. Wolde finished so far ahead, he had finished a full victory lap before Kimihara entered the stadium. Ryan finished only 50 meters back for the bronze.

1. Mamo Wolde (Eth)	2:20:27	4. Ismail Akcay (Tur)	2:25:19
2. Kenji Kimihara (Japan)	2:23:31	5. Bill Adcocks (GB)	2:25:33
3. Mike Ryan (NZ)	2:23:45	6. Merawi Gebru (Eth)	2:27:17

7. Derek Clayton (Aus) 2:27:24; 8. Tim Johnston (GB) 2:28:05; 9. Akio Usami (Jap) 2:28:07; 10. Andy Boychuk (Can) 2:28:41; 11. Gaston Roelants (Bel) 2:29:05; 12. Pat McMahon (Eire) 2:29:21; 13. Alfredo Penaloza (Mex) 2:29:49; 14. Ken Moore (US) 2:29:50; 15. Jurgen Busch (EG) 2:30:43; 16. George Young (US) 2:31:15; 59 of 72 finished.

1972 (73. 10 Sept): Defending champion Wolde was back trying to make it four Ethiopian champions in a row, but Shorter abandoned his usual strategy of moving late in the race and instead took command with only 9000 meters gone. Everyone else let him go, and with Shorter went the gold. He led by 5 seconds at 15-kilos, 31 at 20-kilos and 53 at 25-kilos. He padded his lead at each subsequent 5-kilo mark to finish 2:12 ahead of Lismont, who had been in a group with Wolde, Moore, Kimihara, Bacheler, Hill and Macgregor since 15-kilos. Wolde didn't move away from Moore until just before the stadium where Moore felt a muscle tighten. For Shorter, it was only his fifth marathon ever and made him the first American Olympic champion since 1908. The 1-4-9 finish was the best ever by a trio of US marathoners.

1. Frank Shorter (US)	2:12:20	4. Ken Moore (US)	2:15:40
2. Karel Lismont (Bel)	2:14:32	5. Kenji Kimihara (Japan)	2:16:27
3. Mamo Wolde (Eth)	2:15:09	6. Ron Hill (GB)	2:16:31

7. Don Macgregor (GB) 2:16:35; 8. Jack Foster (NZ) 2:16:57; 9. Jack Bacheler (US) 2:17:39; 10. Lengissa Bedane (Eth) 2:18:37; 11. Seppo Nikkari (Fin) 2:18:50; 12. Akio Usami (Japan) 2:18:58; 13. Derek Clayton (Aus) 2:19:50; 14. Yuriy Velikorodnikh (SU) 2:20:03; 15. Anatoliy Baranov (SU) 2:20:11; 16. Paul Angenvoorth (WG) 2:20:19; 62 finished.

1976 (67. 31 July): Just as Bikila in '68 and Wolde in '72, Shorter was back to defend his title. But like the others, he didn't—because unheralded Cierpinski turned in the equal-4th fastest time ever to win. Cierpinski was like Shorter in one respect, though: It was only the fifth marathon of his life, same as Shorter's '72 winner. The two were always at the front of the pack, along with double winner Viren, back to try the marathon less than 24 hours after winning his second 5000 gold. Viren dogged Shorter's heels, moving with several short bursts made by the defending champion early in the race. At 25-kilos, Shorter poured it on, breaking away from the field, but Cierpinski caught him after about 4 minutes. At 35-kilos, Cierpinski had moved to a slim lead, but by 35k it was 13 seconds and by 40k 32 seconds. Kardong moved steadily through the field and was overtaken by Lismont only a mile from the finish. Viren's finish is admirable coming as it did after 30,000 kilos of tough racing—and in the first marathon of his life.

1. Waldemar Cierpinski (EG)	2:09:55 OR	4. Don Kardong (US)	2:11:16
2. Frank Shorter (US)	2:10:46	5. Lasse Viren (Fin)	2:13:11
3. Karel Lismont (Bel)	2:11:13	6. Jerome Drayton (Can)	2:13:30

7. Leonid Moseyev (SU) 2:13:34; 8. Franco Fava (It) 2:14:25; 9. Aleksandr Gotskiy (SU) 2:15:34; 10. Henri Schoofs (Bel) 2:15:53; 11. Shivnath Singh (Ind) 2:16:22; 12. Chang Sop Choe (NK) 2:16:34; 13. Massimo Magnani (It) 2:16:57; 14. Goran Bengtsson (Swe) 2:17:40; 15. Kazimierz Orzel (Pol) 2:17:44; 16. Hakan Spik (Fin) 2:17:51; 60 finished.

20 KILOMETER WALK

1896–1904 (not contested).

(1908 race was 10M; 1912, 20, 24, 48 & 52 were 10,000m)

1908 (25. F 17 July): An all-British show as Larner scored a convincing win in world record time. He had won the 3500m event 3 days earlier.

1. George Larner (GB)	1:15:58 WR	4.	F. T. Carter (GB)		1:21:21
2. Ernest Webb (GB)	1:17:31	5.	Ernest Larner (GB)		1:24:27
3. Edward Spencer (GB)	1:21:21	—	Williams Palmer (GB)	did not finish

1912 (22. F 11 July): 10 men reached the final, but only 4 finished as 3 were disqualified and another 3 quit. The winner, Goulding, had finished 4th in the 1908 3500m race.

1. George Goulding (GB)	46:28.4 WR	3.	Fernando Altimani (It)	47:37.6
2. Ernest Webb (GB)	46:50.4	4.	Aage Rasmussen (Den)	48:00.0

1920 (25. F 18 Aug): Frigerio won his first race of the Games, in a time almost 2 minutes slower than the OR. He won the 3000m test 3 days later. Pearman's silver was the last walk medal to be won by the U.S. until 1968.

1. Ugo Frigerio (It)	48:06.2	4. Cecil Charles McMaster (S Afr)	
2. Joseph Pearman (US)		5. William Hehir (GB)	
3. Charles Gunn (GB)		6. Thomas Maroney (US)	

1924 (23. F 13 July): Frigerio became walking's only 3-time gold medalist (counting his 3000m win in '20) as Goodwin finished 200m back, with McMaster back another 100.

1. Ugo Frigerio (It)	47:49.0	4. Donato Pavesi (It)	
2. Gordon Goodwin (GB)		5. Arthur Tell Schwab (Switz)	
3. Cecil Charles McMaster (S Afr)		6. F. E. Clarke (GB)	

1948 (19. H 3 Aug; F 7 Aug): Goulding's 36-year-old OR finally fell, to Mikaelsson in a heat (45:03.0). He was 10 seconds slower in leading Sweden to a 1-2 in the final.

1. John Mikaelsson (Swe)	45:13.2	4. Charles Morris (GB)	46:04.0
2. Ingemar Johansson (Swe)	45:43.8	5. Harry Churcher (GB)	46:28.0
3. Fritz Schwab (Switz)	46:00.2	6. Emile Maggi (Fr)	47:02.8

1952 (23. H 25 July; F 27 July): Mikaelsson, the 39-year-old defending champ, jumped into the lead at the 2500m point and never let go in winning by more than 200m. Runner-up Schwab was the son of 1936's 50k silver medallist.

1. John Mikaelsson (Swe)	45:02.8 OR	4. Louis Chevalier (Fr)	45:50.4
2. Fritz Schwab (Switz)	45:41.0	5. George Coleman (GB)	46:06.8
3. Bruno Junk (SU)	45:41.0	6. Ivan Yarmysh (SU)	46:07.0

1956 (20. 28 Nov): The USSR made a memorable occasion of the first-ever Olympic 20-kilo road walk, as Spirin led countrymen Mikenas and Junk to a medal-sweep (only the second by a nation other than the US to then). Spirin was 9th at 5000m, 10th at 10,000 and 3rd at 15,000 when he powered away from leader Mikenas to win.

-61-

1. Leonid Spirin (SU)	1:31:28	4. John Ljunggren (Swe)	1:32:24
2. Antanas Mikenas (SU)	1:32:03	5. Stanley Vickers (GB)	1:32:35
3. Bruno Junk (SU)	1:32:12	6. Donald Keane (Aus)	1:33:52

7. George Coleman (GB) 1:34:02; 8. Ronald Hardy (GB) 1:34:41; 9. Giuseppe Dordoni (It) 1:35:01; 10. Edward Allsopp (Aus) 1:35:43; 11. Abdon Pamich (It) 1:36:04; 12. Henry Laskau (US) 1:38:47; 17 finished.

1960 (36. 2 Sept): Two for two. That was the USSR's record after Vladimir Golubnichiy's close victory. He was near the front from the start and led after halfway. Freeman, who hadn't been over the course previously, started his surge too late and fell 9 seconds short.

1. Vladimir Golubnichiy (SU)	1:34:08	4. Dieter Lindner (EG)	1:35:34
2. Noel Freeman (Aus)	1:34:17	5. Norman Read (NZ)	1:36:59
3. Stanley Vickers (GB)	1:34:57	6. Lennart Back (Swe)	1:37:17

7. John Ljunggren (Swe) 1:37:59; 8. Ladislav Moc (Cze) 1:38:33; 9. Alex Oakley (Can) 1:38:46; 10. Eric Hall (GB) 1:38:54; 28 finished.

1964 (30. 15 Oct): Matthews buried a strong field, winning by almost 2 minutes. Halfway he led by 24 seconds, at 15,000 he had 53. Defender Golubnichiy just held off another late surge from Freeman. Zinn's was the highest placing ever by an American.

1. Ken Matthews (GB)	1:29:34 OR	4. Noel Freeman (Aus)	1:32:07
2. Dieter Lindner (EG)	1:31:14	5. Gennadiy Solodov (SU)	1:32:33
3. Vladimir Golubnichiy (SU)	1:32:00	6. Ron Zinn (US)	1:32:43

7. Boris Khrolovich (SU) 1:32:46; 8. John Edgington (GB) 1:32:46; 9. Gerhard Sperling (EG) 1:33:16; 10. John Paddick (GB) 1:33:29; 26 finished.

1968 (36. 14 Oct): Golubnichiy made history by winning back the title he lost in Tokyo, only narrowly escaping Pedraza's frenzied finish. Golubnichiy led from just before halfway, with Smaga and surprise American Haluza. Pedraza was 4th at 15-kilos but by the last lap on the track was 3rd; he collared Smaga but couldn't quite catch Golubnichiy. Haluza achieved the highest finish ever by an American.

1. Vladimir Golubnichiy (SU)	1:33:59	4. Rudy Haluza (US)	1:35:01
2. Jose Pedraza (Mex)	1:34:00	5. Gerhard Sperling (EG)	1:35:28
3. Nikolay Smaga (SU)	1:34:04	6. Otto Barch (SU)J)	1:36:17

7. Hans-Georg Reimann (EG) 1:36:32; 8. Stefan Ingvarsson (Swe) 1:36:44; 9. Leonida Caraiosifoglu (Rum) 1:37:08; 10. Peter Frenkel (EG) 1:37:21; 11. Arthur Jones (GB) 1:37:32; 12. Pasquale Busca (It) 1:37:32; 29 finishers.

1972 (24. 31 Aug): Frenkel, who had never before won a major title, had his day. The East German trio led from the start, employing team tactics against ageless veteran Golubnichiy. Frenkel assumed the lead in the last few kilos and held off the rush of the defending champion.

1. Peter Frenkel (EG)	1:26:43 OR	4. Gerhard Sperling (EG)	1:27:55
2. Vladimir Golubnichiy (SU)	1:26:56	5. Nikolay Smaga (SU)	1:28:17
3. Hans-Georg Reimann (EG)	1:27:17	6. Paul Nihill (GB)	1:28:45

7. Jan Ornoch (Pol) 1:32:02; 8. Vittorio Visini (It) 1:32:30; 9. Jose Oliveros (Mex) 1:32:41; 10. Larry Young (US) 1:32:54; 11. Jan Rolstad (Nor) 1:33:04; 12. Pedro Aroche (Mex) 1:33:05; 13. Heinz Mayr (WG) 1:33:14; 22 finished.

1976 (38. 23 July): Bautista became Mexico's first-ever Olympic champion as he cruised the fastest time in history. The East Germans again employed team strategy against the formidable Mexican. Evergreen Golubnichiy was out of it before halfway. The first four broke away between 10 and 15 kilos and with 3000m left, Bautista surged away from Reimann and Frenkel to strike gold.

1. Daniel Bautista (Mex)	1:24:41 WR	4. Karl-Heinz Stadtmuller (EG)	1:26:51
2. Hans-Georg Reimann (EG)	1:25:14	5. Raul Gonzalez (Mex)	1:28:19
3. Peter Frenkel (EG)	1:25:30	6. Armando Zambaldo (It)	1:28:26

7. Vladimir Golubnichiy (SU) 1:29:25; 8. Vittorio Visini (It) 1:29:32; 9. Gerard Lelievre (Fr) 1:29:54; 10. Roberto Buccione (It) 1:30:40; 11. Brian Adams (GB) 1:30:47; 12. Ross Haywood (Aus) 1:31:00; 13. Otto Barch (SU) 1:31:13; 36 finishers.

50 KILOMETER WALK

1896-1928 (not contested).

1932 (15. 3 Aug): Green walked to one of the biggest margins of victory (7:10) in the event's history. Three-time gold medalist Frigerio picked up the bronze.

1.	Thomas Green (GB)	4:50:10	4.	Karl Hahnel (Ger)	5:06:06
2.	Janis Dalins (Lat)	4:57:20	5.	Ettore Rivolta (It)	5:07:39
3.	Ugo Frigerio (It)	4:59:06	6.	Paul Sievert (Ger)	5:16:41

1936 (33. 5 Aug): Whitlock chopped almost 20 minutes off the OR as the event's overall quality improved markedly.

1.	Harold Whitlock (GB)	4:30:42 OR	4.	Jaroslav Stork (Cze)	4:34:01
2.	Arthur Schwab (Switz)	4:32:10	5.	Edgar Bruun (Nor)	4:34:54
3.	Adalberts Bubenko (Lat)	4:32:43	6.	Fritz Bleiweiss (Ger)	4:36:49

1948 (23. 31 July): Winner Ljunggren was so far ahead that runner-up Godel thought he had won. The Swiss waved his hat and clasped his hands all around his last lap, seeming to weep for joy until told he was actually 2nd.

1.	John Ljunggren (Swe)	4:41:52	4.	Edgar Bruun (Nor)	4:53:18
2.	Gaston Godel (Switz)	4:48:17	5.	Harry Martineau (GB)	4:53:58
3.	Tebbs Lloyd-Johnson (GB)	4:48:31	6.	Rune Bjurstrom (Swe)	4:56:43

1952 (31. 21 July): Despite persistent rain and a demanding course, Dordoni annexed the title without much trouble. The 26-year-old Italian wisely let defending champ Ljunggren get out in front early, but the Swede had nothing left in the later stages and dropped well back. Dolezal held off a late bid by Roka.

1.	Giuseppe Dordoni (It)	4:28:08 OR	4.	George Whitlock (GB)	4:32:21
2.	Josef Dolezal (Cze)	4:30:18	5.	Sergey Lobastov (SU)	4:32:35
3.	Antal Roka (Hun)	4:31:28	6.	Vladimir Ukhov (SU)	4:32:52

1956 (21. 24 Nov): Read worked his way patiently and steadily through the field, which was led by Maskinskov virtually from the start. The New Zealander took command between 40 and 45 kilos and won by more than 2 minutes.

1.	Norman Read (NZ)	4:30:43	4.	Abdon Pamich (It)	4:39:00
2.	Yevgeniy Maskinskov (SU)	4:32:57	5.	Antal Roka (Hun)	4:50:09
3.	John Ljunggren (Swe)	4:35:02	6.	Raymond Smith (Aus)	4:56:08

7. Adolf Weinacker (US) 5:00:16; 8. Albert Johnson (GB) 5:02:19; 9. Eric Hall (GB) 5:03:59; 10. Ion Barbu (Rum) 5:08:34; 11. Elliott Denman (US) 5:12:14; 12. Leo Sjogren (US) 5:12:34; 13. Ron Crawford (Aus) 5:22:36.

1960 (39. 7 Sept): Thompson, who failed to finish 4 years earlier, and 41-year-old Ljunggren waged a torrid duel over the last half of the distance. The pair took over by the half-way mark and the Swede challenged Thompson to the end. At 45-kilos, Thompson's lead was only a second, but he widened the margin finally to 17 seconds in hot conditions.

1.	Don Thompson (GB)	4:25:30 OR	4.	Aleksandr Shcherbina (SU)	4:31:44
2.	John Ljunggren (Swe)	4:25:47	5.	Thomas Misson (GB)	4:33:03
3.	Abdon Pamich (It)	4:27:56	6.	Alex Oakley (Can)	4:33:09

7. Giuseppe Dordoni (It) 4:33:28; 8. Zora Singh (Ind) 4:37:45; 9. Anatoliy Vedyakov (SU) 4:39:58; 10. Antonio De Gaetano (It) 4:41:02; 11. Ladislav Moc (Cze) 4:42:34; 12. George Hazle (S Afr) 4:43:19; 13. Max Weber (Ger) 4:44:48; 14. Svatopluk Sykara (Cze) 4:46:15; 15. Ajit Singh (Ind) 4:47:29; 28 finished.

1964 (34. 18 Oct): Pamich was challenged by Nihill past the halfway mark, but the Italian gradually widened his margin over the Briton to some 21 seconds at the end of a wet, rain-soaked walk. Super-veteran John Ljunggren was 16th.

1.	Abdon Pamich (It)	4:11:13 OR	4.	Burkhard Leuschke (EG)	4:15:27
2.	Paul Nihill (GB)	4:11:32	5.	Bob Gardiner (Aus)	4:17:07
3.	Ingvar Pettersson (Swe)	4:14:18	6.	Christoph Hohne (EG)	4:17:42

7. Anatoliy Vedyakov (SU) 4:19:56; 8. Kurt Sakowski (Ger) 4:20:31; 9. Charles Sowa (Lux) 4:20:38; 10. Don Thompson (GB) 4:22:40; 11. Ron Crawford (Aus) 4:24:20; 12. Gennadiy Agapov (SU) 4:24:34; 13. Ray Middleton (GB) 4:25:50; 14. Alex Oakley (Can) 4:27:25; 15. Henri Delerue (Fr) 4:27:48; 31 finished.

1968 (36. 17 Oct): Hohne walked a smart, "outlast 'em" race, going out with the leaders and then hanging tough as they dropped off one-by-one. His victory margin of more than 10 minutes is indicative of how well the tactic worked. Young's 3rd and Klopfer's 10th were the highest places ever taken by Americans over a standard Olympic walking distance.

1.	Christoph Hohne (EG)	4:20:14	4.	Peter Selzer (EG)	4:33:10
2.	Antal Kiss (Hun)	4:30:17	5.	Stig-Erik Lindberg (Swe)	4:34:05
3.	Larry Young (US)	4:31:56	6.	Vittorio Visini (It)	4:36:34

7. Bryan Eley (GB) 4:37:33; 8. Jose Pedraza (Mex) 4:37:52; 9. Karl-Heinz Merschenz (Can) 4:37:58; 10. Goetz Klopfer (US) 4:39:14; 11. Horst Magnor (WG) 4:39:44; 12. Frank Clark (Aus) 4:40:14; 13. Stig Andersson (Swe) 4:40:43; 14. Gerhard Weidner (WG) 4:43:27; 15. Sergey Grigoryev (SU) 4:44:40; 28 finished.

1972 (36. 3 Sept): Kannenberg, who had dropped out of the 20-kilo race 3 days earlier with a leg injury, showed no signs of trouble here. He bolted from the stadium, with Soldatenko in hot pursuit, and held the lead throughout to win by more than 2 minutes. Young lowered his American best by more than 12 minutes for his 2nd consecutive bronze.

1.	Bernd Kannenberg (WG)	3:56:12 OR	4.	Otto Barch (SU)	4:01:36
2.	Venyamin Soldatenko (SU)	3:58:24	5.	Peter Selzer (EG)	4:04:06.
3.	Larry Young (US)	4:00:46	6.	Gerhard Weidner (WG)	4:06:26

7. Vittorio Visini (It) 4:08:32; 8. Gabriel Hernandez (Mex) 4:12:09; 9. Paul Nihill (GB) 4:14:10; 10. Charles Sowa (Lux) 4:14:22; 11. Karl-Heinz Stadtmuller (EG) 4:14:29; 12. Hans Tenggren (Swe) 4:16:38; 13. Daniel Bjorkgren (Swe) 4:20:00; 14. Christoph Hohne (EG) 4:20:44; 15. Stefan Ingvarsson (Swe) 4:21:01; 29 finished.

1976 (not contested).

110 HURDLES

1896 (7. H 7 April; F 10 April): Historical debate rages over whether this race was run at 100 or 110 meters. The shorter idea was in vogue for years, but current evidence suggests the race was indeed run at the proper length. In any case, Curtis' time was well off the world record of 15.4.

1. Thomas Curtis (US)   17.6   2. Grantley Goulding (GB)   18.0.
     dns—William Hoyt (US) & Alajos Szokolyi (Hun).

1900 (8. H-F 14 July): Kraenzlein set the initial Olympic record in the first heat with 15.6. In the decisive race, McLean was off the mark first and Kraenzlein did not overtake him until the next to last hurdle, winning by a half meter or so. Moloney finished strongly to take 3rd.

1. Alvin Kraenzlein (US)	15.4 OR	4. Jean Lecuyer (Fr)	
2. John McLean (US)	15.5	5. Norman Pritchard (India)	
3. Fred Moloney (US)			
(Kraenzlein 15.6 OR, H)			

1904 (8. H-F 3 Sept): Shideler (who was reputed to have run the distance in 15.0) and Schule were the leaders in the initial stages and ran abreast to the sixth hurdle. Then Schule's long legs helped him to run away from his shorter opponent. Schule won by almost 2 meters. Third and fourth were well back.

1. Fred Schule (US)	16.0	3. L. Ashburner (US)	16.4
2. Thaddeus Shideler (US)	16.3	4. Frank Castleman (US)	

1908 (25. H 23 July; SF 24 July; F 25 July): Smithson tied the Olympic record (15.4) in his semi. In the final he had an excellent start and gained ground over each hurdle to win by about 5 meters. The race was on grass. There is a picture of Smithson clearing a hurdle while holding a book in his left hand. Whether this was in the prelims or in the final is unknown.

1. Forrest Smithson (US)	15.0 WR	3. Arthur Shaw (US)	
2. John Garrels (US)	15.7	4. William Rand (US)	
(Smithson 15.4 =OR, SF)			

1912 (21. H-SF 11 July; F 12 July): Nicholson and Powell were a fraction behind the rest at the start, but the Englishman drew level at the second flight. Midway, however, Powell began to fade, while Kelly, Wendell and Nicholson were slightly ahead of the others. Nicholson hit the eighth hurdle though, and the final struggle for first was between Kelly and Wendell, with the former forging ahead just before the tape. Hawkins edged Case for third by the narrowest of margins.

1. Fred Kelly (US)	15.1	4. John Case (US)	15.3
2. James Wendell (US)	15.2	5. Kenneth Powell (GB)	15.5
3. Martin Hawkins (US)	15.3	— John Nicholson (US)	dnf

1920 (21. H-SF 17 Aug; F 18 Aug): The fastest time in the heats was Barron's 15.2. The winners of the semis, Barron and Thomson, both returned 15.0 (=OR). In the final Thomson, a Canadian student at Dartmouth College and holder of the world 120 yard hurdles record (14.4), led all the way and won by 2½ meters. Barron and Murray were in contention during the first half of the race, then faded gradually, as Barron came home an easy second.

1. Earl Thomson (Can)	14.8 WR	4. Harry Wilson (NZ)	15.3
2. Harold Barron (US)	15.1	5. Walker Smith (US)	
3. Fred Murray (US)	15.2	6. Carl-Axel Christiernsson (Swe)	
(Barron 15.0 =OR, SF; Thomson 15.0 =OR, SF)			

1924 (27. H-SF 8 July; F 9 July): The fastest time in the prelims was 15.2 by Atkinson (heat) and Guthrie (semi). In the final, Atkinson and Kinsey were off together and ran evenly. Atkinson took the ninth hurdle a few centimeters in front and rose to the last 30 centimeters in front but hit the barrier with his rear foot and stumbled. He had a gallant recovery, however, and the end found him not more than 10 centimeters behind Kinsey. Guthrie finished a close 3rd but was disqualified for knocking down three hurdles: he was officially placed 6th.

1. Dan Kinsey (US)	15.0	4. Carl-Axel Christiernsson (Swe)	15.5
2. Syd Atkinson (S Afr)	15.0	5. Karl Anderson (US)	
3. Sten Pettersson (Swe)	15.4	— George Guthrie (US)	disq

1928 (41. H-SF 31 July; F 1 Aug): Weightman-Smith equaled the Olympic record (14.8) in a heat, and so did Dye and Anderson in winning the first two semis. In the third, Weightman-Smith, hurdling beautifully, lowered the record to 14.6, which also constituted a new world mark for the metric distance. In the final Weightman-Smith shot into the lead with Collier almost level and Anderson and Atkinson next. The decision came about when

Weightman-Smith hit the ninth hurdle, while Anderson and Atkinson, who had been running abreast all the way, passed Collier. In the hectic finish Atkinson edged Anderson by a few centimeters.

1. Syd Atkinson (S Afr)	14.8	4. Leighton Dye (US)	14.9
2. Steve Anderson (US)	14.8	5. George Weightman-Smith (S Afr)	15.0
3. John Collier (US)	14.9	6. Frederick Gaby (GB)	15.2

(Weightman-Smith 14.8 =OR, H; Dye 14.8 =OR, SF; Anderson 14.8 =OR, SF; Weightman-Smith 14.6 WR, SF)

1932 (17. H-SF 2 Aug; F 3 Aug): The semifinals offered some close struggles. In the first, Keller set a new Olympic record of 14.5, and in the second Saling did 14.4 in just beating Beard. The two Americans battled on even terms all the way in the final. Beard was in the lead when he hit the sixth hurdle; despite his gallant recovery he just could not catch Saling, who won by a scant margin. Finlay was a safe 3rd, while Keller just nipped Burghley for 4th. Each of the 6 finalists hit hurdles, Welscher being the greatest offender with four.

1. George Saling (US)	14.6	4. Jack Keller (US)	14.8
2. Percy Beard (US)	14.7	5. David Burghley (GB)	14.8
3. Don Finlay (GB)	14.8	— Willi Welscher (Ger)	disq

(Keller 14.5 OR, SF; Saling 14.4 OR =WR, SF)

1936 (31. H 5 Aug; SF-F 6 Aug): Towns was the fastest qualifier in the first round with 14.5. The next day, aided by a slight wind under the allowable limit, he did 14.1, thus equaling the world record he had set earlier in the season. Finlay won the second semi in 14.5. In the final Pollard led the field until the third hurdle. Then Towns shot into the lead, built up a good margin and was never headed. Finlay moved up from 4th to 2nd in the closing stages. Places 2-4 were tightly bunched.

1. Forrest Towns (US)	14.2	4. Hakan Lidman (Swe)	14.4
2. Don Finlay (GB)	14.4	5. John Thornton (GB)	14.7
3. Fred Pollard (US)	14.4	6. Larry O'Connor (Can)	15.0

(Towns 14.1 OR =WR, SF)

1948 (28. H 3 Aug; SF-F 4 Aug): In the prelims, Dixon did 14.2 twice. Porter won the other semi in 14.1 (=OR) from Scott (14.2). The final saw two distinct races, with the three Americans forming the first division. Porter was off fast and ran a beautiful race. However, he tipped three hurdles and that enabled Dixon to close on him midway. The feud was close until the eighth hurdle, where Porter decisively ran away from his countryman. Scott closed fast to nip Dixon for 2nd. Triulzi was the permanent leader in the second division and took 4th.

1. Bill Porter (US)	13.9 OR	4. Alberto Triulzi (Arg)	14.6
2. Clyde Scott (US)	14.1	5. Peter Gardner (Aus)	
3. Craig Dixon (US)	14.1	6. Hakan Lidman (Swe)	

(Porter 14.1 =OR, SF)

1952 (30. H 23 July; SF-F 24 July): Dillard equaled the Olympic record (13.9) in the first heat, and Davis did 14.0 in the third. The two semis were won by Dillard (14.0) and Davis (14.4). In the final Dillard was off fast, as usual, but Davis also had a good start. At the third hurdle the fast-moving Dillard had a meter lead on Davis. The latter seemed to be closing midway but then knocked down the ninth hurdle and finally lost by a scant meter. Barnard, off badly, picked up to finish an easy 3rd. Bulanchik beat the two Australians—apparently far from their home form—in the race for 4th.

1. Harrison Dillard (US)	13.7 (13.91) OR	4. Yevgeniy Bulanchik (SU)	14.5 (14.74)
2. Jack Davis (US)	13.7 (14.00)	5. Ken Doubleday (Aus)	14.7 (14.82)
3. Art Barnard (US)	14.1 (14.40)	6. Ray Weinberg (Aus)	14.8 (15.15)

(Dillard 13.9 =OR, H)

1956 (24. H 27 Nov; SF-F 28 Nov): Davis won the first semi handily and Calhoun took the second from Shankle by a narrow margin. In the final the runners battled a 1.9 mps wind. Lorger and Calhoun were off fastest. On the fourth hurdle Calhoun led Davis by centimeters, but the latter drew level by the eighth. The two Americans were never more than a few centimetres apart in the closing stages, both using a pronounced lunge for the tape. Calhoun got the verdict after examination of the photo. For the second time in his career, Davis became a co-holder of the Olympic record without winning the gold medal. Shankle was an easy 3rd. Lauer, not yet 20, just beat his European rivals for 4th.

1. Lee Calhoun (US)	13.5 (13.70) OR	4. Martin Lauer (WG)	14.5 (14.67)
2. Jack Davis (US)	13.5 (13.73) =OR	5. Stanko Lorger (Yug)	14.5 (14.68)
3. Joel Shankle (US)	14.1 (14.25)	6. Boris Stolyarov (SU)	14.6 (14.71)

1960 (36. H-QF 3 Sept; SF-F 5 Sept): May won the first semi in 13.7 from Jones (14.1), while Calhoun took the second in 13.7 from Lauer (14.0). In the final, the draw placed May and Calhoun, who appeared the class of the field, head-and-head in lanes 1 and 2. Calhoun was off ahead and had about half a meter on May at the first hurdle. Then May began to chop the disadvantage and his superior speed brought him within centimeters of Calhoun as they went over the last hurdle. On the run-in May closed the gap almost entirely and the champions went through the tape shoulder to shoulder, both using a pronounced lean. Just as in Melbourne four years earlier, Calhoun was declared the winner after examination of the photo finish. The time was "only" 13.8 as a strong wind blew against the hurdlers during the race. Lauer, co-holder of the world-record (13.2), hit three hurdles yet he came up to challenge Jones for 3rd at the end.

1. Lee Calhoun (US)	13.8 (13.98)	4. Martin Lauer (WG)	14.0 (14.20)
2. Willie May (US)	13.8 (13.99)	5. Keith Gardner (W Indies)	14.4 (14.55)
3. Hayes Jones (US)	14.0 (14.17)	6. Valentin Chistyakov (SU)	14.6 (14.71)

1964 (37. H 17 Oct; SF-F 18 Oct): Willie Davenport, surprise winner of the US Trials, injured his leg in training four days before the first round and finished seventh in the first semi-final (won by Mikhailov in 13.9w). Lindgren took the second, also in 13.9, but with little wind assistance. He was followed by Cornacchia, Jones, and Ottoz. As usual, Jones was out fastest of all. But Lindgren was also out better than usual. By the second hurdle Jones had perhaps a 2-foot lead. As they charged over successive flights, Lindgren inched up on Jones. The pair were even over the last three barriers, but Jones's far superior speed made the difference in the run to the tape. Lindgren leaned too soon and just held off the fast-closing Mikhailov. Ottoz closed even faster to get 4th.

1. Hayes Jones (US)	13.6	4. Eddy Ottoz (It)	13.8
2. Blaine Lindgren (US)	13.7	5. Gurbachan Randhawa (Ind)	14.0
3. Anatoliy Mikhailov (SU)	13.7	6. Marcel Duriez (Fr)	14.0

7. Giovanni Cornacchia (It) 14.1; 8. Giorgio Mazza (It) 14.1.

1968 (33. H 16 Oct; SF-F 17 Oct): The favorites came through the first round with little difficulty. Hall set an Olympic record 13.3 in winning the first semi from Ottoz. Davenport outleaned Coleman to take the second semi. Davenport virtually ended the race at the gun as he was off to a superb start and an immediate lead which he never relinquished. Hall and Coleman led the rest until Ottoz edged ahead of the latter when he ticked the sixth hurdle. Hall hung on for the silver.

1. Willie Davenport (US)	13.3 (13.33) =OR	4. Leon Coleman (US)	13.6 (13.67)
2. Erv Hall (US)	13.4 (13.42)	5. Werner Trzmiel (WG)	13.6 (13.68)
3. Eddy Ottoz (It)	13.4 (13.46)	6. Bo Forssander (Swe)	13.7 (13.73)

7. Marcel Duriez (Fr) 13.7 (13.77); 8. Pierre Schoebel (Fr) 14.0 (14.01).

(Ottoz 13.5 =OR, H; Hall 13.3 OR, SF)

1972 (39. H 3 Sept; SF 4 Sept; F 7 Sept): The major result of the first round was the reestablishment of Milburn as the favorite. The top ranked hurdler of '71, he had barely qualified in the US Trials. The only significant casualty was Cuban Alejandro Casanas, who hit the fourth hurdle. The semis dropped no other favorites, the first being won by Hill, winner of

the US Trials, over Drut and the second going to Milburn over Siebeck. Nadenicek was off quickest in the final, but Milburn was in front over the first hurdle and pulled away. He led by nearly two meters off the sixth barrier and though he lost some of this lead to Drut in the closing stages he still won by a comfortable margin. Drut got an indifferent start and nicked hurdle two, but moved from there to pass Hill and then Davenport. Davenport held second place until he socked the eighth barrier. Hill's chances were hampered when he hit hurdle five.

1. Rod Milburn (US)	13.24 =WR	4. Willie Davenport (US)	13.50
2. Guy Drut (Fr)	13.34	5. Frank Siebeck (EG)	13.71
3. Tom Hill (US)	13.48	6. Leszek Wodzynski (Pol)	13.72

7. Lubomir Nadenicek (Cze) 13.76; 8. Petr Cech (Cze) 13.86. Wind +0.3 mps.

1976 (24. H 26 July; SF-F 28 July): With the small field the heats eliminated none of the favorites and produced no surprises. Foster won the first semi over Munkelt and Myasnikov with the fast-starting Owens barely hanging on to qualify. Casanas took the second semi ahead of Drut and Davenport. In the final, Drut was off in front with Davenport close behind while Casanas was almost the last away. By the third hurdle Drut had a slight lead over Davenport, Owens, and Munkelt—these three being virtually even and just inches back, with Foster and Casanas another foot back. Drut and Casanas made their moves off the eighth barrier with Drut holding a scant margin to the line. Davenport couldn't quite keep up with the leaders but had enough left to hold off Foster and Munkelt.

1. Guy Drut (Fr)	13.30	4. Charles Foster (US)	13.41
2. Alejandro Casanas (Cuba)	13.33	5. Thomas Munkelt (EG)	13.44
3. Willie Davenport (US)	13.38	6. James Owens (US)	13.73

7. Vyacheslav Kulebyakin (SU) 13.93; 8. Viktor Myasnikov (SU) 13.94. Wind 0.00 mps.

400 HURDLES

1896 (not contested).

1900 (5. 15 July): This event originated in Europe, and didn't even appear in the US championship program until 1914. Therefore, great was the surprise when the undefeated French champion, Tauzin, was outpaced by Tewksbury, a virtual newcomer to the event, though very well known as a sprinter. The American used his superior speed to good advantage and won handily, while Tauzin barely saved second from Orton.

1. Walter Tewksbury (US)	57.6	3. George Orton (Can)	
2. Henri Tauzin (Fr)	58.3	4. W. F. Lewis (US)	

1904 (4. 31 Aug): The race was run over 2-6 (76 centimeter) hurdles and was won by Hillman in 53.0.

1. Harry Hillman (US)	53.0	3. George Poage (US)	
2. Frank Waller (US)	53.2	4. George Varnell (US)	

1908 (15. H 20 July; SF 21 July; F 22 July): In the heats, Bacon had the fastest time, 57.0 (OR). Defending champion Hillman ran the fastest semi: 56.4 (OR). In the final, Tremeer and Burton were outpaced in the first 150 meters, while Bacon and Hillman ran almost abreast for the greater part of the race and took the last hurdle together. Bacon won on the run-in by 1½ meters.

1. Charlie Bacon (US)	55.0 WR	3. Leonard Tremeer (GB)	57.0
2. Harry Hillman (US)	55.3	— Leslie Burton (GB)	dnf

(Bacon 57.0 OR WR, H; Hillman 56.4 OR WR, SF)

1912 (not contested).

1920 (21. H-SF 15 Aug; F 16 Aug): The fastest time in the heats was Loomis' 54.8 (OR). The semis were won by Desch and Loomis, both in 55.4. In the final, Andre (who won a silver in the '08 high jump) forced the pace in the first 200 meters, after which he was overtaken by Loomis, who won handily in world record time. Norton and Desch passed Andre in the homestretch.

1. Frank Loomis (US)	54.0 WR	4. Geo Andre (Fr)	54.6
2. John Norton (US)	54.3	5. Carl-Axel Christiernsson (Swe)	54.9
3. August Desch (US)	54.5	6. Charles Daggs (US)	
(Loomis 54.8 OR, H)			

1924 (23. H-SF 6 July; F 7 July): In the preliminary rounds, Brookins had the fastest times, 54.8 and 54.6. In the final Andre (by then a 35-year-old warrior), Brookins and Taylor were soon clear of the rest. The Frenchman again dropped back in the second half of the race, and Taylor finally edged Brookins by a good meter. Vilen ran well in the closing stages and finished a safe third. Brookins (2nd in 52.8)—was disqualified for failing to clear a hurdle cleanly and running out of his lane. Even the winner knocked down a hurdle, the last, and his world record time was not allowed under the rule then in force. Vilen thus earned an Olympic record while finishing 3rd! Blackett finished 6th but was disqualified.

1. F. Morgan Taylor (US)	52.6	4. Geo Andre (Fr)	56.2
2. Erik Vilen (Fin)	53.8 OR	− Charles Brookins (US)	disq (52.8)
3. Ivan Riley (US)	54.2	− F.J. Blackett (GB)	disq

1928 (27. H-SF 29 July; F 30 July): The semifinals were won by Taylor (53.4 OR) and Livingstone-Learmonth (54.0). The final was run on a soft track, with the two Britons the early leaders, Burghley in front. Cuhel and Taylor closed fast in the last curve and looked capable of overtaking Burghley. With everyone fading in the homestretch, Burghley, perhaps not a copybook stylist but certainly a great competitor, maintained his lead. Cuhel just edged Taylor for 2nd, while Pettersson finished a close 4th.

1. David Burghley (GB)	53.4=OR	4. Sten Pettersson (Swe)	53.8
2. Frank Cuhel (US)	53.6	5. Thomas Livingstone-Learmonth(GB)	54.2
3. F. Morgan Taylor (US)	53.6	6. Luigi Facelli (It)	55.8
(Taylor 53.4 OR, SF)			

1932 (18. H-SF 31 July; F 1 Aug): The two semis were won by Hardin and Tisdall, both in 52.8 (OR). In the decisive race Tisdall ran well from the start and held his form throughout to win in world record time. A fantastic achievement for a man who before the Games had run the "intermediates" only three times! However, his record time was not allowed because he knocked down a hurdle. Hardin finished strongly to take second from Taylor. Defending champion Burghley faded a bit near the end, yet he finished a fairly close fourth. Facelli, by then 34, was an honorable fifth.

1. Bob Tisdall (Eire)	51.7	4. David Burghley (GB)	52.2
2. Glenn Hardin (US)	51.9 WR	5. Luigi Facelli (It)	53.0
3. F. Morgan Taylor (US)	52.0	6. Kjell Areskoug (Swe)	54.6
(Hardin 52.8 OR, SF; Tisdall 52.8 =OR, SF)			

1936 (32. H 3 Aug; SF-F 4 Aug): The semis were won by Hardin (53.2) and Patterson (52.8). In the final the hurdlers battled against strong winds. Hardin went into the lead early, but White hung on grimly. On the fourth hurdle, the Filipino was actually a fraction ahead of the world record holder (50.6 in '34). Patterson drew level with the two leaders on the fifth hurdle, and the three ran practically even till the eighth barrier, where Hardin finally pulled away. Loaring closed fast, moving up from 4th to 2nd.

1. Glenn Hardin (US)	52.4	4. Joseph Patterson (US)	53.0
2. John Loaring (Can)	52.7	5. Sylvio de Magalhaes Padilha (Brz)	54.0
3. Miguel White (Phil)	52.8	6. Christos Mantikas (Gr)	54.2

1948 (25. H-SF 30 July; F 31 July): The semis offered some hectic struggles. Larsson won the first in 51.9 (OR) from Ault (52.1), White (52.1) and Jean-Claude Arifon of France (52.2). Cochran won the second in 51.9 (=OR) from Cros (52.5). In the final White was off fast but Cochran, after biding his time, opened a gap and won by a huge margin. White had no trouble in saving 2nd from a tiring Larsson.

1. Roy Cochran (US)	51.1 OR	4. Richard Ault (US)	52.4
2. Duncan White (Sri Lanka)	51.8	5. Yves Cros (Fr)	53.3
3. Rune Larsson (Swe)	52.2	6. Ottavio Missoni (It)	54.0

1952 (40. H-QF 20 July; SF-F 21 July): Moore proved the class of the field from the beginning, doing 51.8 and 50.8 (OR), the latter with 200 fractions of 24.6 and 26.2 despite a wet track. The semis were won by Lituyev (51.8) from Holland (52.0), and Yulin (52.1) and by Moore (52.0) from Whittle (52.9) and Filiput (53.0). The final was run about 2½ hours later on a heavy, rain-sodden track. Moore and Lituyev fought it out all the way. With 200 meters to go they were clear of the field. Moore held an advantage at that stage, but Lituyev pulled even on the eighth hurdle. However, Moore was very strong on the run-in and finally won by a clear margin.

1. Charley Moore (US)	50.8 (51.06)=OR	4. Anatoliy Yulin (SU)	52.8 (52.81)
2. Yuriy Lituyev (SU)	51.3 (51.51)	5. Harry Whittle (GB)	53.1 (53.36)
3. John Holland (NZ)	52.2 (52.26)	6. Armando Filiput (It)	54.4 (54.49)
(Moore 50.8 OR, QF)			

1956 (28. H 23 Nov; SF-F 24 Nov): Southern won the first semi in 50.1 (OR) from Davis (50.7), who did not go all out. Culbreath did 50.9 in taking the second from Lean (51.4) and Lituyev (51.8). The final was run 2½ hours later. Southern started fast and had a slight lead on Davis at the third hurdle. This he increased on the next two flights and was timed in 22.5 on top of the fifth hurdle, with Davis showing 22.7. The world record holder started his bid in the last curve and by the eighth hurdle he had overtaken his rival, 35.8 to 35.9. Davis, always a strong finisher, increased his lead in the homestretch, while Southern wound up an easy second. The race for third was close up to the last hurdle: 19-year-old Potgieter held a slight advantage on Culbreath at that stage but hit the last barrier and fell badly. Culbreath took 3rd ahead of Lituyev.

1. Glenn Davis (US)	50.1 (50.29)=OR	4. Yuriy Lituyev (SU)	51.7 (51.91)
2. Eddie Southern (US)	50.8 (50.93)	5. Dave Lean (Aus)	51.8 (51.93)
3. Josh Culbreath (US)	51.6 (51.74)	6. Gert Potgieter (S Afr)	56.0
(Southern 50.1 OR, SF)			

1960 (34. H 31 Aug; SF 1 Sept; F 2 Sept): Davis won the first semi in 51.1 from Rintamaki (51.1) and Janz (51.4), while Cushman took the second in 50.8 from Howard (50.8) and Galliker (51.3), who beat out Salvatore Morale of Italy (51.3). In the final the following day, Davis made several mistakes in the first half of the race, yet hit 24.0 at the halfway point, being a shade behind Janz and just ahead of Howard, while Cushman was lagging in 24.5. Davis came closing fast in the second half and took the lead on the last hurdle, while Cushman gained on everybody in the final stages. Janz hung on grimly and became Europe's first sub-50 man, yet he could not prevent Howard from making it a clean sweep for the U.S.

1. Glenn Davis (US)	49.3 (49.51) OR	4. Helmut Janz (WG)	49.9 (50.04)
2. Cliff Cushman (US)	49.6 (49.77)	5. Jussi Rintamaki (Fin)	50.8 (50.98)
3. Dick Howard (US)	49.7 (49.90)	6. Bruno Galliker (Switz)	51.0 (51.11)

1964 (39. H 14 Oct; SF 15 Oct; F 16 Oct): Cawley took the first semi in an eased-up 49.8. The other qualifiers were Frinolli, Knoke, and Geeroms. Cooper took the second heat in 50.4 with Luck and Morale close. Sixth was sentimental favorite Billy Hardin, whose father won this event in '36. As expected, the two Italians led for the first five hurdles with Luck and Cooper holding down the next two places. Cawley, off slowly, started to move on the turn and caught everyone except Frinolli between the seventh and ninth hurdles. He passed the latter going over the ninth hurdle and finished with his usual burst to win easily. Luck moved well on the turn

but hit the eighth hurdle and then lost his chance for 2nd when he hit the tenth hurdle. Cooper and Morale moved past Frinolli, and Cooper outran Morale in the drive to the tape to get the silver.

1.	Rex Cawley (US)	49.6	4.	Gary Knoke (Aus)	50.4
2.	John Cooper (GB)	50.1	5.	Jay Luck (US)	50.5
3.	Salvatore Morale (It)	50.1	6.	Roberto Frinolli (It)	50.7

7. Vasiliy Anisimov (SU) 51.1; 8. Wilfried Geeroms (Bel) 51.4.

1968 (30. H 13 Oct; SF 14 Oct; F 15 Oct): As in the flat race at this distance, the times turned in during the first round were impressive, the fastest being Whitney's 49.06. Frinolli won the first semi in 49.14 closely followed by Vanderstock, Sherwood, and Schubert, while Hennige took the second in 49.15 with Whitney and Hemery close behind. The next day, Schubert and Hemery went out fast with Whitney lagging. Hemery pulled away after the first barrier and hit the midway point with a substantial lead; his fast early pace seemed to have demoralized the rest and he showed no signs of tiring the rest of the way. Hennige and Vanderstock battled for the second spot, with the German proving stronger in the final stages. Sherwood came up rapidly in the straight to nip the American for the bronze. Hemery's clocking took 0.7 off Vanderstock's pending hand-timed world record.

1.	Dave Hemery (GB)	48.1 (48.12) WR	4.	Geoff Vanderstock (US)	49.0 (49.06)
2.	Gerhard Hennige (WG)	49.0 (49.02)	5.	Vyach Skomorokhov (SU)	49.1 (49.12)
3.	John Sherwood (GB)	49.0 (49.03)	6.	Ron Whitney (US)	49.2 (49.26)

7. Rainer Schubert (WG) 49.2 (49.29); 8. Roberto Frinolli (It) 50.1 (50.13).
(Whitney 49.0 OR, SF)

1972 (37. H 31 Aug; SF 1 Sept; F 2 Sept): Most noteworthy casualty of the heats was Dick Bruggeman, who ran 48.6 in the US Trials. Also lost in the first round was John Sherwood, bronze medalist in '68, who pulled a calf muscle after two hurdles. The second semi saw three other potential finalists bite the dust. Gary Knoke of Australia was confused by an echo from the gun, mistaking it for a recall while Christian Rudolph (European silver medalist in '71) and Dieter Buttner fell. In the final, Akii-Bua was on the inside. Hemery went into an early lead and set a furious pace, even faster than his record run in '68, with Mann close. Akii-Bua began to move after the fifth hurdle and went into the lead at the eighth. He continued to run strongly to an easy win in world record time. Hemery and Mann, both tired, fought it out for the silver, the latter forging ahead in the final ten meters. Seymour, who lost several meters hitting the first barrier, came charging down the straight to be a close 4th.

1.	John Akii-Bua (Uga)	47.82 WR	5.	Rainer Schubert (WG)	49.65
2.	Ralph Mann (US)	48.51	6.	Yevgeniy Gavrilyenko (SU) &	49.66
3.	Dave Hemery (GB)	48.52		Stavros Tziortzis (Gr)	49.66
4.	Jim Seymour (US)	48.64	8.	Yuriy Zorin (SU)	50.25

1976 (22. H 23 July; SF 24 July; F 25 July): The small field made the heats almost a formality and none of the top runners had to strain to make the next round. The semis were won by Shine and Moses, the latter setting a new US record of 48.29. Eliminated in the first was Soviet veteran Dmitriy Stukalov. Jean-Claude Nallet of France lost out in the second as he was outrun in the stretch by Pascoe. Lane assignments for the final put Shine on the inside. Once they were away Moses flew. Gavrilyenko and Shine were also out fast, with Wheeler well back after two hurdles. Pascoe matched Moses for five hurdles and then fell back. Moses and Gavrilyenko hit the curve in front with Shine in close attendance. At the seventh barrier Moses pulled away from Gavrilyenko and came into the straight with a huge lead on Shine—which he held to the tape. Shine held form to get the silver, but Wheeler's late rush from way back wasn't enough to catch Gavrilyenko. The winning time clipped 0.18 off John Akii-Bua's world record.

1.	Edwin Moses (US)	47.64 WR	4.	Quentin Wheeler (US)	49.86
2.	Mike Shine (US)	48.69	5.	Jose Carvalho (Port)	49.94
3.	Yevgeniy Gavrilyenko (SU)	49.45	6.	Yanko Bratanov (Bul)	50.03

7. Damaso Alfonso (Cuba) 50.19; 8. Alan Pascoe (GB) 51.29.

4 X 100 RELAY

1896–1908 (not contested).

1912 (8. H-SF 8 July; F 9 July): The first round was a ridiculous formality, Austria and France being the only victims. The first semi was won by the US in 42.2, but they were disqualified for passing out of the zone, and Great Britain, second in 43.0, advanced to the final. The other semis were won by Sweden (42.5) and Germany (42.3 WR). In the final Germany started on the inside; Britain and Sweden were next, in that order. Sweden had a 1½-meter lead at the end of the second leg but lost it completely in a poor pass, Great Britain moving to the fore. The German anchorman, Richard Rau, ran a great final leg, moving from third to second and just failing to catch Willie Applegarth by a decimeter. But Germany's second pass was out of the zone and they were disqualified.

    1. Great Britain   42.4
(David Jacobs, Harold MacIntosh, Victor d'Arcy, William Applegarth)
    2. Sweden   42.6
(I. Moller, C. Luther, T. Persson, K. Lindberg)
    —Germany   disq.
(Canada 46.2 OR, H; USA 43.7 OR WR, H; Sweden 43.6 OR WR, H; Germany 43.6 =OR =WR, H; Great Britain 43.4 OR WR, SF; Sweden 42.5 OR WR, SF; Germany 42.3 OR WR, SF)

1920 (13. H 21 Aug; F 22 Aug): The final race was essentially between the US and France. As expected, the Americans led all the way and won by 4 meters in world record time.

    1. United States   42.2 WR
(Charley Paddock, Jackson Scholz, Loren Murchison, Morris Kirksey)
    2. France   42.6
(R. Tirard, R. Lorain, R. Mourlon, E. Ali Khan)
    3. Sweden   42.9
(A. Holmstrom, W. Pettersson, S. Malm, N. Sandstrom)
    4. Great Britain
(W. Hill, H. Abrahams, V. d'Arcy, H. Edward)
    5. Denmark
(H. Thorsen, F. Andersen, A. Sorensen, M. Sorensen)
    6. Luxemburg
(J. Colbach, P. Hammer, J. Proess, A. Servais)

1924 (15. H 12 July; SF-F 13 July): Lots of world record action. In the first heat Great Britain bettered the record with 42.0. Holland matched that in the third heat, while the US team pushed the mark down to 41.2 in the sixth heat. In the second round the US improved to 41.0. In the final, from the start it was apparent there were only two teams in the race for first, Great Britain and the US. In fact it was a close race until the end of the third leg. The British bungled the final pass and Alfred Leconey won for the US by 1½ meters, equalling the WR.

    1. United States   41.0=WR
(Francis Hussey, Louis Clarke, Loren Murchison, Alfred Leconey)
    2. Great Britain   41.2
(H. Abrahams, W. Rangeley, L. Royle, W. Nichol)
    3. Holland   41.8
(J. Boot, H. Broos, J. de Vries, M. van den Berge)
    4. Hungary   42.0
(F. Gero, L. Kurunczy, L. Muskat, G. Rozsahegyi)
    5. France   42.2
(M. Degrelle, A. Heise, R. Mourion, A. Mourlon)
    — Switzerland   disq.
(K. Borner, H. Hemmi, J. Imbach, D. Morlaud)
(Great Britain 42.0 OR WR, H; Holland 42.0=OR =WR, H; USA 41.2 OR WR, H; USA 41.0 OR WR, SF)

1928 (13. H 4 Aug; F 5 Aug): The American team won its heat in 41.2, indicating it would be very tough to beat, even by the crack German quartet. In the final, there was little or nothing between the two teams until the final leg in which Henry Russell gained on Helmut Kornig and gave the Americans a win by 1½ meters.

1.	United States	41.0 =WR
(Frank Wykoff, James Quinn, Charley Borah, Henry Russell)		
2.	Germany	41.2
(G. Lammers, R. Corts, H. Houben, H. Kornig)		
3.	Great Britain	41.8
(C. Gill, E. Smouha, W. Rangeley, J. London)		
4.	France	42.0
(A. Cerbonney, G. Auvergne, P. Dufau, A. Mourlon)		
5.	Switzerland	42.6
(E. Goldsmith, W. Weibel, W. Tschopp, H. Niggl)		
—	Canada	disq.
(R. Adams, J. Fitzpatrick, G. Hester, P. Williams)		

1932 (8. H 6 Aug; F 7 Aug): The German team took the first heat in 41.2, but the Americans set a world record of 40.6 in the second. In the final Robert Kiesel gave the US a 2-meter lead at the end of the first leg. The Americans continued to pull away and won by almost 10 meters.

1.	United States	40.0 WR
(Robert Kiesel, Emmett Toppino, Hector Dyer, Frank Wykoff)		
2.	Germany	40.9
(H. Kornig, F. Hendrix, E. Borchmeyer, A. Jonath)		
3.	Italy	41.2
(G. Castelli, R. Maregatti, G. Salviati, E. Toetti)		
4.	Canada	41.3
(P. Williams, J. Brown, H. Wright, B. Pearson)		
5.	Japan	41.3
(T. Yoshioka, C. Nambu, I. Anno, I. Nakajima)		
6.	Great Britain	41.4
(D. Finlay, S. Fuller, S. Englehart, E. Page)		

(USA 40.6 OR WR, H)

1936 (15. H 8 Aug; F 9 Aug): The US team equaled the world record (40.0) in the first heat. In the final Jesse Owens gained a lead of at least 5 meters on the first leg. His teammates increased the lead on each carry. Frank Wykoff (competing in the Olympic relay final for the third time) came home in 39.8 for a new world record. Italy was a surprise second. Holland was chasing Germany for third when Martinus Osendarp dropped the baton 25 meters from home. He finished a shade ahead of Gerd Hornberger, but the Dutch were naturally disqualified.

1.	United States	39.8 WR
(Jesse Owens, Ralph Metcalfe, Foy Draper, Frank Wykoff)		
2.	Italy	41.1
(O. Mariani, G. Caldana, E. Ragni, T. Gonnelli)		
3.	Germany	41.2
(W. Leichum, E. Borchmeyer, E. Gillmeister, G. Hornberger)		
4.	Argentina	42.2
(J. Lavenas, A. Sande, C. Hofmeister, T. Beswick)·		
5.	Canada	42.7
(S. Richardson, B. Humber, L. Orr, H. McPhee)		
—	Holland	disq.
(T. Boersma, W. van Beveren, C. Berger, M. Osendarp)		

(USA 40.0 =OR =WR, H)

1948 (15. H 6 Aug; F 7 Aug): The US had the fastest time in the heats, 41.1. In the final, the Americans led throughout and crossed the finish line well ahead of Britain. They were at first

disqualified due to an allegedly faulty changeover between Barney Ewell and Lorenzo Wright. But after a careful study of the official film, the jury reinstated the US team. Italy, 3rd, won a medal for the third consecutive time.

1. United States	40.6
(Barney Ewell, Lorenzo Wright, Harrison Dillard, Mel Patton)	
2. Great Britain	41.3
(J. Archer, J. Gregory, A. McCorquodale, K. Jones)	
3. Italy	41.5
(M. Tito, E. Perucconi, A. Siddi, C. Monti)	
4. Hungary	41.6
(F. Tima, L. Bartha, G. Csanyi, B. Goldovanyi)	
5. Canada	41.9
(D. McFarlane, J. O'Brien, D. Pettie, E. Haggis)	
6. Holland	41.9
(J. Lammers, J. Meyer, G. Scholten, J. Zwaan)	

1952 (22. H 26 July; SF-F 27 July): The US ran 40.3 in the first round and 40.4 in the second, winning from France (40.8) and the USSR (40.7). The other semi was won by Hungary in 40.9 from France (40.9). In the final the Soviets led over the first two legs, mainly because of their good passes. Lindy Remigino cut their lead considerably in the third leg, and Andy Stanfield was off almost even with Vladimir Sukharyev. The Olympic 200 champion pulled away and gave the US another relay victory. Hungary passed Britain on the last leg to take 3rd.

1. United States	40.1	(40.26)
(Dean Smith, Harrison Dillard, Lindy Remigino, Andy Stanfield)		
2. Soviet Union	40.3	(40.58)
(B. Tokaryev, L. Kalyayev, L. Sanadze, V. Sukharyev)		
3. Hungary	40.5	(40.83)
(L. Zarandi, G. Varasdi, G. Csanyi, B. Goldovanyi)		
4. Great Britain	40.6	(40.85)
(E. McD. Bailey, W. Jack, J. Gregory, B. Shenton)		
5. France	40.9	(41.10)
(A. Porthault, E. Bally, Y. Camus, R. Bonino)		
6. Czechoslovakia	41.2	(41.41)
(F. Broz, J. David, M. Horcic, Z. Pospisil)		

1956 (18. H 30 Nov; SF-F 1 Dec): The heats were won by the US (40.5), Australia (40.6) and the USSR (40.7). The first semi was won by the US in 40.3, the second by the USSR in 40.3. In the final the US was out in front early. Leamon King ran magnificently on the second leg, but two worse-than-average changes caused Bobby Morrow to start with only a narrow lead against Yuriy Konovalov. However, the double Olympic champion came home a safe winner in world record time. The USSR team set a new European record in finishing 2nd, while West Germany just nipped Italy for 3rd.

1. United States	39.5 WR	(39.59)
(Ira Murchison, Leamon King, Thane Baker, Bobby Morrow)		
2. Soviet Union	39.8	(39.92)
(B. Tokaryev, V. Sukharyev, L. Bartenyev, Y. Konovalov)		
3. Germany	40.3	(40.34)
(L. Knorzer, L. Pohl, H. Futterer, M. Germar)		
4. Italy	40.3	(40.43)
(F. Galbiati, G. Ghiselli, G. Gnocchi, V. Lombardo)		
5. Great Britain	40.6	(40.73)
(K. Box, R. Sandstrom, B. Shenton, D. Segal)		
6. Poland	40.6	(40.74)
(M. Foik, J. Jarzembowski, E. Schmidt, Z. Baranowski)		

1960 (19. H 7 Sept; SF-F 8 Sept): In the first round the crack West German quartet tied the world record (39.5) and clearly indicated it was out to challenge the supremacy of the US. The latter, despite indifferent passing, won its heat in 39.7. The other heat winners were Great Britain (40.1) and Italy (40.0). The Germans won the first semi in 39.7. The US took the second, also in 39.7. In the final the first pass by the US was clearly out of the zone. Second man Ray Norton put the US in front only to lose ground with another bad pass. Anchorman Dave Sime started two meters behind Martin Lauer of Germany and finally overhauled him to hit the tape nearly a meter in front. But all was in vain as the US was disqualified, the Germans equalling their world record time of the heats. The USSR, with only fair sprinters but excellent passing, collected its third consecutive silver medal.

1. West Germany	39.5 =WR (39.66)		
(Bernd Cullmann, Armin Hary, Walter Mahlendorf, Martin Lauer)			
2. Soviet Union	40.1	(40.23)	
(G. Kosanov, L. Bartneyev, Y. Konovalov, E. Ozolin)			
3. Great Britain	40.2	(40.32)	
(P. Radford, D. Jones, D. Segal, N. Whitehead)			
4. Italy	40.2	(40.33)	
(A. Sardi, P.G. Cazzola, S. Giannone, L. Barruti)			
5. Venezuela	40.7	(40.83)	
(C. Bonas, L. Murad, E. Romero, R. Romero)			
— United States	disq. (39.4		39.59)
(F. Budd, R. Norton, S. Johnson, D. Sime)			
(West Germany 39.5 =OR =WR, H)			

1964 (21. H-SF 20 Oct; F 21 Oct): In the first round, four teams beat 40 seconds: Italy (39.7) and Poland (39.9) in heat 1, the US (39.8) in 2, and France (39.8) in 3. In the first semi, the US equalled the Olympic record (39.5) in beating France and Jamaica (both 39.6). Italy won the second semi from Poland and Venezuela, all in 39.6, while the USSR was fourth in 39.7. Once again, poor baton passing delayed the Americans in the early stages of the final. Poland and then France were the leaders. Bob Hayes, the US anchor, was off almost 3 meters behind Jocelyn Delecour of France and also behind Poland, the USSR and Britain. But Hayes, the winner of the 100, showed one of the most explosive pick-ups ever seen. He not only made up the deficit but eventually shot ahead to win by three meters in 39.0—a world record. Marian Dudziak finished strongly to edge Delecour for 2nd. In this fantastic race, seven teams equalled or bettered the Olympic record from Rome (39.5), and Britain, last, missed it by 0.1.

1. United States	39.0 WR
(Paul Drayton, Gerry Ashworth, Richard Stebbins, Bob Hayes)	
2. Poland	39.3
(A. Zielinski, W. Maniak, M. Foik, M. Dudziak)	
3. France	39.3
(P. Genevay, B. Laidebeur, C. Piquemal, J. Delecour)	
4. Jamaica	39.4
(P. McNeil, P. Robinson, L. Headley, D. Johnson)	
5. Soviet Union	39.4
(E. Ozolin, B. Zubov, G. Kosanov, B. Savchuk)	
6. Venezuela	39.5
(A. Herrera, L. Murad, R. Romero, H. Fucil)	
7. Italy	39.5
(L. Berruti, E. Preatoni, S. Ottolina, P. Giannattasio)	
8. Great Britain	39.6
(P. Radford, R. Jones, M. Campbell, L. Davies)	
(USA 39.5 =OR, SF)	

1968 (19. H-SF 19 Oct; F 20 Oct): From the standpoint of qualification the first round was a formality, eliminating only three teams. But it revealed that the favored Americans might be in trouble because of the injured leg of leadoff man Charles Greene and that the altitude was going to produce super times. Cuba with 38.7 (38.76), then Jamaica with 38.6 (38.65), bettered the

Olympic record. Jamaica won the first semi in a WR 38.3 (38.39) with East Germany 2nd at 38.7 (38.72)—a new European record. Cuba won the second over the US, both clocking 38.6 (38.63-38.69). Greene's performance was better, but two poor passes slowed the American quartet. Cuba drew the inside lane for the final with the US in 2 and Jamaica in 5. On the first leg Greene was running much better than the day before and US chances looked good. Passes at the first and second exchanges by the three favorites were mediocre to poor. At the final takeover Cuba was off first with nearly a meter on the East German team and almost two on the US. But Jim Hines, blasting off from a near-perfect pass, collared the two men in front of him and was going away at the tape in a world record 38.2 (38.24).

1.	United States	38.2 WR	(38.23)
(Charles Greene, Mel Pender, Ronnie Ray Smith, Jim Hines)			
2.	Cuba	38.3	(38.39)
(H. Ramirez, J. Morales, P. Montes, E. Figuerola)			
3.	France	38.4	(38.42)
(G. Fenouil, J. Delecour, C. Piquemal, R. Bambuck)			
4.	Jamaica	38.4	(38.46)
(E. Stewart, M. Fray, C. Forbes, L. Miller)			
5.	East Germany	38.6	(38.66)
(H. Erbstosser, H. Schelter, P. Haase, H. Eggers)			
6.	West Germany	38.7	(38.76)
(K-P. Schmidtke, G. Wucherer, G. Metz, J. Eigenherr)			
7.	Italy	39.2	(39.21)
(S. Ottolina, E. Preatoni, A. Squazzero, L. Berruti)			
8.	Poland	39.2	(39.22)
(W. Maniak, E. Romanowski, Z. Nowosz, M. Dudziak)			

(Cuba 38.7 OR, H; Jamaica 38.6 OR =WR, H; Jamaica 38.3 OR WR, SF)

1972 (27. H-SF 9 Sept; F 10 Sept): Absent from the first round were highly-touted Jamaica and Trinidad—both having had key men injured in the 100 and 200. A bad pass in the semis eliminated Cuba, which was expected to be in the medal hunt. By this time it was clear that the US was the team to beat as it posted the best times in both preliminary rounds. The Americans drew lane 1 for the final. Their most dangerous rivals were the Soviets and the West Germans. At the gun Aleksandr Kornelyuk was off in front. He led the first leg over Larry Black of the US, but the US went into the lead with Robert Taylor's strong second leg. A near-perfect pass and a fast leg to Gerald Tinker gave the US an 0.3 lead over the Soviets at the final exchange. This margin proved insurmountable as anchorman Eddie Hart poured on the coals, discouraging any attempt by Valeriy Borzov to wrest the gold away. Borzov was apparently happy just to hold 2nd.

1.	United States	38.19 WR
(Larry Black, Robert Taylor, Gerald Tinker, Eddie Hart)		
2.	Soviet Union	38.50
(A. Kornelyuk, V. Lovyetskiy, J. Silovs, V. Borzov)		
3.	West Germany	38.79
(J. Hirscht, K-H. Klotz, G. Wucherer, K. Ehl)		
4.	Czechoslovakia	38.82
(J. Matousek, J. Demec, J. Kynos, L. Bohman)		
5.	East Germany	38.90
(M. Kokot, B. Borth, H-J. Bombach, S. Schenke)		
6.	Poland	39.03
(S. Wagner, T. Cuch, J. Czerbniak, Z. Nowosz)		
7.	France	39.14
(P. Bourbeillon, J-P. Gres, G. Fenouil, B. Cherrier)		
8.	Italy	39.14
(V. Guerini, E. Preatoni, L. Benedetti, P. Mennea)		

1976 (20. H-SF 30 July; F 31 July): The first round dropped only four teams but showed that the US was the team to beat. The US won the first semi by a huge margin over two of the best

teams, Cuba and East Germany. It was now clear that only the Americans could beat the Americans. The leaders ran about even in the final's first leg. The pass from Harvey Glance to Johnny Jones was mediocre, but Jones ran away from the rest on the second carry. Two excellent passes and two more excellent carries served to stretch the margin of victory. Alexander Thieme ran strongly to bring the East Germans home second, while Valeriy Borzov seemed to put out just enough to secure the bronze for the Soviets.

1. United States   38.33
(Harvey Glance, Johnny Jones, Millard Hampton, Steve Riddick)
2. East Germany   38.66
(M. Kokot, J. Pfeifer, K-D. Kurrat, A. Thieme)
3. Soviet Union   38.78
(A. Aksinin, N. Kolyesnikov, J. Silovs, V. Borzov)
4. Poland   38.83
(A. Swierczynski, M. Woronin, B. Grzejszczak, Z. Licznerski)
5. Cuba   39.01
(F. Gomez, A. Casanas, H. Ramirez, S. Leonard)
6. Italy   39.08
(V. Guerini, L. Caravani, L. Benedetti, P. Mennea)
7. France   39.16
(J-C. Amoureux, J. Arame, L. Sainte-Rose, D. Chauvelot)
8. Canada   39.47
(H. Spooner, M. Nash, A. Dukowski, H. Fraser)

4 x 400

1896-1904 (not contested).

1908 (7. F 25 July): Actually, this was a medley relay (200, 200, 400, 800). Only 3 teams were in the final as the U.S. scored an easy 25m victory.

1. United States   3:29.4
(William Hamilton, Nate Cartmell, John Taylor, Mel Sheppard)
2. Germany
(A. Hoffmann, H. Elcke, O. Trieloff, H. Braun)
3. Hungary
(P. Simon, F. Mezey-Wiesner, J. Nagy, O. Bodor)

1912 (7. H 14 July; F 15 July): Three heats were run, with the winners of each (Great Britain 3:19.0, U.S. 3:23.3, France 3:22.5) advancing to the final. Sheppard, '08 800 winner, opened up a good lead for the U.S. and the Americans were never headed, 400 winner Reidpath finishing things off as the team took nearly 2 seconds off the world record. Britain lost its chances to challenge for 2nd when lead-off man Nicol limped around the track.

1. United States   3:16.6 WR
(Mel Sheppard, Edward Lindberg, Ted Meredith, Charley Reidpath)
2. France   3:20.7
(C. Lelong, R. Schurrer, P. Failliot, C. Poulenard)
3. Great Britain   3:23.2
(G. Nicol, E. Henley, J. Soutter, C. Seedhouse)
(Great Britain 3:19.0 OR, H)

1920 (6. 22 Aug; F 23 Aug): The heats were a formality, as all teams advanced to the final, which was marred by two incidents on the first leg. Eby and Krokstrom collided, as did Dafel and Andre. All 4 teams lost ground to the British, who won by a good margin, despite a good anchor by Rudd, the 400 winner.

1. Great Britain	3:22.2
(Cecil Griffiths, Robert Lindsay, John Ainsworth-Davis, Guy Butler)	
2. South Africa	3:24.2
(H. Dafel, C. Oldfield, J. Oosterlaak, B. Rudd)	
3. France	3:24.8
(G. Andre, G. Fery, M. Delvart, J. Deveaux)	
4. United States	3:25.2
(E. Eby, T. Meredith, R. Emory, F. Shea)	
5. Sweden	
(S. Krokstrom, S. Malm, E. Sundblad, N. Engdahl)	
6. Belgium	
(J. Migeot, A. Corteyn, O. Smet, F. Morren)	

1924 (7. H 12 July; F 13 July): In the first round only Finland was eliminated. In the final Edward Toms gave Great Britain a 2-meter lead at the end of the first leg, with the US and Sweden following. But William Stevenson put the US 5 meters in front of Sweden on the second leg with Britain third, another meter back. Guy Butler ran a great anchor for Britain and was only one meter behind Alan Helffrich with 200 meters to go. But he had run himself out and finally had to relinquish 2nd to Sweden's Nils Engdahl.

1. United States	3:16.0 WR
(Con Cochrane, William Stevenson, Olivier McDonald, Alan Helffrich)	
2. Sweden	3:17.0
(A. Svensson, E. Bylehn, G. Wejnarth, N. Engdahl)	
3. Great Britain	3:17.4
(E. Toms, G. Renwick, R. Ripley, G. Butler)	
4. Canada	3:22.8
(H. Aylwin, A. Christie, D. Johnston, W. Maynes)	
5. France	3:23.4
(R. Fritz, G. Fery, F. Galtier, B. Favaudon)	
6. Italy	3:28.0
(G. Cominotto, A. Garginllo, E. Maffiolini, L. Facelli)	

1928 (16. H 4 Aug; F 5 Aug): Great Britain had the fastest time in the heats, 3:20.6. In the final the Americans had a 3-meter lead on Germany at the end of the first leg and increased it considerably on the second. But the third man, Fred Alderman, lost ground, and Ray Barbuti had to fight hard to stave off Hermann Engelhard's attack on the final lap.

1. United States	3:14.2 WR
(George Baird, Bud Spencer, Fred Alderman, Ray Barbuti)	
2. Germany	3:14.8
(O. Neumann, R. Krebs, H. Storz, H. Engelhard)	
3. Canada	3:15.4
(A. Wilson, P. Edwards, S. Glover, J. Ball)	
4. Sweden	3:15.8
(B. Kugelberg, B. von Wachenfeldt, E. Bylehn, S. Pettersson)	
5. Great Britain	3:16.4
(R. Leigh-Wood, W. Craner, J. Rinkel, D. Lowe)	
6. France	3:19.4
(G. Krotoff, J. Jackson, G. Dupont, R. Feger)	

1932 (7. H 6 Aug; F 7 Aug): The US team set a world record 3:11.8 in its heat. In the final the Americans led from the start. Bill Carr started the anchor leg about a dozen meters in front of Great Britain's Godfrey Rampling. The latter made a gallant effort and closed to about five meters, but he could not hold the pace and finally lost more than he had gained.

1. United States	3:08.2 WR
(Ivan Fuqua, Ed Ablowich, Karl Werner, Bill Carr)	
2. Great Britain	3:11.2
(C. Stoneley, T. Hampson, D. Burghley, G. Rampling)	

3. Canada	3:12.8
(R. Lewis, J. Ball, P. Edwards, A. Wilson)	
4. Germany	3:14.4
(J. Buchner, W. Nehb, A. Metzner, O. Peltzer)	
5. Japan	3:14.6
(I. Nakajima, I. Masuda, S. Oki, T. Nishi)	
6. Italy	3:17.8
(G. Carlini, G. Turba, M. De Negri, L. Facelli)	
(USA 3:11.8 OR WR, H)	

1936 (12. H 8 Aug; F 9 Aug): Fastest time in the heats was 3:13.0 by the US. In the final a great run by Godfrey Rampling on the second leg put Britain in the lead. The US team, not using either of its 400 placers, challenged bravely but in vain. Britain won by a wide margin with the second-best mark on record. Rudolf Harbig just saved 3rd for Germany from the attack of John Loaring.

1. Great Britain	3:09.0
(Frederick Wolff 49.2, Godfrey Rampling 46.7, William Roberts 46.4, Godfrey Brown 46.7)	
2. United States	3:11.0
(H. Cagle 48.7, R. Young 47.6, E. O'Brien 46.7, A. Fitch 48.0)	
3. Germany	3:11.8
(H. Hamann 49.3, F. von Stulpnagel 48.3, H. Voigt 46.6, R. Harbig 47.6)	
4. Canada	3:11.8
(M. Limon 47.9, P. Edwards 48.5, W. Fritz 48.3, J. Loaring 47.1)	
5. Sweden	3:13.0
(S. Stromberg, P. Edfeldt, O. Danielsson, B. von Wachenfeldt)	
6. Hungary	3:14.8
(T. Ribenyi, Z. Zsitvai, J. Vadas, J. Kovacs)	

1948 (16. H 6 Aug; F 7 Aug): Fastest time in the heats was 3:12.6 by the US. In the final Arthur Harnden and Cliff Bourland gave the US a big lead. On the third leg Arthur Wint tried to cut down Roy Cochran's advantage but pulled up lame and had to withdraw. The rest of the race was anticlimactic.

1. United States	3:10.4
(Arthur Harnden 48.0, Cliff Bourland 47.3, Roy Cochran 47.8, Mal Whitfield 47.3)	
2. France	3:14.8
(J. Kerebel, F. Schewetta, R. Chefd'hotel, J. Lunis))	
3. Sweden	3:16.0
(K. Lundkvist, L.-E. Wolfbrandt, F. Alnevik, R. Larsson)	
4. Finland	3:24.8
(T. Suvanto, O. Talja, R. Holmberg, B. Storskrubb)	
— Jamaica	did not finish
(G. Rhoden, L. Laing, A. Wint, H. McKenley)	
— Italy	did not finish
(G. Rocca, O. Missoni, L. Paterlini, A. Siddi)	

1952 (18. H 26 July; F 27 July): Jamaica won the first heat in 3:12.1; the US the second in 3:11.5 and Germany the third in 3:10.5. The final was an epic race between the two greatest teams in history. The Jamaicans showed up with the same foursome which had been so unlucky four years earlier in London: in the meantime, all except possibly Wint had grown considerably in stature. The Americans built up a lead on the first two legs giving Herb McKenley a seemingly hopeless task on the third leg against the dependable Charley Moore, the 400 hurdle champion. But the Jamaican ran the race of his life, holding his form to the end after a terrific drive which produced history's fastest split (44.6). He thus sent Rhoden off on his journey with a half-meter lead on Mal Whitfield. Rhoden managed to hold that lead to the end despite Whitfield's challenge in the stretch. Both teams shattered the world record. West Germany in 3rd set a new European mark.

        1. Jamaica   3:03.9 WR
(Arthur Wint 46.8, Leslie Laing 47.0, Herb McKenley 44.6, George Rhoden 45.5)
        2. United States   3:04.0
(O. Matson 46.7, G. Cole 45.5, C. Moore 46.3, M. Whitfield 45.5)
        3. Germany   3:06.6
(H. Geister 47.3, G. Steines 46.9, H. Ulzheimer 46.5, K-F. Haas 45.9)
        4. Canada   3:09.3
(D. Clement 49.0, J. Hutchins 47.0, J. Carroll 46.0, J. Lavery 47.3)
        5. Great Britain   3:10.0
(L. Lewis 47.9, A. Dick 47.4, T. Higgins 47.4, N. Stacey 47.3)
        6. France   3:10.1
(J-P. Goudeau, R. Bart, J. Degats, J-P. Martin du Gard)

1956 (15. H 30 Nov; F 1 Dec): Canada won the first heat in 3:10.5 from the US (3:10.5).
Germany won the second in 3:09.8, Great Britain the third in 3:08.7. In the final the US was
typically in the lead from the start even though world record holder Lou Jones was not at his
best. They won comfortably over a surprisingly good Australian team, which beat such
renowned European foursomes as those of Britain and West Germany.

        1. United States   3:04.7
(Lou Jones 47.1, J.W. Mashburn 46.4, Charley Jenkins 45.5, Tom Courtney 45.7)
        2. Australia   3:06.2
(L. Gregory 47.2, D. Lean 46.3, G. Gipson 46.6, K. Gosper 46.1)
        3. Great Britain   3:07.1
(J. Salisbury 47.6, M. Wheeler 46.8, F. Higgins 46.2, D. Johnson 46.5)
        4. Germany   3:08.1
(J. Kuhl 47.5, W. Oberste 47.3, M. Porschke 47.0, K-F. Haas 46.3)
        5. Canada   3:11.6
(L. Sloan, M. Cockburn, D. Clement, T. Tobacco)
        – Jamaica   disq. (3:10.2)
(K. Gardner, G. Kerr, Mal Spence, Mel Spence)

1960 (19. H-SF 7 Sept; F 8 Sept): First round winners were Germany (3:10.4), West Indies
(3:09.1), Switzerland (3:10.7), and the US (3:10.4). Fast non-qualifiers were Finland (3:11.7)
and Czechoslovakia (3:11.2, Josef Trousil 45.4). South Africa won the first semi in 3:06.4
followed by West Germany (3:07.4) and Great Britain (3:07.5). The 4th and 5th teams, Italy
(3:07.7) and Canada (3:08.2), had faster times than the winner of the second semi. This went
to the US in 3:08.4, followed by the West Indies (3:09.2) and Switzerland (3:09.7).
        In the final Jack Yarman gave the US a 2-meter lead over the West Indies with Germany 5
meters further back in 4th place. Germany's Manfred Kinder, running the fastest leg of all,
cut the US lead down to a scant meter, but veteran Glenn Davis held off Johannes Kaiser's
challenge on the third leg and pulled away to give Otis Davis a solid 6-meter lead on
Carl Kaufmann. The latter closed the gap in the first part of the final lap, but Davis'
quick move with 100 meters to go caught the German unable to give immediate response
and he couldn't gain anything back in the stretch.

        1. United States   3:02.2 WR
(Jack Yerman 46.2, Earl Young 45.6, Glenn Davis 45.4, Otis Davis 45.0)
        2. Germany   3:02.7
(H. Reske 47.0, M. Kinder 44.9, J. Kaiser 45.9, C. Kaufmann 44.9)
        3. West Indies   3:04.0
(Mal Spence 46.5, J. Wedderburn 46.4, K. Gardner 45.8, G. Kerr 45.4)
        4. South Africa   3:05.0
(E. Jefferys 46.7, E. Davis 46.1, G. Day 46.5, M. Spence 45.6)
        5. Great Britain   3:08.3
(M. Yardley 47.1, B. Jackson 47.1, J. Wrighton 47.6, R. Brightwell 46.5)
        6. Switzerland   3:09.4
(R. Weber 48.3, E. Zaugg 46.8, H. Bruder 47.8, C. Wagli 46.5)

1964 (17. H 20 Oct; F 21 Oct): The US won heat I in 3:05.3. Trinidad-Tobago was the winner in II with a 3:05.0. Heat III was the fastest, with Britain (3:04.7) winning from Germany (3:04.9) and Jamaica (3:05.3). The final was a great race from start to finish. Britain was leading after the first leg, but 400 winner Mike Larrabee put the US in the lead with a superb 44.8. After that the Americans were never headed. In the battle for 2nd, Britain's Robbie Brightwell ran his greatest race to edge Wendell Mottley of Trinidad-Tobago, the silver medalist. The first three all beat the world record set by the US in Rome (3:02.2) and Jamaica, 4th, missed it by merely a 10th.

1. United States		3:00.7 WR

(Ollan Cassell 46.0, Mike Larrabee 44.8, Ulis Williams 45.4, Henry Carr 44.5)

2. Great Britain	3:01.6

(T. Graham 45.9, A. Metcalfe 45.5, J. Cooper 45.4, R. Brightwell 44.8)

3. Trinidad	3:01.7

(E. Skinner 46.0, K. Bernard 45.3, E. Roberts 45.4, W. Mottley 45.0)

4. Jamaica	3:02.3

(L. Kahn 46.1, Mal Spence 45.4, Mel Spence 45.2, G. Kerr 45.6)

5. Germany	3:04.3

(J. Juttner 47.1, H-U. Schulz 45.7, J. Schmitt 45.9, M. Kinder 45.6)

6. Poland	3:05.3

(M. Filipiuk 47.5, I. Kluczek 46.0, S. Swatowski 46.3, A. Badenski 45.5)

7. Soviet Union	3:05.9

(G. Sverbyetov 46.8, V. Bichkov 46.3, V. Anisimov 46.5, V. Arkhipchuk 46.3)

8. France	3:07.4

(M. Hiblot 47.1, B. Martin 46.4, G. Nelzy 47.1, J-P. Boccardo 46.8)

1968 (16. H 19 Oct; F 20 Oct): The American quartet consisted of the top four on the all-time 400 list. So, as far as the gold medals were concerned, they could have just mailed their performances in. Still at stake were the other medals and the world record. The prelims were fast; it took 3:04.8 to advance; a surprisingly strong Kenya team clocked 3:00.8 behind the USA's 3:00.7. In the first leg of the final Matthews flew down the back straight to lose all but Kenya's Asati. The latter actually led by three meters at the hand-off, but Freeman ran history's fastest leg to put the US 20 meters ahead and out of reach. However, the record-conscious James and Evans poured it on all the way to clip over three seconds from the world mark. Kenya lost a bit of ground vis-a-vis the other teams on the second and third legs, but anchorman Rudisha was too much for the pursuers and brought his team in for the silver in tying the old mark. West Germany's Jellinghaus just held off Poland's Badenski in a disputed call to get the bronze.

1. United States	2:56.1 WR

(Vince Matthews 45.0, Ron Freeman 43.2, Larry James 43.8, Lee Evans 44.1)

2. Kenya	2:59.6

(C. Asati 44.4, H. Nyamau 45.5, N. Bon 45.1, D. Rudisha 44.6)

3. West Germany	3:00.5

(H. Muller 46.4, M. Kinder 44.7, G. Hennige 44.7, M. Jellinghaus 44.7)

4. Poland	3:00.5

(S. Gredzinski 46.8, J. Balachowski 44.7, J. Werner 44.5, A. Badenski 44.5)

5. Great Britain	3:01.2

(M. Winbolt-Lewis 46.2, C. Campbell 44.9, D. Hemery 44.6, J. Sherwood 45.5)

6. Trinidad	3:04.5

(G. Simon 46.1, E. Bobb 46.7, B. Cayenne 45.9, E. Roberts 45.8)

7. Italy	3:04.6

(S. Ottolina 46.4, G. Puosi 45.8, F. Fusi 46.5, S. Bello 45.9)

8. France	3:07.5

(J-C. Nallet 46.6, J. Carette 45.8, G. Bertould 47.1, J-P. Boccardo 48.0)
(USA 3:00.7 =OR, H)

1972 (21. H 9 Sept; F 10 Sept): The US had been heavily favored to win this event. But with John Smith injured in the 400-meter final and Matthews and Collett disqualified for cavalier behavior during the 400-meter victory ceremony, the Americans were unable to field a team. The heats were hotly contested and it took 3:03.1 to make the final. Just as in Mexico, Kenya's Asati led the first leg, to put his team in front by 0.3 at the exchange. Poland was second and three other teams were bunched a short margin back. Both West Germany and Poland slipped past Kenya on the second leg. The West Germans had a commanding 0.7 lead at the exchange, but everyone gained on them during the third carry and they led by only 0.2 over Poland at the final pass. Honz tried to run away from the field but to no avail. His suicidal first 200 (20.1) took its toll and he was eventually passed by Sang of Kenya, then Jenkins of Great Britain, and finally Carette of France.

    1. Kenya   2:59.8
(Charles Asati 45.5, Hezakiah Nyamau 45.5, Robert Ouko 45.3, Julius Sang 43.5)
    2. Great Britain   3:00.5
(M. Reynolds 46.2, A. Pascoe 45.1, D. Hemery 45.1, D. Jenkins 44.1)
    3. France   3:00.7
(G. Bertould 46.4, D. Velasquez 44.8, F. Kerbiriou 45.2, J. Carette 44.3)
    4. West Germany   3:00.9
(B. Herrmann 46.1, H-R. Schloske 44.2, H. Kohler 45.6, K. Honz 45.0)
    5. Poland   3:01.1
(J. Werner 45.8, J. Balachowski 45.2, Z. Jaremski 45.2, A. Badenski 44.9)
    6. Finland   3:01.1
(S. Lonnqvist 46.5, A. Salin 45.1, O. Karttunen 45.1, M. Kukkoaho 44.4)|
    7. Sweden   3:02.6
(E. Carlgren 46.0, A. Faager 45.5, K. Ohman 45.3, U. Ronner 45.8)
    8. Trinidad   3:03.6
(A. Cooper 46.7, P. Marshall 46.0, C. Joseph 44.5, E. Roberts 46.4)

1976 (16. H 30 July; F 31 July): With Kenya out of the Games no one figured to dispute the US for gold and no one did. The only casualty of the heats was a dropped baton by Great Britain, which put them out of a chance for the silver. Juantorena ran an eased-up 44.1 anchor for Cuba. In the final the Americans led from the gun. The margin increased on each leg, and they eventually won by nearly three seconds in the fastest low-altitude clocking of all time. Poland went into 2nd on the strength of a 44-flat leg by veteran Werner and stayed there the rest of the race. The West Germans were third at the end of the second leg and also held their position to the end for the bronze.

    1. United States   2:58.7
(Herman Frazier 45.3, Benny Brown 44.6, Fred Newhouse 43.8, Maxie Parks 45.0)
    2. Poland   3:01.4
(R. Podlas 46.7, J. Werner 44.0, Z. Jaremski 45.5, J. Pietrzyk 45.2)
    3. West Germany   3:02.0
(F-P. Hofmeister 46.0, L. Krieg 45.3, H. Schmid 45.8, B. Herrmann 44.9)
    4. Canada   3:02.6
(I. Seale 47.0, D. Domansky 45.3, L. Hope 45.5, B. Saunders 44.8)
    5. Jamaica   3:02.8
(L. Priestley 46.4, C. Bradford 46.3, A. Daley 46.3, S. Newman 43.8)
    6. Trinidad   3:03.5
(M. Solomon 46.0, H. Tuitt 45.4, J. Coombs 46.2, C. Joseph 45.9)
    7. Cuba   3:03.8
(E. Gutierrez 46.0, D. Alfonso 46.7, C. Alvarez 46.4, A. Juantorena 44.7)
    8. Finland   3:06.5
(H. Makela 46.3, O. Karttunen 46.7, S. Lonnqvist 46.9, M. Kukkoaho 46.6)

HIGH JUMP

1896 (5. F 10 April): The opening height was 1.50 (4-11). Prizes were awarded only to 1st and 2nd as Clark won with a performance well off the world record level of 1.97 (6-5½). He had won the long jump 3 days earlier. Heights for those behind Clark are controversial.

1. Ellery Clark (US)	1.81	5-11¼	4. Fritz Hofmann (Ger) &	1.62	5-3¾
2. James Connolly (US) &	1.65	5-5	Henrik Sjoberg (Swe)	1.62	5-3¾
Robert Garrett (US)	1.65	5-5			

1900 (11. Q 14 July; F 15 July): Two of the three USA qualifiers—W. P. Remington & W.C. Carroll—refused to compete in the final because it was Sunday. Baxter beat Leahy at 1.90, then attempted to break the world record (1.97) but failed, partly because unrestrained spectators crowding around the standards made it difficult for him to concentrate.

1. Irving Baxter (US)	1.90	6-2¾ OR	4. Carl Albert Andersen (Nor)	1.70	5-7
2. Patrick Leahy (GB-Eire)	1.78	5-10	5. Erik Lemming (Swe)	1.70	5-7
3. Lajos Gonczy (Hun)	1.75	5-9	6. Waldemar Steffen (Ger)	1.70	5-7

1904 (6. F 29 Aug): Jones, a 3-time US champion, won a hotly contested event. Serviss took 2nd from Weinstein in a jumpoff.

1. Samuel Jones (US)	1.80	5-11	4. Lajos Gonczy (Hun)	1.75	5-9
2. Garrett Serviss (US)	1.77	5-9¾	5. Emil Freymark (US)		
3. Paul Weinstein (Ger)	1.77	5-9¾	6. E. J. Barker (US)		

1908 (20. Q-F 21 July): A qualifying round was held in the morning and jumping was done in sections. Presumably, preliminary marks carried over, for nobody except Somodi improved in the final. Porter, the winner, jumped a centimeter above his own height. There was a tie for 2nd-4th and all three were awarded silver medals. Andre was 19 at the time.

1. Harry Porter (US)	1.90	6-2¾ OR	Geo Andre (Fr)	1.88	6-2
2. Con Leahy (GB-Eire),	1.88	6-2	5. Herbert Gidney (US) &	1.85	6-¾
Istvan Somodi (Hun) &	1.88	6-2	Tom Moffitt (US)	1.85	6-¾

7. Neil Patterson (US) 1.83;. . . dnc—A. Hedenlund (Swe).

1912 (26. Q 7 July; F 8 July): Eleven of 26 entrants cleared the qualifying height, 1.83 (6-0). In the final, 7 were still in contention when the bar was raised to 1.87. The height proved too much for only Grumpelt and Johnstone. At 1.89 only Liesche, Horine and Richards cleared the bar, all on second try. Horine, who had set a world record 2.005 (6-7) a few weeks earlier, failed at 1.91, while Liesche went over on his first attempt. When Richards failed twice, the German appeared to have the inside track, but Richards managed to lift his heavy frame over the bar on his last attempt. That was the turning point: while Richards went over 1.93 first time, Liesche, by then too nervous, failed on his three attempts.

1. Alma Richards (US)	1.93	6-4 OR	(Jim Thorpe, US)	1.87, disq)	
2. Hans Liesche (Ger)	1.91	6-3¼	5. Henry Grumpelt (US)	1.85	6-¾
3. George Horine (US)	1.89	6-2½	John Johnstone (US)	1.85	6-¾
4. Egon Erickson (US)	1.87	6-1¾			

7. K-A. Kullerstrand (Swe) 1.83; 8. tie, T. Carroll (GB) & I. Wardener (Hun) 1.75;. . . nh—B. H. Baker (GB) [1.75].
(Liesche 1.91OR; Richards 1.91=OR)

1920 (22. Q 15 Aug; F 17 Aug): An almost continuous rain made it impossible to hold the qualifying at the site scheduled. The competitors thus had to jump from a turf takeoff, which became too soft after the many starters had taken their trial jumps. Twelve men qualified for the final by clearing ı.80 (5-11). In the final, when the bar was raised to 1.80, the four US entrants, plus Ekelund, Baker and Thulin cleared first time, while Lewden needed three attempts. At 1.85 Thulin and Lewden went out, while Murphy, Whalen, Baker and Ekelund

cleared first time, Muller and Landon second time. At 1.90 (6-2¾) Muller cleared first time, Ekelund and Landon second time. At 1.93 (6-4) only Landon went over, on his second attempt. With Baker, Whalen and Murphy knotted at 1.85 a jumpoff was held, the former declining to compete. The other two both cleared 1.89.

1. Dick Landon (US)	1.93	6-4=OR	4. Walter Whalen (US)	1.85	6-¾
2. Harold Muller (US)	1.90	6-2¾	5. John Murphy (US)	1.85	6-¾
3. Bo Ekelund (Swe)	1.90	6-2¾	6. B. Howard Baker (GB)	1.85	6-¾

7. tie, P. Lewden (Fr) & E. Thulin (Swe) 1.80; 9. tie, T. Carroll (GB), H. Jagenburg (Swe), R. Labat (Fr) & T. Swahn (Swe) 1.75.

1924 (21. Q 6 July; F 7 July): In the final, 7 cleared 1.85 (6-¾). Only three went over 1.90 (6-2¾). Lewden, who held the French record at 1.93 (6-4), came close to his best but was outjumped by two Americans. Osborn, the world record holder, cleared all heights through 1.98 (6-6) on his first attempt, then had three tries at 2.02 (6-7½): on the second he went over with his body but dislodged the bar with his hand. There was a jumpoff for 4th and 6th.

1. Harold Osborn (US)	1.98	6-6 OR	4. Thomas Poor (US)	1.88	6-2
2. Leroy Brown (US)	1.95	6-4¾	5. Jeno Gaspar (Hun)	1.88	6-2
3. Pierre Lewden (Fr)	1.92	6-3½	6. Helge Jansson (Swe)	1.85	6-¾

7. P. Guilloux (Fr) 1.85; 8. tie, S. Helgesen (Nor) & L. Roberts (S Afr) 1.83. (Osborne 1.95 OR; Brown 1.95=OR)

1928 (35. F 29 July): Eighteen cleared the qualifying height, 1.83 (6-0). The final, held on a soft takeoff, lasted five hours. King was the only successful jumper at 1.94 (6-4½). Places 2nd-5th were decided in a jumpoff, with defending champ and world record holder Osborn taking the last of those slots.

1. Bob King (US)	1.94	6-4½	4. Simeon Toribio (Phil)	1.91	6-3¼
2. Ben Hedges (US)	1.91	6-3¼	5. Harold Osborn (US)	1.91	6-3¼
3. Claude Menard (Fr)	1.91	6-3¼	6. Kazuo Kimura (Japan)	1.88	6-2

7. tie, A. Cherrier (Fr), P. Lewden (Fr), Charles McGinnis (US) & Mikio Oda (Japan) 1.88; 11. tie, H. Adolfsson (Swe), K. Kesmarki (Hun), F. Koepke (Ger), H. A. Simmons (GB) & E. Tommelstad (Nor) 1.84.

1932 (14. F 31 July): Spitz, holder of the world indoor record at 2.04 (6-8½), was hampered by an injured ankle and went out at 1.90 (6-2¾). The bar was raised to 1.98 (6-6) and on remeasurement found to be 1.97 (6-5½). Four went over. At 2.00 (6-6¾), however, none of the four could make it. Places 1st-4th were then decided on a jumpoff. It should be noted that the winner was the first non-US athlete to win the event.

			1.90	1.94	1.97	2.00
1. Duncan McNaughton (Can)	1.97	6-5½	xo	o	xxo	xxx
2. Robert Van Osdel (US)	1.97	6-5½	xo	xo	o	xxx
3. Simeon Toribio (Phil)	1.97	6-5½	o	xxo	xxo	xxx
4. Cornelius Johnson (US)	1.97	6-5½	o	xo	xo	xxx
5. Ilmari Reinikka (Fin)	1.94	6-4½	xo	xo	xxx	
6. Kazuo Kimura (Japan)	1.94	6-4½				

7. tie, M. Ono (Japan) & Jerzy Plawczyk (Pol) 1.90; 9. tie, B. Haug (Nor), C. Menard (Fr), J. Portland (Can), George Spitz (US) & A. Tommasi (It) 1.85; 14. P. Riesen (Switz) 1.80.

1936 (40. Q-F 2 Aug): Twenty-two mastered the qualifying height, 1.85 (6-¾). In the final, Johnson never had a failure until he missed at a world record 2.08 (6-10). Places 2-4 were decided in a jumpoff, while the four at 1.94 were bracketed in a tie for 6th.

			1.97	2.00	2.03	2.08
1. Cornelius Johnson (US)	2.03	6-8 OR	o	o	o	xxx
2. Dave Albritton (US)	2.00	6-6¾	xo	xxo	xxx	
3. Delos Thurber (US)	2.00	6-6¾	o	xo	xxx	
4. Kalevi Kotkas (Fin)	2.00	6-6¾	o	xxo	xxx	

5. Kimio Yada (Japan)	1.97	6-5½	o	xxx
6. Yoshiro Asakuma (Japan),	1.94	6-4½		
Lauri Kalima (Fin),	1.94	6-4½		
Hiroshi Tanaka (Japan) &	1.94	6-4½		
Gustav Weinkotz (Ger)	1.94	6-4½		

10. tie, G. Gehmert (Ger) & A. Kuuse (Est) 1.90.
(Johnson 2.00 OR; Thurber 2.00=OR; Albritton 2.00=OR; Kotkas 2.00=OR)

1948 (26. F 30 July): Twenty cleared the qualifying height, 1.87 (6-1¾). In the final, the jumpers were hampered by a soft takeoff. Winter was handicapped by a back injury, yet able to clear 1.98 on his first attempt. After that he was obliged to call it a day: fortunately for him, none of his rivals was able to master 1.98. Winter was the last Eastern cutoff jumper to be crowned world champion. Places 2-5 were for the first time decided on the fewer misses rule.

			1.95	1.98
1. John Winter (Aus)	1.98	6-6	xo	o
2. Bjorn Paulson (Nor)	1.95	6-4¾	o	xxx
3. George Stanich (US)	1.95	6-4¾	o	xxx
4. Dwight Eddleman (US)	1.95	6-4¾	o	xxx
5. Georges Damitio (Fr)	1.95	6-4¾	xo	xxx
6. Art Jackes (Can)	1.90	6-2¾		

7. tie, Alan Paterson (GB) & Hans Wahli (Switz) 1.90; 9. tie, P. Lacaze (Fr), A. Jadresic Vargas (Chile) & Goran Widenfelt (Swe) 1.90; 12. A. F. Adedoyin (GB) 1.90; 13. Birger Leirud (Nor) 1.90.

1952 (36. Q-F 20 July): Only 8 failed to make qualifying, 1.87 (6-1¾). In the afternoon's drawn-out final, Davis (a victim of polio at 8) proved the class of the field. Ties were broken on the fewer tries *and* misses rule, under which a pass at any intermediate height is better than clearing on first attempt.

			1.95	1.98	2.01	2.04	2.07
1. Buddy Davis (US)	2.04	6-8½ OR	o	o	o	xo	xxx
2. Ken Wiesner (US)	2.01	6-7¼	o	o	o	xxx	
3. Jose T. da Conceicao (Brz)	1.98	6-6	o	o	xxx		
4. Gosta Svensson (Swe)	1.98	6-6	p	xxo	xxx		
5. Ronald Pravitt (GB)	1.95	6-4¾	o	xxx			
6. Ion Soter (Rum)	1.95	6-4¾	xo	xxx			

7. Arnold Betton (US) 1.95; 8. B. Gundersen (Nor) 1.90; 9. tie, Jacques Delelienne (Bel) & J. Majekodunmi (Nig) 1.90; 11. tie, P. Halme (Fin) & P. Wells (GB) 1.90. 7 others also cleared 1.90.

1956 (28. Q-F 23 Nov): In another fruitless morning of qualifying, only 6 missed 1.92 (6-3½). Bengt Nilsson of Sweden, the European record holder, was handicapped by a ruptured muscle and failed to qualify. The afternoon final lasted five hours. Porter, 20, improved on his PR three times but was finally defeated by 19-year-old Dumas who clinched the gold medal by going over 2.12 on his third attempt.

			2.00	2.03	2.06	2.08	2.10	2.12	2.14
1. Charley Dumas (US)	2.12	6-11½OR	o	xo	o	o	xo	xxo	xxx
2. Chilla Porter (Aus)	2.10	6-10¾	o	o	o	xo	xxo	xxx	
3. Igor Kashkarov (SU)	2.08	6-10	o	o	o	o	xxx		
4. Stig Pettersson (Swe)	2.06	6-9¼	o	o	xxo	xxx			
5. Ken Money (Can)	2.03	6-8	o	xo	xxx				
6. Vladimir Sitkin (SU)	2.00	6-6¾	o	xxx					

7. tie, Phil Reavis (US) & Colin Ridgway (Aus) 2.00; 9. Julius Chigbolu (Nig) 2.00; 10. Vern Wilson (US) 2.00; 11. M. Fournier (Fr) 1.96; 12. tie, P. Etolu (Uga) & Y. Ishikawa (Japan) 1.96. 3 others also cleared 1.96.
(Porter 2.06 OR; 2.06=OR—Kashkarov, Pettersson, Dumas, Money; Dumas 2.08 OR; 2.08=OR—Kashkarov, Porter; Dumas 2.10 OR; Porter 2.10=OR)

1960 (32. Q-F 1 Sept): In the final, Joe Faust, a 7-foot (2.13) jumper from the US, was handicapped by an injured ankle and failed to clear 2 meters. In fact the event turned out to be

the Waterloo of US jumpers. Defending champion Dumas went no higher than 2.03 (6-8) and was 6th. World record holder Thomas was outjumped by two Soviets and tied by another and finally had to be content with 3rd. The winner, 27-year-old Shavlakadze, beat young countryman Brumel, 18, on the countback. He had a flawless record through his winning height.

			2.03	2.06	2.09	2.12	2.14	2.16	2.18
1. Robert Shavlakadze (SU)	2.16	7-1 OR	o	o	o	o	o	o	xxx
2. Valeriy Brumel (SU)	2.16	7-1=OR	o	o	xo	xxo	xo	xo	xxx
3. John Thomas (US)	2.14	7-¼	p	o	o	p	xo	xxx	
4. Viktor Bolshov (SU)	2.14	7-¼	o	o	o	o	xo	xxx	
5. Stig Pettersson (Swe)	2.09	6-10¼	p	xxo	xxo	xxx			
6. Charley Dumas (US)	2.03	6-8	o	p	xxx				

7. tie, Jiri Lansky (Czech), Kjell-Ake Nilsson (Swe) & Theo Pull (WG) 2.03; 10. R. Kotei (Gha) 2.03; 11. C. Porumb (Rum) 2.03; 12. Mahamat Idriss (Fr) 2.03; 13. Sandor Noszaly (Hun) 2.03.
(2.12=OR—Dumas, Bolshov, Shavlakadze, Brumel; Shavlakadze 2.14 OR; 2.14=OR—Brumel, Bolshov, Thomas)

1964 (28. Q 20 Oct; F 21 Oct): Brumel's two misses at the qualifying height of 2.06 (6-9¼) marked the only item of note in the trials, conducted on a wet and dreary field: only 7 were eliminated. In the final it took over two hours and a height of 2.06 to eliminate 3 more. Another 6 failed to clear 2.09. At 2.12 only five made it, the two Russians on their first attempt and Thomas, Rambo, and Pettersson on their second. Major casualty was Poland's Edward Czernik, who had been thought to be the biggest threat to Brumel for the gold. Czernik missed once at 2.09, then passed to 2.12 where two misses (one close) put him out. At 2.14 Pettersson and Shavlakadze missed their first attempts. Then Rambo made it and was in the lead after misses by Brumel and Thomas. Only Pettersson succeeded on second attempt, but the other three made it on their third tries. At 2.16 Brumel was the only one to clear on first attempt and this jump won him the gold. Thomas cleared on second attempt and Rambo on third. Brumel and Thomas both cleared 2.18 on first attempt with Rambo missing three. Arch-rivals Brumel and Thomas both missed three at 2.20, and it was over.

			2.06	2.09	2.12	2.14	2.16	2.18	2.20
1. Valeriy Brumel (SU)	2.18	7-1¾ OR	o	o	o	xxo	o	o	xxx
2. John Thomas (US)	2.18	7-1¾=OR	o	o	xo	xxo	xo	o	xxx
3. John Rambo (US)	2.16	7-1	o	o	xo	o	xxo	xxx	
4. Stig Pettersson (Swe)	2.14	7-¼	o	o	xo	xo	xxx		
5. Robert Shavlakadze (SU)	2.14	7-¼	o	o	o	xxo	xxx		
6. Ralf Drecoll (Ger) &	2.09	6-10¼	o	o	xxx				
Kjell-Ake Nilsson (Swe)	2.09	6-10¼	o	o	xxx				

8. Ed Caruthers (US) 2.09; 9. Mahamat Idriss (Chad) 2.09; 10. Lawrie Peckham (Aus) 2.09. (2.16=OR—Brumel, Thomas, Rambo)

1968 (39. Q 19 Oct; F 20 Oct): Fosbury used his radical back-to-the-bar style to defeat the traditional straddlers with an Olympic (and American) record 2.24 (7-4¼). By 2.16 (7-1), Spielvogel, Crosa, the two Soviets and three Americans were left and the Italian and West German bowed out at their final jump. At 2.18 (7-1¾), Brown missed badly twice and then barely brushed the bar off on his last try. Fosbury sailed over on his first leap, matching the Olympic record. Caruthers needed all his jumps to clear, while Gavrilov played a psych game by passing. Skvortsov missed thrice, so the medalists were determined. All three easily cleared 2.20 (7-2¾) on their first attempts. At 2.22 (7-3½), Fosbury used the full two minutes of his pre-jump preparation and cleared. Caruthers made it on his second try, while Gavrilov looked tired and missed all. 2.24: both Americans missed twice (Fosbury's first misses of the day), but Fos arched over on his last try. Caruthers couldn't clear and the boyishly-enthusiastic Fosbury was Olympic champion. He unsuccessfully tried three times at a world record 2.29 (7-6¼), after more than three hours of jumping.

Dick Fosbury's Mexico win brought his flop style to worldwide attention and revolutionized the face of high jumping forever.

			2.14	2.16	2.18	2.20	2.22	2.24	2.29
1. Dick Fosbury (US)	2.24	7-4¼ OR	o	p	o	o	o	xxo	xxx
2. Ed Caruthers (US)	2.22	7-3½	xxo	p	xxo	o	xo	xxx	
3. Valentin Gavrilov (SU)	2.20	7-2¾	o	o	p	o	xxx		
4. Valeriy Skvortsov (SU)	2.16	7-1	o	xxo	xxx				
5. Reynaldo Brown (US)	2.14	7-¼	o	p	xxx				
6. Giacomo Crosa (It)	2.14	7-¼	o	xxx					

7. Gunther Spielvogel (WG) 2.14; 8. Lawrie Peckham (Aus) 2.12; 9. tie, Robert Sainte-Rose (Fr) & Ingomar Sieghart (WG) 2.09; 11. Luis Garriga (Sp) 2.09; 12. Ahmed Senoussi (Chad) 2.09; 13. Miodrag Todosijevic (Yug) 2.06.
(2.18=OR—Fosbury, Caruthers; Gavrilov 2.20 OR; 2.20=OR—Fosbury, Caruthers; Fosbury 2.22 OR; Caruthers 2.22=OR)

1972 (40. Q 9 Sept; F 10 Sept): Tarmak became the third Soviet in four Olympics to win the HJ, his 2.23 (7-3¼) the highest of 14 finishers who cleared at least 2.15 (7-¾). Eleven jumpers were still in the fray at 2.18 (7-1¾), but only Tarmak, Stones, Junge, Magerl and Szepesi moved on to 2.21 (7-3). Tarmak missed once and then cleared strongly, as did fellow-straddler Junge. Flopper Stones needed three tries but made it, while Magerl missed by the slimmest of margins on his final effort. The medalists were known as the bar was raised to 2.23 (7-3¾). All missed their initial tries, but Tarmak rolled over in his classic straddle style on his second. Junge missed

badly on his final two jumps, while Stones's second was close but his third hit the bar off on the way up. Stones, at 18, became the youngest medalist of men's track. Tarmak tried unsuccessfully to raise the Olympic record to 2.26 (7-5) but wasn't close on any of three attempts. The drawn-out competition lasted nearly four hours, finishing in the rain and dark and ending the track competition of the '72 Games.

			2.05	2.10	2.15	2.18	2.21	2.23	2.26
1. Juri Tarmak (SU)	2.23	7-3¾	p	o	o	o	xo	xo	xxx
2. Stefan Junge (EG)	2.21	7-3	xo	o	o	o	xo	xxx	
3. Dwight Stones (US)	2.21	7-3	p	o	o	o	xxo	xxx	
4. Hermann Magerl (WG)	2.18	7-1¾	o	o	xo	o	xxx		
5. Adam Szepesi (Hun)	2.18	7-1¾	o	o	o	xxo	xxx		
6. John Beers (Can) &	2.15	7-¾	o	o	o	xxx			
Istvan Major (Hun)	2.15	7-¾	o	o	o	xxx			

8. Rustam Akhmyetov (SU) 2.15; 9. John Hawkins (Can) 2.15; 10. Enzo Dal Forno (It) 2.15; 11. Jan Dahlgren (Swe) 2.15; 12. tie, Vassilios Papadimitriou (Gr) & Kestutis Sapka (SU) 2.15; 14. Bernard Gauthier (Fr) 2.15; 15. Henri Elliott (Fr) 2.10; 16. Serban Ioan (Rum) 2.10; 17. Marco Schivo (It) 2.10; 18. Lawrie Peckham (Aus) 2.10; 19. Hidehiko Tomizawa (Japan) 2.05.

1976 (38. Q 30 July; F 31 July): Six weeks before Montreal, Stones upped his own world record to 2.31 (7-7) and went to the Games a heavy favorite. But the one foe Stones couldn't control—rain—did him in as 19-year-old Wszola scaled an Olympic record 2.25 (7-4½) for the victory. Stones was relegated to his second consecutive bronze medal as home-son Joy gave the Canadians plenty to go wild about with his silver medal. Stones's concentration may have suffered, too, after some of his typically-brash statements about the French-Canadian organizers brought a hail of boos both in the qualifying round and early in the finals. Only four jumpers were out when the bar was raised to 2.18 (7-1¾), but by the time 2.21 (7-3) had been finished only the three medalists plus Budalov remained. And it had started raining. At 2.21 (7-3), Stones, Wszola and Joy all cleared on their first tries, but Wszola led by virtue of his one fewer attempt than Stones. At 2.23 (7-3¾), Wszola again cleared initially and Joy needed three. Stones, whose style relied heavily on speed, tried in vain to squeegee away the water from the takeoff but he couldn't dry it well enough and he missed all and was out. Wszola recorded his first miss at 2.25 but then cleared on his second; Joy took one and then passed to 2.27 (7-5½) which he couldn't clear. Wszola took two tries at 2.27 and one at 2.29 (7-6½) before bowing out. Four days later, Stones upped his own record to 2.32 (7-7¼).

			2.14	2.18	2.21	2.23	2.25	2.27	2.29
1. Jacek Wszola (Pol)	2.25	7-4½ OR	o	o	o	o	xo	xxp	x
2. Greg Joy (Can)	2.23	7-3¾	xo	xxo	o	xxo	xpp	xx	
3. Dwight Stones (US)	2.21	7-3	o	o	o	xxx			
4. Sergey Budalov (SU)	2.21	7-3	o	o	xo	xpp	xx		
5. Sergey Senyukov (SU)	2.18	7-1¾	o	o	xxx				
6. Rodolfo Bergamo (It)	2.18	7-1¾	xo	o	xxx				

7. Rolf Beilschmidt (EG) 2.18; 8. Jesper Torring (Den) 2.18; 9. Terje Totland (Nor) 2.18; 10. Rune Almen (Swe) 2.18; 11. James Barrineau (US) 2.14; 12. Claude Ferragne (Can) 2.14; 13. Bill Jankunis (US) 2.10; 14. Leif-Roar Falkum (Nor) 2.10.

POLE VAULT

1896 (5. F 10 April): A drawn-out contest, held in cool weather. After being outjumped, the Greek competitors "became interested spectators and were most energetic in rubbing the limbs of the two Americans after each jump."

1. William Hoyt (US)	3.30	10-10		4. Ioan. Theodoropoulos (Gr)	2.80	9-2¼
2. Albert Tyler (US)	3.25	10-8		5. Vasilios Xydas (Gr)	2.50	8-2½
3. Evangelos Damaskos (Gr)	2.85	9-4¼				

1900 (8. F 15 July): Three leading American entrants—D.S. Horton, Bascom Johnson and Charles Dvorak—did not compete in the event, which was held on a Sunday. In fact, the last two did go to the field on Sunday—only to be told that the final would not be held on that day. So they left. The event was run off later in the day, and Baxter, who was still lingering around the field, joined in and won. "To appease the indignant visitors from across the sea," the French Committee staged a special vault at a later date. In this Horton did 3.45 (11-3¾) to beat Dvorak's 3.40 (11-1¾), but Johnson (3.55/11-8 a month earlier in the US) did not participate.

1. Irving Baxter (US)	3.30	10-10	4. Eric Lemming (Swe),		3.10	10-2
2. M. B. Colkett (US)	3.25	10-8	Jakab Kauser (Hun) &		3.10	10-2
3. Carl-Albert Andersen (Nor)	3.20	10-6	Louis Gontier (Fr)		3.10	10-2

7. K. G. Staaf (Swe) 2.80; 8. Aug. Nilsson (Swe) 2.60.

1904 (7. F 3 Sept): After clearing the winning height, Dvorak tried for a new world record of 3.71 (12-2) but failed on all his attempts. After his disappointment at the previous Games, it must have been a sweet victory, indeed.

1. Charles Dvorak (US)	3.50	11-6 OR	4. Ward McLanahan (US)	3.35	11-0
2. Leroy Samse (US)	3.43	11-3	5. Walter Dray (US)		
3. L. Wilkins (US)	3.43	11-3	6. Claude Allen (US)		

7. Paul Weinstein (Ger).
(Dvorak 3.35 OR; 3.35=OR—Samse, Wilkins, McLanahan; Dvorak 3.43 OR; 3.43=OR—Dvorak, Samse, Wilkins)

1908 (14. F 24 July): In the qualifying round, jumping was done in sections. Cooke had the best mark, 3.71. This was equaled by Gilbert in the final and the two were bracketed in a tie for 1st. Each received a gold medal!

1. Edward Cooke (US) &	3.71	12-2 OR	Bruno Soderstrom (Swe)	3.58	11-9
Alfred Gilbert (US)	3.71	12-2 OR	6. Sam Bellah (US) &	3.50	11-6
3. Ed Archibald (Can),	3.58	11-9	Georgios Banikas (Gr)	3.50	11-6
Charles Jacobs (US) &	3.58	11-9			

8. K. Szathmary (Hun) 3.35
(3.50=OR Q—Dvorak, Gilbert, Soderstrom, Archibald, Jacobs; Gilbert 3.58OR Q; 3.58=OR Q—Soderstrom, Archibald; Gilbert 3.66OR Q; Cooke 3.66=OR Q; Cooke 3.71OR Q; 3.71=OR—Gilbert, Cooke)

1912 (24. Q 10 July; F 11 July): Only 11 mastered the qualifying height, 3.65 (11-11¾). In the final, no less than 7 beat the listed Olympic record. At 3.80 Babcock, Nelson and world record holder Wright—history's first 4-meter man—cleared first time, Happenny, Murphy and Uggla second time. Happenny sustained an injury in vaulting at that height and was unable to continue. Babcock, Nelson and Wright cleared 3.85. But at 3.90 (12-9½) only Babcock was successful and he went on to clear 3.95. Only the world record height of 4.06 (13-3¾) proved too much for him. Two silver and three bronze medals were awarded.

1. Harry Babcock (US)	3.95	12-11½ OR	4. Bertil Uggla (Swe),	3.80	12-5½
2. Frank Nelson (US) &	3.85	12-7½	William Happenny (Can) &	3.80	12-5½
Marc Wright (US)	3.85	12-7½	Frank Murphy (US)	3.80	12-5½

7. Sam Bellah (US) 3.75; 8. tie, Frank Coyle, Gordon Dukes & Bill Fritz (all US) 3.65; 11. R. Pasemann (Ger) 3.40.
(Nelson 3.75 OR; 3.75=OR—Uggla, Wright, Happenny, Murphy, Bellah; Nelson 3.80 OR; 3.80=OR—Babcock, Wright, Uggla, Happenny, Murphy; Babcock 3.85 OR; 3.85=OR—Nelson, Wright; Babcock 3.90 OR)

1920 (14. F 20 Aug): The useless qualifying round (3.60) eliminated only one. In the final, the initial height was 3.30 (10-10), with the bar raised 10cm each time. Only Foss and Petersen cleared 3.70 and at the next height, 3.80 (12-5½), Foss was the only one to succeed. When the bar was raised to 4.00 (13-1½), he failed on his first attempt, after which he chose to take his second at 4.10 (13-5½). He went over and thus set a new world record, which upon recheck was

found to be 4.09. Places 3-6 were decided in a jumpoff.

1. Frank Foss (US)	4.09	13-5 WR	4. Edward Knourek (US)	3.60	11-9¾
2. Henry Petersen (Den)	3.70	12-1¾	5. Ernfrid Rydberg (Swe)	3.60	11-9¾
3. Edwin Myers (US)	3.60	11-9¾	6. Lauritz Jorgensen (Den)	3.60	11-9¾

7. Eldon Jenne (US) 3.60. Other finalists: A. Franquenelle (Fr), Mattsson (Swe), J. Rouho (Fin), 6. Hogstrom (Swe), P. Lagarde (Fr) & R. Powell (Bel).

1924 (20. Q 9 July; F 10 July): Seven qualified by going over 3.66 (12-0). The winner, Barnes, was a California high schooler. He clinched the gold by defeating Graham in a jumpoff. It should be noted that Charles Hoff of Norway, the world record holder, was handicapped by a foot injury and failed to appear here, although he started in the 400 and 800 meters.

1. Lee Barnes (US)	3.95	12-11½	4. Henry Petersen (Den)	3.90	12-9½
2. Glenn Graham (US)	3.95	12-11½	5. Victor Pickard (Can)	3.80	12-5½
3. James Brooker (US)	3.90	12-9½	6. Ralph Spearow (US)	3.70	12-1¾

7. M. Henrijean (Bel) 3.66.

1928 (20. F 1 Aug): Nine men qualified for the final by clearing 3.66 (12-0). Defending champion Barnes, who had raised the world record to 4.30 (14-1½) in April, could only duplicate his 1924 mark and had to be content with 5th after a jumpoff. Carr, history's first 14-footer (4.26), won with a new Olympic record, then failed at the world record height of 4.31 (14-1¾). Places 3-5 were decided in a jumpoff, with McGinnis clearing 4.10 to clinch the bronze.

1. Sabin Carr (US)	4.20	13-9¼ OR	4. Victor Pickard (Can)	3.95	12-11½
2. William Droegemuller (US)	4.10	13-5½	5. Lee Barnes (US)	3.95	12-11½
3. Charles McGinnis (US)	3.95	12-11½	6. Yonataro Nakazawa (Japan)	3.90	12-9½

7. H. Lindblad (Swe) 3.90; 8. J. Karlovits (Hun) 3.80; 9. J. Muller (Ger) 3.65. (Carr 4.10 OR; Droegmuller 4.10=OR)

1932 (8. F 3 Aug): The event, with a very limited entry, was featured by two major upsets. Graber, the man who had set a world record of 4.37 (14-4¼) at the US Trials in July, had to be content with 4th. Nishida, the 22-year-old Japanese who had come to the meet with a personal best of 4.15, improved by 15 centimeters. But Miller, America's second string, was able to reproduce his form of the Final Trials (4.31) and that sufficed for a narrow win. At the decisive height, 14-2 (which upon remeasurement turned out to be 14-1 7/8), Nishida had a close failure on his last attempt, brushing off the bar with his chest. Miller then made it on his last attempt—his arm hit the bar, which jiggled but stayed on.

			4.15	4.20	4.25	4.30	4.31
1. Bill Miller (US)	4.31	14-1¾ OR	xxo	o	o	o	xxo
2. Shuhei Nishida (Japan)	4.30	14-1¼	o	xo	xxo	xxo	xxx
3. George Jefferson (US)	4.20	13-9½	p	o	xxx		
4. Bill Graber (US)	4.15	13-7½	xxo	p	xxx		
5. Shizuo Mochizuki (Japan)	4.00	13-1½					
6. Lucio De Castro (Brazil)	3.90	12-9½					

7. P. Chlentzos (Gr) 3.75; . . . nh—C.J. Nelli (Brz).

1936 (30. F 5 Aug): A qualifying round at 3.80 (12-5½) eliminated only 5, so the final lasted 5 hours and was completed under floodlights. Meadows, who went on to set a world record the next year, was the only one successful at 4.35. Places 2-4 were decided in a jumpoff. Nishida and Oe did 4.15 to move Sefton, who missed, out of the medals. The two Japanese were given a tie for 2nd, although the team leader wanted the silver to go to Nishida, who had fewer misses (that rule not being in force at the time). The two finally decided to cut the medals in half so that each had a share of silver and bronze. The lack of a tie-breaking procedure knotted 11 men in a tie for 6th. World record holder George Varoff (4.43/14-6½) didn't make the U.S. team.

			4.15	4.25	4.35	4.45
1. Earle Meadows (US)	4.35	14-3¼ OR	o	xo	xo	xxx
2. Shuhei Nishida (Japan)	4.25	13-11¼	o	o	xxx	
Sueo Oe (Japan)	4.25	13-11¼	o	xo	xxx	
4. Bill Sefton (US)	4.25	13-11¼	xxo	o	xxx	
5. Bill Graber (US)	4.15	13-7½	xo	xxx		

6. tie, K. Adachi (Japan), Syl Apps (Can), P. Bacsalmasi (Hun), J. Haunzwickel (Aut), Danilo Innocenti (It), J. Korejs (Czech), Bo Ljungberg (Swe), A. Proksch (Aut), Wilhelm Sznajder (Pol), Dick Webster (GB) & Viktor Zsuffka (Hun) 4.00.

1948 (19. F 2 Aug): Twelve men qualified for the final by clearing 4.00 (13-1½). It rained during the final, and the water-logged runway made the vaulting precarious. When the bar was raised to 4.30, Kataja led on fewer misses. But at that height only Smith succeeded. It was a hard-won victory, as Smith was hampered by a tightly strapped, painful knee.

			4.10	4.20	4.30	4.40
1. Guinn Smith (US)	4.30	14-1¼	xo	o	xxo	x
2. Erkki Kataja (Fin)	4.20	13-9½	o	o	xxx	
3. Bob Richards (US)	4.20	13-9½	xo	xo	xxx	
4. Erling Kaas (Nor)	4.10	13-5½	o	xxx		
5. Ragnar Lundberg (Swe)	4.10	13-5½	xxo	xxx		
6. Richmond Morcom	3.95	12-11½	p	xxx		

7. tie, H. Gollors (Swe) & Valto Olenius (Fin) 3.95; 9. tie, J. Barbosa (P Rico), Victor Sillon (Fr) & J. Vicente (P Rico) 3.95; 12. Allan Lindberg (Swe) 3.80.

1952 (25. F 22 July): Nineteen qualified by clearing 4.00 (13-1½). The final lasted well over 5 hours. Richards, a great competitor, cleared the winning height on his third attempt to eliminate the threat of a jumpoff.

			4.20	4.30	4.40	4.50	4.55	4.60
1. Bob Richards (US)	4.55	14-11¼OR	o	o	o	xo	xxo	xxx
2. Don Laz (US)	4.50	14-9¼	o	o	o	xo	xxx	
3. Ragnar Lundberg (Swe)	4.40	14-5¼	o	xo	o	xxx		
4. Pyotr Denisyenko (SU)	4.40	14-5¼	xo	o	o	xxx		
5. Valto Olenius (Fin)	4.30	14-1¼	xo	xo	xxx			
6. Bunkichi Sawada (Japan)	4.20	13-9½	o	xxx				

7. Vladimir Brazhnik (SU) 4.20; 8. Viktor Knyazev (SU) 4.20; 9. George Mattos (US) 4.20; 10. Erkki Kataja (Fin) 4.10; 11. tie, Tomas Homonnay (Hun) & Lennart Lind (Swe) 4.10; 13. Milan Milakov (Yug) 4.10.
(Lundberg 4.40 OR; 4.40=OR–Laz, Denisyenko, Richards; Laz 4.50 OR; Richards 4.50=OR)

1956 (19 Q 24 Nov; F 26 Nov): Fourteen qualified by clearing 4.15. It was in the qualifying round that defending champ Richards found himself on the verge of a dramatic failure: at 4.00 (13-1½) he missed twice, partly because of a gusty wind which threw off his timing. On his third try at that height, Richards cleared with about 30 centimeters to spare! In the final, he was his true self again and became the first vaulter to win the event twice. Roubanis, surprising with one of the first fiberglass poles, added 9cm to his previous best to split the American trio.

			4.35	4.40	4.45	4.50	4.53	4.56	4.59
1. Bob Richards (US)	4.56	14-11½OR	o	o	o	o	o	xo	xxx
2. Bob Gutowski (US)	4.53	14-10¼	xo	xo	xxo	o	o	xxx	
3. Georgios Roubanis (Gr)	4.50	14-9¼	xo	o	o	o	xxx		
4. George Mattos (US)	4.35	14-3¼	o	xxx					
5. Ragnar Lundberg (Swe)	4.25	13-11¼							
6. Zenon Wazny (Pol)	4.25	13-11¼							

7. Eeles Landstrom (Fin) 4.25; 8. Manfred Preussger (EG) 4.25; 9. tie, Vladimir Bulatov (SU) & G. Chiesa (It) 4.15; 11. A. Petrov (SU) 4.15; 12. Zbigniew Janiszewski (Pol) 4.15.

1960 (29. Q 5 Sept; F 7 Sept): The qualifying round was a long, drawn-out affair which lasted about 7 hours. At the end, only 10 had mastered the qualifying height, 4.40—a mark previously achieved by only 6 men in Olympic competition. Since the rules state that at least 12 must be in the final, those who had fewer misses at the preceding height, 4.30—Morris, Khlebarov and Krzesinki—were advanced to the final. Among those who missed out were such highly touted vaulters as Manfred Preussger (East Germany), Dave Clark (US) and Georgios Roubanis (Greece). The final lasted a solid 6½ hours. Bragg (the world record holder) and Morris made it another US 1-2.

			4.50	4.55	4.60	4.70	4.82
1. Don Bragg (US)	4.70	15-5 OR	o	o	o	o	xxx
2. Ron Morris (US)	4.60	15-1¼	xo	o	xo	xxx	
3. Eeles Landstrom (Fin)	4.55	14-11¼	xo	o	xxx		
4. Rolando Cruz (P Rico)	4.55	14-11¼	o	xo	xxx		
5. Gunther Malcher (Ger)	4.50	14-9¼	o	xxx			
6. Igor Petrenko (SU) &	4.50	14-9¼	o	xxx			
Matti Sutinen (Fin)	4.50	14-9¼	o	xxx			

8. Rudolf Tomasek (Czech) 4.50; 9. Leon Lukman (Yug) 4.40; 10. Khristo Khristov (Bul) 4.40; 11. Dimiter Khlebarov (Bul) 4.30; 12. Andrzej Krzesinski (Pol) 4.30; 13. Janis Krasovskis (SU) 4.30.

(Bragg 4.60 OR; Morris 4.60=OR)

1964 (30. Q 15 Oct; F 17 Oct): In the qualification round, 18 made 4.60 (15-1¼). The fiberglass era had arrived. Among the non-qualifiers were two 16-footers, Rolando Cruz (Puerto Rico) and Wlodzimierz Sokolowski (Poland). C.K. Yang (Taiwan) qualified but withdrew from the final to save himself for the decathlon. Nine of the 18 finalists cleared 4.80 for a new Olympic record. 17-footer John Pennel of the US passed this height but failed at the next one. He had a bad back which pained him so much he had to have it taped after the first qualifying vault. At 5.05, Hansen passed and Reinhardt cleared on his first attempt. The rest were eliminated. The bar was raised to 5.10 and Hansen had to clear in order to win. Both missed on their first two attempts. Then Hansen cleared. Reinhardt had one jump left, but he had to clear that and beat Hansen at the next height in order to win. He hit the bar with his knees, leaving Hansen the winner. He declined to try for any higher height. The competition lasted an exhausting 9 hours. .

			4.80	4.85	4.90	4.95	5.00	5.05	5.10
1. Fred Hansen (US)	5.10	16-8¾ OR	o	o	p	p	o	p	xxo
2. Wolfgang Reinhardt (WG)	5.05	16-6¾	xo	p	xo	p	o	o	xxx
3. Klaus Lehnertz (WG)	5.00	16-5	o	o	o	xo	o	xxx	
4. Manfred Preussger (EG)	5.00	16-5	o	p	o	p	o	xxx	
5. Gennadiy Bliznyetsov (SU)	4.95	16-3	p	o	p	o	xp	xx	
6. Rudolf Tomasek (Czech)	4.90	16-1	xo	p	o	p	xxp	x	

7. Pentti Nikula (Fin) 4.90; 8. Billy Pemelton (US) 4.80; 9. Igor Fyeld (SU) 4.80; 10. Gerry Moro (Can) 4.70; 11. John Pennel (US) 4.70; 12. Risto Ankio (Fin) 4.70; 13. Roman Lesek (Yug) 4.70; 14. Taisto Laitinen (Fin) 4.60; 15. tie, Herve D'Encausse (Fr), Ignacio Sola (Sp) & Sergey Dyemin (SU) 4.40; 18. Chris Papanicolaou (Gr) 4.40.

(4.70=OR—Bliznyetsov, Hansen, Nikula, Pemelton, Lehnertz, Moro, Tomasek, Pennel, Ankio, Lesek, Fyeld; Hansen 4.80 OR; 4.80=OR—Pemelton, Preussger, Lehnertz, Reinhardt, Tomasek, Fyeld, Nikula; Bliznyetsov 4.85 OR; 4.85=OR—Lehnertz, Nikula; Nikula 4.90 OR; 4.90=OR—Preussger, Lehnertz, Tomasek, Reinhardt, Bliznyetsov, Lehnertz; Bliznyetsov 4.95 OR; Lehnertz 4.95=OR; Hansen 5.00 OR; 5.00=OR—Reinhardt, Preussger, Lehnertz; Reinhardt 5.05 OR)

1968 (23. Q 14 Oct; F 16 Oct): Seagren had set a world record of 5.41 (17-9) in winning the US Olympic Trials, but he got a stiff tussle from unheralded Schiprowski (pre-Olympic best of 5.18 [17-0]) and European champ Nordwig. The only notables to fall in the qualifying were high-schooler Casey Carrigan and Tokyo bronze winner Klaus Lehnertz. When 11 finalists had bested the Olympic record of 5.10 (16-8¾) by clearing 5.15 (16-10½), a long competition was in store. By the time the bar was raised to 5.35 (17-6¾), six were still in. Only Bliznyetsov

surrendered as everyone cleared except Seagren, who passed. At 5.40 (17-8½) all missed their first efforts. But Seagren made it on his second to take the lead. Schiprowski followed to move into the runner-up position. Nordwig needed three, while Papanicolaou and Pennel went out. The final height was a world record 5.45 (17-10½); Schiprowski came close only once, but both Seagren and Nordwig had two very close efforts. Schiprowski's final miss ended the competition 7½ hours after it had begun. It was the first time all 3 medallists had the same height.

			5.15	5.20	5.25	5.30	5.35	5.40	5.45
1. Bob Seagren (US)	5.40	17-8½ OR	p	xo	p	o	p	xo	xxx
2. Claus Schiprowski (WG)	5.40	17-8½	p	o	xo	o	xo	xo	xxx
3. Wolfgang Nordwig (EG)	5.40	17-8½	p	o	p	o	o	xxo	xxx
4. Chris Papanicolaou (Gr)	5.35	17-6¾	o	p	xo	xo	o	xxx	
5. John Pennel (US)	5.35	17-6¾	p	xo	p	xo	xxo	xxx	
6. Gennadiy Bliznyetsov (SU)	5.30	17-4¾	p	o	p	xo	xxx		

7. Herve D'Encausse (Fr) 5.25; 8. Heinfried Engel (WG) 5.20; 9. Ignacio Sola (Sp) 5.20; 10. Kjell Isaksson (Swe) 5.15; 11. Kiyoshi Niwa (Japan) 5.15; 12. Aleksandr Malyutin (SU) 5.00; 13. Mike Bull (GB) 5.00; 14. Altti Alarotu (Fin) 5.00;... nh—Erkki Mustakari (Fin) [4.80].
(5.10=OR—Bliznyetsov, Niwa, Schiprowski, Sola, Engel; Sola 5.15 OR; 5.15=OR—Papanicolaou, Isaksson, Niwa, D'Encausse; Bliznyetsov 5.20 OR; 5.20=OR—Nordwig, Engel, Schiprowski, Seagren, Pennel, Sola; D'Encausse 5.25 OR; 5.25=OR—Papanicolaou, Schiprowski; Nordwig 5.30 OR; 5.30=OR—Seagren, Schiprowski, Papanicolaou, Bliznyetsov, Pennel; Papanicolaou 5.35 OR; 5.35=OR—Nordwig, Schiprowski, Pennel; Seagren 5.40 OR; 5.40=OR—Schiprowski, Nordwig).

1972 (21. Q 1 Sept; F 2 Sept): Controversy swirled around this competition in the form of vacillating IAAF rulings on the acceptability of certain "new" poles and thus slightly diminished Nordwig's victory with an Olympic record 5.50 (18-½). The final banning decision came the night before the qualifying and 14 of 21 vaulters entered were forced to jump on poles they had never seen before. For the final, cold, windy weather hampered the jumpers as well, so that only four men jumped higher than 5.20 (17-¾). Kuretzky led the competition after a PR clearance at 5.30 (17-4¾), but he went out at 5.35 while Nordwig, defending champ Seagren and Johnson cleared. Johnson missed at 5.40 (17-8½) while the others cleared and it became a two-man duel. Nordwig made his first try at 5.45 (17-10½) to put the pressure on Seagren. But the controversy and the competition had taken their toll and Seagren missed all his tries. The East German then needed three jumps to make the Olympic record height of 5.50 before he missed at 5.56 (18-3). But he had come out on top of the comparatively short competition (less than six hours) to become the first non-American to win the event.

			5.20	5.30	5.35	5.40	5.45	5.50	5.56
1. Wolfgang Nordwig (EG)	5.50	18-½ OR	p	xo	o	xo	o	xxo	xxx
2. Bob Seagren (US)	5.40	17-8½	o	p	o	xxo	xxx		
3. Jan Johnson (US)	5.35	17-6¾	xo	p	xo	xxx			
4. Reinhard Kuretzky (WG)	5.30	17-4¾	xo	o	xxx				
5. Bruce Simpson (Can)	5.20	17-¾	o	xxx					
6. Volker Ohl (WG)	5.20	17-¾	xo	xxx					

7. Hans Lagerqvist (Swe) 5.20; 8. Francois Tracanelli (Fr) 5.10; 9. Ingemar Jernberg (Swe) 5.10; 10. Wojciech Buciarski (Pol) 5.00; 11. Chris Papanicolaou (Gr) 5.00;... nh—Antti Kalliomaki (Fin) [5.20], Herve D'Encausse (Fr) [5.10] & Tadeusz Slusarski (Pol) [5.00].
(5.40=OR—Nordwig, Seagren; Nordwig 5.45 OR)

1976 (27. Q 24 July; F 26 July): This was a surprising competition in many respects: winner Slusarski was only the No. 2 Polish vaulter, Kalliomaki wasn't tabbed for a spot in the top six beforehand and Roberts was rated highly after setting a world record 5.70 (18-8¼) in the US Trials. Other favorites Kozakiewicz and Bell didn't live up to expectations. Kalliomaki opened at 5.10 (16-8¾), while Slusarski, Buciarski and Bell opened at 5.20 (17-¾). Abada started at 5.30 (17-4¾), a height equaling his seasonal best. Roberts opened at 5.35 (17-6¾) and missed his first try, which turned out to be the difference between gold and bronze. He made his second and passed to 5.50 (18-½). Abada got a PR at 5.45 and when the bar moved to 5.50,

seven men were still in it. The three medalists all cleared first-time, to tie the Olympic record. Abada and Bell passed as they had no other hope of moving into the medals. At 5.55 (18-2½), Roberts made a critical error by passing, while everyone else missed and went out. Then Roberts missed all his tries at 5.60 (18-4½). Rain and a headwind severely hampered the vaulters in the final.

			5.30	5.35	5.40	5.45	5.50	5.55	5.60
1. Tadeusz Slusarski (Pol)	5.50	18-½=OR	p	p	o	p	o ·	xxx	
2. Antti Kalliomaki (Fin)	5.50	18-½=OR	o	p	o	o	o	xxx	
3. Dave Roberts (US)	5.50	18-½=OR	p	xo	p	p	o	p	xxx
4. Patrick Abada (Fr)	5.45	17-10½	xo	p	p	xo	p	xxx	
5. Wojciech Buciarski (Pol)	5.45	17-10½	p	xo	p	xo	xp	xx	
6. Earl Bell (US)	5.45	17-10½	p	o	p	xxo	p	xxx	

7. Jean-Michel Bellot (Fr) 5.40; 8. Itsuo Takanezawa (Japan) 5.40; 9. Gunther Lohre (WG) 5.35; 10. Yuriy Prokhoryenko (SU) 5.25; 11. Wladyslaw Kozakiewicz (Pol) 5.25; 12. Don Baird (Aus) 5.25; 13. tie, Vladimir Kishkun (SU) & Terry Porter (US) 5.20; 15. Tapani Haapakoski (Fin) 5.20; 16. Brian Hooper (GB) 5.00;. . . nh—Francois Tracanelli (Fr) [5.30], Kjell Isaksson (Swe) [5.20], Roberto More (Cuba) [5.10] & Bruce Simpson (Can) [5.00].
(5.50=OR—Kalliomaki, Slusarski, Roberts)

LONG JUMP

1896 (8. F 7 April): Little is known of this competition. Each man had only three tries, as the US scored the first Olympic medal sweep.

1. Ellery Clark (US)	6.35	20-10	4. Alexandre Tuffere (Fr)	5.98	19-7½
2. Robert Garrett (US)	6.18	20-3¼	5. A. Grisel (Fr)	5.83	19-1½
3. James Connolly (US)	6.11	20-½	6. Alex. Chalkokondilis (Gr)	5.74	18-10

7. Karl Schumann (EG) 5.70 (not tabbed).

1900 (12. Q 14 July; F 15 July): Prinstein was in the lead after the qualifying round but was prevented by the leaders of his university (Syracuse) from competing in the Sunday final. Kraenzlein, one of the greatest talents of the time, bettered Prinstein's mark by 1cm in the final. Earlier in the year, Prinstein had set a world record of 7.50 (24-7¼).

1. Alvin Kraenzlein (US)	7.18	23-6¾ OR	4. William Remington (US)	6.82	22-4½
2. Myer Prinstein (US)	7.17	23-6¼	5. Albert Delannoy (Fr)	6.75	22-1¾
3. Patrick Leahy (GB-Eire)	6.95	22-9½	6. John McLean (US)	6.43	21-1¼

(Prinstein 7.17 OR)

1904 (7. F 1 Sept): All the contestants were Americans; world record holder Peter O'Connor was among the absent. Prinstein, a most reliable competitor who won the AAU title four times, scored an easy victory.

1. Myer Prinstein (US)	7.34	24-1 OR	4. Fred Englehardt (US)	6.63	21-9
2. Daniel Frank (US)	6.89	22-7¼	5. G. H. Van Cleve (US)		
3. Robert Stangland (US)	6.88	22-7	6. John Percy Hagerman (US)		

1908 (30. Q-F 22 July): In the qualifying round, Irons did 7.44 (24-5). It would appear that only the first three were admitted to the final. Among those who failed to survive was Tim Ahearne of Ireland and Great Britain, who did 7.57 (24-10) a couple of weeks later to become No. 2 ever. In the final, Irons was the only one to improve. His mark ranked him 3rd on the all-time world list, after Peter O'Connor and Myer Prinstein.

1. Frank Irons (US)	7.48	24-6½ OR	4. Edward Cooke (US)	6.97	22-10½
2. Dan Kelly (US)	7.09	23-3¼	5. John Brennan (US)	6.86	22-6¼
3. Calvin Bricker (Can)	7.08	23-3	6. Frank Mountpleasant (US)	6.82	22-4½

7. A. Weinstein (Ger) 6.77; 8. Timothy Ahearne (GB) 6.72; 9. D. Murray (GB) 6.71; 10. G. Ronstrom (Swe) 6.66.
(Irons 7.44 OR)

1912 (32. Q-F 12 July): In the qualifying round the jumpers were divided into three groups. The three best were allowed three more trials in the final. Defending champion Irons started with 6.80, but countryman Allen improved to 6.94. Then Aberg took the lead with 7.04 (23-1¼). But then Gutterson, a 7.33 (24-½) jumper, killed the opposition with a great 7.60: second only to Peter O'Connor's world record 7.61 (24-11¾). Bricker led the second group with 7.21 (23-7¾) and Worthington the third with 7.03. The Swede was the only one to improve in the final.

1. Albert Gutterson (US)	7.60	24-11¼	(7.60	7.48	7.25	7.18	7.09	7.09)
2. Calvin Bricker (Can)	7.21	23-7¾	(6.92	7.07	7.21	7.04	6.85	?)
3. Georg Aberg (Swe)	7.18	23-6¾	(7.04	6.70	6.99	6.98	7.18	6.63)
4. Harry Worthington (US)	7.03	23-¾						
5. Eugene Mercer (US)	6.97	22-10½	6. Fred Allen (US)				6.94	22-9¼

7. R. Pasemann (Ger) 6.82; 8. Frank Irons (US) 6.80; 9. H. S. O. Ashington (GB) 6.78.

1920 (29. Q 17 Aug; F 18 Aug): Pettersson led the qualifiers with 6.94 (22-9¼). The pre-meet favorite, Sol Butler, who had done 7.52 (24-8) at the US Trials, sustained a muscle injury on his first jump and had to call it a day. In the final the loose runway kept the marks down. Even so, all but Franksson were able to improve on their qualifying efforts. On the whole, the Swedes had quite a day.

1. William Pettersson (Swe)	7.15	23-5½	4. Dink Templeton (US)	6.95	22-9½
2. Carl Johnson (US)	7.09	23-3¼	5. Erling Aastad (Nor)	6.88	22-7
3. Eric Abrahamsson (Swe)	7.08	23-2¾	6. Rolf Franksson (Swe)	6.73	22-1

7. Sol Butler (US) 6.60; 8. E. Raeder (Nor) 6.58; 9. G. Bladin (Swe) 6.57; 10. J. Johannessen (Nor) 6.56; 11. Jack Merchant (US) 6.50; 12. E. Coulon (Fr) 6.50.

1924 (34. Q-F 8 July): Robert LeGendre (US), who had set a world record of 7.77 (25-6) during the pentathlon, was not entered. Bill Comins, a 7.57 (24-8) man from the US, pulled a muscle in the qualifying and was unable to go on. In the final pool, Hubbard—probably the greatest long jumper of the pre-Owens era—had a magnificent jump in the vicinity of LeGendre's newly-set record but fell back and thus lost many vital centimeters. As it was, that jump amply sufficed to earn gold for him.

1. Dettart Hubbard (US)	7.44	24-5	4. Vilho Tuulos (Fin)	7.07	23-2¼
2. Ed Gourdin (US)	7.27	23-10¼	5. Louis Wilhelme (Fr)	6.99	22-11¼
3. Sverre Hansen (Nor)	7.26	23-9¾	6. Christopher Macintosh (GB)	6.92	22-8½

7. Virgilio Tommasi (It) 6.89; 8. J. Boot (Hol) 6.86; 9. Albert Rose (US) 6.85; 10. tie, Mikio Oda (Japan) & P. Sandstrom (Fin) 6.83; 12. Silvio Cator (Haiti) 6.81.

1928 (41. O-F 31 July): In the qualifying round, the jumpers were divided into four sections. All the good marks occurred in this preliminary phase. In the final, which was held on another runway, nobody was able to improve. De Boer was admitted to the final as the sixth man on the strength of his better second mark vis-a-vis Gordon. In the final, world record holder Hamm did 7.66 (25-1½) and 7.22 (23-8¼), then passed up his third and last trial. Defending champion Hubbard was hampered by a weak ankle and failed to make the final.

1. Ed Hamm (US)	7.73	25-4¼ OR	4. Willi Meier (Ger)	7.39	24-3
2. Silvio Cator (Haiti)	7.58	24-10½	5. Erich Kochermann (Ger)	7.35	24-1½
3. Alfred Bates (US)	7.40	24-3¼	6. Hannes de Boer (Hol)	7.32	24-¼

7. Ed Gordon (US) 7.32; 8. E. Svensson (Swe) 7.29; 9. Chuhei Nambu (Japan) 7.25; 10. O. Hallberg (Swe) 7.18; 11. tie, DeHart Hubbard (US), Mikio Oda (Japan) & Vilho Tuulos (Fin) 7.11; 14. E. Aastad (Nor) 7.07.

1932 (12. F 2 Aug): Three of the non-qualifiers at Amsterdam—Gordon, Nambu, Svensson— figured prominently here, four years later, while the Amsterdam silver medallist, Cator

(injured), had the worst day of his career. All the best jumps occurred in the early rounds. Nambu, holder of the world record, had sustained a slight injury in practice, yet he reached 7.45 on his first jump. Redd opened with a hairline foul of about 7.85 (25-9). Still in the first round, Gordon produced a fine 7.64—the eventual winning mark. Redd had a 7.60 in the second round. After that, no major changes were registered.

1. Ed Gordon (US)	7.64	25-¾	(7.64	7.00	7.43	f	f	f)
2. Lambert Redd (US)	7.60	24-11¼	(f	7.60	f	7.39	f	7.49)
3. Chuhei Nambu (Japan)	7.45	24-5¼	(7.45	f	f	7.32	7.39	f)
4. Eric Svensson (Swe)	7.41	24-3¾	(7.27	7.24	7.41	7.06	p	p)
5. Richard Barber (US)	7.39	24-3						
6. Naoto Tajima (Japan)	7.15	23-5½						

7. H. Berra (Arg) 6.66; 8. C. de Figueiredo Raposo (Braz) 6.43; 9. Silvio Cator (Haiti) 5.93; 10. E. Crespo (Mex) 5.83; 11. Erich Kochermann (Ger) 5.72;. . . nm—L. Hutton (Can).

1936 (43. Q-F 4 Aug): The favorites, Owens and Long, needed two trials to qualify. In the afternoon of the same day, there was a "semi-final" (3 tries) and a final (3 tries), with the latter held on a runway parallel to the homestretch. According to the Official Report, "the wind velocity was between 3.5 and 3.7 m/s, the jumping being in the direction of the wind." The wind was particularly strong during the final pool. However, no readings were announced for the individual jumps. It should be noted that Long's 7.87 was not accepted as a German record. Long and Maffei achieved personal bests, Tajima equaled his best of 1935, Owens and Leichum came fairly close to their best ever marks.

1. Jesse Owens (US)	8.06	26-5¼w	(7.74	7.87	7.75	f	7.94	8.06)
2. Luz Long (Ger)	7.87	25-9¾w	(7.54	7.74	7.84	7.73	7.87	f)
3. Naoto Tajima (Japan)	7.74	25-4¾	(7.65	f	7.74	7.52	7.60	f)
4. Arturo Maffei (It) &	7.73	25-4¼w	(7.50	7.47	7.73	7.22	7.42	7.39)
Wilhelm Leichum (Ger)	7.73	25-4¼	(f	f	7.52	7.38	7.25	7.73)
6. Bob Clark (US)	7.67	25-2	(f	7.60	7.54	7.60	7.67	7.57),

7. John Brooks (US) 7.41; 8. Robert Paul (Fr) 7.34; 9. A. Baumle (Ger) 7.32; 10. tie, Ake Stenqvist (Swe) & Otto Berg (Nor) 7.30; 12. G. Caldana (It) 7.26.

1948 (21. Q-F 31 July): In the qualifying round, only four jumpers achieved the qualifying distance, 7.20 (23-7½). Steele led the qualifiers with a magnificent 7.78 (25-6¼), with Wright 2nd at 7.53 (24-8½). In the final Steele, though handicapped by a badly hurt leg, had jumps of 7.82 and 7.68 (25-2¼), then retired. Bruce came very close to his best ever and took 2nd, 1cm ahead of Douglas. Wright didn't quite match his qualifying distance.

1. Willie Steele (US)	7.82	25-8				
(7.82	7.68	p	p	p	p)	
2. Thomas Bruce (Aus)	7.55	24-9¼				
3. Herbert Douglas (US)	7.54	24-9				
4. Lorenzo Wright (US)	7.45	24-5¼				
5. Adeg. F. Adedoyin (GB)	7.27	23-10¼				
6. Georges Damitio (Fr)	7.07	23-2¼				

7. Harry Whittle (GB) 7.03; 8. F. Wurth (Aut) 7.00; 9. H. Askew (GB) 6.93; 10. Enrique Kistenmacher (Arg) 6.80; 11. Edward Adamczyk (Pol) 6.73. (Steele 7.78 OR Q).

Jesse Owens at Berlin.

1952 (27. Q-F 21 July): Only 7 achieved the qualifying distance, 7.20 (23-7½). The leading qualifiers were Gourdine 7.41 (24-3¾), Biffle 7.40 (24-3¼), Price 7.36 (24-1¾) and Brown 7.32 (24-¼). It rained during the early rounds of the final. Price had an injured leg and was unable to do himself justice. Brown, an 8.00 (26-3¼) performer, who was probably the most prohibitive favorite in these Games, fouled three times and was eliminated: his last effort would have been worth a medal, if measured from takeoff.

1. Jerome Biffle (US)	7.57	24-10	(7.21	f	7.57	f	f	f)
2. Meredith Gourdine (US)	7.53	24-8½	(7.38	6.58	7.53	7.49	7.36	7.51)
3. Odon Foldessy (Hun)	7.30	23-11½	(7.04	7.23	f	7.17	7.30	7.12)
4. Ary Facanha de Sa (Braz)	7.23	23-8¾	(7.15	6.77	7.06	7.22	7.20	7.23)
5. Jorma Valtonen (Fin)	7.16	23-6	(f	7.06	7.16	f	f	6.97)
6. Leonid Grigoryev (SU)	7.14	23-5¼	(f	7.14	6.92	5.55	f	6.67)

7. K.-E. Israelsson (Swe) 7.10; 8. Paul Faucher (Fr) 7.02; 9. P. Snellman (Fin) 7.02; 10. Masaji Tajima (Japan) 7.00; 11. Neville Price (S Afr) 6.40;. . . nm—George Brown (US), Henk Visser (Hol).

1956 (32. Q-F 24 Nov): Thirteen achieved the qualifying distance, a regressive 7.15 (23-5½). Grabowski led the qualifiers with 7.52 (24-8), followed by Bennett 7.50 (24-7½) and Fyedoseyev 7.42 (24-4¼). Conditions during the final were not conducive to good performances. The wind ranged from 14 mps adverse to 9 mps favorable. The short, loose runway was another deterrent. However, Bell and Bennett achieved their best distances against stiff winds. "They were the worst conditions I ever jumped under," said Bell.

1. Greg Bell (US)	7.83	25-8¼	(6.98	7.83	7.77	f	p	7.16)
2. John Bennett (US)	7.68	25-2¼	(7.68	7.61	f	p	f	p)
3. Jorma Valkama (Fin)	7.48	24-6½	(7.11	f	7.48	7.07	7.22	7.00)
4. Dmitriy Bondarenko (SU)	7.44	24-5	(7.44	f	7.13	f	6.89	6.99)
5. Karim Olowu (Nig)	7.36	24-1¾	(7.28	6.77	7.36	6.42	f	6.91)
6. Kaz. Kropidlowski (Pol)	7.30	23-11½	(7.27	6.92	7.30	6.95	7.03	6.94)

7. Neville Price (S Afr) 7.28; 8. Olyeg Fyedoseyev (SU) 7.27; 9. Arthur Cruttenden (GB) 7.15; 10. Henryk Grabowski (Pol) 7.15; 11. Ken Wilmshurst (GB) 7.14; 12. Fermin Donazar (Urg) 6.57;. . . nm—Igor Ter-Ovanesyan (SU).

1960 (49. Q-F 2 Sept): Roberson led the qualifiers with 7.81 (25-7½), followed by Ter-Ovanesyan 7.79 (25-6¾), Visser 7.72 (25-4) and Steinbach 7.70 (25-3¼). In the final, Roberson and Boston quickly took the lead with impressive 8-meter jumps. Going into the last round, it looked as if Boston's 8.12 was untouchable. But then came the fireworks: first Ter-Ovanesyan moved to 2nd with a new European record of 8.04, then Steinbach produced a new German record of 8.00 but fell short of a medal. Finally, Roberson sailed for a great 8.11, thus failing to catch Boston by a centimeter. Had he tied Boston at 8.12 he would have been the winner on the basis of having a longer second jump.

1. Ralph Boston (US)	8.12	26-7¾ OR	(7.82	f	8.12	7.80	f	7.96)
2. Bo Roberson (US)	8.11	26-7¼	(f	8.03	7.88	7.75	7.62	8.11)
3. Igor Ter-Ovanesyan (SU)	8.04	26-4½	(7.90	7.80	f	f	7.68	8.04)
4. Manfred Steinbach (WG)	8.00	26-3	(7.81	f	7.76	f	f	8.00)
5. Jorma Valkama (Fin)	7.69	25-2¾	(7.52	7.69	7.36	7.31	f	7.29)
6. Christian Collardot (Fr)	7.68	25-2½	(7.61	f	7.68	6.96	7.50	f)

7. Henk Visser (Hol) 7.66; 8. Dmitriy Bondarenko (SU) 7.58; 9. Manfred Molzberger (WG) 7.49; 10. Attilio Bravi (It) 7.47; 11. Dimitrios Maglaras (Gr) 7.45; 12. Paul Foreman (W Indies) 7.26; 12. Fred Alsop (GB) 7.25;. . . dnc—Takayuki Okazaki (Japan). (Roberson 8.03 OR)

1964 (32. Q-F 18 Oct): The weather was cold, rainy, and windy. In the morning qualifying only five men were able to meet the standard of 7.60 (24-11¼) so the next seven were added to make a twelve man field for the finals. Among the non-qualifiers were 26 footers Leonid Barkovskiy (USSR), Phil Shinnick (US), Klaus Beer (EG) and Pentti Eskola (Finland). By the afternoon finals the rain had made the runway quite slippery. After the first three rounds Boston led with 7.85, Ter-Ovanesyan was second at 7.78, and Davies was third with 7.59. One

of the pre-meet favorites, Hopkins, fouled all three of his jumps. The three leaders all improved on the fourth round with Boston still ahead at 7.88. In round 5 Boston fouled. Then Davies came thundering down the runway to post a new personal record of 8.07 and took over the lead. Ter-Ovanesyan also passed Boston with a leap of 7.99. Boston had one jump left. It was a gallant effort—8.03—but not good enough to win. Neither Davies nor Ter-Ovanesyan improved on their final jumps. "I prayed for rain and I got it," revealed Davies.

1.	Lynn Davies (GB)	8.07	26-5¾	(7.45	f	7.59	7.78	8.07	7.74)
2.	Ralph Boston (US)	8.03	26-4¼	(7.76	7.85	7.62	7.88	f	8.03)
3.	Igor Ter-Ovanesyan (SU)	7.99	26-2½	(7.78	f	7.64	7.80	7.99	7.81)
4.	Wariboko West (Nig)	7.60	24-11¼	(7.56	7.51	7.50	7.40	7.60	f)
5.	Jean Cochard (Fr)	7.44	24-5	(f	f	7.44	7.43	7.26	7.10)
6.	Luis Felipe Areta (Sp)	7.34	24-1	(7.20	7.31	7.34	5.16	f	6.99)

7. Mike Ahey (Gha) 7.30; 8. Andrzej Stalmach (Pol) 7.26; 9. Hiroomi Yamada (Japan) 7.16; 10. Wolfgang Klein (WG) 7.15; 11. John Morbey (GB) 7.09;... nm—Gayle Hopkins (US).

1968 (35. Q 17 Oct; F 18 Oct): 17 achieved the qualifying distance, 7.65 (25-1¼). At the beginning, things did not look promising for pre-meet favorite Beamon: he fouled on his first two jumps, one by a massive margin; on his third, he took off with about 30cm to spare, yet managed 8.19 (26-10½). This was bettered only by Boston, who had qualified on his first jump with a beautiful, windless OR of 8.27 (27-1½). In the final, fouls by the first three jumpers acted as an anonymous introduction to trackdom's most legendary performance—Beamon's 8.90, an effort surpassing the previous world record by an unheard of margin of 55cm. Everything went right with that jump, including wind assistance, the maximum permissible at 2.0 m/s. It looked as if the heavens too were impressed, for shortly afterwards the rains came. In the brief interim, Mays narrowly fouled on a jump of about 8.60 (28-2½). The rain further dampened the reactive power of Beamon's most feared rivals—yet three of the finalists, Beer, Lepik and Crawley, defied the elements to chalk up new PRs in the rarefied atmosphere.

1.	Bob Beamon (US)	8.90	29-2½ WR	(8.90	8.04	p	p	p	p)
2.	Klaus Beer (EG)	8.19	26-10½	(7.97	8.19	f	7.62	f	f)
3.	Ralph Boston (US)	8.16	26-9½	(8.16	8.05	7.91	f	f	7.97)
4.	Igor Ter-Ovanesyan (SU)	8.12	26-7¾	(8.12	8.09	f	f	8.10	8.08)
5.	Tonu Lepik (SU)	8.09	26-6½	(7.82	8.09	7.63	7.36	7.84	7.75)
6.	Allen Crawley (Aus)	8.02	26-3¾	(f	8.01	f	7.80	f	8.02)

7. Jacques Pani (Fr) 7.97; 8. Andrzej Stalmach (Pol) 7.94; 9. Lynn Davies (GB) 7.94; 10. Hiroomi Yamada (Japan) 7.93; 11. Leonid Barkovskiy (SU) 7.90; 12. Reinhold Boschert (WG) 7.89; 13. Mike Ahey (Gha) 7.71; 14. Lars-Olof Hook (Swe) 7.66; 15. Vic Brooks (Jam) 7.51; 16. Gerard Ugolini (Fr) 7.44;... nm—Charley Mays (US). (Boston 8.27 OR Q)

1972 (36. Q 8 Sept; F 9 Sept): Igor Ter-Ovanesyan, competing in his fifth Olympics, just failed to qualify with 7.77 (25-6) and 13th place. Lynn Davies, the '64 champion, also failed. Williams qualified on his first try with a superb and windless 8.34 (27-4¼), a mark excelled only once in Olympic history. In the final, Williams, sensing a twinge in his takeoff leg, decided to put all he had into his first jump, which resulted in a fine 8.24 (27-½), the eventual winner. The only serious threat to him came from Baumgartner, who reached a PR of 8.18 (26-10) in round 3, then fouled on a jump which might well have won the competition. Williams, who turned 19 only a couple of weeks earlier, was the youngest winner of the Games. The only other jumpers to exceed 8 meters were Robinson and Owusu.

1.	Randy Williams (US)	8.24	27-½	(8.24	7.32	7.72	7.80	7.77	p)
2.	Hans Baumgartner (WG)	8.18	26-10	(f	7.99	8.18	f	7.83	8.05)
3.	Arnie Robinson (US)	8.03	26-4¼	(f	7.89	7.95	f	8.03	f)
4.	Josh Owusu (Ghana)	8.01	26-3½	(7.71	7.77	7.88	7.70	7.98	8.01)
5.	Preston Carrington (US)	7.99	26-2½	(7.99	f	f	7.95	7.63	7.69)
6.	Max Klauss (EG)	7.96	26-1½	(7.51	7.94	7.96	7.86	6.13	7.88)

7. Alan Lerwill (GB) 7.91; 8. Leonid Barkovskiy (SU) 7.75; 9. Valeriy Podluzhniy (SU) 7.72; 10. Jacques Rousseau (Fr) 7.65; 11. Ari Vaananen (Fin) 7.62; 12. Grzegorz Cybulski (Pol) 7.58.

1976 (33. Q 28 July; F 29 July): The wind was never a factor, the highest reading throughout the competition being only 1.0 mps. Defending champion Williams (7.97/26-1¾), Robinson (7.95/26-1), Larry Myricks (7.92/25-11¼) and European champion Podluzhniy (7.90/25-11) led the qualifiers as only nine men mastered the qualifying distance of 7.80 (25-7). The next three were also admitted to the final. In the final Myricks, the revelation of 1976, broke a bone in his foot on a warmup jump. Robinson was first to jump—and he struck early and hard as his opening effort, against a slight breeze of 0.60 m/s, was 8.35 (27-4¾)—the best in Olympic history apart from the Beamon classic at Mexico City. There was no adequate reply, even though four others also achieved their best for the day in the same round. Considering the uninspiring conditions (a dead runway, an ungiving board, no wind), the overall result, with five men at 8 meters (26-3) or more, was excellent.

1. Arnie Robinson (US)	8.35	27-4¾	(8.35	8.26	f	8.04	8.16	7.91)
2. Randy Williams (US)	8.11	26-7¼	(8.11	7.81	f	f	f	7.81)
3. Frank Wartenberg (EG)	8.02	26-3¾	(7.81	f	f	8.02	7.84	f)
4. Jacques Rousseau (Fr)	8.00	26-3	(8.00	7.82	7.67	7.91	f	7.62)
5. Joao Oliveira (Braz)	8.00	26-3	(8.00	f	7.76	p	p	7.85)
6. Nenad Stekic (Yug)	7.89	25-10¾	(7.75	7.81	7.89	7.80	f	7.77)

7. Valeriy Podluzhniy (SU) 7.88; 8. Hans Baumgartner (WG) 7.84; 9. Rolf Bernhard (Switz) 7.74; 10. Aleksey Pereverzyev (SU) 7.66; 11. Fletcher Lewis (Bah) 7.61;. . . dnc—Larry Myricks (US) (injured).

TRIPLE JUMP

1896 (10. F 6 April): Connolly, chronologically the first athlete to be crowned Olympic champion in the modern Games, took two hops with his right foot and one jump.

1. James Connolly (US)	13.71 44-11¾	4. Alajos Szokolyi (Hun)	12.30 40-4¼
2. Alexandre Tuffere (Fr)	12.70 41-8	5. Christos Zoumis (Gr)	
3. Ioannis Persakis (Gr)	12.52 41-1	6. Alek. Chalkokondilis (Gr)	

1900 (9. F 16 July): Prinstein, who had withdrawn from the long jump final the day before (a Sunday), beat defending champion Connolly by a convincing margin even though Connolly improved by almost a foot over his Athens mark.

1. Myer Prinstein (US)	14.47 47-5¾ OR	4. Albert Delannoy (Fr)
2. James Connolly (US)	13.97 45-10	5. Alexandre Tuffere (Fr)
3. Lewis P. Sheldon (US)	13.64 44-9	

1904 (7. F 1 Sept): Prinstein successfully defended his triple jump title and on the same day also won the long jump.

1. Myer Prinstein (US)	14.35 47-1	4. John Fuhler (US)	12.91 42-4½
2. Fred Englehardt (US)	13.90 45-7¼	5. G. H. Van Cleve (US)	
3. Robert Stangland (US)	13.36 43-10	6. John Percy Hagerman (US)	

1908 (19. F. 25 July): Ahearne led the qualifiers with 14.72 (48-3¾). Apparently, everybody improved in the final and Ahearne's winning effort was made before MacDonald's runner-up performance. Although there are marks on record farther than Ahearne's, his 14.91 is generally accepted as a world record as the better efforts were almost certainly made with a hop-hop-jump style.

1. Timothy Ahearne (GB-Eire)	14.91 48-11 WR	4. Calvin Bricker (Can)	14.09 46-2¾
2. J. Garfield MacDonald (Can)	14.76 48-5¼	5. Platt Adams (US)	14.07 46-2
3. Edvard Larsen (Nor)	14.39 47-2½	6. Frank Mountpleasant (US)	13.97 45-10

1912 (22. Q-F 15 July): In qualifying the jumping was done in 3 groups. All the good marks were made in this preliminary phase and nobody managed to improve in the 3 final trials as the Swedes scored a sweep.

1. Gustaf Lindblom (Swe)	14.76 48-5	4. Erling Vinne (Nor)	14.14 46-4¾
2. Georg Aberg (Swe)	14.51 47-7¼	5. Platt Adams (US)	14.09 46-2¾
3. Eric Almlof (Swe)	14.17 46-5¾	6. Edvard Larsen (Nor)	14.06 46-1½

1920 (19. Q 19 Aug; F 21 Aug): In the qualifying round, Tuulos reached 14.50 on his first effort—the eventual winning mark. The next best qualifiers were Almlof 14.19 (46-6¾), Jansson 14.16 (46-5½) and Landers 14.00 (45-11¼). World record holder Ahearn, by then 32, barely qualified with 13.75 (45-1¼), 1 centimeter ahead of Nylund. In the three final jumps all but Tuulos improved. Jansson's best effort was probably good for 1st but he fell back to his 14.48.

1. Vilho Tuulos (Fin)	14.50 47-7	4. Ivar Sahlin (Swe)	14.17 46-6
2. Folke Jansson (Swe)	14.48 47-6	5. Sherman Landers (US)	14.17 46-5¾
3. Eric Almlof (Swe)	14.27 46-9¾	6. Dan Ahearn (US)	14.08 46-2¼

7. O. Nylund (Fin) 13.74; 8. B. H. Baker (GB) 13.67; 9. K. Bache (Nor) 13.64; 10. S. Runstrom (Swe) 13.63; 11. E. Juul (Nor) 13.59; 12. Kaufman Geist (US) 13.52.

1924 (20. Q-F 12 July): Brunetto took the lead early with a magnificent 15.42, which was well over his South American record. "Nick" Winter trailed with 15.18 (49-9¾), followed by Jansson 14.97 (49-1¼), Rainio 14.94 (49-¼), defending champ Tuulos 14.84 (48-8¼) and Oda 14.35. Winter, whose best before the Games was just 15.15 (49-8½), moved to first in the final with a world record 15.52, which consisted of a 5.78 (18-11½) hop, a 3.97 (13-¼) step and a 5.77 (18-11¼) jump.

1. Anthony Winter (Aus)	15.52 50-11 WR	4. Vaino Rainio (Fin)	15.01 49-3
2. Luis Brunetto (Arg)	15.42 50-7	5. Folke Jansson (Swe)	14.97 49-1¼
3. Vilho Tuulos (Fin)	15.37 50-5	6. Mikio Oda (Japan)	14.35 47-1

1928 (24. Q-F 2 Aug): In the qualifying round the men were divided into two groups. Oda led in the first with 15.21 from Tuulos 14.73 (48-4), and Tulikoura 14.70 (48-2¾). Nambu led the second with 15.01 from Casey 14.93 (48-11¾) and Jarvinen 14.65. Tuulos, now 33, improved to 15.11 (49-7) in the final; then came Casey with a PR 15.17. But neither was able to go farther and Oda won Japan's first Olympic track gold.

1. Mikio Oda (Japan)	15.21 49-10¾	4. Chuhei Nambu (Japan)	15.01 49-3
2. Levi Casey (US)	15.17 49-9¼	5. Toimi Tulikoura (Fin)	14.70 48-2¾
3. Vilho Tuulos (Fin)	15.11 49-7	6. Erkki Jarvinen (Fin)	14.65 48-¾

7. Willem Peters (Hol) 14.55; 8. Vaino Rainio (Fin) 14.41; 9. tie, Sid Bowman (US) & J. Blankers (Hol) 14.35; 11. L. Bourgeois (US) 14.28; 12. Anthony Winter (Aus) 14.15.

1932 (16. F 4 Aug): Svensson led till the 5th round, when Nambu gathered himself up and clinched the gold medal with a world record 15.72. Segments: 6.40 (21-0), 4.39 (14-4¾), 4.93 (16-2¼). At the time he also held the world record for the long jump (7.98/26-2¼). He is the last to have excelled in such a double capacity. Defending champion and previous world record holder Oda was injured.

1. Chuhei Nambu (Japan)	15.72 51-7 WR	(15.07	14.67	15.22	14.89	15.72	14.85)
2. Eric Svensson (Swe)	15.32 50-3¼	(14.21	15.32 f		14.70	14.77 f)	
3. Kenkichi Oshima (Japan)	15.12 49-7¼	(f	f	15.05 f		14.85	15.12)
4. Eamonn Fitzgerald (Eire)	15.01 49-3						
5. Willem Peters (Hol)	14.93 48-11¾						
6. Sol Furth (US)	14.88 48-9¾						

7. Sid Bowman (US) 14.87; 8. Rolland Romero (US) 14.85; 9. P. Bacsalmasi (Hun) 14.33; 10. F. Tabai (It) 14.29; 11. O. Rajasaari (Fin) 14.20; 12. Mikio Oda (Japan) 13.97 (inj).

1936 (31. F 6 Aug): There was a slight and generally assisting wind during the final. Tajima's world record was, however, fully legitimate. Segments: 6.20 (20-4), 4.00 (13-1½), 5.80 (19-½). It should be noted that he had a pre-Games best of 15.40 (50-6¼).

1. Naoto Tajima (Japan)	16.00 52-6 WR	(15.76 f		15.44	16.00	15.65 f)
2. Masao Harada (Japan)	15.66 51-4½	(15.39	15.45	15.42	15.50	15.27 15.66)

1932—Chuhei Nambu took the TJ gold and the LJ bronze.

3. Jack Metcalfe (Aus)	15.50	50-10¼	(15.50 f	14.67	14.83 f	15.20)
4. Heinz Wollner (Ger)	15.27	50-1¼	(15.27 f	f	14.53 f	14.23)
5. Rolland Romero (US)	15.08	49-5¾	(14.68 f	14.90 f	15.08	15.04)
6. Kenkichi Oshima (Japan)	15.07	49-5¼	(15.07 f	f	f	f

7. E. Joch (Ger) 14.88; 8. Dudley Wilkins (US) 14.83; 9. O. Suomela (Fin) 14.72; 10. Luz Long (Ger) 14.62; 11. Edward Luckhaus (Pol) 14.61; 12. L. Somlo (Hun) 14.60; 13. Onni Rajasaari (Fin) 14.59.
(Tajima 15.76 OR)

1948 (29. F 3 Aug): Avery led the qualifiers with 15.33 (50-3¾), followed by Rautio 14.86 (48-9). In the final, Ahman went into the lead early with 15.40 (50-6¼). Only fine technician Avery was able to threaten the Swede as both notched PRs.

1. Arne Ahman (Swe)	15.40 50-6¼	(15.40	14.68	14.89	14.58 f	-)
2. George Avery (Aus)	15.36 50-4¾	(15.36 f		14.67	14.32 14.78	-)
3. Ruhi Sarialp (Tur)	15.02 49-3¼	(14.23	15.02	14.91	15.02 f	-)
4. Preben Larsen (Den)	14.83 48-7¾					
5. Geraldo de Oliveira (Braz)	14.82 48-7½					
6. Valdemar Rautio (Fin)	14.70 48-2¾					

7. Les McKeand (Aus) 14.53; 8. Helio Coutinho da Silva (Braz) 14.49; 9. A. Hallgren (Swe) 14.48; 10. Bill Albans (US) 14.33; 11. Adhemar Ferreira da Silva (Braz) 14.31; 12. Won Kwon Kim (Kor) 14.25; 13. Lennart Moberg (Swe) 14.21;. . . nm—Henry Rebello (Ind).

1952 (35. Q-F 23 July): Da Silva led the qualifiers with 15.32 (50-3¼), followed by Devonish 15.24 (50-0) and Shcherbakov 15.05 (49-4½). In the final he offered a great exhibition of competitive ability topping the world record on four of six tries! Segments: 6.02 (19-9), 4.22 (13-10), 5.98 (19-7½).

1. Adhemar F. da Silva (Braz)	16.22 53-2½ WR	(15.95	16.12	15.54	16.09	16.22	16.05)
2. Leonid Shcherbakov (SU)	15.98 52-5¼	(15.07	15.26	15.18	15.98	15.84 f)	
3. Arnoldo Devonish (Ven)	15.52 50-11	(15.04	15.52 injured, withdrew)				
4. Walt Ashbaugh (US)	15.39 50-6	(15.05	15.39	14.56	14.50	15.38 f)	
5. Rune Nilsen (Nor)	15.13 49-7¾	(15.13	14.21 f		14.70 f		f)
6. Yoshio Iimuro (Japan)	14.99 49-2¼	(14.99 f		f		f	14.66 13.70)

7. Geraldo de Oliveira (Braz) 14.95; 8. Roger Norman (Swe) 14.89; 9. R. Hiltunen (Fin) 14.85; 10. Zygfryd Weinberg (Pol) 14.76; 11. Jim Gerhardt (US) 14.69; 12. Rui Ramos (Port) 14.69;. . . 15. Arne Ahman (Swe) 14.05.
(da Silva 16.12 OR)

1956 (32. Q-F 27 Nov): Kogake, who had done 16.48 (54-¾) at the Japanese Championships, led the qualifiers with 15.63 (51-3¼), followed by Shcherbakov 15.59 (51-1¾). In the final, the surprising Einarsson produced a PR in the 2nd round, only to be outdone by the consistent da Silva in the 4th round, as the Brazilian successfully defended his title. Kreyer took 3rd with a PR.

1. Adhemar F. da Silva (Braz)	16.35 53-7¾ OR	(15.69	16.04	15.90	16.35	16.26	16.21)
2. Vilhjalmur Einarsson (Ice)	16.26 53-4¼	(f		16.26	15.81 f		15.61 p)
3. Vitold Kreyer (SU)	16.02 52-6¾	(15.83 f		16.02	15.51 f		f)
4. Bill Sharpe (US)	15.88 52-1¼	(15.88 f		14.15 injured, withdrew)			
5. Martin Rehak (Czech)	15.85 52-0	(15.58 f		15.85 f		15.10 15.63)	
6. Leonid Shcherbakov (SU)	15.80 51-10	(15.75 f		15.58 f		15.80 15.12)	

7. Koji Sakurai (Japan) 15.73; 8. Teruji Kogake (Japan) 15.64; 9. Ken Wilmshurst (GB) 15.54; 10. Ryszard Malcherczyk (Pol) 15.54; 11. Ira Davis (US) 15.40; 12. George Shaw (US) 15.33; 13. Hiroshi Shibata (Japan) 15.25.

1960 (39. Q-F 6 Sept): World record holder Schmidt led the qualifiers with a new Olympic record—16.44 (53-11¼), followed by Goryayev 16.21 (53-2¼). Defending champion da Silva qualified with 15.61 (51-2½). In the final, Schmidt killed the opposition in the early rounds and won with his second best ever mark. Places 2-5 were decided in the closing rounds. Ira Davis set a new US record but had to be content with 4th.

1. Jozef Schmidt (Pol)	16.81 55-1¾ OR	(16.78 f		16.81 f		16.63 13.48)	
2. Vladimir Goryayev (SU)	16.63 54-6¾	(16.11	16.39	15.55	16.63	16.28 f)	
3. Vitold Kreyer (SU)	16.43 53-11	(16.21	16.00	15.96	16.01	15.91 16.43)	
4. Ira Davis (US)	16.41 53-10	(f		16.41 f		16.13 f	16.05)
5. Vilhjalmur Einarsson (Ice)	16.37 53-8½	(16.37	16.06	15.90	16.24 f		16.36)
6. Ryszard Malcherczyk (Pol)	16.01 52-6¼	(15.87	16.01	15.83	15.82	13.18 14.66)	

7. Manfred Hinze (EG) 15.93; 8. Kari Rahkamo (Fin) 15.84; 9. Ian Tomlinson (Aus) 15.71; 10. Yevgeniy Mikhailov (SU) 15.67; 11. Sten Erickson (Swe) 15.49; 12. Fred Alsop (GB)

15.49; 13. John Baguley (Aus) 15.22; 14. Adhemar Ferreira da Silva (Braz) 15.07;...
nm—Pierluigi Gatti (It).
(Schmidt 16.44 OR Q, 16.78 OR)

1964 (34. Q-F 16 Oct): Defending champion Schmidt, with only one competition to his credit in the pre-Olympic season, impressed by qualifying on his first try with 16.18 (53-1). Alsop had to try harder but finally made it on his third attempt with an excellent 16.41 (53-10), bucking an adverse wind of 1.74. That was a new British record. Five others bettered 16 meters (52-6). In the first round of the final, Alsop improved his record to 16.46 (54-0) and took the lead. But Schmidt went 16.65 (54-7½) on his second attempt and eventually broke his own Olympic record in the last round with 16.85. This last was made against a wind of 1.26. Fyedoseyev and Kravchenko also passed Alsop. Most of the best marks were made with slightly adverse winds.

1. Jozef Schmidt (Pol)	16.85 55-3½ OR	(16.37	16.65	16.58	f		14.55	16.85)
2. Olyeg Fyedoseyev (SU)	16.58 54-4¾	(15.73	15.67	16.35	16.20	16.58	16.38)
3. Viktor Kravchenko (SU)	16.57 54-4½	(16.14	16.38	16.17	16.57	16.10	15.99)
4. Fred Alsop (GB)	16.46 54-0	(16.46	f		16.14	f	f	16.14)
5. Serban Ciochina (Rum)	16.23 53-3	(15.79	16.23	15.70	16.10	15.79	15.77)
6. Manfred Hinze (EG)	16.15 52-11¾	(15.81	16.06	16.15	f		13.63	f)

7. Georgi Stoikovski (Bul) 16.10; 8. Hans-Jurgen Ruckborn (EG) 16.09; 9. Ira Davis (US) 16.00; 10. Takayuki Okazaki (Japan) 15.90; 11. Bill Sharpe (US) 15.84; 12. Jan Jaskolski (Pol) 15.82; 13. Mansour Dia (Sen) 15.44.

1968 (34. Q 16 Oct; F 17 Oct): The world triple jump record had been broken five times in Olympic history, yet here Schmidt's 17.03 (55-10½) was improved on just as many times—all in one competition! The stage for this bonanza was set in the qualifying round, when Gentile sailed a record 17.10 (56-1¼) in windless conditions on his second try. Thirteen mastered the qualifying standard, 16.10 (52-10). In the final, Gentile again set the style of things to come as he improved to 17.22 (56-6) on his first try. In the third round, Saneyev wrested both lead and record from the Italian by going 17.23 (56-6¼). Prudencio, who had come to the Games with a PR of just 16.30 (53-5¾), reached a record 17.27 (56-8) in the fifth round, but Saneyev regained the lead for good with a splendid 17.39 (57-¾) on his last try. Curiously enough, on the last three mentioned efforts the wind invariably blew at + 2.0 mps. Schmidt jumped 16.89 (55-5), better than his OR of '64, yet finished only 7th. May had to pass up his last try because of injury.

1. Viktor Saneyev (SU)	17.39 57-¾ WR	(16.49	16.84	17.23	17.02	16.81' 17.39)
2. Nelson Prudencio (Braz)	17.27 56-8	(16.33	17.05	16.75	f	17.27 17.15)
3. Giuseppe Gentile (It)	17.22 56-6	(17.22	f	f	16.54' f)
4. Art Walker (US)	17.12 56-2w	(15.43	16.45	16.77' 16.48	f	17.12')
5. Nikolay Dudkin (SU)	17.09 56-¾w	(16.15	16.70	16.37' 16.73' 17.09'16.53')
6. Phil May (Aus)	17.02 55-10	(15.48	16.58	16.51 17.02	f	p)

7. Jozef Schmidt (Pol) 16.89; 8. Mansour Dia (Sen) 16.73w; 9. Georgi Stoikovski (Bul) 16.46; 10. Henrik Kalocsai (Hun) 16.45; 11. Joachim Kugler (WG) 15.90; 12. Luis Felipe Areta (Sp) 15.75; 13. Serban Ciochina (Rum) 15.62.
(Gentile 17.10 WR, OR Q; 17.22 WR, OR; Saneyev 17.23 WR, OR; Prudencio 17.27 WR, OR; Saneyev 17.39 WR, (OR); '=wind-aided.

1972 (36. Q 3 Sept; F 4 Sept): In the qualifying round, world record holder Pedro Perez of Cuba, suffering from injury, withdrew after two feeble attempts, the best of which (15.72/51-7) was far short of the qualifying standard, 16.20 (53-1¾). Others who failed to make it were Giuseppe Gentile, the bronze medalist of '68, and 17m man Dave Smith. Saneyev led the qualifiers with a windy 16.85 (55-3½). Exactly 12 mastered the qualifying standard. In the final, Saneyev produced the winning jump on his first effort: a windy 17.35 (56-11). Drehmel did 17.02 (55-10) on his second try, then, after a foul estimated at 17.40 (57-1), he chalked up a new PR of 17.31. Prudencio, who in the whole of his career had excelled 17m only once, in the memorable Mexico final, did it again with 17.05 on his last try, nailing the bronze.

-103-

1. Viktor Saneyev (SU)	17.35 56-11w	(17.35	16.71 17.19 f	16.98 f)
2. Jorg Drehmel (EG)	17.31 56-9½	(f	17.02 f f	17.31 15.34)
3. Nelson Prudencio (Braz)	17.05 55-11¼	(16.87	16.61 16.35 16.88 f	17.05)
4. Carol Corbu (Rum)	16.85 55-3½w	(16.62	16.85 16.40 f	13.72 ip)
5. John Craft (US)	16.83 55-2½	(16.77	16.75 16.83 16.26 p	f)
6. Mansour Dia (Sen)	16.83 55-2½w	(16.77	16.83 f f	16.15 f)

7. Michal Joachimowski (Pol) 16.69; 8. Kristen Flogstad (Nor) 16.44; 9. Mikhail Bariban (SU) 16.30; 10. Bernard Lamitie (Fr) 16.27w; 11. Samuel Igun (Nig) 16.03; 12. Toshiaki Inoue (Japan) 15.88.

1976 (25. Q 29 July; F 30 July): World record holder Oliveira led the qualifying with 16.81 (55-1¾) ahead of two-time Olympic champion Saneyev (16.77/55-¼) and surprising Kolmsee, who chalked up a new PR of 16.68 (54-8¾). Shut out, among others, were Nelson Prudencio of Brazil, a medal winner in '68 and '72, and Michal Joachimowski of Poland, who missed by one centimeter. Former world record holder Perez took the lead in the first round of the final with 16.81 (53-1¾) but lost it in round 3 as Saneyev went 17.06 (55-11¾). In the next round, Butts answered with a PR of 17.18 (56-4½), even though the gun for a race was fired just as he was in the air. The irrepressible Saneyev was not to be denied: in round 5 he reached a zero-wind 17.29 (56-8¾)—and thus nailed his third gold medal. Oliveira lost valuable ground by sailing diagonally more than once, yet finished 3rd with 16.90 (55-5½). Just as in the long jump final the day before, there was no wind.

1. Viktor Saneyev (SU)	17.29 56-8¾	(f	16.71 17.06 f	17.29 f)
2. James Butts (US)	17.18 56-4½	(16.69	16.76 14.80 17.18 16.55	16.61)
3. Joao Oliveira (Braz)	16.90 55-5½	(f	16.15 16.85 14.91 16.69	16.90)
4. Pedro Perez (Cuba)	16.81 55-1¾	(16.81	16.24 16.48 16.47 f	f)
5. Tommy Haynes (US)	16.78 55-¾	(15.46	f 16.68 16.78 16.71	16.71)
6. Wolfgang Kolmsee (WG)	16.68 54-8¾	(16.23	f 16.68 16.58 16.31	f)

7. Eugeniusz Biskupski (Pol) 16.49; 8. Carol Corbu (Rum) 16.43; 9. Jiri Vycichlo (Czech) 16.28; 10. Pentti Kuukasjarvi (Fin) 16.23; 11. Bernard Lamitie (Fr) 16.23; 12. Rayfield Dupree (US) 16.23.

SHOT

1896 (7. F 7 April): The implement was thrown from a 7-foot (2.13) square. Garrett had won the discus the previous day.

1. Robert Garrett (US)   11.22 36-9¾   4. Geo. Stuart Robertson (GB) 9.95 32-7¾
2. Miltiades Gouskos (Gr)   11.20 36-9   5. Louis Adler (Fr)
3. Georgios Papasideris (Gr) 10.36 34-0   6. Sotirios Versis (Gr)
    7. Ch. Winckler (Den).

1900 (10. F 15 July): Again, the implement was thrown from a 7-foot (2.13) square. Defending champ Garrett was more than a meter better than at Athens, but slipped to 3rd.

1. Richard Sheldon (US)   14.10 46-3¼ OR   4. Rezso Crettier (Hun)   12.05 39-6½
2. Josiah McCracken (US)   12.85 42-2   5. Pan. Paraskevopoulos (Gr) 11.29 37-½
3. Robert Garrett (US)   12.37 40-7   6. Gustaf Soderstrom (Swe)   11.18 36-8¼
(Sheldon 13.80 OR Q)

1904 (8. F 31 Aug): For the first time in Olympic history, the shot was thrown from a 7-foot (2.13) *circle.* Rose, a 20-year-old giant standing 6-6 (1.98) and weighing 235 pounds (106), bettered 47 feet in qualifying. In the final he opened with 14.35 (47-1), but Coe responded with a toss of 14.40 (47-3). Then Rose unleashed an impressive 14.81 (48-7)—a new world record, although it should be noted that Coe had attained exactly the same distance unofficially before the Games. Nicolaos Georgantas of Greece exceeded 13.10 (43-0) twice but was disqualified for *throwing* the shot—a violation of the rule already in force in the US.

Big Ralph Rose was a prolific medal winner in the early Games: 1904—shot gold (WR), discus silver, hammer bronze; 08—shot gold; 12—shot silver.

1. Ralph Rose (US)	14.81 48-7 WR	4. Martin Sheridan (US)	12.39 40-8
2. Wesley Coe (US)	14.40 47-3	5. Charles Chadwick (US)	
3. Leon Feuerbach (US)	13.37 43-10½	6. Albert Johnson (US)	

(Rose 14.35 OR; Coe 14.40 OR)

1908 (26. F 16 July): Rose successfully defended his title from the assault of Dennis Horgan, the Irish stalwart who between 1893 and 1912 won the British title 13 times. Places 4-8 are uncertain, as the throwing was done in sections and some of the non-qualifying marks were not measured.

1. Ralph Rose (US)	14.21 46-7½	4. Wesley Coe (US)	13.07 42-10½
2. Dennis Horgan (GB)	13.62 44-8¼	5. Edmond Barrett (GB)	12.89 42-3½
3. John Garrels (US)	13.18 43-3	6. Marquis Horr (US)	12.82 42-1

7. J. Sauli (Fin) 12.58; 8. Lee Talbott (US) 11.63.

1912 (22. F 10 July): Defending champion Rose was the leader in the early rounds with puts of 14.98 (49-1¾) and 15.25 (50-½), with Irish-born McDonald a distant 2nd at 14.78 (48-6). The first three in the qualifying round were admitted to the final, in which each had three trials. It was here that McDonald shot into the lead with his first toss—15.34.

1. Pat McDonald (US)	15.34 50-4 OR	4. Elmer Niklander (Fin)	13.65 44-9½
2. Ralph Rose (US)	15.25 50-½	5. George Philbrook (US)	13.13 43-1
3. Lawrence Whitney (US)	13.93 45-8½	6. Imre Mudin (Hun)	12.81 42-¼

7. Einar Nilsson (Swe) 12.62; 8. P. Quinn (GB) 12.53; 9. A. Tison (Fr) 12.41; 10. P. Aho (Fin) 12.40.
(Rose 14.98 OR, 15.25 OR)

1920 (20. Q 17 Aug; F 18 Aug): Niklander led the qualifiers with 14.15 (46-5), followed by defending champion McDonald 14.08 (46-2¼), Porhola 14.03 (46-¼). In the final, Porhola improved to 14.81 (48-7) and that settled the issue as far as 1st place was concerned. Liversedge moved to 3rd, a half centimeter behind Niklander.

1. Ville Porhola (Fin)	14.81 48-7	4. Pat McDonald (US)	14.08 46-2¼
2. Elmer Niklander (Fin)	14.15 46-5¼	5. Einar Nilsson (Swe)	13.87 45-6
3. Harry Liversedge (US)	14.15 46-5	6. Harald Tammer (Estonia)	13.60 44-7½

7. George Bihlman (US) 13.57; 8. Howard Cann (US) 13.52; 9. B. Jansson (Swe) 13.27; 10. Armas Taipale (Fin) 12.94; 11. O. Petersen (Den) 12.52; 12. R. Paoli (Fr) 12.48.

1924 (28. F 8 July): Houser led the qualifiers with 14.99. That was to remain the longest put and he thus won the first of his two gold medals in the space of 5 days. Hartranft, who had done 14.40 (47-3) in the qualifying round, improved to 14.89 in the final.

1. Clarence Houser (US)	14.99 49-2¼	4. Hannes Torpo (Fin)	14.45 47-5
2. Glenn Hartranft (US)	14.89 48-10¼	5. Norman Anderson (US)	14.29 46-10½
3. Ralph Hills (US)	14.64 48-½	6. Elmer Niklander (Fin)	14.26 46-9½

7. Ville Porhola (Fin) 14.10; 8. B. Jansson (Swe) 13.76; 9. R. Paoli (Fr) 13.53; 10. S. Sundstrom (Swe) 13.53; 11. A. Takala (Fin) 13.31; 12. H. Tammer (Est) 13.28.

1928 (22. F 29 July): Most of the good marks occurred in the qualifying round, with Brix leading at 15.75, followed by Hirschfeld 15.72, Kuck 15.03 (49-3¾), Krenz 14.99, Wahlstedt and Uebler both 14.69. In the final, only Kuck managed to improve and did so with a new world record of 15.87. Brix and previous world record holder Hirschfeld were consistent in the 15-meter-plus range but could not match Kuck's effort. Wahlstedt beat Uebler in the throw-off for 5th place, 13.92 to 13.82.

1. John Kuck (US)	15.87 52-¾ WR	4. Eric Krenz (US)	14.99 49-2¼
2. Herman Brix (US)	15.75 51-8	5. Armas Wahlstedt (Fin)	14.69 48-2¼
3. Emil Hirschfeld (Ger)	15.72 51-7	6. Wilhelm Uebler (Ger)	14.69 48-2¼

7. Harlow Rothert (US) 14.68; 8. Jozsef Daranyi (Hun) 14.35; 9. Paavo Yrjola (Fin) 14.01; 10. W. Nuesch (Switz) 13.77; 11. E. Duhour (Fr) 13.72; 12. N. Feldmann (Est) 13.54.
(Hirschfeld 15.72 OR; Brix 15.75 OR)

1932 (15. F 31 July): Sexton, a consistent 52-plus performer throughout the season, took the lead in the third round and finally wound up with an OR toss of 16.00, just 5 cm off the WR of Heljasz (9th). Sexton improved the WR to 16.16 (53-¼) a month later.

1. Leo Sexton (US)	16.00 52-6 OR	(15.60 15.56 15.72 15.94 15.48 16.00)
2. Harlow Rothert (US)	15.67 51-5	(15.67 15.67 15.43 14.99 f f)
3. Frantisek Douda (Czech)	15.61 51-2½	(15.61 15.24 14.49 15.05 15.22 15.33)
4. Emil Hirschfeld (Ger)	15.56 51-½	
5. Nelson Gray (US)	15.46 50-8½	6. Hans-Heinrich Sievert (Ger) 15.07 49-5¼

7. Jozsef Daranyi (Hun) 14.67; 8. Jules Noel (Fr) 14.53; 9. Z. Heljasz (Pol) 14.49; 10. H. Hart (S Afr) 14.22.
(Sexton 15.94 OR)

1936 (22. F 2 Aug): In the final, Wollke and Barlund alternated in the lead. The German decisively took the lead in the fifth round. World record holder Torrance, obviously far from his 1934 form—when he did 17.40 (57-1)—was a disappointing 5th as the US was shut out of the medals for the first time.

1. Hans Wollke (Ger)	16.20 53-1¾ OR	(15.96	14.76	15.72	15.90	16.20	14.98)
2. Sulo Barlund (Fin)	16.12 52-10¾	(15.68	16.03	14.98	15.52	16.12	15.42)
3. Gerhard Stock (Ger)	15.66 51-4½	(15.56	15.56	15.14	15.29	14.78	15.66)
4. Sam Francis (US)	15.45 50-8¼	(15.45	15.09	15.09 f		14.57	13.61)
5. Jack Torrance (US)	15.38 50-5½	(15.38	14.40	15.34	14.79	14.57	14.56)
6. Dimitri Zaitz (US)	15.32 50-3¼	(15.32	14.16	14.09	14.09 f		14.85)

7. Frantisek Douda (Czech) 15.28; 8. Arnold Viiding (Est) 15.23; 9. Gunnar Bergh (Swe) 15.01; 10. Hans-Heinrich Sievert (Ger) 14.79.
(Barlund 16.03 OR)

1948 (24. F 3 Aug): Fuchs led the qualifiers with 15.87 (52-¾), followed by Thompson 15.09 (49-6) and Delaney 14.97 (49-1¼). In the final, "Moose" Thompson had his day of days and won easily. His last throw, a foul, was in the vicinity of 17.30 (56-9). Americans swept the medals for the fifth time.

1. Wilbur Thompson (US)	17.12 56-2 OR	(16.47	17.12	16.97	16.67	16.80	f)
2. Jim Delaney (US)	16.68 54-8¾	(16.14	16.68	15.88	16.03	16.03	16.28)
3. Jim Fuchs (US)	16.42 53-10½	(16.32	16.42	15.60	15.56	14.82	16.28)
4. Mieczyslaw Lomowski (Pol)	15.43 50-7½						
5. Gosta Arvidsson (Swe)	15.37 50-5						
6. Yrjo Lehtila (Fin)	15.05 49-4½						

7. J. Jouppila (Fin) 14.59; 8. C. Kalina (Cze) 14.55; 9. C. Yataganas (Gr) 14.54; 10. Witold Gerutto (Pol) 14.37; 11. John Giles (GB) 13.73; 12. S. Sigurdsson (Ice) 13.66.
(Fuchs 16.32 OR; Thompson 16.47 OR; Delaney 16.68 OR)

1952 (20. F 21 July): O'Brien led the qualifiers with 16.05 (52-8), followed by Grigalka 15.90 (52-2), Nilsson 15.81 (51-10½), Hooper 15.48 (50-9½) and Fuchs 15.29 (50-2). In the final, O'Brien opened with an Olympic record 17.41. Arch-rival Darrow Hooper came dangerously close to matching that performance on his last try but had to settle for 2nd. World record holder Fuchs, with an injured hand, made it another sweep for the US.

1. Parry O'Brien (US)	17.41 57-1½ OR	(17.41	17.21	16.79	16.87	17.12	16.53)
2. Darrow Hooper (US)	17.39 57-¾	(17.02	16.59	17.08	16.90	16.93	17.39)
3. Jim Fuchs (US)	17.05 55-11¾	(16.93 p	p	p		17.06 p)	
4. Otto Grigalka (SU)	16.78 55-¾	(16.53	16.78	15.91	16.27	16.29	16.33)
5. Roland Nilsson (Swe)	16.55 54-3½	(16.55	16.08	16.33 f		f	f)
6. John Savidge (GB)	16.19 53-1½	(16.17	16.18 f		16.19	16.03 f)	

7. G. Fyodorov (SU) 16.06; 8. P. Stavem (Nor) 16.02; 9. Jiri Skobla (Czech) 15.92; 10. T. Krzyzanowski (Pol) 15.08; 11. L. Guiller (Fr) 14.84; 12. Angiolo Profeti (It) 14.74; 13. A. Schwabl (Aut) 14.45.

1956 (14. Q-F 28 Nov): Skobla led the qualifiers with 17.15 (56-3¼), followed by Nieder 16.76 (54-11¾) and O'Brien 16.63 (54-6¾). In the final, the first four surpassed the Olympic record 12 times. Defending champion O'Brien was the class of the field and led from the first round. Skobla prevented another US sweep.

1. Parry O'Brien (US)	18.57 60-11¼ OR	(17.92	18.47	18.37	18.45	18.57	18.23)
2. Bill Nieder (US)	18.18 59-7¾	(f	17.61	17.81	16.82	18.18 f)	
3. Jiri Skobla (Czech)	17.65 57-11	(17.39	16.70	17.34	17.51	17.05	17.65)
4. Ken Bantum (US)	17.48 57-4¼	(16.99 f		16.27	17.48 f		f)
5. Boris Balyayev (SU)	16.96 55-7¾	(16.96	16.05	16.58	15.96	16.11	16.24)
6. Erik Uddebom (Swe)	16.65 54-7½	(16.54 f		16.65	15.74	16.06	16.31)

7. Karl-Heinz Wegmann (WG) 16.63; 8. Georgios Tsakanikas (Gr) 16.56; 9. Barry Donath (Aus) 16.52; 10. Silvano Meconi (It) 16.28; 11. Robert Hanlin (Aus) 16.08; 12. Barclay Palmer (Aus) 15.81; 13. Vladimir Loshchilov (SU) 15.62; 14. Raymond Thomas (Fr) 15.31. (O'Brien 17.92 OR)

1960 (24. Q-F 31 Aug): Among those who fell by the wayside in qualifying was Arthur Rowe of Britain, the European record holder—he could do no better than 16.68 (54-8¾). Lipsnis and Long led the qualifiers with 17.65 (57-11), followed by Skobla 17.32 (56-10), O'Brien 17.29 (56-8¾), Lindsay 17.28 (56-8¼), Lucking 17.20 (56-5¼) and Nieder 17.14 (56-3¾). In the final, O'Brien went into the lead early and held it till the fifth round, when Nieder, the world record holder, shot ahead with a toss of 19.68. Long, 20, completed the US sweep.

1. Bill Nieder (US)	19.68 64-6¾ OR	(18.67	18.77 f	18.67	19.68 f)
2. Parry O'Brien (US)	19.11 62-8½	(18.77	19.11 f	18.64	17.41 18.39)
3. Dallas Long (US)	19.01 62-4½	(16.80	18.88 18.66	18.25 f	19.01)
4. Viktor Lipsnis (SU)	17.90 58-8¾	(17.28	17.90 17.51 f	f	17.83)
5. Mike Lindsay (GB)	17.80 58-4¾	(17.63	17.61 17.80	17.09 17.39	17.43)
6. Alfred Sosgornik (Pol)	17.57 57-7¾	(17.57	17.40 f	f	17.52 17.39)

7. Dieter Urbach (WG) 17.47; 8. Martyn Lucking (GB) 17.43; 9. Jiri Skobla (Cze) 17.39; 10. Jaroslav Plihal (Czech) 17.36; 11. Les Mills (NZ) 17.06; 12. Hermann Lingnau (WG) 16.98; 13. Silvano Meconi (It) 16.73; 14. Zsigmond Nagy (Hun) 16.67; 15. Warwick Selvey (Aus) 16.18. (Nieder 18.67 OR; O'Brien 18.77 OR; Long 18.88 OR; O'Brien 19.11 OR)

1964 (22. Q-F 17 Oct): In the trials, thirteen made the qualifying standard of 17.80 (58-4¾). The major casualty was Poland's Alfred Sosgornik, who went out with 17.75 (58-2¾), which ironically bettered the mark that had earned him 6th at Rome four years earlier. World record holder Long led the qualifiers with 19.51 (64-¼), followed by Matson 18.92 (62-1) and Lipsnis 18.90 (62-0). In the final, Long took the lead early but was passed in third round by 19-year-old Matson, who raised the OR to 19.88 (65-2¾). And Matson went farther in round 4, when he produced his best-ever throw, 20.20. But the reliable Long, throwing right after his younger countryman, offered a quick reply with a toss of 20.33 that eventually won the gold for him. Veteran O'Brien, competing in his fourth Games, lost 3rd to Varju, the No. 1 European. The Hungarian had four throws better than O'Brien's longest—19.20. This was the best mark ever made by O'Brien in the Olympics, but for the first time he had to step out of the ring without a medal.

1. Dallas Long (US)	20.33 66-8½ OR	(19.61	19.55 19.34	20.33 19.90 f)
2. Randy Matson (US)	20.20 66-3¼	(18.53	19.19 19.88	20.20 f	19.62)
3. Vilmos Varju (Hun)	19.39 63-7½	(19.23 f	19.39 19.29	18.97 19.25)
4. Parry O'Brien (US)	19.20 63-0	(18.95	18.86 19.20	18.32 18.64 18.84)
5. Zsigmond Nagy (Hun)	18.88 61-11¼	(18.77 f	18.50 18.43 f	18.88)
6. Nikolay Karasyov (SU)	18.86 61-10½	(18.86	18.26 f	18.14 17.98 18.18)

7. Les Mills (NZ) 18.52; 8. Adolfas Varanauskas (SU) 18.41; 9. Wladyslaw Komar (Pol) 18.20; 10. Viktor Lipsnis (SU) 18.11; 11. Rudolf Langer (EG) 17.29; 12. Dieter Hoffmann (EG) 17.11; 13. Georgios Tasakanikas (Gr) 16.87. (Matson 19.88 OR, 20.20 OR)

1968 (19. Q 13 Oct; F 14 Oct): Matson made simple work of this competition. He was the first thrower in the ring for the finals and his 20.54 (67-4¾) opener proved unbeatable. The first five placers, in fact, all got their best efforts on their first throws. No one, Matson included, came within a foot of his opening heave. The Texan, who had reached an Olympic record 20.68 (67-10¼) in the qualifying, had two other throws which would have beaten Woods's best of 20.12 (66-¼).

1. Randy Matson (US)	20.54 67-4¾	(20.54	20.09 18.67	20.15	20.02 20.18)
2. George Woods (US)	20.12 66-¼	(20.12 f	f	f	19.19 f)
3. Eduard Gushchin (SU)	20.09 65-11	(20.09	19.45 19.69 f	f	19.41)
4. Dieter Hoffmann (EG)	20.00 65-7½	(20.00	19.33 19.75	19.68 19.85 19.86)
5. Dave Maggard (US)	19.43 63-9	(19.43	19.33 18.46	18.90 19.15 f)
6. Wladyslaw Komar (Pol)	19.28 63-3¼	(18.66	19.28 18.54 f	f	19.21)

7. Uwe Grabe (EG) 19.03; 8. Heinfried Birlenbach (WG) 18.80; 9. Pierre Colnard (Fr) 18.79; 10. Jeff Teale (GB) 18.65; 11. Les Mills (NZ) 18.18; 12. Traugott Glockler (WG) 18.14. (Matson 20.69 OR Q)

1972 (29. Q 8 Sept; F 9 Sept): Komar was rated as only an outside contender for the gold, but his first throw reached a PR and Olympic record 21.18 (69-9), and it held up. But the onslaught was fierce. Briesenick hit his 21.14 (69-4¼) in round 4 to match countryman Gies's opening effort. Four throws after Briesenick, Woods punched the ball tantalizingly close with 21.17 (69-5½). Feuerbach and Oldfield both reached their place-winning marks in the fifth round. Up for his last chance, Woods popped the ball out—and it struck the small metal flag marking Komar's Olympic record put. Woods (and many other observers) felt he should receive another throw since the flight of his shot was impeded but officials saw it differently and measured the throw at 21.05 (69-¾). So a bare centimeter separated the two, Woods winning his second consecutive silver while Komar became the first Pole to win a shot medal. Briesenick and Gies were separated by better second throw, the difference again being a centimeter (21.02 [68-11½] —21.01 [68-11¼]).

1. Wladyslaw Komar (Pol)	21.18 69-6 OR	(21.18 f	20.55 20.74 20.80 f)
2. George Woods (US)	21.17 69-5½	(20.55 20.17 20.71 21.17 20.88 21.05)	
3. Hartmut Briesenick (EG)	21.14 69-4¼	(20.97 20.91 21.02 21.14 20.61 20.54)	
4. Hans-Peter Gies (EG)	21.14 69-4¼	(21.14 21.00 21.01 20.62 f f)	
5. Al Feuerbach (US)	21.01 68-11¼	(20.90 20.29 f 20.86 21.01 20.28)	
6. Brian Oldfield (US)	20.91 68-7¼	(20.85 20.60 20.87 20.54 20.91 20.13)	

7. Heinfried Birlenbach (WG) 20.37; 8. Vilmos Varju (Hun) 20.10; 9. Jaromir Vlk (Czech) 20.09; 10. Jaroslav Brabec (Czech) 19.86; 11. Heinz-Joachim Rothenburg (EG) 19.74; 12. Yves Brouzet (Fr) 19.61; 13. Ralf Reichenbach (WG) 19.48; 14. Rimantas Plunge (SU) 19.30; 15. Lahcen Samsam (Mor) 19.11; 16. Seppo Simola (Fin) 19.06; 17. Bruce Pirnie (Can) 18.90; 18. Traugott Glockler (WG) 18.85.
(Briesenick 20.97 OR; Gies 21.14 OR)

1976 (23. Q 23 July; F 24 July): The better-known throwers with the longer seasonal bests fell to 20-year-old Beyer, who was named to the East German team only a week before the Games opened. His 21.05 (69-¾) proved unbeatable as the throwing was well below its pre-Games level (steroid testing?). Feuerbach, Woods, Capes, Barishnikov and Mironov had all been over 70 feet prior to the Games, with Barishnikov setting a world record 22.00 (72-2¼). Barishnikov, a "spinner," highlighted the qualifying with an Olympic record 21.32 (69-11½) but only 11 could meet the modest 19.40 (63-7¾) qualifying standard. Woods made the final only as the 12th man after reaching 19.35 (63-5¾). Barishnikov led the first round of the final before giving way to Feuerbach in round 2, who was then eclipsed by Barishnikov in round 3. Beyer was in a medal position from the beginning and his 5th-round 21.05 put him at the front. Mironov came up with his so-close 21.03 (69-0) in the same round, but no one could exceed Beyer. Gies was more than two feet off his pre-Games best, Feuerbach was off three feet and Woods and Capes were four feet off.

1. Udo Beyer (EG)	21.05 69-¾	(20.38 20.50 20.49 f 21.05 20.45)	
2. Yevgeniy Mironov (SU)	21.03 69-0	(19.67 20.38 20.14 20.17 21.03 20.06)	
3. Aleksandr Barishnikov (SU)	21.00 68-10¾	(20.53 20.27 21.00 20.96 20.58 f)	
4. Al Feuerbach (US)	20.55 67-5	(19.74 20.55 20.07 20.21 20.10 20.32)	
5. Hans-Peter Gies (EG)	20.47 67-2	(19.98 20.19 20.47 20.45 20.11 20.13)	
6. Geoff Capes (GB)	20.36 66-9½	(20.15 20.21 20.36 20.32 20.31 f)	

7. George Woods (US) 20.26; 8. Hans Hoglund (Swe) 20.17; 9. Pete Shmock (SU) 19.89; 10. Heinz-Joachim Rothenburg (EG) 19.79; 11. Jaroslav Brabec (Czech) 19.62; 12. Reijo Stahlberg (Fin) 18.99.
(Barishnikov 21.32 OR Q)

DISCUS

1896 (11. F 6 April): Garrett, captain of the Princeton team and a novice in this event, came to Athens on his own after practicing for a while with a steel discus. His Olympic victory thus came as a major surprise—especially to the Greeks, who claimed to have several specialists. The implement was thrown from a 2.50 m (8-2½) square. It is related that Versis threw 29.50 (96-9) in a special event which was not part of the Olympic program.

1. Robert Garrett (US)   29.14 95-7   4. Louis Adler (Fr)
2. Pan. Paraskevopoulos (Gr) 28.94 94-11   5. Georgios Papasideris (Gr)
3. Sotirios Versis (Gr)   28.78 94-5   6. George Stuart Robertson (GB)

1900 (11. F 15 July): The implement was thrown in a lane amid some beautiful trees in the *Bois de Boulogne*. Several competitors, including defending champion Garrett, consistently threw into the trees! Even so, the winner, 21-year-old "Rezso" Bauer, reached a distance which was very good in those days.

1. Rudolf Bauer (Hun)   36.04 118-3 OR   4. Pan. Paraskevopoulos (Gr)   34.04 111-8
2. Frantisek Janda-Suk (Boh) 35.24 115-7   5. Rezso Crettier (Hun)   33.64 110-4
3. Richard Sheldon (US)   34.60 113-6   6. Gustaf Soderstrom (Swe)   33.30 109-3

1904 (6. F 3 Sept): Each man was allowed six throws. At the end of the competition, Sheridan and Rose had reached the same distance, so there was a throw-off (the only one for 1st in history) in which Sheridan beat his opponent by about 1.5m.

1. Martin Sheridan (US)   39.28 128-10=OR 4. John Flanagan (US)   36.14 118-7
2. Ralph Rose (US)   39.28 128-10 OR   5. John Biller (US)
3. Nicolaos Georgantas (Gr) 37.68 123-7   6. James Mitchell (US)

1908 (41. F 16 July): Competitors were divided into 8 sections. The three best—Giffin 40.70, Sheridan 40.56 (133-1) and Horr 39.44—were admitted to the final, in which defending champ Sheridan moved from 2nd to 1st.

1. Martin Sheridan (US)   40.88 134-1 OR   4. Werner Jarvinen (Fin)   39.42 129-4
2. Merritt Giffin (US)   40.70 133-6   5. Arthur Dearborn (US)   38.52 126-4
3. Marquis Horr (US)   39.44 129-5   6. Gyorgy Luntzer (Hun)   38.34 125-9
     7. A. Tison (Fr) 38.30; 8. W. G. Burroughs (US) 37.42.
(Griffin 40.70 OR)

1912 (40, F 12 July): The three best from 5 sections—Taipale 43.90 (144-0), Byrd 42.32 and Duncan 42.28—were admitted to the final, in which only Taipale improved, reaching 44.34 (145-6) on his first try and 45.20 on his last.

1. Armas Taipale (Fin)   45.20 148-3 OR   4. Elmer Niklander (Fin)   42.08 138-1
2. Richard Byrd (US)   42.32 138-10   5. Hans Tronner (Aut)   41.24 135-3
3. James Duncan (US)   42.28 138-8   6. Arlie Mucks (US)   40.92 134-3
     7. George Philbrook (US) 40.92; 8. E. Magnusson (Swe) 39.90; 9. R. Ujlaky (Hun) 39.82; 10. E. Nilsson (Swe) 39.68; 11. Ralph Rose (US) 39.64.
(Taiplae 43.90 OR, 44.34 OR)

1920 (28. Q 21 Aug; F 22 Aug): All the good marks were made in the qualifying phase. In the final Zallhagen was the only one to improve, moving from 5th at 40.16 (131-9) to 4th at 41.06. Defending champion Taipale, who appeared to be in record form during practice sessions, unexpectedly lost to arch-rival Niklander.

1. Elmer Niklander (Fin)   44.68 146-7   4. Otto Zallhagen (Swe)   41.06 134-8
2. Armas Taipale (Fin)   44.18 144-11   5. William Bartlett (US)   40.86 134-1
3. Gus Pope (US)   42.12 138-2   6. Allan Eriksson (Swe)   39.40 129-3
     7. W. Jensen (Den) 38.22.

1924 (32. F 13 July): Again, all the good marks were made in the qualifying round. Houser, who had won the shot five days earlier, is the last man to have scored a shot-discus double.

1. Bud Houser (US)	46.14	151-4 OR	4. Gus Pope (US)	44.42	145-8
2. Vilho Niittymaa (Fin)	44.94	147-5	5. Ketil Askildt (Nor)	43.40	142-4
3. Thomas Lieb (US)	44.82	147-0	6. Glenn Hartranft (US)	42.48	139-4

7. Elmer Niklander (Fin) 42.08; 8. H. Malmivirta (Fin) 41.16; 9. S. Toldy (Hun) 41.08; 10. K. Marvalits (Hun) 40.82; 11. P. Bermingham (Eire) 40.42; 12. Armas Taipale (Fin) 40.20.

1928 (34. F 1 Aug): Defending champ Houser, by now a veteran of 27, led the qualifiers with 47.32. Among those who fell by the wayside were Paulus, a 2.02 (6-7½) giant, and Hoffmeister, both of Germany. The latter, who had broken the world record before the Games, could manage no better than 39.16 (128-6). In the final, all but Houser and Kentta improved, but Houser still won with his qualifying round mark.

1. Bud Houser (US)	47.32	155-3 OR	4. Harald Stenerud (Nor)	45.80	150-3
2. Antero Kivi (Fin)	47.22	154-11	5. John Anderson (US)	44.86	147-2
3. James Corson (US)	47.10	154-6	6. Eino Kentta (Fin)	44.16	144-10

7. E. Paulus (Ger) 44.14; 8. J. Trandem (Nor) 43.96; 9. Fred Weicker (US) 43.80; 10. G. Kalkun (Est) 43.08; 11. H. Taskinen (Fin) 43.00; 12. J. Jordans (Lat) 42.78. (Corson 47.00 OR Q)

1932 (18. F 3 Aug): Anderson showed great improvement over his Amsterdam form. In the first round of the final, however, Noel got one off which appeared to be in the neighborhood of Anderson's top mark. At that very moment, the officials had their minds and eyes on the dramatic vault duel between Miller and Nishida. When they wanted to measure Noel's throw later on, no trace could be found in the ground, and much to his despair Noel received no recognition for his effort. He was allowed to take one more try at the end of the regular competition, but he failed to do himself justice. World record holder Jessup could do no better than 8th.

1. John Anderson (US)	49.48	162-4 OR	(47.86 48.86 49.38 49.38 49.48 47.98)	
2. Henri Jean Laborde (US)	48.46	159-0	(48.22 f	48.44 f	48.46 47.14)
3. Paul Winter (Fr)	47.84	157-0		
4. Jules Noel (Fr)	47.74	156-7		
5. Istvan Donogan (Hun)	47.08	154-5		
6. Endre Madarasz (Hun)	46.52	152-7		

7. Kalevi Kotkas (Fin) 45.86; 8. Paul Jessup (US) 45.24; 9. Jozsef Remecz (Hun) 45.02; 10. E. Janausch (Aut) 44.82; 11. Hans-Heinrich Sievert (Ger) 44.50; 12. H. Hart (S Afr) 43.32. (Anderson 47.86 OR; Laborde 48.22 OR; Anderson 48.86 OR; 49.38 OR)

1936 (31. F 5 Aug): Schroder, the world record holder, barely won access to the final by beating Bergh in a throwoff. Harald Andersson of Sweden, Europe's most consistent thrower, was suffering from an injured right hand and unable to qualify. In the final, Carpenter moved from 3rd to 1st on his next-to-last trial.

1. Ken Carpenter (US)	50.48	165-7 OR	(f 44.52 48.98 f	50.48 47.48)
2. Gordon Dunn (US)	49.36	161-11	(f 49.36 48.04 47.20 47.76 f)	
3. Giorgio Oberweger (It)	49.22	161-6	(46.66 46.64 49.22 47.28 f	f)
4. Reidar Sorlie (Nor)	48.76	159-11	(47.00 48.76 46.78 47.66 48.64 47.86)	
5. Willy Schroder (Ger)	47.92	157-3	(44.78 47.22 45.00 47.38 47.80 47.92)	
6. Nicolaos Sylias (Gr)	47.74	156-7	(47.74 44.58 47.06 45.34 47.58 47.66)	

7. Gunnar Bergh (Swe) 47.22; 8. Ake Hedvall (Swe) 46.20; 9. J. Wotapek (Aut) 46.04; 10. H. Sivertsen (Nor) 45.88; 11. H. Fritsch (Ger) 45.10; 12. Jules Noel (Fr) 44.56.

1948 (35. Q-F 2 Aug): Consolini led the qualifiers with 51.08 (167-7), a new Olympic record, with Tosi 50.56 (165-10) and Gordien 48.40 (158-9) following. In the final, most of the good throws were made in the early rounds. Then drizzle turned into rain and the water-logged circle precluded spectacular advances.

1. Adolfo Consolini (It)	52.78	173-2 OR	(49.66 52.78 47.94 f	50.50 50.42)
2. Giuseppe Tosi (It)	51.78	169-10	(51.78 48.80 50.10 50.08 f	51.18)
3. Fortune Gordien (US)	50.76	166-6	(47.94 49.20 50.76 f	48.74 f)

4. Ivar Ramstad (Nor)   49.20   161-5   6. Veikko Nyqvist (Fin)   47.32   155-3
5. Ferenc Klics (Hun)   48.20   158-2
   7. Nicolaos Syllas (Gr) 47.24; 8. Stein Johnsen (Nor) 46.54; 9. A. Huutoniemi (Fin) 45.28;
10. U. Fransson (Swe) 45.24; 11. H. Tunner (Aut) 44.42; 12. E. Julve (Peru) 44.04.
(Consolini 51.08 OR Q; Tosi 51.78 OR)

1952 (32. Q-F 22 July): Defending champion Consolini led the qualifiers with 51.88 (170-2),
followed by Gordien 50.34 (165-2), Grigalka 48.92 (160-6) and Iness 48.90 (160-5). In the
final, Iness, a 22-year-old giant, beat the listed Olympic record on all 6 throws. It was the
greatest discus competition in history, with four over 170-feet.

1. Sim Iness (US)	55.02	180-6 OR	(53.46	54.60	55.02	53.48	54.12	52.82)
2. Adolfo Consolini (It) .	53.78	176-5	(51.68	53.78	53.44	50.62	50.08	51.20)
3. Jim Dillion (US)	53.28	174-9	(52.46	48.06	51.76	53.28 f		52.28)
4. Fortune Gordien (US)	52.66	172-9	(52.52	52.66	51.70	51.48 f		49.92)
5. Ferenc Klics (Hun)	51.12	167-9	(48.74	49.06	51.12 f		49.78	f)
6. Otto Grigalka (SU)	50.70	166-4	(50.70 f		47.84 f		f	f)

   7. Roland Nilsson (Swe) 50.06; 8. Giuseppe Tosi (It) 49.02; 9. Nicolaos Syllas (Gr) 48.98;
10. B. Matveyev (SU) 48.70; 11. B. Butyenko (SU) 48.14; 12. Veikko Nyqvist (Fin) 47.72.
(Innes 53.46 OR, 54.60 OR)

1956 (20. Q-F 27 Nov): The leading qualifiers were Oerter 51.18 (167-11), Du Plessis 50.68
(166-3), Bukhantsev 49.64 (162-10). In the final, the 20-year-old Oerter killed the opposition with
his very first throw, a personal best and a new Olympic record. "I was keyed up. I was inspired,"
he said. Consolini, 39, and Gordien, 34, placed among the first six for the third time. The
Italian was partly handicapped by an injury to the index finger of his right hand.

1. Al Oerter (US)	56.36	184-11 OR	(56.36	53.80	53.22	55.08	53.28	54.92)
2. Fortune Gordien (US)	54.80	179-9	(54.74	49.18	51.40	53.84	52.74	54.80)
3. Des Koch (US)	54.40	178-6	(50.52 f		53.54	53.64	54.40	54.02)
4. Mark Pharaoh (GB)	54.26	178-0	(52.52 f		53.26	49.84	54.26	53.16)
5. Otto Grigalka (SU)	52.36	171-9	(51.24	50.08	52.36	49.44 f		50.12)
6. Adolfo Consolini (It)	52.20	171-3	(51.92	52.20	52.12 f		51.28	52.00)

   7. Ferenc Klics (Hun) 51.82; 8. Dako Radosevic (Yug) 51.68; 9. Boris Matveyev (SU)
51.38; 10. Gerald Carr (GB) 50.72; 11. Gunter Kruse (Arg) 49.88; 12. Kim Bukhantsev (SU)
48.58; 13. Stephanus Du Plessis (S Afr) 48.48; 14. Erik Uddebom (Swe) 48.28; 15. Musulami
Rakura (Fiji) 47.24; 16. Herman Haddad (Chile) 46.00.

1960 (35. Q 6 Sept; F 7 Sept): Defending champion Oerter passed the world record in a
warmup throw, then needed two trials to qualify. Even so, his second throw was 58.42 (191-8),
a new Olympic record. Other leading qualifiers were Szecsenyi 55.52 (182-2), Repo 54.84
(179-11) and Babka 54.48 (178-9). In the final, Babka took the lead with his first throw but
Oerter shot past his rival with his fifth throw, clinching the gold for the second time—again with
a PR.

1. Al Oerter (US)	59.18	194-2 OR	(57.64	56.72	56.52	56.72	59.18	57.18)
2. Rink Babka (US)	58.02	190-4	(58.02	55.32	56.14	54.92	57.52	57.40)
3. Dick Cochran (US)	57.16	187-6	(f	54.74	48.70	54.50	57.16	54.48)
4. Jozsef Szecsenyi (Hun)	55.78	183-0	(54.58 f		54.86	55.22	55.78	55.60)
5. Edmund Piatkowski (Pol)	55.12	180-10	(54.06	51.52	54.28 f		55.12	f)
6. Viktor Kompanyeyets (SU)	55.06	180-8	(55.06	53.38 f		53.52 f		51.08)

   7. Carmelo Rado (It) 54.00; 8. Kim Bukhantsev (SU) 53.60; 9. Pentti Repo (Fin) 53.44; 10.
Ferenc Klics (Hun) 53.36; 11. Stein Haugen (Nor) 53.36; 12. Lothar Milde (EG) 53.32; 13.
Zdenek Cihak (Czech) 53.28; 14. Zenon Begier (Pol) 53.18; 15. Vladimir Trusenyov (SU)
52.92; 16. Manfred Grieser (EG) 52.68; 17. Adolfo Consolini (It) 52.44; 18. Antonios
Kounadis (Gr) 52.42; 19. Zdenek Nemec (Czech) 52.14; 20. Todor Todorov (Bul) 52.12; 21.
Warwick Selvey (Aus) 49.34; 22. Kees Koch (Hol) 49.20.
(Oerter 58.42 OR Q)

1964 (29. Q-F 15 Oct): The defending champion from Melbourne and Rome, Oerter had been bothered by a cervical disc injury for some time. Here he also had torn cartilages in his lower rib cage and threw against medical advice. But when he led the qualifiers with an Olympic record 60.54 (198-7), it became apparent that he was not totally disabled. Danek, the Czech who had taken away Oerter's world record, qualified with 58.88 (193-2). Next best were Jay Silvester, 57.80 (189-7), and Viktor Kompanyeyets, 57.40 (188-4). Danek took the lead early in the final and improved to 60.52 (198-7) in the fourth round. Weill and Silvester also had better marks than Oerter, who was thus lying 4th by the time he stepped into the ring for his penultimate try. But it was right there that he proved to be one of the greatest competitors in Olympic history. His 61.00 gave him his third consecutive gold medal in the same event—a feat previously achieved only by hammer thrower John Flanagan (1900-04-08).

1. Al Oerter (US)	61.00	200-1 OR	(57.64	58.34	55.10	54.36	61.00 p)
2. Ludvik Danek (Czech)	60.52	198-7	(59.72	58.82 f		60.52	58.38 57.16)
3. Dave Weill (US)	59.48	195-2	(f	59.48	56.24	56.14	55.94 52.44)
4. Jay Silvester (US)	59.08	193-10	(56.98 f		57.54	57.46	59.08 f)
5. Jozsef Szecsenyi (Hun)	57.22	187-9	(54.34	52.14	56.96	57.22 f	54.66)
6. Zenon Begier (Pol)	57.06	187-2	(57.06	52.44	55.82 f	f	56.68)

7. Edmund Piatkowski (Pol) 55.80; 8. Vladimir Trusenyov (SU) 54.78; 9. Kim Bukhantsev (SU) 54.38; 10. Roy Hollingsworth (GB) 53.78; 11. Hartmut Losch (EG) 52.08; 12. Viktor Kompanyeyets (SU) 51.96.
(Oerter 60.54 OR Q)

1968 (27. Q 14 Oct; F 15 Oct): Three-time winner Oerter threw himself into Olympic history by becoming the only athlete to win four consecutive titles, this one with an Olympic record 64.78 (212-6). It was his third career best of his four victories. Teammate Silvester reached an Olympic record 63.34 (207-10) in the qualifying while Oerter qualified on his first throw (59.36). In the finals, Oerter stood only 4th after two rounds as Milde led with 63.08 (206-11), but Oerter proved to be the supreme competitor as he winged his 3rd throw to 64.78 to shatter the field and lock up his gold medal. Silvester, who came into the Games with a PR 17 feet ahead of Oerter's, then fouled three of his next four throws and finished 5th. Danek got his longest of the day in the third frame to win the bronze. But no one could match his throws before Oerter's bomb. Of course, who came closest but Oerter himself, with throws of 64.74 (212-4) and 64.04 (210-1). Said Oerter, "I guess I'm a little jealous of my gold medal. I don't want to give it up."

1. Al Oerter (US)	64.78	212-6 OR	(61.78 f		64.78	62.42	64.74 64.04)
2. Lothar Milde (EG)	63.08	206-11	(62.44	63.08	62.58	59.98	60.24 58.00)
3. Ludvik Danek (Czech)	62.92	206-5	(60.62 f		62.92 f		61.28 61.34)
4. Hartmut Losch (EG)	62.12	203-10	(62.12	61.68	60.34	59.48	58.94 59.50)
5. Jay Silvester (US)	61.78	202-8	(61.10	61.78 f		f	f 60.44)
6. Gary Carlsen (US)	59.46	195-1	(58.62	59.26	59.46	59.30	52.60 58.54)

7. Edmund Piatkowski (Pol) 59.40; 8. Ricky Bruch (Swe) 59.28; 9. Hein-Direck Neu (WG) 58.66; 10. Gunter Schaumburg (EG) 58.62; 11. Ferenc Tegla (Hun) 58.36; 12. Robin Tait (NZ) 57.68.
(Silvester 63.34 OR Q)

1972 (29. Q 1 Sept; F 2 Sept): Danek finally reached the top step of the victory platform, completing his set of medals with a triumph of 64.40 (211-3). And Silvester finally won a medal in his third Olympics, after a 4th and a 5th. The leaders established themselves right away in the final: five of the eventual first six finishers were in those positions, while Danek stood 9th. In round 2, Powell took command with 62.82 (206-1), but Silvester moved ahead in frame 3 with 63.50 (208-4) while Danek jumped to 5th with 62.38 (204-8). Bruch came to life in round 4 with a 62.76 (205-10) spin while Danek improved for the fourth consecutive throw, this time to 62.54 (205-2). Bruch moved to 2nd in round 5 with his 63.40 (208-0). Danek threw second in the order and on his final throw he winged it his winning 64.40. Only Fejer responded, getting his best of the day (62.62/205-5). Silvester and Bruch kept their positions, but Powell lost a chance to regain a medal when he fouled his last throw. The medal winners said the wind conditions (left rear) were the worst they had ever seen in a major competition.

-113-

1. Ludvik Danek (Czech)   64.40   211-3   (58.12 60.38 62.38 62.54 61.70 64.40)
2. Jay Silvester (US)   63.50   208-4   (62.12 f   63.50 f   f   62.86)
3. Ricky Bruch (Swe)   63.40   208-0   (59.12 f   61.52 62.76 63.40 62.60)
4. John Powell (US)   62.82   206-1   (61.92 62.82 60.44 f   61.38 f)
5. Geza Fejer (Hun)   62.62   205-5   (62.50 62.56 f   61.50 62.62)
6. Detlef Thorith (EG)   62.42   204-9   (61.74 62.42 61.06 f   59.88 f)
    7. Ferenc Tegla (Hun) 60.60; 8. Tim Vollmer (US) 60.24; 9. Pentti Kahma (Fin) 59.66; 10. Silvano Simeon (It) 59.34; 11. Jorma Rinne (Fin) 59.22; 12. Janos Muranyi (Hun) 57.92; 13. Namakoro Niare (Mali) 56.48; 14. Les Mills (NZ) 55.86.

1976 (30. Q 24 July; F 25 July): Wilkins added nearly a dozen feet to the Olympic record with his soaring 68.28 (224-0) in the qualifying, which saw the exit of '72 bronze winner Ricky Bruch and highly-rated Finn Markku Tuokko. In the finals, Wilkins' first throw was a paltry 61.78 (202-8) as Schmidt 63.68 (208-11) led from Kahma (63.12/207-1) and Powell (62.48/205-0). Wilkins wasted no time in rectifying this mistake with 67.50 (221-5) in the second round. Powell moved to second in round 3 with 65.70 (215-7) and Schmidt to third with 65.16 (213-9). Thiede moved to 4th in round 5 with 64.30 (210-11). In the final round, Powell hit his second 64.24 of the day. Two throws later, Schmidt connected and popped 66.22 (217-3) to claim the silver medal and leave Powell with no recourse. Wilkins got his second-longest of the day (66.14/217-0) and on the competition's last throw Pachale reached his 64.24 (210-9) best. The medal-winning heaves were all the more impressive because of the enclosed stadium, which was virtually windless.

1. Mac Wilkins (US)   67.50   221-5   (61.78 67.50 63.44 63.52 f   66.14)
2. Wolfgang Schmidt (EG)   66.22   217-3   (63.68 f   65.16 f   63.96 66.22)
3. John Powell (US)   65.70   215-7   (62.48 64.24 65.70 60.48 60.20 64.24)
4. Norbert Thiede (EG)   64.30   210-11   (62.40 61.66 61.98 63.02 64.30 63.04)
5. Siegfried Pachale (EG)   64.24   210-9   (59.62 64.04 60.02 61.08 59.62 64.24)
6. Pentti Kahma (Fin)   63.12   207-1   (63.12 61.22 f   f   f   61.94)
    7. Knut Hjeltnes (Nor) 63.06; 8. Jay Silvester (US) 61.98; 9. Ludvik Danek (Czech) 61.28; 10. Velko Velev (Bul) 60.94; 11. Ferenc Tegla (Hun) 60.54; 12. Hein-Direck Neu (WG) 60.46; 13. Josef Silhavy (Czech) 58.42; 14. Janos Farago (Hun) 57.48; 15. Armando De Vincentiis (It) 55.86.
(Wilkins 68.28 OR Q)

HAMMER

1896 (not contested).

1900 (3. F 17 July): The implement was thrown from a 9 ft. (2.74) circle. World record holder Flanagan was an easy winner.

1. John Flanagan (US)   49.72 163-1   3. Josiah McCracken (US)   42.46 139-4
2. Truxton Hare (US)   49.12 161-2

1904 (5. F 29 Aug): The ring was the now-standard 7 feet (2.13). Flanagan, the world record holder and defending champ, achieved the winning distance on his first trial.

1. John Flanagan (US)   51.22 168-0 OR   4. Charles Chadwick (US)   42.78 140-4
2. John DeWitt (US)   50.26 164-11   5. James Mitchell (US)
3. Ralph Rose (US)   45.72 150-0
(DeWitt 50.26 OR)

1908 (18. F 14 July): McGrath led the qualifiers with 51.18 (167-11), followed by Flanagan 50.36 (165-3). In the final, Flanagan moved to 1st, winning his third gold medal in the event.

1. John Flanagan (US)   51.92 170-4 OR   4. Thomas Nicolson (GB)   48.08 157-9
2. Matt McGrath (US)   51.18 167-11   5. Lee Talbott (US)   47.86 157-0
3. Con Walsh (US)   48.50 159-2   6. Marquis Horr (US)   46.94 154-0
    7. Simon Gillis (US) 45.58.

1912 (14. F 14 July): In the absence of arch-rival Pat Ryan, McGrath was an easy winner. His best marks were 54.12 (177-7) and 54.74 (179-7).

1. Matt McGrath (US)	54.74 179-7 OR	4. Robert Olsson (Swe)	46.50 152-6
2. Duncan Gillis (Can)	48.38 158-9	5. Carl Johan Lind (Swe)	45.60 149-7
3. Clarence Childs (US)	48.16 158-0	6. Denis Carey 36.26;	43.78 143-8

7. Nils Linde (Swe) 43.32; 8. Carl Jahnzon (Swe) 42.58; 9. Ralph Rose (US) 42.58; 10. A. Aberg (Swe) 41.10.
(McGrath 54.12 OR)

1920 (12. Q-F 18 Aug): World holder Ryan led the qualifiers with 52.82 (173-3). Defending champion McGrath injured a knee and had to withdraw after his second preliminary throw. Nicolson arrived at the stadium after the completion of the qualifying round but was nonetheless allowed to take his three throws: he shunted Linde to 7th and qualified for the final. Only Ryan and "Massa" Lind managed to improve in the closing rounds.

1. Pat Ryan (US)	52.86 173-5	4. Malcolm Svensson (Swe)	47.28 155-1
2. Carl Johan Lind (Swe)	48.42 158-10	5. Matt McGrath (US)	46.66 153-1
3. Basil Bennet (US)	48.24 158-3	6. Thomas Nicolson (GB)	45.70 149-11

7. Nils Linde (Swe) 44.88; 8. James McEachen (US) 44.70; 9. S. McPermott (Can) 44.66; 10. R. Olsson (Swe) 44.18; 11. J. Pettersson (Fin) 41.76;. . . nm—J. Cameron (Can).

1924 (15. F 10 July): Tootell led the qualifiers at 50.60 (166-0), followed by Nokes 48.86, Eriksson 47.96 (157-4) and McGrath 47.04 (154-4). All but Nokes improved in the final. Tootell won in fine style from McGrath, by now a veteran of 46.

1. Fred Tootell (US)	53.28 174-10	4. Erik Eriksson (Fin)	48.74 159-11
2. Matt McGrath (US)	50.84 166-9	5. Ossian Skiold (Swe)	45.28 148-6
3. Malcolm Nokes (GB)	48.86 160-4	6. James McEachern (US)	45.22 148-4

7. Carl Johan Lind (Swe) 44.78; 8. J. Murdock (Can) 42.48; 9. John Merchant (US) 41.44; 10. Robert Saint-Pe (Fr) 36.26; 11. C. Jensen (Den) 36.26; 12. P. Zaidin (Fr) 36.14.

1928 (16. F 30 July): Skiold led the qualifiers with 51.28 followed by Black 49.02 and O'Callaghan 47.48 (155-9). In the final O'Callaghan, who had only one year of experience in the hammer circle, clinched the gold medal on his next-to-last trial. He and Poggioli, 40, were the only ones who managed to improve.

1. Pat O'Callaghan (Eire)	51.38 168-7	4. Armando Poggioli (It)	48.36 158-8
2. Ossian Skiold (Swe)	51.28 168-3	5. Donald Gwinn (US)	47.14 154-8
3. Edmund Black (US)	49.02 160-10	6. Frank Connor (US)	46.74 153-4

7. Federico Kleger (Arg) 46.60; 8. R. Bayer (Chile) 46.34; 9. Erik Eriksson (Fin) 46.22; 10. H. Kamerbeek (Hol) 46.02; 11. Malcolm Nokes (GB) 45.36; 12. Ken Caskey (US) 44.80.

1932 (14. F 1 Aug): Porhola, the Olympic shot champion of 1920, led until the last round, when defending champion O'Callaghan came through to win.

1. Pat O'Callaghan (Eire)	53.92	176-11	(47.76 52.20 50.86 51.80 51.84 53.92)
2. Ville Porhola (Fin)	52.26	171-5	(51.26 52.26 f f 50.86 51.76)
3. Peter Zaremba (US)	50.32	165-1	4. Ossian Skiold (Swe) 49.24 161-6
5. Grant McDougall (US)	49.12	161-2	6. Federico Kleger (Arg) 48.32 158-6

7. Gunnar Jansson (Swe) 47.78; 8. Armando Poggioli (It) 46.90; 9. Fernando Vandelli (It) 45.16; 10. Y. Nagao (Japan) 43.40.

1936 (27. F 3 Aug): The German duo Hein-Blask came out on top after a hard fight with Warngard. All three achieved new personal bests, with Hein less than a meter off the WR.

1. Karl Hein (Ger)	56.48	185-4 OR	(52.12 52.44 f 54.70 54.84 56.48)
2. Erwin Blask (Ger)	55.04	180-7	(52.54 55.04 f 54.10 54.48 f)
3. Fred Warngard (Swe)	54.82	179-10	(52.04 52.98 54.02 54.82 53.30 50.60)
4. Gustaf Koutonen (Fin)	51.90	170-3	(f 50.00 51.90 49.10 49.90 f)
5. William Rowe (US)	51.66	169-6	(51.52 51.04 49.28 50.32 51.66 f)
6. Donald Favor (US)	51.00	167-4	(50.78 50.02 51.00 48.48 50.32 47.70)

7. B. Greulich (Ger) 50.60; 8. K. Annamaa (Est) 50.46; 9. Henry Dreyer (US) 50.44; 10. S. Heino (Fin) 49.92; 11. Ville Porhola (Fin) 49.88; 12. Gunnar Jansson (Swe) 49.28. (Blask 55.04 OR)

1948 (23. F 31 July): Nemeth, a fine technician who had set a WR earlier in the month, led the qualifiers with 54.02 (177-3). In the final, he took the lead early and was never threatened.

1. Imre Nemeth (Hun)	56.06	183-11	(53.58	55.44	54.94	50.04 f		56.06)
2. Ivan Gubijan (Yug)	54.26	178-0	(f	f	54.26	51.76	54.22 f)	
3. Bob Bennett (US)	53.72	176-3	(52.52	51.10	52.08	53.72	51.20	49.80)
4. Sam Felton (US)	53.66	176-0						
5. Lauri Tamminen (Fin)	53.08	174-2						
6. Bo Ericson (Swe)	52.98	173-10						

7. Teseo Taddia (It) 51.74; 8. E. Soderqvist (Swe) 51.48; 9. Henry Dreyer (US) 51.36; 10. Svend Aage Frederiksen (Den) 50.06; 11. Duncan McD. Clark (GB) 48.34; 12. Hans Houtzager (Hol) 45.68.

1952 (33. Q-F 24 July): Csermak led the qualifiers with 57.20 (187-8), a new Olympic record. Then came Storch 55.32 (181-6) and Strandli 54.96 (180-4). In the final, 20-year-old Csermak killed the opposition on his third throw—a record-shattering 60.34—history's first 60-meter effort. Storch, the 39-year-old German, was a good 2nd ahead of former record holder Nemeth, the defending champ.

1. Jozsef Csermak (Hun)	60.34	197-11 WR	(58.44	57.28	60.34	49.68 f		f)
2. Karl Storch (Ger)	58.86	193-1	(f	56.44	58.18	58.86	57.80	58.34)
3. Imre Nemeth (Hun)	57.74	189-5	(54.92	55.04	56.82	54.94	57.74	56.30)
4. Jiri Dadak (Czech)	56.80	186-4	(54.00	56.80 f		51.72	55.60	54.04)
5. Nikolay Ryedkin (SU)	56.54	185-6	(53.08	56.54	52.30	53.54 f		54.16)
6. Karl Wolf (Ger)	56.48	185-4	(56.48	54.98	53.78	53.60 f		56.40)

7. Sverre Strandli (Nor) 56.36; 8. G. Dibyenko (SU) 55.02; 9. Ivan Gubijan (Yug) 54.54; 10. Teseo Taddia (It) 54.26; 11. Sam Felton (US) 53.32; 12. Constantin Dumitru (Rum) 52.76; 13. Bob Backus (US) 52.10. (Csermak 57.20 OR Q, 58.44 OR)

1956 (22. Q-F 24 Nov): Samotsvyetov led the qualifiers with 59.52 (195-3), followed by Racic 59.06 (193-9) and Connolly 59.04 (193-8). In the final, world record holder Krivonosov took the lead in the second round and increased slightly in the third. Connolly, who had a long foul in his opening trial, wrested the lead from the Soviet in the next-to-the-last round for a narrow win.

1. Hal Connolly (US)	63.18	207-3 OR	(f	60.92	62.64	61.76	63.18 f)	
2. Mikhail Krivonosov (SU)	63.02	206-9	(60.58	63.00	63.02 f		f	f)
3. Anat. Samotsvyetov (SU)	62.56	205-3	(62.10	58.12	61.94	60.22	59.20	62.56)
4. Al Hall (US)	61.96	203-3	(57.76	61.82 f		61.58 f		61.96)
5. Jozsef Csermak (Hun)	60.70	199-2	(58.26	58.42	60.70 f		59.10 f)	
6. Kresimir Racic (Yug)	60.36	198-0	(57.98	60.36 f		f	58.06	55.08)

7. Dmitriy Yegorov (SU) 60.22; 8. Sverre Strandli (Nor) 59.20; 9. Peter Allday (GB) 58.00; 10. Alfons Niklas (Pol) 57.70; 11. Muhammad Iqbal (Pak) 56.96; 12. Donald Anthony (GB) 56.72; 13. Guy Husson (Fr) 55.02; 14. Tadeusz Rut (Pol) 53.42; . . . nm—Birger Asplund (Swe). (Samotsvyetov 62.10 OR; Krivonosov 63.00 OR, 63.02 OR)

1960 (28. Q 2 Sept; F 3 Sept): Rudenkov led the qualifiers with an Olympic record 67.02 (219-10), followed by Zsivotzky 64.80 (212-7), and Samotsvyetov 64.66 (212-2). In the final, world record holder Connolly surprisingly failed to survive for the last three rounds. Rudenkov won comfortably and had a very consistent series of throws, capped by another OR.

1. Vasiliy Rudenkov (SU)	67.10	220-2 OR	(65.60	64.98	67.10	66.62	64.58	66.22)
2. Gyula Zsivotzky (Hun)	65.78	215-10	(60.82	63.82	64.86	65.78 f		65.10)
3. Tadeusz Rut (Pol)	65.64	215-4	(64.50	65.64	64.94 f		64.84	63.54)
4. John Lawlor (Eire)	64.94	213-1	(f	62.58	64.08	64.94 f		f)

5. Olgierd Cieply (Pol)   64.56   211-10   (60.02 64.06 62.26 64.56 64.48 62.06)
6. Zvonko Bezjak (Yug)   64.20   210-8   (61.96 64.20 63.54 63.94 62.86 f)
7. Anatoliy Samotsvyetov (SU) 63.60; 8. Hal Connolly (US) 63.58; 9. Heinrich Thun (Aut) 63.52; 10. Yuriy Nikulin (SU) 63.10; 11. Sverre Strandli (Nor) 63.04; 12. Muhammad Iqbal (Pak) 61.78; 13. Noboru Okamoto (Japan) 60.08; 14. Al Hall (US) 59.76; 15. Mike Ellis (GB) 54.22.
(Zsivotsky 64.80 OR Q; Rudenkov 67.02 OR Q)

1964 (24. Q-F 18 Oct): In the morning trials, the Olympic record was bettered by Zsivotzky 67.98 (223-0) and Connolly 67.40 (221-1), and equaled by Klim, 67.10 (220-2). In the first round, Zsivotzky threw 69.08 to take the lead, while Uwe Beyer did 68.08—the longest distance ever achieved by a thrower under 20. But neither was able to improve later, and the veteran Klim unleashed a winning toss of 69.74 on his fourth throw. That was a personal best for the 31-year-old Soviet. Another USSR veteran, 33-year-old Nikulin, was fourth. World record holder Connolly did better than in Melbourne and Rome distance-wise, but had to be content with 6th.

1. Romuald Klim (SU)   69.74   228-10   (67.18 64.64 68.58 69.74 68.80 68.16)
2. Gyula Zsivotzky (Hun)   69.08   226-8   (69.08 66.20 68.46 67.42 67.84 67.32)
3. Uwe Beyer (WG)   68.08   223-4   (68.08 65.64 62.90 f   67.70 f)
4. Yuriy Nikulin (SU)   67.68   222-1   (67.08 67.00 67.68 f   f   65.60)
5. Yuriy Bakarinov (SU)   66.72   218-11   (65.90 66.50 65.38 65.24 66.72 f)
6. Hal Connolly (US)   66.64   218-8   (f   62.94 66.64 f   64.72 f)
7. Ed Burke (US) 65.66; 8. Olgierd Cieply (Pol) 64.82; 9. Josef Matousek (Cze) 64.58; 10. Tadeusz Rut (Pol) 64.52; 11. Sandor Eckschmidt (Hun) 63.82; 12. Al Hall (US) 63.82; 13. Takeo Sugawara (Japan) 63.68; 14. Zdzislaw Smolinski (Pol) 62.90; 15. Heinrich Thun (Aut) 62.76.
(Klim 67.10=OR Q; Connolly 67.40 OR Q; Zsivotzky 67.98 OR Q, 69.08 OR)

1968 (22. Q 16 Oct; F 17 Oct): The final was featured by a hot duel between defending champion Klim and world record holder Zsivotzky. Throwing in that order, they opened with 72.24 and 72.26. This was the beginning of a ding-dong battle which ended in Zsivotzky's favor when he reached 73.36 (240-8) in the fifth round, merely 8cm farther than Klim's best. Lovasz and Sugawara ended with the same result, 69.78 (228-11), with the Hungarian clinching the bronze on the strength of second-best throw.

1. Gyula Zsivotzky (Hun)   73.36   240-8 OR   (72.26 72.46 72.54 f   73.36 72.22)
2. Romuald Klim (SU)   73.28   240-5   (72.24 68.96 72.82 73.28 71.16 71.64)
3. Lazar Lovasz (Hun)   69.78   228-11   (64.76 f   69.78 f   69.38 f)
4. Takeo Sugawara (Japan) 69.78   228-11   (67.24 68.12 f   69.06 69.78 61.40)
5. Sandor Eckschmidt (Hun) 69.46   227-11   (67.84 68.50 69.46 f   67.64 68.08)
6. Gennadiy Kondrashov (SU) 69.08   226-8   (69.08 67.00 68.64 67.10 67.98 67.70)
7. Reinhard Theimer (EG) 68.84; 8. Helmut Baumann (EG) 68.26; 9. Anatoliy Shchuplyakov (SU) 67.74; 10. Howard Payne (GB) 67.62; 11. Hans Fahsl (WG) 66.36; 12. Ed Burke (US) 65.72; 13. Yoshihisa Ishida (Japan) 65.04.
(Zsivotzky 72.60 OR Q; Klim 72.82 OR, 73.28 OR)

1972 (31. Q 4 Sept; F 7 Sept): The qualifying standard of 66.00 (216-6) proved too easy as no less than 20 made it. Bondarchuk led with 72.88 (239-1). In the early rounds of the final, long waits between throws were the obvious consequence of the large field. Bondarchuk opened with an impressive OR 75.50 (247-8), which proved to be a killer. The 32-year-old Soviet continued with a good series of throws in the 71/74 range. The only serious challenge came in round 5, when Sachse fouled on a 75-meter throw.

1. Anatoliy Bondarchuk (SU) 75.50   247-8 OR   (75.50 72.62 71.76 73.78 73.50 72.90)
2. Jochen Sachse (EG)   74.96   245-11   (71.54 f   73.70 71.26 f   74.96)
3. Vasiliy Khmyelevskiy (SU) 74.04   242-11   (68.82 71.62 74.04 68.16 f   f)
4. Uwe Beyer (WG)   71.52   234-8   (70.32 71.52 f   68.98 69.90 f)
5. Gyula Zsivotzky (Hun)   71.38   234-2   (71.38 70.44 70.48 f   70.66 70.20)
6. Sandor Eckschmidt (Hun) 71.20   233-7   (71.20 f   67.26 69.24 67.90 68.86)

7. Edwin Klein (WG) 71.14; 8. Shigenobu Murofushi (Japan) 70.88; 9. Mario Vecchiato (It) 70.58; 10. Karl-Hans Riehm (WG) 70.12; 11. Istvan Encsi (Hun) 70.06; 12. Tom Gage (US) 69.50; 13. Reinhard Theimer (EG) 69.16; 14. Srecko Stiglic (Yug) 68.34; 15. Stavros Moutaftsidis (Gr) 68.30; 16. Barry Williams (GB) 68.18; 17. Peter Sternad (Aut) 66.64; 18. Iosif Gamskiy (SU) 66.26; 19. Jacques Accambray (Fr) 65.06; 20. Takeo Sugawara (Japan) 64.70.

1976 (20. Q 26 July; F 28 July): Former world record holder Riehm led the 10 who reached the qualifying distance with 74.46 (244-3). Syedikh and his coach, defending champion Bondarchuk, were next best. In the final the three Soviet entries had things going their way from the beginning. After round 1 they were 1-2-3, Spiridonov-Syedikh-Bondarchuk, with Riehm a close 4th. In round 2, the 21-year-old Syedikh produced the winning throw, 77.52 (254-4). In round 4, Riehm missed Bondarchuk's 3rd-place mark by the narrowest of official margins—2 centimeters.

1. Yuriy Syedikh (SU)	77.52	254-4 OR	(75.64 77.52 f	f	75.58 76.40)
2. Aleksey Spiridonov (SU)	76.08	249-7	(75.74 73.94 75.28 75.60 f		76.08)
3. Anatoliy Bondarchuk (SU)	75.48	247-8	(75.48 f	74.64 74.16 f	75.46)
4. Karl-Hans Riehm (WG)	75.46	247-7	(75.00 73.08 f	75.46 75.42 74.62)	
5. Walter Schmidt (WG)	74.72	245-2	(72.58 74.72 74.36 73.52 74.72 72.42)		
6. Jochen Sachse (EG)	74.30	243-9	(71.90 72.84 72.80 73.14 74.30 73.70)		

7. Chris Black (GB) 73.18; 8. Edwin Klein (WG) 71.34; 9. Jacques Accambray (Fr) 70.44; 10. Manfred Seidel (EG) 70.02; 11. Shigenobu Murofushi (Japan) 68.88; 12. Peter Farmer (Aut) 68.00.
(Syedikh 75.64 OR; Spiridonov 75.74 OR)

JAVELIN

1896—1904 (not contested).

1908 (16. F 17 July): Distances were measured only for the first five. Lemming led the qualifiers with 53.68 (176-1). In the final he improved to 54.82.

1. Eric Lemming (Swe)	54.82 179-10 WR	4. Aarne Salovaara (Fin)	45.88 150-6
2. Arne Halse (Nor)	50.56 165-11	5. Armas Pesonen (Fin)	45.18 148-3
3. Otto Nilsson (Swe)	47.10 154-6	6. Juho Halme (Fin)	
(Nilsson 47.10 OR Q; Lemming 53.58 OR Q)		7. Jalmari Sauli (Fin)	

1912 (25. F 6 July): Lemming led qualifiers with 57.42 (188-5) which was not too far from his own world record, 58.26 (191-2). In the opening round of the final, Lemming brought the crowd to its feet with a great 60.64—history's first 60-meter-plus mark. Saaristo also beat the listed record in finishing 2nd. Three days later, in the javelin both hands, Saaristo totalled 109.42 (359-0) and bettered Lemming's record with a right hand throw of 61.00 (200-1).

1. Eric Lemming (Swe)	60.64	198-11 WR	(53.02 54.78 57.42 60.64 ?		"59")
2. Juho Saaristo (Fin)	58.66	192-5	(54.74 55.36 ?	56.20 ?	58.66)
3. Mor Koczan (Hun)	55.50	182-1			
4. Juho Halme (Fin)	54.64	179-3			
5. Vaino Siikaniemi (Fin)	52.42	172-0			
6. Richard Abrink (Swe)	52.20	171-3			

7. Arne Halse (Nor) 51.98; 8. Jonni Myyra (Fin) 51.32; 9. Urho Peltonen (Fin) 49.20; 10. Otto Nilsson (Swe) 49.18; 11. H. Sonne (Swe) 47.84; 12. D. W. Johansen (Nor) 47.60.
(Saaristo 55.36 OR Q; Lemming 57.42 OR Q)

1920 (30. F 15 Aug): At the end of the qualifying round (3 trials) Peltonen led with 63.50, followed by Johansson 63.08 and Myyra 60.62 (198-11). In the first round of the final Myyra moved to first with an OR 65.78, missing his own world record by 32 cm.

1. Jonni Myyra (Fin)	65.78	215-10 OR	4. Juho Saaristo (Fin)	62.38	204-8
2. Urho Peltonen (Fin)	63.50	208-4	5. Aleksander Klumberg (Est)	62.38	204-8
3. Paavo Johansson (Fin)	63.08	207-0	6. Gunnar Lindstrom (Swe)	60.52	198-7

7. Milton Angier (US) 59.26; 8. Erik Blomqvist (Swe) 58.18; 9. James Lincoln (US) 57.86; 10. H. Lillier (Swe) 56.44.
(Peltonen 63.50 OR Q)

1924 (29. F 6 July): Myyra, by now 32, successfully defended his title, beating Lindstrom, who later in the season set a world record of 66.62 (218-7).

1. Jonni Myyra (Fin)	62.96	206-7	4. Yrjo Ekqvist (Fin)	57.56	188-10
2. Gunnar Lindstrom (Swe)	60.92	199-10	5. William Neufeld (US)	56.96	186-10
3. Eugene Oberst (US)	58.34	191-5	6. Erik Blomqvist (Swe)	56.84	186-6

7. Urho Peltonen (Fin) 55.66; 8. Paavo Johansson (Fin) 55.10; 9. A. Cejzik (Pol) 54.86; 10. Taka Gangue (Fr) 54.64; 11. L. B. Priester (US) 54.50; 12. H. Welchel (US) 52.98

1928 (28. F 2 Aug): Lundqvist achieved his winning throw on the opening round of the competition. In fact, none of the leaders improved in the final. World record holder Penttila had an injured foot.

1. Erik Lundqvist (Swe)	66.60	218-6 OR	4. Paavo Liettu (Fin)	63.86	209-6
2. Bela Szepes (Hun)	65.26	214-1	5. Bruno Schlokat (Ger)	63.40	208-0
3. Olav Sunde (Nor)	63.96	209-10	6. Eino Penttila (Fin)	63.20	207-4

7. S. Lay (NZ) 62.88; 8. J. Meimer (Est) 61.46; 9. A. Lampuu (Fin) 61.44; 10. Arthur Sager (US) 60.46; 11. E. Stoschek (Ger) 59.86; 12. Doral Pilling (Can) 59.16.

1932 (13. F 4 Aug): Jarvinen was the class of the field and proved it in no uncertain manner, with 5 throws good enough to win. Sippala moved from 4th to 2nd in the last round.

1. Matti Jarvinen (Fin)	72.70	238-6 OR	(71.24 70.42 72.70 71.30 72.56 67.92)
2. Martti Sippala (Fin)	69.80	229-0	(68.14 63.18 66.52 62.98 61.22 69.80)
3. Eino Penttila (Fin)	68.70	225-5	(60.04 64.12 64.28 65.40 68.70 66.86)
4. Gottfried Weimann (Ger)	68.18	223-8	
5. Lee Bartlett (US)	64.46	211-6	
6. Ken Churchill (US)	63.24	207-6	

7. M. W. Metcalf (US) 61.88; 8. K. Sumiyoshi (Japan) 61.14; 9. Olav Sunde (Nor) 60.80; 10. S. Nagao (Japan) 59.82.
(Jarvinen 71.24 OR)

1936 (28. F 6 Aug): World record holder Jarvinen, the defending champ, had a back injury and was short on condition. Stock, a good all-around thrower who already had a bronze in the shot, clinched the gold in the fifth round.

1. Gerhard Stock (Ger)	71.84	235-8	(f	68.10	65.50*66.00*71.84	65.00*)
2. Yrjo Nikkanen (Fin)	70.76	232-2	(f	70.76	f	62.00*62.00*63.00*)
3. Kalervo Toivonen (Fin)	70.72	232-0	(62.00	67.00	68.76 f	70.72 f)
4. Lennart Atterwall (Swe)	69.20	227-0	(67.14	69.20	f	65.00*61.00*62.00*)
5. Matti Jarvinen (Fin)	69.18	227-0	(68.30	69.18	f	64.00*f	66.00*)
6. Alton Terry (US)	67.14	220-3	(67.10	67.14	f	64.00*65.00*62.00*)

*=estimated distance (throw not measured)

7. E. Lokajski (Pol) 66.38; 8. Jozsef Varszegi (Hun) 65.30; 9. Gottfried Weimann (Ger) 63.58; 10. W. Turczyk (Pol) 63.36; 11. Gustav Sule (Est) 63.26; 12. Lee Bartlett (US) 61.14.

1948 (22. F 4 Aug): Biles led the qualifiers with 67.68 (222-0), followed by Berglund 67.02 (219-10), Rautavvara 64.88 (212-10) and Pettersson 64.04 (210-1). They were the only throwers to attain the qualifying distance, 64.00 (210-0). In the opening round of the final, Rautavvara reached 69.76, the eventual winning mark. Marks were below par due to a sloppy runway. Biles was unable to reproduce his form of the preliminary round, which would have earned him a silver medal.

1. Tapio Rautavaara (Fin)	69.76	228-11	(69.76 f 57.68 59.42 61.86 58.94)
2. Steve Seymour (US)	67.56	221-8	(f 62.36 67.56 61.72 63.58 61.00)

3. Jozsef Varszegi (Hun)   67.02   219-11   (67.02 58.14 60.28 57.52 59.70 58.34)
4. Pauli Vesterinen (Fin)   65.88   216-2   (65.44 60.96 63.00 61.76 65.88 65.78)
5. Odd Maehlum (Nor)   65.32   214-4   (65.32 62.00 61.66 59.22 60.58 59.32)
6. Marty Biles (US)   65.16   213-9   (58.70 65.08 65.18 59.08 64.10 62.26)
7. Mirko Vujacic (Yug) 64.88; 8. Bob Likens (US) 64.50; 9. Gunnar Pettersson (Swe) 62.80; 10. Per-Arne Berglund (Swe) 62.62; 11. Lumir Kiesewetter (Cze) 60.24; 12. Soini Nikkinen (Fin) 58.04.

1952 (26. Q-F 23 July): Hyytiainen led the qualifiers with 71.28 (223-10), followed by Berglund (71.28) 233-10, and Tsibulenko 69.42 (227-9). In the final, Young made the winning throw in the second round to give the US its first gold in this event.

1. Cy Young (US)   73.78   242-0 OR   (68.44 73.78 72.80 65.72 71.72 f)
2. Bill Miller (US)   72.46   237-9   (72.46 71.64 63.94 65.40 66.96 70.44)
3. Toivo Hyytiainen (Fin)   71.88   235-10   (71.88 71.24 70.24 70.00 69.54 71.16)
4. Viktor Tsibulenko (SU)   71.72   235-4   (71.72 70.44 66.48 71.36 66.48 f)
5. Branko Dangubic (Yug)   70.54   231-5   (66.20 61.08 70.54 58.94 f   f)
6. Vladimir Kuznyetsov (SU)   70.36   230-10   (70.36 65.70 64.80 56.16 58.08 60.10)
7. Ragnar Ericzon (Swe) 69.04; 8. Soini Nikkinen (Fin) 68.80; 9. Bud Held (US) 68.42; 10. Per-Arne Berglund (Swe) 67.46; 11. Otto Bengtsson (Swe) 65.50; 12. Herbert Koschel (WG) 64.54.

1956 (21. Q-F 26 Nov): Young led the qualifiers with 74.76 (245-3), followed by Danielsen 74.14 (243-3) and Kuznyetsov 73.88 (242-5)—all over the old Olympic record. In the final, Danielsen moved from 6th to 1st with a real killer—a world record of 85.70. He was Norway's first world record holder in the event.

1. Egil Danielsen (Nor)   85.70   281-2 WR   (72.60 68.48 70.74 85.70 72.60 68.86)
2. Janusz Sidlo (Pol)   79.98   262-5   (72.78 f   79.98 79.70 75.78 73.50)
3. Viktor Tsibulenko (SU)   79.50   260-10   (74.96 75.84 71.74 79.50 72.98 63.24)
4. Herbert Koschel (Ger)   74.68   245-0   (74.68 60.80 69.88 71.66 f   61.28)
5. Jan Kopyto (Pol)   74.28   243-8   (71.82 73.32 73.08 74.28 57.20 73.26)
6. Giovanni Lievore (It)   72.88   239-1   (71.26 72.88 67.46 65.58 64.86 55.78)
7. Michel Macquet (Fr) 71.84; 8. Aleksandr Gorshkov (SU) 70.32; 9. Heiner Will (Ger) 69.86; 10. Phil Conley (US) 69.74; 11. Cy Young (US) 68.64; 12. Vladimir Kuznyetsov (SU) 67.14; 13. Sandor Krasznai (Hun) 66.32; 14. Muhammad Nawaz (Pak) 62.54;. . . nm—Benny Garcia (US).
(Danielsen 74.14 OR Q; Young 74.76 OR Q; Tsibulenko 74.96 OR, 75.84 OR; Sidlo 79.98 OR)

1960 (28. Q 7 Sept; F 8 Sept): Sidlo led the qualifiers with a great 85.14 (279-4), followed by Cantello 79.72 (261-6) and Tsibulenko 79.70 (261-6). In the final, 30-year-old Tsibulenko opened with 84.64—his best ever. Most of the favorites fell by the wayside and none was able to approach Tsibulenko's distance. In the closing rounds, adverse weather conditions made the throwing particularly difficult.

1. Viktor Tsibulenko (SU)   84.64   277-8   (84.64 76.58 76.46 f   67.72 f)
2. Walter Kruger (Ger)   79.36   260-4   (79.36 66.50 71.28 76.22 72.60 f)
3. Gergely Kulcsar (Hun)   78.56   257-9   (78.56 77.60 68.56 73.20 f   f)
4. Vaino Kuisma (Fin)   78.40   257-2   (78.40 74.08 74.44 67.74 76.38 74.68)
5. Willy Rasmussen (Nor)   78.36   257-1   (f   67.62 78.36 f   f   69.54)
6. Knut Fredriksson (Swe)   78.32   256-11   (69.70 78.32 64.28 72.52 78.00 68.50)
7. Zbigniew Radziwonowicz (Pol) 77.30; 8. Janusz Sidlo (Pol) 76.46; 9. Carlo Lievore (It) 75.20; 10. Al Cantello (US) 74.70; 11. Mart Paama (SU) 74.56; 12. Hermann Salomon (WG) 74.10;. . . dnc—Terje Pedersen (Nor).

1964 (25. Q-F 14 Oct): On a rainy day, the qualifying mark of 77.00 (252-7) really proved too difficult. In fact, only one thrower made it—von Wartburg, who achieved a PR 79.92 (262-2) on his second attempt. Eleven others were admitted to the final with marks ranging from Sidlo's

76.92 (252-4) to 72.30 (237-2). Terje Pedersen, the Norwegian world record holder at 91.72 (300-11), was a disappointing 13th with 72.10 (236-6). The final was started less than two hours later. Sidlo soon went into the lead, only to be passed by Lusis in the next round. But the real fireworks came in round 4: the bronze medalist from Rome, Kulcsar, threw 82.32, a lifetime best, but Nevala quickly replied with 82.66—good enough to earn him a gold medal and add new luster to the Finnish tradition.

1. Pauli Nevala (Fin)	82.66	271-2	(76.42	78.38	f	82.66	f	f)
2. Gergely Kulcsar (Hun)	82.32	270-1	(75.00	77.28	78.28	82.32	78.56	79.78)
3. Janis Lusis (SU)	80.56	264-4	(72.50	80.56	79.84	78.94	78.06	f)
4. Janusz Sidlo (Pol)	80.16	263-0	(80.16	f	f	f	76.96	78.16)
5. Urs von Wartburg (Switz)	78.72	258-3	(78.72	76.84	76.36	73.08	63.12	f)
6. Jorma Kinnunen (Fin)	76.94	252-5	(72.32	76.36	71.80	76.94	f	f)

7. Rolf Herings (WG) 74.72; 8. Vladimir Kuznyetsov (SU) 74.26; 9. Wladyslaw Nikiciuk (Pol) 73.10; 10. Christos Pierrakos (Gr) 72.64; 11. Ed Red (US) 71.52; 12. Hans Schenk (Ger) 69.82.

1968 (27. Q 15 Oct; F 16 Oct): The qualifying standard (80.00/262-5) again proved a bit too tough. It was mastered by 11. Top qualifier was Nilsson at 84.74 (278-0). In the opening round of the final, Kinnunen upped the OR to 86.30 (283-2), only to be surpassed by pre-meet favorite Lusis in round 2. Veteran Kulcsar managed to interfere in round 4 as he reached a new PR of 87.06 (285-7). But the closing fireworks belonged to Lusis and Kinnunen, as the Soviet threw 90.10 (295-7) on his last try, to which the Finn responded with a bold but insufficient 88.58 (290-7), a new national record.

1. Janis Lusis (SU)	90.10	295-7 OR	(81.74	86.34	82.66	84.40	f	90.10)
2. Jorma Kinnunen (Fin)	88.58	290-7	(86.30	f	f	79.00	85.82	88.58)
3. Gergely Kulcsar (Hun)	87.06	285-7	(83.10	f	83.32	87.06	85.14	83.40)
4. Wladyslaw Nikiciuk (Pol)	85.70	281-2	(f	85.70	82.24	f	82.32	80.44)
5. Manfred Stolle (EG)	84.42	277-0	(f	76.86	81.52	84.42	f	79.72)
6. Ake Nilsson (Swe)	83.48	273-11	(83.48	f	f	f	76.74	79.76)

7. Janusz Sidlo (Pol) 80.58; 8. Urs von Wartburg (Switz) 80.56; 9. Mark Murro (US) 80.08; 10. Walter Pektor (Aut) 77.40; 11. Aurelio Janet Torres (Cuba) 74.88; 12. Hermann Salomon (WG) 73.50.
(Kinnunen 86.30 OR; Lusis 86.34 OR; Kulcsar 87.06 OR)

1972 (23. Q 2 Sept; F 3 Sept): Once again, qualifying (80.00) proved too tough: only 7 made it. Main casualty was Gergely Kulcsar, a medalist in the three previous Games. Wolfermann led the qualifiers with 86.22 (282-10), followed by Lusis (82.82/271-9). In the final, Siitonen opened the parade with 84.32 (276-8), but a few minutes later Lusis got one off to 88.88. The Soviet improved in round 3, at which stage he led from the nearest competitor, Wolfermann, by almost 3 meters. The German closed the gap on his fourth try, then forged ahead with a new OR of 90.48 (296-10). The great Lusis was equal to his reputation; in the last round his 90.46 missed the Wolfermann mark by the minimum unit of measurement allowed for this event. Schmidt moved to third in round 2 with 84.42 and never relinquished that position. Siitonen, aiming for big things, fouled five times.

1. Klaus Wolfermann (WG)	90.48	296-10 OR	(86.68	85.14	f	88.40	90.48	84.70)
2. Janis Lusis (SU)	90.46	296-9	(88.88	f	89.54	f	81.66	90.46)
3. Bill Schmidt (US)	84.42	277-0	(75.96	84.42	f	79.92	84.12	f)
4. Hannu Siitonen (Fin)	84.32	276-8	(84.32	f	f	f	f	f)
5. Bjorn Grimnes (Nor)	83.08	272-7	(71.86	82.38	83.08	f	f	f)
6. Jorma Kinnunen (Fin)	82.08	269-3	(f	82.08	75.76	f	f	77.60)

7. Miklos Nemeth (Hun) 81.98; 8. Fred Luke (US) 80.06; 9. Manfred Stolle (EG) 79.32; 10. Milt Sonsky (US) 77.94; 11. Lolesio Tuita (Fr) 76.34; 12. Jozsef Csik (Hun) 76.14.

1976 (23. Q 25 July; F 26 July): Pre-meet favorite Hovinen led with 89.76 (294-6) from Nemeth (89.28) and surprising Phil Olsen, who chalked up a new World Junior Record of 87.76 (287-11). In the first round of the final, Nemeth—son of the 1948 Olympic hammer champion, Imre Nemeth—uncorked a stupendous throw, 94.58 (310-4), a new world record. That killed

the opposition. Hovinen managed no better than 84.26 (276-5) and had to be content with 7th. His countryman Siitonen was a distant second, ahead of Rumania's Megelea, who produced a PR to take the bronze. Lusis, 37, competing in his fourth Games, made it to the final rounds and wound up 8th.

1. Miklos Nemeth (Hun)	94.58	310-4 WR	(94.58	p	p	83.32	84.76	86.84)
2. Hannu Siitonen (Fin)	87.92	288-5	(87.92	f	86.58	f	f	80.92)
3. Gheorghe Megelea (Rum)	87.16	285-11	(87.16	83.16	82.92	82.10	f	f)
4. Pyotr Bielczyk (Pol)	86.50	283-9	(f	77.90	86.50	81.00	82.28	82.94)
5. Sam Colson (US)	86.16	282-8	(77.70	85.08	86.16	f	f	f)
6. Vasiliy Yershov (SU)	85.26	279-9	(85.26	f	77.06	f	78.32	82.50)

7. Seppo Hovinen (Fin) 84.26; 8. Janis Lusis (SU) 80.26; 9. Michael Wessing (WG) 79.06; 10. Terje Thorslund (Nor) 78.24; 11. Phil Olsen (Can) 77.70; 12. Amado Morales (P Rico) 75.54; 13. Bjorn Grimnes (Nor) 74.88; 14. Valentin Dzonev (Bul) 73.88; 15. Anthony Hall (US) 71.70;. . . dnc—Jorma Jaakola (Fin).

DECATHLON

1896—1908 (not contested).

(Multiple scores are given in nearly all cases, representing the score on the tables in effect at the time and on the current [1962] tables. The 1962 tables have had two minor revisions, in 1971 [automatic timing tables for 100 and 110H] and again in 1977 [auto timing for 400].

1912 (29. 13-14-15 July): The only 3-day contest in Olympic history, with three events on the first and third days. Thorpe, the American Indian who went on to be rated by some as the greatest all-around athlete ever, won by an overwhelming margin. But months later he was declared a professional for playing semi-pro baseball and his victories were forfeited. This left a grand-slam for Sweden. Avery Brundage, later president of the IOC, failed to finish. Points were calculated with reference to the existing Olympic records through 1908.

										1912 A	1962
— Jim Thorpe (US) (disqualified)										8412 WR	6756
(11.2	6.79	12.89	1.87	52.2	15.6	36.98	3.25	45.70	4:40.1)		
1. Hugo Wieslander (Swe)										7724	6161
(11.8	6.42	12.14	1.75	53.6	17.2	36.28	3.10	50.40	4:45.0)		
2. Charles Lomberg (Swe)										7413	5943
(11.8	6.87	11.67	1.80	55.0	17.6	35.34	3.25	41.82	5:12.2)		
3. Gosta Holmer (Swe)										7347	5956
(11.4	5.98	10.98	1.70	53.2	17.0	31.78	3.20	46.28	4:41.9)		
4. James Donahue (US)										7083	5836
(11.8	6.48	9.67	1.65	51.6	16.2	29.94	3.40	37.08	4:44.0)		
5. Eugene Mercer (US)										7074	5927
(11.0	6.84	9.76	1.65	49.9	16.4	21.94	3.60	32.32	4:46.3)		
6. Woldemar Wickholm (Fin)										7058	5778
(11.5	5.95	11.09	1.60	52.3	17.0	29.78	3.25	42.58	4:43.9)		

7. E. Kugelberg (Swe) 6758/5499; 8. K. von Halt (Ger) 6682/5269; 9. J. Schafer (Aut) 6568/5458; 10. A. Schulz (Russia) 6134/5094.

1920 (23. 20-21 Aug): Lovland won in the last event, passing Hamilton (who was to become one of America's most famous coaches and head of the 1952 Olympic team). Fourth-placer Holmer also became a world-renowned coach while Alek sander Klumberg of Estonia, the world record breaker in 1922, dropped out after eight events. Points were awarded with reference to the 1912 Olympic records.

									1912 B	1962
1. Helge Lovland (Nor)									6804	5970
(12.0	6.28	11.19	1.65	54.8	16.2	37.34	3.20	48.06	4:48.4)	
2. Brutus Hamilton (US)									6770	5912
(11.4	6.32	11.61	1.60	55.0	17.3	36.14	3.20	48.08	4:57.8)	
3. Bertill Olsson (Swe)									6579	5825
(12.0	6.43	11.07	1.65	55.0	17.0	37.78	3.30	39.88	4:50.6)	
4. Gosta Holmer (Swe)									6533	5740
(11.8	5.92	11.06	1.70	56.5	16.6	34.82	3.20	47.62	5:01.6)	
5. Evert Nilsson (Swe)									6434	5624
(12.2	5.67	11.39	1.75	55.7	20.0	34.76	3.40	49.28	4:45.6)	
6. Woldemar Wickholm (Fin)									6406	5806
(11.6	6.12	11.44	1.60	52.4	16.8	32.30	3.00	42.76	4:45.6)	

7. Gene Vidal (US) 6359/5673; 8. E. Gyllenstolpe (Swe) 6332/5653; 9. Ernst Gerspach (Switz) 5948/5263; 10. Harry Goelitz (US) 5324/5065.

1924 (36. 11-12 July): Osborn was an easy winner, setting a new world record and becoming the only man ever to win an individual event and the decathlon as he won the high jump on 7 July. He set the world high jump record in May at 2.03.

									1912B	1962
1. Harold Osborn (US)									7710 WR	6668 WR
(11.2	6.92	11.45	1.97	53.2	16.0	34.50	3.50	46.68	4:50.0)	
2. Emerson Norton (US)									7350	6340
(11.6	6.92	13.04	1.92	53.0	16.6	33.12	3.80	42.08	5:38.0)	
3. Aleksander Klumberg (Estonia)									7329	6260
(11.6	6.96	12.27	1.75	54.4	17.6	36.78	3.30	57.70	5:16.0)	
4. Anton Huusari (Fin)									7005	6119
(12.0	6.16	12.02	1.70	53.4	16.6	33.14	3.20	53.64	4:37.2)	
5. Edward Sutherland (S Afr)									6794	5943
(11.6	6.67	10.86	1.80	56.0	16.6	39.82	3.30	51.00	5:19.0)	
6. Ernst Gerspach (Switz)									6743	5959
(11.4	6.46	10.35	1.70	53.4	16.8	33.90	3.40	44.82	5:08.2)	

7. Helge Jansson (Swe) 6656/5861; 8. Harry Frieda (US) 6618/5754; 9. Paavo Yrjola (Fin) 6548/5742; 10. H.J. M. de Keyser (Hol) 6509/5702.

1928 (38. 3-4 Aug): Finland won the gold and silver with Yrjola improving on his own world record. Jarvinen, who was to set the WR in 1930, was the older brother of Matti Jarvinen, 10-time javelin record breaker. Leading the American contingent was Doherty, another famous coach-to-be and a future prolific technical writer.

									1912B	1962
1. Paavo Yrjola (Fin)									8053 WR	6774
(11.8	6.72	14.11	1.87	53.2	16.6	42.08	3.30	55.70	4:44.0)	
2. Akilles Jarvinen (Fin)									7931	6815 WR
(11.2	6.87	13.64	1.75	51.4	15.6	36.94	3.30	55.58	4:52.4)	
3. Ken Doherty (US)									7706	6593
(11.6	6.61	11.85	1.80	52.0	15.8	38.72	3.30	56.56	4:54.0)	
4. James Stuart (US)									7624	6530
(11.2	6.61	13.04	1.87	52.8	16.6	40.90	3.30	48.06	5:17.0)	
5. Thomas Churchill (US)									7417	6364
(11.6	6.32	12.28	1.70	52.2	16.8	38.18	3.60	50.92	4:55.0)	
6. Helge Jansson (Swe)									7286	6434
(11.4	6.85	13.59	1.87	53.2	16.6	36.82	3.30	41.72	5:27.0)	

7. L. Vesely (Aut) 7274/6393; 8. Albert Andersson (Swe) 7109/6211; 9. H. Lindblad (Swe) 7071/6106; 10. W. Ladewig (Ger) 6881/6131.

1932 (14. 5-6 Aug): Only 5th at the end of the first day, Bausch relied on his strong

throwing and vaulting to pile up a world record total. Jarvinen was again 2nd with Sievert, soon to be a two-time world record breaker, 5th. For the first time, the winner's marks were superior to Thorpe's.

										1912B	1962
1.	Jim Bausch (US)									8462 WR	6896
	(11.7	6.95	15.32	1.70	54.2	16.2	44.58	4.00	61.90	5:17.0)	
2.	Akilles Jarvinen (Fin)									8292	7038 WR
	(11.1	7.00	13.11	1.75	50.6	15.7	36.80	3.60	61.00	4:47.0)	
3.	Wolrad Eberle (Ger)									8030	6830
	(11.4	6.77	13.22	1.65	50.8	16.7	41.34	3.50	57.48	4:34.4)	
4.	Wilson Charles (US)									7985	6901
	(11.2	7.24	12.56	1.85	51.2	16.2	38.70	3.40	47.72	4:39.8)	
5.	Hans-Heinrich Sievert (Ger)									7941	6699
	(11.4	6.97	14.50	1.78	53.6	16.1	44.54	3.20	53.90	5:18.0)	
6.	Paavo Yrjola (Fin)									7688	6566
	(11.8	6.59	13.68	1.75	52.6	17.0	40.76	3.10	56.12	4:37.4)	

7. Clyde Coffman (US) 7534/6480; 8. Bob Tisdall (Eire) 7327/6557; 9. E. Wegner (Ger) 7179/6331; 10. P. Bacsalmasi (Hun) 7001/6011; 11. H. Hart (S Afr) 6799/5891;. . . dnf—H. Berra (Arg), Janis Dimza (Lat), Z. Siedlecki (Pol).

1936 (28. 7-8 Aug): For the fourth straight time the world record was broken. Morris led an American sweep in his third and last decathlon, topping a 1-year career which saw him break the American record in his first try and the world mark in his next two efforts. All the leading contestants scored personal bests and a new set of tables was used.

										1934	1962
1.	Glenn Morris (US)									7900 WR	7421
	(11.1	6.97	14.10	1.85	49.4	14.9	43.02	3.50	54.52	4:33.2)	
2.	Bob Clark (US)									7601	7226
	(10.9	7.62	12.68	1.80	50.0	15.7	39.38	3.70	51.12	4:44.4)	
3.	Jack Parker (US)									7275	6918
	(11.4	7.35	13.52	1.80	53.3	15.0	39.10	3.50	56.46	5:07.8)	
4.	Erwin Huber (Ger)									7087	6811
	(11.5	6.89	12.70	1.70	52.3	15.8	35.46	3.80	56.44	4:35.2)	
5.	Reindert Brasser (Hol)									7046	6758
	(11.6	6.69	13.49	1.90	51.5	16.2	39.44	3.40	55.74	5:06.0)	
6.	Armin Guhl (Switz)									7033	6790
	(11.3	7.04	12.30	1.80	52.3	15.6	40.96	3.30	51.02	4:49.2)	

7. Olle Bexell (Swe) 7024/6743; 8. H. Bonnet (Ger) 6939/6672; 9. Jerzy Plawczyk (Pol) 6871/6637; 10. E. Natvig (Hun) 6759/6490; 11. A. Reinikka (Fin) 6755/6528; 12. P. Bacsalmasi (Hun) 6395/6206; 13. F. Dallenbach (Switz) 6311/6206; 14. L. Doichev (Bul) 6307/6157; 15. Wenzel (Chile) 6058/5999.

1948 (35. 5-6 Aug): Mathias, only 17-years-old, overcame rain, darkness, a long-drawn-out schedule and his own inexperience to score a dramatic, long-remembered win. Post World War II marks were considerably poorer than in the 1936 Games.

										1934	1962
1.	Bob Mathias (US)									7139	6825
	(11.2	6.61	13.04	1.86	51.7	15.7	44.00	3.50	50.32	5:11.0)	
2.	Ignace Heinrich (Fr)									6974	6740
	(11.3	6.89	12.85	1.86	51.6	15.6	40.94	3.20	40.98	4:43.8)	
3.	Floyd Simmons (US)									6950	6711
	(11.2	6.72	12.80	1.86	51.9	15.2	32.72	3.40	51.98	4:58.0)	
4.	Enrique Kistenmacher (Arg)									6929	6726
	(10.9	7.08	12.67	1.70	50.5	16.3	41.10	3.20	45.06	4:49.6)	
5.	Erik Peter Andersson (Swe)									6877	6669
	(11.6	6.59	12.66	1.75	52.0	15.9	36.06	3.60	51.04	4:34.0)	
6.	Peter Mullins (Aus)									6739	6527
	(11.2	6.64	12.75	1.83	53.2	15.2	33.94	3.40	51.32	5:17.6)	

7. Per Eriksson (Swe) 6731/6552; 8. Irv Mondschein (US) 6715/6538; 9. Edward Adamczyk (Pol) 6712/6514; 10. Godtfred Holmvang (Nor) 6663/6492; 11. P. Stavem (Nor) 6552/6348; 12. Orn Clausen (Ice) 6444/6355.

1952 (28. 25-26 July): Now a mature veteran, although only 21, Mathias made a shambles of the opposition, winning by 912 points, by far the greatest margin of all Olympics, then and now. He became the only two-time winner of the event as he scored the third universal record of his career. It was an American sweep. Still another scoring table was introduced.

										1952	*1962*
1.	Bob Mathias (US)									7887 WR	7731 WR
	(10.9	6.98	15.30	1.90	50.2	14.7	46.88	4.00	59.20	4:50.8)	
2.	Milt Campbell (US)									6975	7132
	(10.7	6.74	13.89	1.85	50.9	14.5	40.50	3.30	54.54	5:07.2)	
3.	Floyd Simmons (US)									6788	7069
	(11.5	7.06	13.18	1.92	51.1	15.0	37.76	3.60	54.68	4:53.4)	
4.	Vladimir Volkov (SU)									6674	7030
	(11.4	7.09	12.62	1.75	51.2	15.8	38.04	3.80	56.68	4:33.2)	
5.	Sepp Hipp (WG)									6449	6882
	(11.4	6.85	13.26	1.75	51.3	16.1	45.84	3.50	54.14	4:57.2)	
6.	Goran Widenfelt (Swe)									6388	6850
	(11.4	6.76	11.61	1.94	51.3	16.1	39.52	3.50	49.38	4:38.6)	

7. Kjell Tannander (Swe) 6308/6797; 8. Friedel Schirmer (WG) 6118/6647; 9. Geoff Elliott (GB) 6044/6542; 10. Sergey Kuznyetsov (SU) 5937/6523; 11. H. Frayer (Fr) 5772/6335; 12. B. Iriarte (Ven) 5770/6400. 21 finishers.

1956 (15. 29-30 Nov): Johnson, the world record holder and early favorite, began competition with a bad knee and added a pulled stomach muscle. But even in top condition he would have had his hands full with Campbell, 2nd-placer in 1952, who scored the second-highest total ever.

										1952	*1962*
1.	Milt Campbell (US)									7937 OR	7708
	(10.8	7.33	14.76	1.89	48.8	14.0	44.98	3.40	57.08	4:50.6)	
2.	Rafer Johnson (US)									7587	7568
	(10.9	7.34	14.48	1.83	49.3	15.1	42.16	3.90	60.26	4:54.2)	
3.	Vasiliy Kuznyetsov (SU)									7465	7461
	(11.2	7.04	14.49	1.75	50.2	14.9	44.32	3.95	65.12	4:53.8)	
4.	Uno Palu (SU)									6930	7186
	(11.5	6.65	13.39	1.89	50.8	15.4	40.38	3.60	61.58	4:35.6)	
5.	Martin Lauer (WG)									6853	7072
	(11.1	6.83	12.86	1.83	48.2	14.7	39.38	3.10	50.66	4:43.8)	
6.	Walter Meier (EG)									6773	7111
	(11.3	6.80	12.99	1.86	49.3	16.1	37.58	3.70	47.98	4:20.6)	

7. Torbjorn Lassenius (Fin) 6565/6938; 8. C.K. Yang (Tai) 6521/6850; 9. Pat Leane (Aus) 6427/6884; 10. John Cann (Aus) 6278/6678; 11. Ian Bruce (Aus) 6025/6589; 12. Reze Farabi (Iran) 5103/5887; 13. Bob Richards (US) 5781/6090. (9 events). 12 finishers.

1960 (30. 5-6 Sept): Johnson, who set his third world mark in the Olympic Trials, was not figured to have an easy time with Kuznyetsov, two-time record breaker, or Yang. The former was injured and finished a weak 3rd. But Yang battled his college teammate to the final tape, smashing the Olympic record but trailing by 58 points.

										1952	*1962*
1.	Rafer Johnson (US)									8392 OR	8001
	(10.9	7.35	15.82	1.85	48.3	15.3	48.48	4.10	69.76	4:49.7)	
2.	Chuan-Kwang Yang (Taiwan)									8334	7930
	(10.7	7.46	13.33	1.90	48.1	14.6	39.82	4.30	68.22	4:48.5)	
3.	Vasiliy Kuznyetsov (SU)									7809	7624
	(11.1	6.96	14.46	1.75	50.2	15.0	50.52	3.90	71.20	4:53.8)	

4. Yuriy Kutyenko (SU) 7567 7513
(11.4 6.93 13.97 1.80 51.1 15.6 45.62 4.20 71.44 4:44.2)
5. Evert Kamerbeek (Hol) 7236 7361
(11.3 7.21 13.76 1.80 51.1 14.9 44.30 3.80 57.48 4:43.6)
6. Franco Sar (Italy) 7195 7291
(11.4 6.69 13.89 1.80 51.3 14.7 49.58 3.80 55.74 4:49.2)

7. Markus Kahma (Fin) 7112/7316; 8. Klaus Grogorenz (EG) 7032/7265; 9. Joze Brodnik (Yug) 6918/7140; 10. Manfred Bock (WG) 6894/7165; 11. Fritz Vogelsang (Switz) 6767/7040; 12. Seppo Suutari (Fin) 6751/7053. 23 finishers.

1964 (22. 19-20 Oct): Yang, runner-up last time and current record holder, was not in the best of shape and his chances were further lessened by the last-minute adoption of new scoring tables which hurt him more than it did others. He finished 5th as the four ahead of him were within 100 points of each other. Holdorf led from the fifth event although the final result was always in doubt.

											1962
1. Willi Holdorf (WG)											7887
(10.7	7.00	14.95	1.84	48.2	15.0	46.04	4.20	57.36	4:34.3)		
2. Rein Aun (SU)											7842
(10.9	7.22	13.82	1.93	48.8	15.9	44.18	4.20	59.06	4:22.3)		
3. Hans-Joachim Walde (WG)											7809
(11.0	7.21	14.45	1.96	49.5	15.3	43.14	4.10	62.90	4:37.0)		
4. Paul Herman (US)											7787
(11.2	6.97	13.89	1.87	49.2	15.2	44.14	4.35	63.34	4:25.4)		
5. Chuan-Kwang Yang (Taiwan)											7650
(11.0	6.80	13.23	1.81	49.0	14.7	39.58	4.60	68.14	4:48.4)		
6. Horst Beyer (WG)											7647
(11.2	7.02	14.32	1.90	49.8	15.2	45.16	3.80	58.16	4:23.6)		

7. Vasiliy Kuznyetsov (SU) 7569; 8. Mikhail Storozhenko (SU) 7464; 9. Russ Hodge (US) 7325; 10. Dick Emberger (US) 7292; 11. Bill Gairdner (Can) 7147; 12. Valbjorn Thorlaksson (Ice) 7135. 18 finishers.

1968 (33. 18-19 Oct): Toomey enjoyed a 115-point margin at the end of the first day, 4499-4384 over Kirst. He had scored heavily in the sprints and long jump, his strongest areas and those most aided by Mexico's altitude. He sprinted 10.4, leaped 7.87 (25-9¾), surrendered the lead to Kirst after the shot but rolled to an impressive 45.6 400 to take back first place for good. The West German duo of Walde-Bendlin was always in the top six with '64 bronze winner Walde in the top three up to the 1500. Toomey almost came to grief in the vault when he needed three jumps to clear his 3.60 (11-9¾) opening height. World record holder Bendlin was hampered by an injured elbow which held him back in the javelin, one of his strongest events. His best throw doubled him over in pain. The 1500 not only finalized Toomey's win but also determined places 2-5.

1. Bill Toomey (US)										8193 OR
(10.4	7.87	13.75	1.95	45.6	14.9	43.68	4.20	62.80	4:57.1)	
2. Hans-Joachim Walde (WG)										8111
(10.9	7.64	15.13	2.01	49.0	14.8	43.54	4.30	71.62	4:58.5)	
3. Kurt Bendlin (WG)										8064
(10.7	7.56	14.74	1.80	48.3	15.0	46.78	4.60	75.42	5:09.8)	
4. Nikolay Avilov (SU)										7909
(10.9	7.64	13.41	2.07	49.9	14.5	46.64	4.10	60.12	5:00.8)	
5. Joachim Kirst (EG)										7861
(10.5	7.61	16.43	1.98	50.2	15.6	46.88	4.15	57.02	5:20.1)	
6. Tom Waddell (US)										7720
(11.3	7.47	14.45	2.01	51.2	15.3	43.72	4.50	63.70	5:04.5)	

7. Rick Sloan (US) 7692; 8. Steen Smidt-Jensen (Den) 7648; 9. Eduard De Noorlander (Hol) 7554; 10. Manfred Tiedtke (EG) 7551; 11. Lennart Hedmark (Swe) 7481; 12. Walter Diessl (Aut) 7465. 20 finishers.

1972 (33. 7-8 Sept): The hurdles decided a lot of things: Avilov ran the fastest time and took a lead which he never relinquished en route to a world record 8454; contenders Kirst (who led the first day), Skowronek and Bannister all fell to end their chances; Litvinyenko and Katus started their surges toward medals. Avilov was hot both days, scoring personal bests in 7 events and matching another in totalling the best second-day score ever (4109). The battle for the places behind Avilov was tight and tense, the 1500 deciding it as Litvinyenko jumped from 8th to 2nd thanks to his quick 4:05.9. Bennett ran in the first 1500 heat and was just edged for 3rd. Herbrandt won the tie for 6th by winning 6 events to Smidt-Jensen's 4. The first to congratulate Avilov following the 1500 was deposed Olympic champ and recordman Bill Toomey, in Munich as a television announcer.

								1962	*1971*	*1977*
1. Nikolay Avilov (SU)								8454	8454 WR	8456
(11.00	7.68	14.36	2.12	48.45	14.31	46.98	4.55	61.66	4:22.8)	
2. Leonid Litvinyenko (SU)								8045	8035	8034
(11.13	6.81	14.18	1.89	48.40	15.03	47.84	4.40	58.94	4:05.9)	
3. Ryszard Katus (Poland)								7981	7984	7983
(10.89	7.09	14.39	1.92	49.11	14.41	43.00	4.50	59.96	4:31.9)	
4. Jeff Bennett (US)								7979	7974	7977
(10.73	7.26	12.82	1.86	46.25	15.58	36.58	4.80	57.48	4:12.2)	
5. Stefan Schreyer (EG)								7954	7950	7948
(10.82	7.44	15.02	1.92	49.51	15.00	45.08	4.40	60.70	4:48.2)	
6. Freddy Herbrand (Bel)								7944	7947	7948
(11.00	7.30	13.91	2.04	49.78	14.87	47.12	4.40	50.42	4:27.7)	

7. Steen Smidt-Jensen (Den) 7947; 8. Tadeusz Janczenko (Pol) 7861; 9. Sepp Zeilbauer (Aut) 7741; 10. Bruce Jenner (US) 7722; 11. Regis Ghesquiere (Bel) 7677; 12. Yves Leroy (Fr) 7675. 21 finishers.

1976 (28. 29-30 July): Jenner totaled an impressive world record 8618, setting four personal bests and equaling two along the way. Even though he had set a world mark in the US Trials, Jenner felt he would be around 6th or 7th at the end of the first day. But he stood 3rd (4298) behind young Kratschmer (4333) and defending champ Avilov (4315) and with Jenner's extraordinary strength in the second five events, the outcome was a foregone conclusion. He didn't take the lead until the vault, but he pulled away from there and even finished with a career-low in the 1500 to bow out with the gold and record. Kratschmer and Avilov were valiant in defeat, while Pihl was a surprise. Only Jenner, Kratschmer, and Pihl set personal best totals. Litvinyenko (7th) and Katus (12th) were well off their medal-winning showings in Munich; Dixon, a pre-meet medal favorite, nearly fell in the hurdles and then no-heighted in the vault. Jenner, who had prepared so thoroughly and confidently both mentally and physically, retired immediately after the competition.

								1962	*1971*	*1977*
1. Bruce Jenner (US)								8631	8618 WR	8617
(10.94	7.22	15.35	2.03	47.51	14.84	50.04	4.80	68.52	4:12.6)	
2. Guido Kratschmer (WG)								8397	8411	8411
(10.66	7.39	14.74	2.03	48.19	14.58	45.70	4.60	66.32	4:29.1)	
3. Nikolay Avilov (SU)								8375	8369	8371
(11.23	7.52	14.81	2.14	48.16	14.20	45.60	4.45	62.28	4:26.3)	
4. Raimo Pihl (Swe)								8224	8218	8220
(10.93	6.99	15.55	2.00	47.97	15.81	44.30	4.40	77.34	4:28.8)	
5. Ryszard Skowronek (Pol)								8112	8113	8113
(11.02	7.26	13.74	1.91	47.91	14.75	45.34	4.80	62.22	4:29.9)	
6. Siegfried Stark (EG)								8032	8048	8045
(11.35	6.98	15.08	1.91	49.14	15.65	45.48	4.65	74.18	4:24.9)	

7. Leonid Litvinyenko (SU) 8025; 8. Lennart Hedmark (Swe) 7974; 9. Aleksandr Grebenyuk (SU) 7803; 10. Claus Marek (WG) 7767; 11. Johannes Lahti (Fin) 7711; 12. Ryszard Katus (Pol) 7616. 23 finishers.

Above left, James B. Connolly, American triple jumper 1896, first modern Olympic champion. Above right, Ray Ewry, who garnered 8 gold medals in jumping events, 1900-1908. Below left, Hannes Kolehmainen, star of the 1912 Olympics, heralding Finnish domination of the distance events until World War II. Below right, one of the Games' most famous occurrences, the illegal assistance given marathoner Dorando Pietri, 1908, leading to his disqualification.

Above left, Wilma Rudolph, triple gold medalist 1960. Above right, Fanny Blankers-Koen, 1948 quadruple gold medalist. Below, Betty Cuthbert (right), seen anchoring 4x100 win for Australia in 1956. Cuthbert won three gold medals at Melbourne, and eight years later added another in the Tokyo 400.

Above left, Harrison Dillard, 1948 100 and 1952 110H champion. Above right, Vladimir Kuts, hero of the '56 Games (5000-10,000 victor). Below left, Rafer Johnson, 1960 decathlon gold medalist. Below right, Abebe Bikila, only marathon repeat winner (1960-1964).

Ed Lacey

Bob Beamon's winning long jump at Mexico City, 1968, considered by many the greatest single performance in the history of track and field.

Don Wilkinson

Don Chadez

1500 champions, and then some: above left, Kip Keino, 1968 1500 winner and 1972 steeplechase champion (plus a silver medal in both Games); above right, Herb Elliott, whose 1960 1500 smashed the world record; right, Tatyana Kazankina, 1976 800-1500 doubler.

Double winners: above left, Alberto Juantorena, 1976 400-800 champion; Lasse Viren, 5000-10,000 winner in both 1972 and 1976; and Valeriy Borzov, 1972 100-200 champion.

Women's Results

Women's results are presented in exactly the same format as the men's. In the case of women who appeared in Olympic results under both a maiden and married name, we have carried them only with their married name. However, we have asterisked (*) them where they were competing under their maiden name (e.g., in the 100, Shirley de la Hunty is presented without an asterisk in 1952, when she was married, but with an asterisk in 1948, when she was Shirley Strickland). A compilation of maiden names appears at the end of the women's results section.

No women's events were contested in the Olympics until the 1928 Games.

100 METERS

1896–1924 (not contested).

1928 (31. H-SF 30 July; F 31 July): Robinson, who had lowered the best on record to 12.0 nearly 2 months before, became the first woman to win an Olympic track medal as she lowered the OR by 0.2. Only 16, she was nicknamed "Babe."

1. Elizabeth Robinson (US)	12.2	4. Erna Steinberg (Ger)	12.4
2. Fanny Rosenfeld (Can)	12.3	— Myrtle Cook (Can)	disq
3. Ethel Smith (Can)	12.3	— Leni Schmidt (Ger)	disq

(Anni Holdmann [Ger] 13.0 OR, H; Steinberg 12.8 OR, H; Kinue Hitomi [Jap] 12.8 =OR, H; Leni Junker [Ger] 12.8 =OR, H; Schmidt 12.8 =OR H; Rosenfeld 12.6 OR, H; Smith 12.6 =OR, H; Rosenfeld 12.4 OR, SF; Robinson 12.4 =OR, SF)

1932 (20. F 2 Aug): The winner, a U.S. resident whose real name was Stanislawa Walasiewiczowna, equalled the World Record in all 3 rounds, with Strike matching her in the final.

1. Stella Walsh (Pol)	11.9 =WR	4. Maria Dollinger (Ger)	12.2
2. Hilde Strike (Can)	11.9 =WR	5. Eileen Hiscock (GB)	12.3
3. Wilhelmina Von Bremen (US)	12.0	6. Elizabeth Wilde (US)	

(Dollinger 12.2 =OR H; Walsh 11.9 OR, =WR, H-SF)

1936 (30. H-SF 3 Aug; F 4 Aug): Defending champ Walsh found herself matched against Stephens, who had beaten her in the AAU meet the previous year. Stephens, who never lost a race in her career, scored an easy win in 11.5 (wind-aided).

1. Helen Stephens (US)	11.5w	4. Maria Dollinger (Ger)	12.0
2. Stella Walsh (Pol)	11.7	5. Annette Rogers (US)	12.2
3. Kathe Krauss (Ger)	11.9	6. Emmi Albus (Ger)	12.3

(Stephens 11.4w H)

1948 (38. H 31 July; SF-F 2 Aug): Blankers-Koen began her fabled quadruple by scoring a huge 0.3 margin of victory in equalling the OR.

1. Fanny Blankers-Koen (Hol)	11.9=OR	4. Viola Myers (Can)	
2. Dorothy Manley (GB)	12.2	5. Patricia Jones (Can)	
3. Shirley de la Hunty* (Aus)	12.2	6. Cynthia Thompson (Jam)	

1952 (56. H-QF 21 July; SF-F 22 July): Jackson, the meet's outstanding woman performer, quickly chopped 0.3 off the OR in her heat (11.6), then matched that in the semi. She was untouchable in the final, equalling the WR (11.5) in winning by a wide margin.

1.	Marjorie Jackson (Aus)	11.5 (11.65) =WR	4.	Winsome Cripps (Aus)	11.9 (12.15)
2.	Daphne Hasenjager (SAfr)	11.8 (12.04)	5.	Maria Sander (WG)	12.0 (12.26)
3.	Shirley de la Hunty (Aus)	11.9 (12.10)	6.	Mae Faggs (US)	12.1 (12.26)

(Catherine Hardy US 11.9 =OR, H; Jackson 11.6 OR, H-SF)

1956 (34. H-SF 24 Nov; F 26 Nov): For the second Games in a row, an Australian sprinter was the outstanding performer. The young (18) Cuthbert lowered the OR to 11.4 in her heat, then took the final in 11.5. (Note that the automatic timer halved her winning margin over hand timing.)

1.	Betty Cuthbert (Aus)	11.5 (11.82)	4.	Isabelle Daniels (US)	11.8 (11.98)
2.	Christa Stubnick (EG)	11.7 (11.92)	5.	Giuseppina Leone (It)	11.9 (12.07)
3.	Marlene Matthews (Aus)	11.7 (11.94)	6.	Heather Armitage (GB)	12.0 (12.10)

(Matthews 11.5 OR, H; Cuthbert 11.4 OR, H)

1960 (31. H-QF 1 Sept; SF-F 2 Sept): Rudolph showed her clear superiority in every round, matching the 11.3 world record in her semi. Defending champ Cuthbert was eliminated in the second round. After 30m of the final, Rudolph accelerated away to an easy win, her 11.0 being barely wind-aided.

1.	Wilma Rudolph (US)	11.0 (11.18)	4.	Mariya Itkina (SU)	11.4 (11.54)
2.	Dorothy Hyman (GB)	11.3 (11.43)	5.	Catherine Capdeville (Fr)	11.5 (11.64)
3.	Giuseppina Leone (It)	11.3 (11.48)	6.	Jennifer Smart (Aus)	11.6 (11.72)

(Rudolph 11.3 OR =WR, SF)

1964 (44. H-QF 15 Oct; SF-F 16 Oct): Tyus matched the WR of 11.2 in the quarter-finals before surging the next day to the championships in 11.4 ahead of teammate McGuire, up to then the more renowned of the two. And the U.S. nearly made it a sweep as White was just edged for 3rd by Klobukowska (both 11.6).

1.	Wyomia Tyus (US)	11.4	4.	Marilyn White (US)	11.6
2.	Edith McGuire (US)	11.6	5.	Miguelina Cobian (Cuba)	11.7
3.	Ewa Klobukowska (Pol)	11.6	6.	Marilyn Black (Aus)	11.7

7. Halina Gorecka (Pol) 11.8; 8. Dorothy Hyman (GB) 11.9.
(Tyus 11.2 OR =WR, QF)

1968 (41. H-QF 14 Oct; SF-F 15 Oct): Tyus was an undisputed leader, winning every round before taking the final in a record 11.0 (11.08). Ferrell excelled herself to take 2nd from the fast-closing Szewinska.

1.	Wyomia Tyus (US)	11.0 (11.08) WR	4.	Raelene Boyle (Aus)	11.1 (11.19)
2.	Barbara Ferrell (US)	11.1 (11.15)	5.	Margaret Bailes (US)	11.3
3.	Irena Szewinska (Pol)	11.1 (11.19)	6.	Dianne Burge (Aus)	11.4

7. Chi Cheng (Tai) 11.5; 8. Miguelina Cobian (Cuba) 11.6.
(Tyus 11.2 =OR, H; Bailes 11.2 =OR, H; Ferrell 11.2 =OR, H; Szewinska 11.1 OR =WR, QF; Tyus 11.0w QF)

1972 (47. H-QF 1 Sept; SF-F 2 Sept): The only real contest was for the non-winning spots as Stecher proved to be head and shoulders above the rest with her world record 11.07. The East German star asserted herself after the first few meters and was never headed.

1.	Renate Stecher (EG)	11.07 WR	4.	Iris Davis (US)	11.32
2.	Raelene Boyle (Aus)	11.23	5.	Annegret Richter (WG)	11.38
3.	Silvia Chivas (Cuba)	11.24	6.	Alice Annum (Gha)	11.41

7. Barbara Ferrell (US) 11.45; 8. Eva Gleskova (Czech) 11.48.

1976 (39. H-QF 24 July; SF-F 25 July): Overshadowed by teammate Helten early in the year, Munich 5th-placer Richter was indomitable at Montreal. She recorded 3 of the top 8 times ever

(and 2 of 3), highlighted by a WR 11.01 in her semi. Even with Helten and defending champ Stecher at the halfway mark, Richter pulled away in the second 50 to record a narrow victory. US champ Brenda Morehead strained a hamstring in her semi.

1. Annegret Richter (WG)	11.08	4. Raelene Boyle (Aus)	11.23
2. Renate Stecher (EG)	11.13	5. Evelyn Ashford (US)	11.24
3. Inge Helten (WG)	11.17	6. Chandra Cheeseborough (US)	11.31

    7. Andrea Lynch (GB) 11.32; 8. Marlies Oelsner (EG) 11.34.
(Richter 11.05 OR, QF; Richter 11.01 OR, WR, SF)

200 METERS

1896—1936 (not contested).

1948 (33. H-SF 5 Aug; F 6 Aug): Blankers-Koen won the third of her individual medals by the largest margin ever recorded in this event in the Games—0.7. Her 24.4 was a 10th off the OR she had set in the semis.

1. Fanny Blankers-Koen (Hol)	24.4	4. Shirley de la Hunty* (Aus)	
2. Audrey Williamson (GB)	25.1	5. Margaret Walker (GB)	
3. Audrey Patterson (US)	25.2	6. Daphne Hasenjager* (S Afr)	

(Blankers-Koen 25.7 OR, H; Cynthia Thompson [Jam] 25.6 OR, H; Hasenjager* 25.3 OR, H; Blankers-Koen 24.3 OR, SF)

1952 (38. H-SF 25 July; F 26 July): Improved standards found the first 4 finishing inside Blankers-Koen's winning time of 4 years earlier. The winner, Jackson (23.7), did her best running the prelims, equalling the WR (23.6) in her heat and lowering it to 23.4 in the semis.

1. Marjorie Jackson (Aus)	23.7 (23.89)	4. Winsome Cripps (Aus)	24.2 (24.41)
2. Bertha Brouwer (Hol)	24.2 (24.25)	5. Helga Klein (WG)	24.6 (24.71)
3. Nadyezhda Khnykina (SU) 24.2 (24.37)		6. Daphne Hasenjager (SAf)) 24.6 (24.72)	

(Khnykina 24.3 =OR, H; Jackson 23.6 OR =WR H; Jackson 23.4 OR WR, SF)

1956 (27. H-SF 29 Nov; F 30 Nov): For the only time in Olympic history (men or women), all the sprint medals went to the same trio (in the same order). Cuthbert, who equalled the OR with her 23.4, had 0.3 on Stubnick this time (against 0.2 in the 100), while Stubnick added a 10th to her margin over Matthews.

1. Betty Cuthbert (Aus)	23.4 (23.55) =OR	4. Norma Croker (Aus)	24.0 (24.22)
2. Christa Stubnick (EG)	23.7 (23.89)	5. June Paul-Foulds (GB)	24.3 (24.30)
3. Marlene Matthews (Aus)	23.8 (24.10)	6. Gisela Kohler (EG)	24.3 (24.68)

1960 (29. H 3 Sept; SF-F 5 Sept): Rudolph's dominance was even greater here than the 100. She set an OR 23.2 in her heat (next fastest qualifiers were 0.5 slower), was fastest by 0.3 in the semis and was unchallenged in the final. Long-legged Heine collared Hyman in the final 30m to take the silver.

1. Wilma Rudolph (US)	24.0 (24.13)	4. Mariya Itkina (SU)	24.7 (24.85)
2. Jutta Heine (WG)	24.4 (24.58)	5. Barbara Sobotta* (Pol)	24.8 (24.96)
3. Dorothy Hyman (GB)	24.7 (24.82)	6. Giuseppina Leone (It)	24.9 (25.00)

(Rudolph 23.2 OR, H)

1964 (29. H-SF 18 Oct; F 19 Oct): McGuire made good on her rating as favorite, setting an OR of 23.0 to take the gold. She won by a foot from rising Polish star Szewinska and surprise Aussie Black.

1. Edith McGuire (US)	23.0 OR	4. Una Morris (Jam)		23.5
2. Irena Szewinska* (Pol)	23.1	5. Lyudmila Samotyesova (SU)		23.5
3. Marilyn Black (Aus)	23.1	6. Barbara Sobotta (Pol)		23.9

7. Janet Simpson (GB) 23.9; 8. Daphne Arden (GB) 24.0.

1968 (36. H-SF 17 Oct; F 18 Oct): Szewinska steamrolled through the turn en route to a World Record 22.5, while young revelations Boyle and Lamy turned back Ferrell. Tyus ran hard early but faded to 6th.

1. Irena Szewinska (Pol)	22.5 (22.58) WR	4. Barbara Ferrell (US)	22.9 (22.92)
2. Raelene Boyle (Aus)	22.7 (22.73)	5. Nicole Montandon (Fr)	23.0 (23.08)
3. Jennifer Lamy (Aus)	22.8 (22.88)	6. Wyomia Tyus (US)	23.0 (23.08)

7. Margaret Bailes (US) 23.1 (23.18); 8. Jutta Stock (WG) 23.2 (23.24).
(Boyle 23.0 =OR, H; Ferrell 22.9 OR, H; Boyle 22.9 =OR, SF; Ferrell 22.8 OR, SF)

1972 (37. H-QF 4 Sept; SF-F 7 Sept): Stecher was nearly as dominant as she had been in the 100, although she did get a surprisingly strong battle in the stretch from Boyle. who picked up another silver. Stecher's reward was another world record, 22.40 (wind 1.1).

1. Renate Stecher (EG)	22.40 WR	4. Ellen Streidt* (EG)	22.75
2. Raelene Boyle (Aus)	22.45	5. Annegret Kroniger (WG) &	22.89
3. Irena Szewinska (Pol)	22.74	Christina Heinich (EG)	22.89

7. Alice Annum (Gha) 22.99; 8. Rose Allwood (Jam) 23.11.

1976 (36. H 25 July; QF 26 July; SF-F 28 July): Not a strong contender for the East German team early in the year, Eckert's ever-improving season first saw her as a challenger with a 22.85 semi. Still, she surprised by leading off the turn. 100 champ Richter made a furious bid down the stretch but lost out on the lean-in as Eckert moved to No. 2 all-time.

1. Barbel Eckert (EG)	22.37 OR	4. Carla Bodendorf (EG)	22.64
2. Annegret Richter (WG)	22.39	5. Inge Helten (WG)	22.68
3. Renate Stecher (EG)	22.47	6. Tatyana Prorochenko (SU)	23.03

7. Denise Robertson (Aus) 23.05; 8. Chantal Rega (Fr) 23.09.

400 METERS

1896—1960 (not contested).

1964 (23. H 15 Oct; SF 16 Oct; F 17 Oct): Eight years after her golden Games at Melbourne in the sprints, Cuthbert returned to claim the first-ever Olympic 400 title with an OR 52.0. She nosed out eventual 800 winner Packer (52.2), with teammate Amoore a solitary 3rd.

1. Betty Cuthbert (Aus)	52.0 OR	4. Antonia Munkacsi (Hun)	54.4
2. Ann Packer (GB)	52.2	5. Mariya Itkina (SU)	54.6
3. Judy Amoore (Aus)	53.4	6. Tilly van der Zwaard (Hol)	55.2

7. Gertrude Schmidt (EG) 55.4; 8. Evelyne Lebret (Fr) 55.5.
(Munkacsi 54.4 OR, H; Packer 53.1 OR, H; Packer 52.7 OR, SF)

1968 (29. H 14 Oct; SF 15 Oct; F 16 Oct): Pre-Games favorite Board led the field into the stretch, but with about 30m to go, lightly-regarded Besson spurted and passed Board just before the line.

1. Colette Besson (Fr)	52.0 (52.03) =OR	4. Janet Simpson (GB)	52.5 (52.57)
2. Lillian Board (GB)	52.1 (52.12)	5. Aurelia Penton (Cuba)	52.7
3. Natalya Petschenkina (SU)	52.2 (52.25)	6. Jarvis Scott (US)	52.7

7. Helga Henning (WG) 52.8; 8. Myrna van der Hoeven (Hol) 53.0.

1972 (49. H 2 Sept; QF 3 Sept; SF 4 Sept; F 7 Sept): Zehrt, still a teenager but already holder of the world record, established herself early, leading through the 200 (24.2) and 300 (36.8) marks, with Wilden always following. To the joy of the West German crowd, Wilden made a gallant stretch run, but Zehrt solidified her lead in the closing stages.

1. Monika Zehrt (EG)	51.08 OR		4. Helga Seidler (EG)		51.86
2. Rita Wilden (WG)	51.21		5. Mable Fergerson (US)		51.96
3. Kathy Hammond (US)	51.64		6. Charlene Rendina (Aus)		51.99

7. Dagmar Kasling (EG) 52.19; 8. Gyorgyi Balogh (Hun) 52.39.
(Rendina 51.94 OR, H; Balogh 51.71 OR, QF; Zehrt 51.47 OR, SF)

1976 (39. H 25 July; SF 28 July; F 29 July): An eagerly awaited duel between world record setters Szewinska and Brehmer was anti-climactic as the Pole completely dominated her younger rival in the stretch to chop 0.46 from her own world record. The US entries broke the NR 4 times.

1. Irena Szewinska (Pol)	49.29 WR		4. Pirjo Haggman (Fin)		50.56
2. Christine Brehmer (EG)	50.51		5. Rosalyn Bryant (US)		50.65
3. Ellen Streidt (EG)	50.55		6. Sheila Ingram (US)		50.90

7. Riitta Salin (Fin) 50.98; 8. Debra Sapenter (US) 51.66.
(Szewinska 50.48 OR, SF)

800 METERS

1896—1924 (not contested).

1928 (25. H 1 Aug; F 2 Aug): Radke, who had become the first woman to break 2:20 just a month earlier, chopped 2.8 off her own WR with 2:16.8 as all the medallists eclipsed the old mark. Her mark wasn't officially bettered until 1944.

1. Lina Radke (Ger)	2:16.8 WR		4. Jenny Thompson (Can)		2:21.6
2. Kinuye Hitomi (Japan)	2:17.6		5. Fanny Rosenfeld (Can)		2:22.4
3. Inga Gentzel (Swe)	2:17.8		6. Florence McDonald (US)		2:22.6

7. Marie Dollinger (Ger) 2:23.0; 8. Gertrude Kilosowna (Pol); 9. Elfriede Wever (Ger).
(Dollinger 2:22.4OR H)

1932—1956 (not contested).

1960 (27. H 6 Sept; F 7 Sept): The first Olympic 800 final since 1928 produced a rousing competition. Willis led the field past 400 with world record holder Shevtsova right behind. Willis held the edge until some 150m remained when the Soviet pulled ahead. This pair, plus Jones and Donath, ran abreast down the final stretch before Willis abruptly stepped off the track. Jones edged ahead but Shevtsova squeezed back in front just before the wire to win in a record-equaling 2:04.3.

1. Lyudmila Shevtsova (SU)	2:04.3 =WR		4. Vera Kummerfeldt (EG)		2:05.9
2. Brenda Jones (Aus)	2:04.4		5. Antje Gleichfeld (WG)		2:06.5
3. Ursula Donath (EG)	2:05.6		6. Joyce Jordan (GB)		2:07.8

7. G. Csoka (Hun) 2:08.0; 8. Beata Zbikowska (Pol) 2:11.9;. . . dnf—Dixie Willis (Aus).
(Gleichfeld 2:10.9 OR, H; Donath 2:07.8 OR, H; Willis 2:05.9 OR, H)

1964 (23. H 18 Oct; SF 19 Oct; F 20 Oct): France's Dupureur set an OR in the semis, but no one could match the stretch speed of 400 runner-up Packer. Her WR 2:01.1 gave her a comfortable 1.7-second margin ahead of Dupureur, who just held off the closing rush of Chamberlain.

1. Ann Packer (GB)	2:01.1 WR		4. Zsuzsa Nagy-Szabo (Hun)		2:03.5
2. Maryvonne Dupureur (Fr)	2:01.9		5. Antje Gleichfeld (WG)		2:03.9
3. Marise Chamberlain (NZ)	2:02.8		6. Laine Erik (SU)		2:05.1

7. Gerda Kraan (Hol) 2:05.8; 8. Anne Smith (GB) 2:05.8.
(Dupureur 2:04.1 OR, SF)

1968 (24. H 17 Oct; SF 18 Oct; F 19 Oct): Manning and Silai set a 59.1 pace and then the young American ran the final bend hard to open an unbeatable gap. Silai and Gommers attacked only in the final 50m as Manning won with an Olympic Record.

1. Madeline Manning (US)	2:00.9 OR	4. Sheila Taylor (GB)	2:03.8
2. Ileana Silai (Rum)	2:02.5	5. Doris Brown (US)	2:03.9
3. Maria Gommers (Hol)	2:02.6	6. Pat Lowe (GB)	2:04.2

7. Abby Hoffman (Can) 2:06.8; 8. Maryvonne Dupureur (Fr) 2:08.2.

1972 (38. H 31 Aug; SF 1 Sept; F 3 Sept): Two minutes ceased to be an Olympic barrier in the second heat, as Zlateva's 1:58.9 missed the world record by only 0.4! In the final, virtually everyone was still in contention at the end of the 600, Zlateva leading at 1:28.0. Coming off the curve, Falck made a sudden burst of speed to pull clear; she moved away from everyone but Sabaite, who produced a fierce closing rush which fell just short.

1. Hildegard Falck (WG)	1:58.6 OR	4. Svetla Koleva* (Bul)	1:59.7
2. Niole Sabaite (SU)	1:58.7	5. Vera Nikolic (Yug)	2:00.0
3. Gunhild Hoffmeister (EG)	1:59.2	6. Ileana Silai (Rum)	2:00.0

7. Rosemary Stirling (GB) 2:00.2; 8. Abby Hoffman (Can) 2:00.8.
(Zlateva 1:58.9 OR, H)

1976 (34. H 23 July; SF 24 July; F 26 July): Everybody expected a world record—nobody was let down, with the first 4 breaking the old standard. What did surprise was the winner, Kazankina, who thought of herself as a 1500 specialist. Added to the 800 squad at the last minute, she showed a superb turn of speed off the last curve to score a big win. The prelims were so fast that Judy Pollock broke 2:00 in her semi and didn't make the final.

1. Tatyana Kazankina (SU)	1:54.9 WR	4. Anita Weiss (EG)	1:55.7
2. Nikolina Shtereva (Bul)	1:55.4	5. Svyetlana Styrkina (SU)	1:56.4
3. Elfi Zinn (EG)	1:55.6	6. Svetla Koleva (Bul)	1:57.2

7. Doris Gluth (EG) 1:59.0; 8. Mariana Suman (Rum) 2:02.2.
(Weiss 1:56.5 OR, SF)

1500 METERS

1896–1968 (not contested).

1972 (36. H 4 Sept; SF 7 Sept; F 9 Sept): Bragina got Olympic 1500 running off to a flying start by winning the first heat in a world record (4:06.5). Amazingly, she produced another in the semis (4:05.1) and yet another (4:01.4) in the final. Bragina picked up most of her winning margin with a surprise burst just before the 800. The all-time list was completely revised.

1. Lyudmila Bragina (SU)	4:01.4 WR	4. Karin Burneleit (EG)	4:04.1
2. Gunhild Hoffmeister (EG)	4:02.8	5. Sheila Carey (GB)	4:04.8
3. Paola Cacchi (It)	4:02.9	6. Ilja Keizer (Hol)	4:05.1

7. Tamara Pangelova (SU) 4:06.5; 8. Jenny Orr (Aus) 4:12.2; 9. Bernie Boxem (Hol) 4:13.1;. . . dnf—Ellen Wellmann* (WG).
(Bragina 4:06.5 OR, WR H; Bragina 4:05.1 OR, WR, SF)

1976 (35. H 28 July; SF 29 July; F 30 July): Already the world record holder in this event, and coming off a WR win in the 800, Kazankina was a big favorite. She let no one down, finishing in 56.9 and dusting her East German rivals in the straight. Francie Larrieu (4:07.2) and Merrill (4:02.6) broke the AR in the prelims, which were less tactical than the final.

1. Tatyana Kazankina (SU)	4:05.5	4. Nikolina Shtereva (Bul)	4:06.6
2. Gunhild Hoffmeister (EG)	4:06.0	5. Lyudmila Bragina (SU)	4:07.2
3. Ulrike Klapezynski (EG)	4:06.1	6. Gabriella Dorio (It)	4:07.3

7. Ellen Wellmann (WG) 4:07.9; 8. Jan Merrill (US) 4:08.5; 9. Nina Holmen (Fin) 4:10.0.

100 HURDLES

1896–1928 (not contested).

Races held at 80m through 1968.

1932 (9. F 4 Aug): Didrikson, the outstanding woman competitor of the Games, won her second medal, in a tight finish with Hall as both clipped a 10th off the WR Didrikson had equalled in her heat.

1. Mildred Didrikson (US)	11.7 WR	4. Simone Schaller (US)	11.9
2. Evelyne Hall (US)	11.7 =WR	5. Violet Webb (GB)	11.9
3. Marjorie Clark (S Afr)	11.8	6. Alda Wilson (Can)	12.0

(Didrikson 11.8 OR =WR, H)

1936 (22. H-SF 5 Aug; F 6 Aug): Valla was declared the winner of a blanket finish which found the first 4 given the same time. Only a photo could separate them. The Italian had run 11.6 in her semi, a mark accepted as a WR by the IAAF even though it was aided by an illegal 2.8 mps wind.

1. Trebisonda Valla (It)	11.7 OR	4. Claudia Testoni (It)	11.7 =C
2. Anny Steuer (Ger)	11.7 =OR	5. Catharina Elisabeth ter Braake (Hol)	11.8
3. Elizabeth Taylor (Can)	11.7 =OR	6. Doris Eckert (Ger)	12.0

(Valla 11.6w, SF)

1948 (21. H-SF 3 Aug; F 4 Aug): Blankers-Koen had chopped an incredible 0.3 off her own WR (to 11.0) 2 months before the Games, but got a good battle from local favorite Gardner as they set an OR 11.2. De la Hunty's time was obviously in error, as she finished no more than a half-meter behind the winner.

1. Fanny Blankers-Koen (Hol)	11.2 OR	4. Yvette Monginou (Fr)	
2. Maureen Gardner (GB)	11.2 =OR	5. Maria Oberbreyer (Aut)	
3. Shirley de la Hunty* (Aus)	11.4	6. Libuse Lomska (Czech)	

(Blankers-Koen 11.3 OR, H)

1952 (33. H 23 July; SF-F 24 July): De la Hunty was in control all the way, equalling Blankers-Koen's 4-year-old WR in her heat, running a windy 10.8 in the semi, then lowering the WR to 10.9 in the final.

1. Shirley de la Hunty (Aus) 10.9 (11.03) WR		4. Annel. Seonbuchner (WG) 11.2 (11.46)	
2. Mariya Golubnichaya (SU) 11.1 (11.24)		5. Jean Desforges (GB) 11.6 (11.75)	
3. Maria Sander (WG) 11.1 (11.38)		— Fanny Blankers-Koen (Hol)dnf	

(de la Hunty 11.0 OR, =WR, H; de la Hunty 10.8w SF)

1956 (22. H-SF 27 Nov; F 28 Nov): De la Hunty became the only successful defender in this event's history, chopping a 10th off the OR she had set in the heats and tied (with medallists Birkemeyer and Thrower) in the semis. World Record holder Gastl (10.6) started with an OR in her heat but failed to make the final.

1. Shirley de la Hunty (Aus) 10.7 (10.96) OR		4. Galina Bystrova (SU) 11.0 (11.25)	
2. Gisela Birkemeyer* (EG) 10.9 (11.12)		5. Mariya Golubnichaya (SU) 11.3 (11.50)	
3. Norma Thrower (Aus) 11.0 (11.25)		6. Gloria Cooke (Aus) 11.4 (11.60)	

(Zenta Gastl WG 10.9 =OR, H; de la Hunty 10.8 OR, H; Thrower 10.8 =OR, H; de la Hunty 10.8 =OR,SF; Kohler 10.8 =OR, SF)

1960 (28. H-SF 31 Aug; F 1 Sept): The powerful Press, younger sister of shot/discus star Tamara, tied the Olympic record in the heats and set a new one in the semis. Press rocketed to an immediate lead in the final (zero wind), which she never relinquished despite the snappy performance by the relatively unknown Quinton.

1. Irina Press (SU)	10.8 (10.94)	4. Mary Rand* (GB)	11.1 (11.22)
2. Carol Quinton (GB)	10.9 (10.99)	5. Galina Bystrova (SU)	11.2 (11.26)
3. Gisela Birkemeyer (EG)	11.0 (11.13)	6. Rimma Koshelyeva (SU)	11.2 (11.29)

(Press 10.7 =OR, H; Press 10.6 OR, SF)

1964 (27. H 18 Oct; SF-F 19 Oct): After Ryan and Balzer matched the OR (10.6) in the semis, the final figured to be a blazer. And it was as the East German got to the line first in 10.5—which would have tied the WR but for the 2.23 wind pushing the hurdlers. The proverbial blanket could have covered the first 4, as Pole Ciepla slipped in ahead of Ryan for the silver and pentathlon champ Press was hot on the heels of the medalists.

1. Karin Balzer (EG)	10.5	4. Irina Press (SU)	10.6
2. Tereza Ciepla (Pol)	10.5	5. Ikuko Yoda (Japan)	10.7
3. Pam Ryan* (Aus)	10.5	6. Maria Piatkowska (Pol)	10.7

7. Draga Stamejcic (Yug) 10.8; 8. Rosie Bonds (US) 10.8.
(Kilborn 10.6 =OR, SF; Balzer 10.6 =OR, SF; Piatkowska 10.6w H; Bonds 10.6w H)

1968 (32. H 17 Oct; SF-F 18 Oct): The final 80m race in Olympic history (the event was replaced by the 100m barriers immediately after this final) went to 17-year-old Caird, the youngest track winner in Mexico. She moved ahead after 4 hurdles, with Kilborn and Cheng also clear in their positions. Young van Wolvelaere placed the best of an American since Babe Didrikson's '32 victory.

1. Maureen Caird (Aus)	10.3 OR	4. Patty van Wolvelaere (US)	10.5
2. Pam Ryan* (Aus)	10.4	5. Karin Balzer (EG)	10.6
3. Chi Cheng (Tai)	10.4	6. Danuta Straszynska (Pol)	10.6

7. Elzbieta Zebrowska (Pol) 10.6; 8. Tatyana Talisheva (SU) 10.7.
(Kilborn 10.4 OR, H; Caird 10.4 =OR, H; Kilborn 10.4 =OR, SF)

1972 (25. H 4 Sept; SF 7 Sept; F 8 Sept): Despite running into a light headwind (0.6), Ehrhardt produced a stunning world record of 12.59, annihilating the field by 0.25 seconds.

1. Annelie Erhardt (EG)	12.59 WR	4. Pam Ryan (Aus)	12.98
2. Valeria Stefanescu* (Rum)	12.84	5. Teresa Nowak (Pol)	13.17
3. Karin Balzer (EG)	12.90	6. Danuta Straszynska (Pol)	13.18

7. Annerose Krumpholz (EG) 13.27; 8. Grazyna Rabsztyn (Pol) 13.44.
(Ehrhardt 12.70 OR, H)

1976 (23. H 28 July; H-SF 28 July; F 29 July): There were surprises aplenty here with co-favorites Rabsztyn and Annelie Ehrhardt (defending champ) out of the medals. Ehrhardt was eliminated in the rerun of a disputed semifinal. The final was close all the way, with medals sorted out by the finish picture.

1. Johanna Schaller (EG)	12.77	4. Gudrun Berend (EG)	12.82
2. Tatyana Anisimova (SU)	12.78	5. Grazyna Rabsztyn (Pol)	12.96
3. Natalya Lebedyeva (SU)	12.80	6. Ester Rot (Isr)	13.04

7. Valeria Stefanescu (Rum) 13.35; 8. Ileana Ongar (It) 13.51.

4 X 100

1896-1924 (not contested).

1928 (8. H 4 Aug; F 5 Aug): The crack Canadian foursome—which included 3 finalists from the 100—hacked 0.4 off the WR in the first heat and went on to demolish that with a 48.4 final. The first 4 teams ended up better than the WR going into the meet.

1. Canada	48.4 WR
(Fanny Rosenfeld, Ethel Smith, Florence Bell, Myrtle Cook)	
2. United States	48.8
(M. Washburn, J. Gross, L. McNeil, E. Robinson)	
3. Germany	49.0
(R. Kellner, L. Schmidt, A. Holdmann, L. Junker)	
4. France	49.6
(G. Gagneux, Y. Plancke, M. Radideau, L. Velu)	
5. Holland	49.8
(M. Aengenendt, M. Briejer, J. Grooss, E. ter Horst)	
6. Italy	53.6
(L. Bonfanti, G. Marchini, D. Polazzo, V. Vivenza)	

(Canada 49.3 OR WR, H)

1932 (6. F 7 Aug): Canada's WR had remained inviolate during the Olympiad, but was crushed by both the Americans and the Canadians, as they finished in 47.0. It wasn't that close, however, and some sources list the US time as 46.9.

1. United States	47.0 WR
(Mary Carew, Evelyn Furtsch, Annette Rogers, Wilhelmina Von Bremen)	
2. Canada	47.0 =WR
(Mildred Frizzel, L. Palmer, Mary Frizzel, H. Strike)	
3. Great Britain	47.6
(E. Hiscock, G. Porter, V. Webb, N. Halstead)	
4. Holland	
(J. Dalmolen, C. Aalten, E. du Mee, T. Schuurman)	
5. Japan	
(M. Muraoka, M. Nakanishi, A. Dogura, S. Watanabe)	
6. Germany	
(G. Heublein, E. Braumuller, T. Fleischer, M. Dollinger)	

1936 (8. H 8 Aug; F 9 Aug): The uniforms were familiar, as the US and Canada scored medals for the third time in a row, Great Britain for the second. The US foursome included a member from each of the 1928 and '32 squads. The favored German team, which had twice lowered the WR before the Games, and did so again in the second heat, failed to finish.

1. United States	46.9
(Harriet Bland, Annette Rogers, Elizabeth Robinson, Helen Stephens)	
2. Great Britain	47.6
(E. Hiscock, V. Olney, A. Brown, B. Burke)	
3. Canada	47.8
(D. Brookshaw, M. Dolson, H. Cameron, A. Meagher)	
4. Italy	48.7
(L. Bongiovanni, T. Valla, F. Bullano, C. Testoni)	
5. Holland	48.8
(C. ter Braake, F. Blankers-Koen*, A. de Vries, E. Koning)	
—. Germany	did not finish
(E. Albus, K. Krauss, M. Dollinger, I. Dorffeldt)	(dropped baton)

(Germany 46.4 OR WR, H)

1948 (10. H 6 Aug; F 7 Aug): Blankers-Koen had run an inconspicuous second leg on Holland's 5th-place team 12 years earlier. Here, she picked up her fourth gold of the meet in leading her team to victory in a time (47.6) slower than any other winner since the first time the event was held.

1. Holland	47.5

(Xenia Stad de Jong, Jeanette Witziers-Timmer, Gerda v.d. Kade-Koudijs, Fanny Blankers-Koen)

2. Australia	47.6

(S. de la Hunty*, J. Maston, B. McKinnon, J. King)

3. Canada	47.8

(V. Myers, N. Mackay, D. Foster, P. Jones)

4. Great Britain	48.0

(D. Manley, M. Pletts, M. Walker, M. Gardner)

5. Denmark	48.2

(G. Lovsoe-Nielsen, B. Bergendorff, B. Nielsen, H. Nissen)

6. Austria	49.2

(G. Jenny, E. Steurer, G. Pavlousek, M. Oberbreyer)

1952 (15. H 27 July; H-F 27 July): The Australians were clearly favored, with hurdle winner de la Hunty leading off and a 100/200 champ Jackson anchoring. Their 46.1 performance in the heats did nothing to dispel that role, as it chopped 0.3 off Germany's 16-year-old WR. But when Jackson fumbled the baton in the final it was the end of the game as the US edged Germany by inches in another WR.

1. United States	45.9 (46.14) WR

(Mae Faggs, Barbara Jones, Janet Moreau, Catherine Hardy)

2. West Germany	45.9 (46.18) =WR

(U. Knab, M. Sander, H. Klein, M. Petersen)

3. Great Britain	46.2 (46.41)

(S. Cheeseman, J. Foulds, J. Desforges, H. Armitage)

4. Soviet Union	46.3 (46.41)

(I. Turova, Y. Setschenova, N. Khnykina, V. Kalashnikova)

5. Australia	46.6 (46.84)

(S. de la Hunty, V. Johnson, W. Cripps, M. Jackson)

6. Holland	47.8 (47.16)

(G. de Jongh, B. Brouwer, N. Buch, W. Lust)

(Australia 46.1 OR WR, H)

1956 (9. H-F 1 Dec): The Australians produced another crack team, even though only lead-off de la Hunty remained from Helsinki. Pushed to the wire in a 44.9 (WR) heat win, the Aussies axed that down to 44.5 in the final.

1. Australia	44.5 (44.65) WR

(Shirley de la Hunty, Norma Croker, Fleur Mellor, Betty Cuthbert)

2. Great Britain	44.7 (44.70)

(A. Pashley, J. Scriven, J. Paul-Foulds, H. Armitage)

3. United States	44.9 (45.04)

(M. Faggs, M. Matthews, W. Rudolph, I. Daniels)

4. Soviet Union	45.6 (45.81)

(V. Krepkina, G. Restshikova, M. Itkina, I. Boshkaryova)

5. Italy	45.7 (45.81)

(M. Musso, L. Bertoni, M. Greppi, G. Leone)

6. Germany	47.2 (47.29)

(M. Sander, C. Stubnick, G. Kohler, B. Mayer)

(Australia 44.9 OR WR, H; Germany 44.9 =OR =WR, H)

1960 (10. H 7 Sept; F 8 Sept): No question about which team was the favorite after the U.S. won its heat by matching the world record of 44.4 with incomparable double sprint champ Rudolph anchoring. The final went in 44.5 as the Americans easily handled Germany.

1. United States	44.5 (44.72)

(Martha Hudson, Lucinda Williams, Barbara Jones, Wilma Rudolph)

2. Germany	44.8 (45.00)

(M. Pensberger*, A. Biechl, B. Hendrix, J. Heine)

3. Poland	45.0 (45.19)

(T. Ciepla*, B. Janiszewska, C. Jesionowska, H. Gorecka*)

4. Soviet Union	45.2 (45.39)

(V. Krepkina, V. Maslovskaya, M. Itkina, I. Press)

5. Italy	45.6 (45.80)

(L. Bertoni, S. Valenti, P. Tizzoni, G. Leone)

—. Great Britain   did not finish
(C. Quinton, D. Hyman, J. Smart, M. Rand*)
(USA 44.4 OR WR, H)

1964 (15. H 20 Oct; F 21 Oct): With sprint gold medalists McGuire and Tyus, it looked like the U.S. had the inside track, but the smooth-passing Polish foursome carried the day, getting a WR 43.6 to boot. Fine running considering the damp track. The 3 medal-winning teams all came home under the old WR. Szewinska won her 3rd medal of the Games (2 silver, 1 gold), while Rand completed a set (LJ gold, pentathlon silver).

1. Poland	43.6 WR
(Tereza Ciepla, Irena Szewinska*, Gorecka, Ewa Klobukowska)	
2. United States	43.9
(W. White, W. Tyus, M. White, E. McGuire)	
3. Great Britain	44.0
(J. Simpson, M. Rand, D. Arden, D. Hyman)	
4. Soviet Union	44.4
(G. Gaide, R. Latse, L. Samotyesova, G. Popova)	
5. Germany	44.7
(K. Frisch, E. Pollmann, M. Pensberger, J. Heine)	
6. Australia	45.0
(D. Bowering, M. Black, M. Burvill, J. Bennett)	
7. Hungary	45.2
8. France	46.1

1968 (14. H 19 Oct; F 20 Oct): The World Record was beaten in the first heat and then matched in the second heat. The final was even faster as the American foursome won by a half-second in another WR, despite the usual ragged U.S. passing. The altitude was an important factor in the fast times.

1. United States	42.8 (42.87) WR
(Barbara Ferrell, Margaret Bailes, Mildrette Netter, Wyomia Tyus)	
2. Cuba	43.3 (43.35)
(M. Elejarde, F. Romay, V. Quesada, M. Cobian)	
3. Soviet Union	43.4 (43.41)
(L. Maslakova*, G. Bukarina, V. Popkova, L. Samotyesova)	
4. Holland	43.4 (43.44)
(G. Hennipman, M. Sterk, C. Bakker, W. van den Berg)	
5. Australia	43.4 (43.50)
(J. Lamy, J. Bennett, R. Boyle, D. Burge)	
6. West Germany	43.6 (43.70)
(R. Meyer, J. Stock, R. Wilden*, I. Mickler*)	
7. Great Britain	43.7
(M. Tranter, A. Neil, L. Board, J. Simpson)	
8. France	44.2
(M. Alayrangues, G. Meyer, N. Montandon, S. Telliez)	

(USA 43.4 OR, WR, H; Holland 43.4 =OR =WR, H)

1972 (15. H 9 Sept; F 10 Sept): The West Germans got the baton to anchor Heide Rosendahl a meter ahead of East Germany. But the Easterners had double sprint champ Renate Stecher. Surprisingly, the multi-talented Rosendahl refused to yield more than half the margin and flashed across the tape in a world record equalling 42.81 (superior to its "equal," which was at altitude). It had been obvious that a hot race was in the offing in the second heat, when the East topped the West 42.88 to 42.97, only the second time that 43 seconds had been broken.

1. West Germany	42.81 WR
(Christiane Kraus, Ingrid Mickler*, Annegret Richter, Heide Rosendahl)	
2. East Germany	42.95
(E. Kaufer, C. Heinich, B. Struppert, R. Stecher)	
3. Cuba	43.36
(M. Elejarde, C. Valdes, F. Romay, S. Chivas)	
4. United States	43.39
(M. Watson, M. Render, M. Netter, I. Davis)	
5. Soviet Union	43.59

(M. Sidorova, G. Bukarina, L. Maslakova*, N. Besfamilnaya)
```
     6. Australia                                43.61
(M. Caird, R. Boyle, M. Hoffman, P. Gillies)
     7. Great Britain                            43.71
(A. Lynch, D. Pascoe, J. Vernon, A. Neil)
     8. Poland                                   44.20
(H. Kerner, B. Bakulin, U. Jozwik, D. Jedrejek)
```

1976 (10. H 30 July; F 31 July): Although the world record holder, East Germany looked to be the underdog after the Germans from the West matched them in the sprints and set an OR in the heats. But the East had 200 winner Barbel Eckert on the anchor, while the West had run Inge Helten and Annegret Richter early in 2-3, and Eckert ran down Annegret Kroniger, who had a couple of meters lead.

```
     1. East Germany                             42.55 OR
(Marlies Oelsner, Renate Stecher, Carla Bodendorf, Barbel Eckert)
     2. West Germany                             42.59
(E. Possekel, I. Helten, A. Richter, A. Kroniger)
     3. Soviet Union                             43.09
(T. Prorochenko, L. Maslakova, N. Besfamilnaya, V. Anisimova)
     4. Canada                                   43.17
(M. Howe, P. Loverock, J. McTaggart, M. Bailey)
     5. Australia                                43.18
(B. Wilson, D. Wells, D. Robertson, R. Boyle)
     6. Jamaica                                  43.24
(L. Hodges, R. Allwood, C. Cummings, J. Pusey)
     7. United States                            43.35
(M. Watson, E. Ashford, D. Armstrong, C. Cheeseborough)
     8. Great Britain                            43.79
(W. Clarke, D. Ramsden, S. Colyear, A. Lynch)
```

(West Germany 42.61 OR, H)

4 X 400

1896—1964 (not contested).

1972 (14. H 9 Sept; F 10 Sept): No contest, as the East Germans quickly took over this event by lowering their own world record in the heats. The first 4 ended up under that mark in the final, but the East Germans won by more than 2 seconds as Rita Kuhne blew the race open on the second leg.

```
     1. East Germany                             3:23.0 WR
(Dagmar Kasling 52.2, Rita Kuhne 50.0, Helga Seidler 50.5, Monika Zehrt 50.3)
     2. United States                            3:25.2
(M. Fergerson 51.8, M. Jackson 51.9, C. Toussaint 51.3, K. Hammond 50.2)
     3. West Germany                             3:26.6
(A. Ruckes 53.1, I. Bodding 51.6, H. Falck 51.2, R. Wilden 50.6)
     4. France                                   3:27.6
(M. Duvivier 53.0, C. Besson 52.1, B. Martin 51.8, N. Duclos 50.6)
     5. Great Britain                            3:28.8
(V. Elder* 53.1, J. Simpson 52.0, J. Roscoe 51.8, R. Stirling 51.8)
     6. Australia                                3:28.9
(A. Ross-Edwards 53.4, R. Boyle 50.8, C. Peasley 53.9, C. Rendina 50.7)
     7. Finland                                  3:29.5
(M. Haggman* 53.3, P. Lindholm* 52.4, T. Rautanan 52.6, M-L. Pursiainen* 51.1)
     8. Soviet Union                             3:31.9
(L. Runtso 54.0, O. Syrovatskaya 53.2, N. Chistyakova 52.6, N. Ilyina* 52.1)
```

(West Germany 3:29.3 OR, H; East Germany 3:28.5 OR, WR, H)

1976 (11. H 30 July; F 31 July): The big question was how low could the East Germans take the record. They beat a 50-sec. average (49.7) in crushing their own WR. The race for the other medals was closer, with Rosalyn Bryant annihilating Nadyezhda Ilyina on the anchor for a new AR.

1. East Germany   3:19.2 WR
(Doris Maletzki 50.5, Brigitte Rohde 49.5, Ellen Streidt 49.5, Christine Brehmer 49.7)
2. United States   3:22.8
(D. Sapenter 51.8, S. Ingram 50.0, P. Jiles 51.3, R. Bryant 49.7)
3. Soviet Union   3:24.2
(I. Klimovicha 51.4, L. Aksenova, N. Sokolova, N. Ilyina)
4. Australia   3:25.6
(J. Canty 52.4, V. Burnard 51.2, C. Rendina 51.6, B. Nail 50.4)
5. West Germany   3:25.7
(C. Steger 52.4, D. Fuhrmann 51.3, E. Barth 51.5, R. Wilden 50.5)
6. Finland   3:25.9
(M. Lindholm 52.8, P. Haggman 51.4, M-L. Pursiainen 52.0, R. Salin 50.6)
7. Great Britain   3:28.1
(E. Barnes 52.5, G. Taylor 52.6, V. Elder 52.6, D. Murray 50.3)
8. Canada   3:28.9
(M. Stride 53.1, J. Yakubowich 51.6, R. Campbell 52.5, Y. Saunders 51.7)

HIGH JUMP

1896–1924 (not contested).

1928 (20. F Aug 5): The initial Olympic high jump competition was so competitive that Canadian Catherwood had to clear a WR 1.59 to win, boosting the former record by 1cm. Places 2-5 were decided by jump-offs.

1. Ethel Catherwood (Can)	1.59	5-2½ WR	4. Jean Shiley (US)	1.51	4-11½
2. Carolina Gisolf (Hol)	1.56	5-1½	5. Marjorie Clark (S Afr)	1.48	4-10¼
3. Mildred Wiley (US)	1.56	5-1½	6. Helma Notte (Ger)	1.48	4-10¼

7. Inge Braumuller (Ger) 1.48; 8. Catherine Maguire (US) 1.48; 9. Marion Holley (US) 1.48; 10. Louise Stevens (Bel) 1.48.
(Catherwood 1.58 OR)

1932 (10. F 7 Aug): This competition was just as competitive as 4 years previously, but between American teammates Shiley and Didrikson. Both cleared a WR 1.65, upping the old mark by 5cm. In a jump-off, both then cleared 1.67 (5-5¾), but judges ruled that Didrikson illegally dove over head-first and thus disallowed her jump. According to the rules of the day, the 1.67 could not be ratified as a WR as it occurred in a jump-off.

1. Jean Shiley (US)	1.65	5-5 WR	4. Carolina Gisolf (Hol)	1.58	5-2¼
2. Mildred Didrikson (US)	1.65	5-5	5. Marjorie Clark (S Afr)	1.58	5-2¼
3. Eva Dawes (Can)	1.60	5-3	6. Annette Rogers (US)	1.58	5-2¼

7. Helma Notte (Ger) 1.55; 8. Yuriko Hiroashi (Japan) 1.48; 9. Yayeko Sagara (Japan) 1.46; 10. Inge Braumuller (Ger) 1.46.
(Shiley 1.60 OR; 1.60=OR–Didrikson, Dawes; Shiley 1.62 OR; Didrikson 1.62=OR)

1936 (17. F 9 Aug): Yet another closie, with 3 jumpers topping 1.60. Csak cleared 1.62 in a jump-off to win. Tyler, just 16, would have won the competition under modern count-back rules. Ratjen was barred from women's competition 2 years later after she won the European title but was found to be a hermaphrodite.

1. Ibolya Csak (Hun)	1.60	5-3	5. Marguerite Nicolas (Fr)	1.58	5-2¼
2. Dorothy Tyler* (GB)	1.60	5-3	6. Doris Carter (Aus),	1.55	5-1
3. Elfriede Kaun (Ger)	1.60	5-3	Fanny Blankers-Koen* (Hol)	1.55	5-1
4. Dora Ratjen (Ger)	1.58	5-2¼	& Annette Rogers (US)	1.55	5-1

8. tie, Nelly Carrington (GB), Margaret Bell (Can), Alice Arden (US), Kathlyn Kelly (US) & Wanda Nowak (Aut) 1.50.

1948 (19. F 7 Aug): Eight years after her Berlin silver, Tyler again came up 2nd despite clearing the same height as the winner. Coachman cleared an OR 5-6¼ before Tyler could and so took the gold. Ostermeyer in 3rd added a bronze to her golds in the SP-DT.

1. Alice Coachman (US)	1.68	5-6¼ OR	4. Vinton Beckett (Can) &	1.58	5-2¼
2. Dorothy Tyler (GB)	1.68	5-6¼ =OR	Doreen Dredge (Can)	1.58	5-2¼
3. Micheline Ostermeyer (Fr)	1.61	5-3½	6. Bertha Crowther (GB)	1.58	5-2¼

7. I. Steinegger (Aut) 1.55; 8. Dorothy Gardner (GB) 1.55; 9. tie, Anne Iversen (Den) & Simone Ruas (Fr) 1.50; 11. tie, S. Gordon (Can), C. Phipps (Jam) & Bernice Robinson (US) 1.50; 14. tie, Triny Bourkel (Lux), Anne-Marie Colchen (Fr) & Emma Reed (US) 1.40; 17. tie, Clara Muller (Braz) & Olga Gyarmati (Hun) 1.40; 19. K. Silburn (Can) 1.40.
(Coachman 1.66 OR; Tyler 1.68=OR)

1952 (17. F 27 July): The WR stood at 1.72 (5-7¾), but the wet conditions held winner Brand to 5cm below that ceiling.

1. Esther Brand (S Afr)	1.67	5-5¾	4. Thelma Hopkins (GB)	1.58	5-2¼
2. Sheila Lerwill (GB)	1.65	5-5	5. Olga Modrachova (Czech)	1.58	5-2¼
3. Aleksandra Chudina (SU)	1.63	5-4¼	6. Feodora Schenk (Aut)	1.58	5-2¼

7. tie, Nina Kossova (SU) & Dorothy Tyler (GB) 1.58; 9. Gunhild Larking (Swe) 1.55; 10. Alice Whitty (Can) 1.55; 11. Galina Ganyeker (SU) 1.55; 12. D. de Castro (Braz) 1.50; 13. D. Josephs (Can) 1.50; 14. Solveig Ericsson (Swe) 1.50; 15. S. Pontinen (Fin) 1.50; 16. S. Heikkila (Fin) 1.40; 17. T. Mettal (Isr) 1.40.

1956 (19. Q-F 1 Dec): Twenty-three-year-old "Babe" McDaniel not only beat the WR with her 1.76 clearance, but beat record-holder Balas in the bargain. The Rumanian could manage only 5th, but equalled McDaniels' WR a year later.

1. Mildred McDaniel (US)	1.76	5-9¼ WR	4. Gunhild Larking (Swe)	1.67	5-5¾
2. Maria Pisaryeva (SU) &	1.67	5-5¾	5. Iolanda Balas (Rum)	1.67	5-5¾
Thelma Hopkins (GB)	1.67	5-5¾	6. Michele Brown* (Aus)	1.67	5-5¾

7. Mary Donaghy (NZ) 1.67; 8. tie, Hermina Geyser (S Afr) & Jirina Voborilova (Czech) 1.64; 10. Olga Modrachova (Czech) 1.64; 11. Valentina Ballod (SU) 1.60; 12. tie, Reinelde Knapp (Aus) & Dorothy Tyler (GB) 1.60; 14. C. Bernoth (Aus) 1.60; 15. Janice Cooper (Aus) 1.55; 16. tie, Audrey Bennett (GB) & Alice Whitty (Can) 1.55; 17. Inge Kilian (WG) 1.55.
(McDaniel 1.70 OR)

1960 (23. Q 7 Sept; F 8 Sept): The long-legged Balas moved up from 5th at Melbourne to the victory platform this time, her unique scissors-like style getting her over an Olympic Record 1.85. No one else could manage higher than 1.71, where Shirley and Jozwiakowska knotted for the silver medal.

1. Iolanda Balas (Rum)	1.85	6-¾ OR	5. Taisiya Chenchik (SU)	1.68	5-6¼
2. Dorothy Shirley (GB) &	1.71	5-7¼	6. Helen Frith (Aus),	1.65	5-5
Jaroslawa Jozwiakowska (Pl)	1.71	5-7¼	Inga-Britt Lorentzen (Swe)&	1.65	5-5
4. Galina Dolya (SU)	1.71	5-7¼	Frances Slaap (GB)	1.65	5-5

9. tie, Ingrid Becker* (WG), Olga Gere (Yug), Florence Petry (Fr), Marlene Schmitz-Portz (WG) & Petronella Zwier (Pol) 1.65; 14. Neomia Rogers (US) 1.65; 15. Valentina Ballod (SU) 1.65.
(Balas 1.77 OR, 1.81 OR)

1964 (27. Q-F 15 Oct): Balas continued as untouchable as ever, clearing an OR 1.90 with second-placer Brown a full 10cm. behind. Balas so dominated things that she needed only 8 jumps to win, clearing every height including 1.90 on her 1st try, before missing thrice at 1.92 (6-4).

1. Iolanda Balas (Rum) 1.90 6-2¾ OR   4. Aida dos Santos (Braz) 1.74 5-8½
2. Michele Brown (Aus) 1.80 5-11   5. Dianne Gerace (Can) 1.71 5-7¼
3. Taisiya Chenchik (SU) 1.78 5-10   6. Frances Slaap (GB) 1.71 5-7¼

7. Olga Pluic (Yug) 1.71; 8. Eleanor Montgomery (US) 1.71; 9. Karin Schulze* (EG) 1.71; 10. Jaroslawa Bieda (Pol) 1.71; 11. Robyn Woodhouse (Aus) 1.71; 12. Gerda Kupferschmid (EG) 1.68; 13. Leena Kaaran (Fin) 1.65;... nh—Terrezene Brown (US) [1.65], Ulla Flegel (Aut) [1.65].
(Balas 1.86 OR)

1968 (24. Q 16 Oct; F 17 Oct): As in the hurdles, youth won the day as 18-year-old Hubnerova cleared 1.82 to turn back Soviets Okorokova and Kozyr (both 1.80). She cleared 1.78 (5-10) and 1.80 (5-11) on her initial tries, but needed all 3 before making 1.82. She then missed 1.84/6-½.

			1.71	1.74	1.76	1.78	1.80	1.82	1.84
1. Miloslava Hubnerova* (Cze)	1.82	5-11¾	xo	xo	xo	o	o	xxo	xxx
2. Antonina Okorokova (SU)	1.80	5-11	p	o	p	xo	o	xxx	
3. Valentina Kozyr (SU)	1.80	5-11	o	o	o	xo	xxo	xxx	
4. Jaroslava Valentova (Cze)	1.78	5-10	o	p	xo	o	xxx		
5. Rita Schmidt (EG)	1.78	5-10	o	xxo	o	xo	xxx		
6. Maria Mracnova* (Cze)	1.78	5-10	o	xo	o	xxo	xxx		

7. Karin Schulze (EG) 1.76; 8. Ilona Gusenbauer (Aut) 1.76; 9. tie, Ghislaine Barnay (Fr) & Magda Csabi (Hun) 1.71; 11. Maria Cypriano (Braz) 1.71; 12. Vera Grushkina (SU) 1.71; 13. Barbara Inkpen (GB) 1.68; 14. Snezana Hrepevnik (Yug) 1.68.

1972 (40. Q 3 Sept; F 4 Sept): Coming from the proverbial nowhere, 16-year-old Meyfarth barely made the West German team, yet added 7cm to her PR to equal the world record and beat back a sterling field. The youngest champion in track history, the 16-year-old Meyfarth clinched at least a medal with a perfect record through 1.88, then ensured the gold by being the only one over 1.90.

			1.79	1.82	1.85	1.88	1.90	1.92	1.94
1. Ulrike Meyfarth (WG)	1.92	6-3½=WR	o	o	o	o	xo	o	xxx
2. Yordanka Blagoyeva (Bul)	1.88	6-2	o	o	o	o	xxx		
3. Ilona Gusenbauer (Aut)	1.88	6-2	o	o	xxo	xo	xxx		
4. Barbara Inkpen (GB)	1.85	6-¾	o	o	o	xxx			
5. Rita Schmidt (EG)	1.85	6-¾	o	o	xo	xxx			
6. Sara Simeoni (It)	1.85	6-¾	o	xo	xo	xxx			

7. Rosemarie Ackermann* (EG) 1.85; 8. Debbie Brill (Can) 1.82; 9. Andrea Bruce (Jam) 1.82; 10. Ellen Mundinger (WG) 1.82; 11. Audrey Reid (Jam) 1.82; 12. tie, Grith Ejstrup (Den) & Rita Gildemeister (EG) 1.82; 14. Renate Gartner (WG) 1.82; 15. Miloslava Hubnerova (Czech) 1.82; 16. tie, Ria Ahlers (Hol) & Erika Rudolf (Hun) 1.79; 18. Alena Proskova (Czech) 1.79; 19. Cornelia Popa* (Rum) 1.76; 20. Snezana Hrepevnik (Yug) 1.76; 21. Solveig Langkilde (Den) 1.76; 22. Milada Karbanova (Czech) 1.76; 23. Magdolna Komka (Hun) 1.71.
(Meyfarth 1.90=OR)

1976 (35. Q 26 July; F 28 July): Overcoming some boredom-breaking misses at lower heights, world record holder Ackermann exhibited her tremendous style in clearing 1.93 (6-4) or better for the 9th time. It was a case of being familiar at a height where everyone else was a stranger. An 84% success rate at the first three heights left 19 in after 2 hours of competition, 13 after 3.

			1.81	1.84	1.87	1.89	1.91	1.93	1.97
1. Rosemarie Ackermann (EG)	1.93	6-4 OR	o	o	o	xo	o	xo	xxx
2. Sara Simeoni (It)	1.91	6-3¼	o	o	o	o	o	xxx	
3. Yordanka Blagoyeva (Bul)	1.91	6-3¼	o	o	o	o	xo	xxx	
4. Maria Mracnova (Cze)	1.89	6-2½	o	o	o	xxx			
5. Joni Huntley (US)	1.89	6-2½	xxo	o	xo	xxx			
6. Tatyana Shlyakto (SU)	1.87	6-1¾	o	o	o	xxx			

7. Annette Tannander (Swe) 1.87; 8. Cornelia Popa (Rum) 1.87; 9. Andrea Matay (Hun) 1.87; 10. Julie White (Can) 1.87; 11. Brigitte Holzapfel (WG) 1.87; 12. tie, Ria Ahlers (Hol),

Galina Filatova (SU) & Snezana Hrepevnik (Yug) 1.84; 15, tie Marie-Christine Debourse (Fr) & Susann Sundqvist (Fin) 1.84; 17. Anne Pira (Bel) 1.84; 18. Paula Girven (US) 1.84; 19. Milada Karbanova (Czech) 1.81; 20. Louise Walker (Can) 1.78; 21. Audrey Reid (Jam) 1.78.

LONG JUMP

1896–1936 (not contested).

1948 (27. Q-F 4 Aug): Gyarmati took the initial Olympic competition with a mark well off the WR of 6.25 (20-6), held by Fanny Blankers-Koen.

1. Olga Gyarmati (Hun)   5.69   18-8   4. Gerda van der Kade (Hol)   5.57   18-3¼
2. Noemi S. De Portela (Arg) 5.60   18-4½   5. Nelly Karelse (Hol)   5.54   18-2¼
3. Ann-Britt Leyman (Swe)   5.57   18-3¼   6. Kathleen Russell (Jam)   5.49   18-¼
7. Judy Canty (Aus) 5.38; 8. Yvonne Curtet-Chabot (Fr) 5.35; 9. Maria Oberbreyer (Aut) 5.24; 10. Ilse Steinegger (Aut) 5.19; 11. V. Beckett (Jam) 5.14; 12. Emma Reed (US) 4.83.

1952 (34. Q-F 23 July): Williams missed the WR by 1cm to best Chudina by 10. Chudina later won the HJ bronze and javelin silver for a unique triple. And the versatile Williams took 6th in the shot.

1. Yvette Williams (NZ)   6.24   20-5¾ OR (f   f   5.90   6.24   6.11   5.99)
2. Aleksandra Chudina (SU) 6.14   20-1¾   (5.99   6.14 5.74   5.90   5.95   6.07)
3. Shirley Cawley (GB)   5.92   19-5   (5.92   f   5.53   5.46   5.78   5.82)
4. Irmgard Schmelzer (WG)   5.90   19-4¼   (5.89   5.76 5.90   f   5.84   f)
5. Wilhelmina Lust (Hol)   5.81   19-¾   (5.68   5.65 5.79   f   5.81   f)
6. Nina Tyurkina (SU)   5.81   19-¾   (5.61   5.81 5.76   5.52   f   f)
7. Mabel Landry (US) 5.75; 8. Verna Johnson (Aus) 5.74; 9. Marie Osterdahl (Fin) 5.73; 10. Olga Gyarmati (Hun) 5.67; 11. Valentina Lituyeva (SU) 5.65; 12. Elzbieta Dunska (Pol) 5.65; 13. A. Millard (Chile) 5.59; 14. Elfriede von Nitzsch (WG) 5.57; 15. Leni Hofknecht (WG) 5.54; 16. Ayako Yoshikawa (Japan) 5.54; 17. D. Josephs (Can) 5.47; 18. G. Erbetta (Arg) 5.47; 19. C. Willoughby (GB) 5.47; 20. G. Magnusson (Swe) 5.43; 21. W. dos Santos (Braz) 5.36; 22. T. Jones (Berm) 5.33; 23. Yvonne Curtet (Fr) 5.30; 24. H. de Menezes (Braz) 4.98.
(Williams 6.16OR Q)

1956 (19. Q-F 27 Nov): Krzesinka killed the competition by matching her 3-month-old WR. Runner-up White, only 17, took the silver by 2cm from Dvalishvili.

1. Elzbieta Krzesinska (Pol) 6.35 20-10=WR 4. Erika Fisch (WG)   5.89   19-4
2. Willye White (US)   6.09 19-11¾   5. Marthe Lambert (Fr)   5.88   19-3½
3. Nadyezhda Dvalishvili (SU) 6.07 20-11   6. Valentina Shaprunova (SU)   5.85   19-2¼
7. Beverly Weigel (NZ) 5.85; 8. Nancy Borwick (Aus) 5.82; 9. Maria Kusion (Pol) 5.79; 10. Helga Hoffmann (EG) 5.73; 11. Olga Gyarmati (Hun) 5.66; 12. Genovefa Minicka (Pol) 5.64.

1960 (30. Q-F 31 Aug): The first gold medal awarded in these Games went to the 100m world record co-holder—for producing an Olympic record 6.37 long jump. Krepkina bested defender Krzesinska by 10cm, with world record holder Claus 3rd. Rand, qualifying leader at 6.33/20-9¼, was far off form in the finals, fouling twice.

1. Vyera Krepkina (SU)   6.37   20-10¾ OR (6.17   6.00 6.22   6.37   6.17   f)
2. Elzbieta Krzesinska (Pol) 6.27   20-7   (f   6.17 f   6.25   f   6.27)
3. Hildrun Laufer* (EG)   6.21   20-4½   (6.21   6.18 f   f   6.13   6.11)
4. Renate Junker (WG)   6.19   20-3¾   (6.17   5.93 6.05   6.19   6.11) 6.10)
5. Lyudmila Radchenko (SU)   6.16   20-2½   (5.99   6.00 6.16   5.83   5.91   5.90)
6. Helga Hoffmann (EG)   6.11   20-½   (6.02   5.88 6.11   5.90   f   6.09)
7. Johanna Bijleveld (Hol) 6.11; 8. V. Shaprunova (SU) 6.00; 9. Mary Rand* (GB) 6.00; 10. Beverly Weigel (NZ) 5.98; 11. Maria Chojnacka (Pol) 5.98; 12. Fumiko Ito (Japan) 5.98; 13. Maria Bibro (Pol) 5.86; 14. Madeleine Thetu (Fr) 5.77; 15. Norma Fleming (Aus) 5.77; 16.

Willye White (US) 5.77; 17. Helen Frith (Aus) 5.57; 18. Brita Johansson (Fin) 5.57; 19. Chris Persighetti (GB) 5.57.

1964 (31. Q-F 14 Oct): Rand was hot from the start. A favorite 4 years earlier in Rome who fell to 9th place, she set an OR 6.52 in the qualifying. She never trailed in the finals, reaching 6.59 in the opening round. In the 5th frame, she unloaded a WR 6.76. Szewinska also got her best in the 5th round as this duo dominated the competition.

1.	Mary Rand (GB)	6.76	22-2¼ WR	(6.59	6.56	6.57	6.63	6.76	6.61)
2.	Irena Szewinska* (Pol)	6.60	21-7¾	(5.86	6.43	6.56	6.03	6.60	f)
3.	Tatyana Schelkanova (SU)	6.42	21-¾	(6.21	6.09	6.42	6.34	6.39	f)
4.	Ingrid Mickler* (WG)	6.40	21-0	(5.97	6.24	6.34	6.25	6.38	6.40)
5.	Vior. Viscopoleanu (Rum)	6.35	20-10	(f	6.35	f	6.32	f	6.32)
6.	Diana Yorgova (Bul)	6.24	20-5¾	(6.24	6.01	6.21	f	5.63	6.06)

7. Hildrun Laufer (EG) 6.24; 8. Helga Hoffmann (EG) 6.23; 9. Berit Berthelsen (Nor) 6.19; 10. Tatyana Talisheva (SU) 6.18; 11. Aida Chuiko (SU) 6.13; 12. Willye White (US) 6.07; 13. Sheila Sherwood* (GB) 6.04; 14. Maria Vittoria Trio (It) 6.98; 15. Johanna Bijleveld (Hol) 5.98; 16. Oddrun Hoklant (Nor) 5.68; 17. Louise Jamieson (GB) 5.66.
(Rand 6.59 OR, 6.63 OR)

1968 (27. Q 13 Oct; F 14 Oct): Only 6 jumps into the finals, Viscopoleanu pulled a killer: a World Record 6.82/22-4½. That did it, as Sherwood got her best in round 5 and Talisheva in round 2. All jumped with either nil or negative wind.

1.	Vior. Viscopoleanu (Rum)	6.82	22-4½ WR	(6.82	f	6.64	6.54	6.52	6.57)
2.	Sheila Sherwood (GB)	6.68	21-11	(6.60	f	6.50	6.59	6.68	6.61)
3.	Tatyana Talisheva (SU)	6.66	21-10¾	(6.55	6.66	5.38	6.38	4.49	f)
4.	Burghild Wieczorek (EG)	6.48	21-3¼	(f	6.48	6.45	6.33	6.42	6.25)
5.	Miroslawa Sarna (Pol)	6.47	21-2¾	(6.47	f	4.98	6.44	6.31	6.45)
6.	Ingrid Mickler (WG)	6.43	21-1¼	(f	6.32	f	6.43	f	6.27)

7. Berit Berthelsen (Nor) 6.40; 8. Heide Rosendahl (WG) 6.40; 9. Violet Odogwu (Nig) 6.23; 10. Martha Watson (US) 6.20; 11. Willye White (US) 6.08; 12. Maureen Barton (GB) 5.95; 13. Ann Wilson (GB) 5.90; 14. Barbel Lohnert (EG) 4.49.

1972 (33. Q-F 31 Aug): The favored Rosendahl appeared to lock up the gold medal with a first-round bound of 6.78, just 6cm off her own World Record. But Yorgova added spice to the proceedings in stanza five, reaching 6.77. As the last jumper in the competition, Yorgova had a final chance, and landed in the vicinity of a winning mark, but fouled.

1.	Heide Rosendahl (WG)	6.78	22-3	(6.78	6.76	6.69	6.52	6.73	6.71)
2.	Diana Yorgova (Bul)	6.77	22-2½	(6.43	6.12	6.62	6.77	6.53	f)
3.	Eva Suranova (Czech)	6.67	21-10¼	(6.51	6.60	f	6.67	f	6.27)
4.	Marcia Garbey (Cuba)	6.52	21-4¾	(6.26	6.52	3.96	5.94	f	f)
5.	Heidi Schuller (WG)	6.51	21-4¼	(6.32	6.18	6.51	f	f	6.25)
6.	Meta Antenen (Switz)	6.49	21-3½	(f	6.49	f	6.16	6.39	f)

7. Viorica Viscopoleanu (Rum) 6.48; 8. Margrit Olfert (EG) 6.46; 9. Sheila Sherwood (GB) 6.41; 10. Ilona Bruzsenyak (Hun) 6.39; 11. Willye White (US) 6.27; 12. Jarmila Nygrynova (Czech) 6.24; 13. Angelika Liebsch (EG) 6.23; 14. Elena Vintila (Rum) 6.13.

1976 (30. Q-F 23 July): Known as a big-meet choker, early-season record setter Voigt found her opener good enough to win as nearly all jumpers complained of poor conditions. In the last round she had to sweat out the final jumps of placers 2-5, who jumped after her. Jumping last, young McMillan landed between the OR and WR flags, but had marginally scratched.

1.	Angela Voigt (EG)	6.72	22-½	(6.72	f	6.50	6.53	f	6.57)
2.	Kathy McMillan (US)	6.66	21-10¼	(f	6.31	6.43	6.47	6.66	f)
3.	Lidia Alfeyeva (SU)	6.60	21-7¾	(6.46	f	6.34	6.60	6.46	6.39)
4.	Sigrun Siegl (EG)	6.59	21-7½	(6.51	6.36	6.59	4.87	6.55	6.57)
5.	Ildiko Erdelyi (Hun)	6.57	21-6¾	(6.51	6.51	6.57	6.40	6.47	f)
6.	Jarmila Nygrynova (Czech)	6.54	21-5½	(6.04	6.15	6.54	f	6.36	6.50)

7. Heidi Wycisk (EG) 6.39; 8. Elena Vintila (Rum) 6.38; 9. Sue Reeve (GB) 6.27; 10. Aniko Milassin (Hun) 6.19; 11. Diane Jones (Can) 6.13;. . . nm—Lilyana Panayotova (Bul).

SHOT

1896–1936 (not contested).

1948 (19. Q-F 4 Aug): Multi-talented Ostermeyer (DT winner as well as HJ 3rd-placer) took the gold with a mark more than 5 feet off the WR (14.89/48-10¼). The medal-winning nations (France, Italy, Austria) have never again even had anyone in the top 8.

1. Micheline Ostermeyer (Fr)	13.75	45-1¼	4. Paulette Veste (Fr)		12.98	42-7
2. Amelia Piccinini (It)	13.09	42-11½	5. Jaroslava Komarkova (Cze)	12.92	42-4¾
3. Ine Schaffer (Aut)	13.08	42-11	6. Anni Bruk (Aut)		12.50	41-¼

7. Maria Radosaljevic (Yug) 12.35; 8. Bevis Reid (GB) 12.16; 9. Ingeborg Pfuller* (Arg) 12.08; 10. Paulette Laurent (Fr) 12.02; 11. Eivor Olsson (Swe) 11.84; 12. M. Schlager (Aut) 11.77.

1952 (20. F 26 July): Zybina's WR 15.28 boosted her own global mark from 15.19 (49-10) as the Soviets first showed their power here.

1. Galina Zybina (SU)	15.28	50-1½ WR	(15.00 14.58 14.04 14.55 14.33 15.28)
2. Marianne Werner (WG)	14.57	47-9¾	(13.89 13.91 f f 14.04 14.57)
3. Klaudia Tochenova (SU)	14.50	47-7	(14.42 f 14.50 14.11 14.06 14.35)
4. Tamara Tishkyevich (SU)	14.42	47-3¾	(14.42 14.13 13.57 14.00 13.45 13.88)
5. Gertrud Kille (WG)	13.84	45-5	(f 12.49 13.48 13.77 13.74 13.84)
6. Yvette Williams (NZ)	13.35	43-9½	(12.27 11.54 13.35 12.68 12.28 11.73)

7. Maria Radosaljevic (Yug) 13.30; 8. Meeri Saari (Fin) 13.02; 9. Paulette Veste (Fr) 12.96; 10. Magdalena Bregulanka (Pol) 12.93; 11. Dorothea Kress (WG) 12.91; 12. Jaroslava Kritkova (Czech) 12.73; 13. Eivor Olsson (Swe) 12.46; 14. Nadya Kotlusek (Yug) 11.98. (Tochenova 14.42 OR; Tishkyevich 14.42=OR; Zabina 15.00 OR)

1956 (18. Q-F 30 Nov): The massive Tishkyevich bested defender Zybina, who had set a WR of 16.76 (55-0) in October. Sixth-placer Brown boosted her American best by more than 3 feet.

1. Tamara Tishkyevich (SU)	16.59	54-5¼ OR	4. Zinaida Doynikova (SU)	15.54	50-11¾
2. Galina Zybina (SU)	16.53	53-2¾	5. Valerie Young* (NZ)	15.34	50-4
3. Marianne Werner (WG)	15.61	51-2½	6. Earlene Brown (US)	15.12	49-7¼

7. Regina Branner (Aut) 14.60; 8. Nadya Kotlusek (Yug) 14.56; 9. Milena Usenik (Yug) 14.49; 10. Jacqueline MacDonald (Can) 14.31; 11. Johanna Hubner* (EG) 13.88; 12. Anne-Katrine Lafrenz (WG) 12.72; 13. Valerie Lawrence (Aus) 13.12; 14. Lois Testa (US) 13.06; 15. Suzanne Allday (GB) 12.71. (Zabina 16.35 OR, 16.48 OR, 16.53 OR)

1960 (18. Q-F 2 Sept): Press had no trouble winning with an Olympic record 17.32, but the next 3 battled throughout. Hubner got her medal-winner in the final round as did American Brown (the only American ever to place in the first 6 in the Olympic shot, let alone win a medal). Zybina, '52 champ, took 7th with a mark better than her Helsinki winner.

1. Tamara Press (SU)	17.32	56-10 OR	(16.08 17.32 16.40 16.19 16.20 f)
2. Johanna Hubner* (EG)	16.61	54-6	(16.21 15.59 15.74 15.20 15.40 16.61)
3. Earlene Brown (US)	16.42	53-10½	(15.73 16.34 16.07 15.80 15.95 16.42)
4. Val Young* (NZ)	16.39	53-9¾	(16.11 16.26 15.72 16.39 16.21 16.07)
5. Zinaida Doynikova (SU)	16.13	52-11	(f 15.72 15.40 15.65 16.13 15.52)
6. Renate Boy* (EG)	15.94	52-3½	(15.61 15.94 15.40 15.07 15.20 15.60)

7. Galina Zybina (SU) 15.56; 8. Wilfriede Hoffmann (EG) 15.14; 9. Vera Cerna (Czech) 15.08; 10. Jadwiga Klimaj (Pol) 14.67; 11. Eugenia Rusink (Pol) 14.55; 12. Milene Usenik (Yug) 14.20.

1964 (26. Q-F 20 Oct): Defending champion Press came back a day after winning the discus to complete a weight double with an OR 18.14. ¿She led from the beginning, although Boy got close on two efforts, before putting things away in the closing round with her OR. Helsinki champ Zybina showed she still had what it takes by taking 3rd, with Irina Press 6th.

1. Tamara Press (SU)	18.14	59-6¼ OR	(17.51 17.72 17.18 16.49 f	18.14)
2. Renate Boy* (EG)	17.61	57-9¼	(17.41 17.10 16.38 17.61 17.00 17.01)	
3. Galina Zybina (SU)	17.45	57-3	(17.38 17.25 17.45 17.42 16.65 17.36)	
4. Val Young (NZ)	17.26	56-7½	(17.08 15.84 16.81 17.26 17.24 17.23)	
5. Margitta Gummel* (EG)	16.91	55-5¾	(16.67 15.87 f	16.60 16.91 16.34)
6. Irina Press (SU)	16.71	54-10	(f	16.50 f	15.81 15.78 16.71)

7. Nancy McCredie (Can) 15.89; 8. Ana Salagean (Rum) 15.83; 9. Johanna Hubner (EG) 15.77; 10. Ivanka Khristova (Bul) 15.69; 11. Judit Bognar (Hun) 15.65; 12. Earlene Brown (US) 14.80.
(Press 17.51 OR, 17.72 OR)

1968 (14. F 9.0 Oct): Lange took the lead in Round 1 with 18.78 and held it until the 3rd frame when Gummel reached 19.07. Then in round 5, Gummel exploded to a World Record 19.61 to salt away the gold.

1. Margitta Gummel (EG)	19.61	64-4 WR	(18.53 17.88 19.07 18.30 19.61 18.59)	
2. Maritta Lange (EG)	18.78	61-7½	(18.78 f	18.17 18.47 18.20 18.26)
3. Nadyezhda Chizova (SU)	18.19	59-8¼	(18.19 f	18.03 17.62 17.49 17.26)
4. Judit Bognar (Hun)	17.78	58-4	(17.14 17.30 17.21 17.78 17.75 16.83)	
5. Renate Boy (EG)	17.72	58-1¼	(17.67 17.15 17.68 17.49 17.72 17.69)	
6. Ivanka Khristova (Bul)	17.25	56-7¼	(16.65 17.25 16.85 f	f	17.20)

7. Marlene Fuchs (WG) 17.11; 8. Els Van Noorduyn (Hol) 16.23; 9. Irina Solontsova (SU) 15.88; 10. Gertrud Schafer (WG) 15.26; 11. Maren Seidler (US) 14.86; 12. Rosa Molina (Chile) 12.85; 13. Ok-Ja Paik (S Kor) 12.67; 14. Rosario Martinez (El Sal) 10.18.
(Gummel 18.53 OR, 19.07 WR, OR)

1972 (18. Q 4 Sept; F 7 Sept): In a Games where first-round marks were the key to winning field events, Chizova overpowered her opposition by nearly a meter with an opening world record of 21.03. It was history's first 21m put and the game was over.

1. Nadyezhda Chizova (SU)	21.03	69-0 WR	(21.03 20.36 20.58 19.97 f	f)
2. Margitta Gummel (EG)	20.22	66-4	(18.46 18.83 19.55 20.22 19.53 f)	
3. Ivanka Khristova (Bul)	19.35	63-5¾	(19.35 f	19.22 f	18.82 18.95)
4. Svet. Krachevskaya* (SU)	19.24	63-1½	(18.43 19.24 f	18.74 f	f)
5. Marianne Adam (EG)	18.94	62-1¾	(18.75 f	18.58 18.94 18.91 18.71)
6. Maritta Lange (EG)	18.85	61-10¼	(f	18.46 18.29 18.85 18.38 18.71)

7. Helena Fibingerova (Czech) 18.81; 8. Yelena Stoyanova (Bul) 18.34; 9. Antonia Ivanova (SU) 18.28; 10. Ludwika Chewinska (Pol) 18.24; 11. Judit Bognar (Hun) 18.23; 12. Radostina Vasekova (Bul) 17.86; 13. Valentina Cioltan (Rum) 16.62.

1976 (13. F 31 July): Bulgaria's first-ever track gold went to Khristova, who set 2 WRs just before the Games. It wasn't easy, however, as she didn't take the lead to stay until the 5th round. Chizova completed her set of medals in second, while the East Germans were shut out in their only whitewash of the Games.

1. Ivanka Khristova (Bul)	21.16	69-5 OR	(19.96 20.88 20.67 20.47 21.16 20.19)	
2. Nadyezhda Chizova (SU)	20.96	68-9¼	(20.84 20.96 f	p	14.16 f)
3. Helena Fibingerova (Cze)	20.67	67-9¾	(f	19.68 20.15 f	20.67 f)
4. Marianne Adam (EG)	20.55	67-5	(20.55 f	f	18.15 19.50)
5. Ilona Schoknecht (EG)	20.54	67-4¾	(20.52 19.78 19.65 19.80 19.72 20.54)	
6. Margitta Droese (EG)	19.79	64-11¼	(f	17.53 19.15 f	19.64 19.79)

7. Eva Wilms (WG) 19.29; 8. Yelena Stoyanova (Bul) 18.89; 9. Svyetlana Krachevskaya (SU) 18.36; 10. Faina Myelnik (SU) 18.07; 11. Maria Sarria (Cuba) 16.31; 12. Maren Seidler (US) 15.60; 13. Lucette Moreau (Can) 15.48.

DISCUS

1896—1924 (not contested).

1928 (21. F 31 July): Konopacka upped the WR from 39.18 (128-6) to win from Copeland by more than 2½ meters.

1. Halina Konopacka (Pol) 39.62 130-0 WR 4. Milly Reuter (Ger) 35.86 117-8
2. Lillian Copeland (US) 37.08 121-8 5. Grete Heublein (Ger) 35.56 116-8
3. Ruth Svedberg (Swe) 35.92 117-10 6. Liesl Perkaus (Aut) 33.54 110-0
  7. Maybelle Reichardt (US) 33.52; 8. Genovefa Kobielska (Pol) 39.72; 9. Charlotte Mader (Ger) 32.22; 10. Lucienne Vellu (Fr) 31.28; 11. Leni Michaelis (Hol) 31.04; 12. Paula Mollenhauer (Ger) 30.94.
(Heublein 35.56 OR; Copeland 36.33 OR; Konopacka 39.16 OR)

1932 (9. F 2 Aug): Copeland moved up to the top notch this time, setting an OR as teammate Osborn took 2nd, the best-ever U.S. showing. Note the presence of 100 winner Walsh.

1. Lillian Copeland (US) 40.58 133-2 OR 4. Tilly Fleischer (Ger) 36.12 118-6
2. Ruth Osborn (US) 40.12 131-7 5. Grete Heublein (Ger) 34.66 113-8
3. Jadwiga Marcinkiewicz*(Pol)38.74 127-1 6. Stella Walsh (Pol) 33.60 110-3
  7. Mitsue Ishizu (Japan) 33.48; 8. Ellen Braumuller (Ger) 33.14; 9. Margaret Jenkins (US) 30.22.
(Osborn 40.12 OR)

1936 (19. F 4 Aug): Mauermeyer, touted before the Games as the classic example of Arayan women, added more than 7 meters to the former OR in winning comfortably. Silver winner Marcinkiewicz threw 6m farther than Copeland had to win 4 years earlier.

1. Gisela Mauermeyer (Ger) 47.62 156-3 OR (47.62 41.64 40.70 36.26 43.54 44.26)
2. Jadwiga Marcinkiewicz*(Pol)46.22 151-8 (44.68 31.98 46.22 43.36 f 42.88)
3. Paula Mollenhauer (Ger) 39.80 130-7 (38.58 37.44 33.26 35.82 f 39.80)
4. Ko Nakamura (Japan) 38.24 125-5
5. Hide Mineshima (Japan) 37.34 122-6
6. Birgit Lundstrom (Swe) 35.92 117-10
  7. Anna Niesink*(Hol) 35.20; 8. Gertrude Wilhemsen (US) 34.42; 9. Helen Stephens (US) 34.32; 10. Ljubica Gabric (It) 34.30.
(Wajsowna 44.68 OR)

1948 (21. F 30 July): Post-war standards had dropped. Ostermeyer was able to win with a throw nearly 6m short of the OR and more than 8m short of the WR of 50.50 (165-8).

1. Micheline Ostermeyer (Fr) 41.92 137-6 4. Jad. Marcinkiewicz* (Pol) 39.30 128-11
2. Edera Gentile (It) 41.16 135-0 5. Lotte Haidegger (Aut) 38.80 127-3
3. Jacqueline Mazeas (Fr) 40.46 132-9 6. Anna Niesink (Hol) 38.74 127-1
  7. Majken Aberg (Swe) 38.48; 8. Ingeborg Mello (Arg) 38.44; 9. Freida Tiltsch (Aut) 37.18; 10. Paulette Veste (Fr) 36.84; 11. Frances Kaszubski (US) 36.50; 12. G. Arenander (Swe) 36.24; 13. P. Roos-Looder (Hol) 36.14; 14. Bevis Reid (GB) 35.84; 15. M. Schlager (Aut) 34.78; 16. Dorothy Dodson (US) 34.68; 17. Gabric Calvesi (It) 34.12; 18. Pong Sik Pak (Kor) 33.80; 19. M. Birtwhistle (GB) 33.02; 20. E. Whyte (GB) 32.46; 21. Julia Matej (Yug) 30.22.

1952 (20. Q-F 20 July): Soviet Olympic power was exemplified by this sweep of a technical event. The Soviet trio was the first ever to win all 3 medals in a women's event. Winner Ponomaryeva took her first of 3 medals in this event.

1. Nina Ponomaryeva* (SU) 51.42 168-8 OR (45.16 50.84 51.42 47.24 44.66 49.36)
2. Yeliz. Bagryantseva (SU) 47.08 154-5 (43.58 47.08 44.26 43.96 44.58 43.00)
3. Nina Dumbadze (SU) 46.28 151-10 (45.84 40.24 44.10 46.28 45.10 41.04)
4. Toyoko Yoshino (Japan) 43.80 143-8 (41.70 42.66 37.14 41.58 43.80 42.02)
5. Lotte Haidegger (Aut) 43.48 142-8 (35.66 43.48 40.02 f f 41.32)

6. Lia Manoliu (Rum)   42.64   139-11   (41.56 42.64 41.48 36.04 41.20 40.78)
7. Ingeborg Pfuller   (Arg) 41.74; 8. Ilona Jozsa (Hun) 41.60; 9. Marianne Werner (WG)
41.02; 10. Yvette Williams (NZ) 40.46; 11. K. Koivuniemi (Fin) 40.32; 12. Ingeborg Mello
(Arg) 39.04; 13. L. Novakova (Czech) 38.82; 14. Edera Gentile (It) 38.22; 15. S. Farmer (GB)
37.96; 16. Paulette Veste (Fr) 37.64; 17. G. Bollinger (Switz) 36.36; 18. Frieda Tiltsch (Aut)
27.84.
(Ponomaryeva* 50.84 OR)

1956 (22. Q-F 23 Nov): Connolly, who created as many headlines with her romance with
hammer winner Hal Connolly, turned back the Soviets with an OR as defending champ
Ponomaryeva slipped to 3rd. Brown took 4th with an AR by more than 20 feet!

1. Olga Connolly* (Czech)   53.68   176-1 OR 4. Earlene Brown (US)   51.34 168-5
2. Irina Beglyakova (SU)   52.54   172-4   5. Albina Yelkina (SU)   48.20 158-2
3. Nina Ponomaryeva (SU)   52.02   170-8   6. Isabel Avellan (Arg)   46.72 153-3
    7. Jirina Voborilova (Czech) 45.84; 8. Stepanka Mertova (Czech) 45.78; 9. Lia Manoliu
(Rum) 43.90; 10. Marianne Werner (WG) 43.34; 11. Paola Paternoster (It) 42.82; 12. Nadya
Kotlusek (Yug) 42.16; 13. L. Jackman (Aus) 40.84.
(Beglyakova 51.77 OR; Connolly* 52.04 OR; Beglyakova 52.54 OR, 52.54=OR)

1960 (24. Q 3 Sept; F 5 Sept): Ponomaryeva showed her competitive verve by winning back
the title she had first taken in Helsinki, but lost in Melbourne. She dominated shot winner Press
with 3 throws longer than anyone else's. Defending champ Fikotova-Connolly took 7th (one
place higher than husband Hal in the hammer).

1. Nina Ponomaryeva (SU)   55.10   180-9 OR (44.48 52.40 53.40 51.66 55.10 54.40)
2. Tamara Press (SU)   52.58   172-4   (51.64 46.82 f   50.90 f   52.58)
3. Lia Manoliu (Rum)   52.36   171-9   (52.36 f   46.28 50.58 48.78 46.94)
4. Kriemhild Limberg* (WG) 51.46   168-10   (51.46 f   45.28 47.40 48.10 46.38)
5. Yevgenia Kuznyetsova (SU) 51.42   168-8   (51.42 51.38 50.96 49.68 50.62 51.24)
6. Earlene Brown (US)   51.28   168-3   (51.28 35.82 47.26 f   35.18 45.80)
    7. Olga Connolly (US) 50.32; 8. Jirina Nemcova (Czech) 50.10; 9. Irene Schuch (EG) 49.86;
10. Val Young* (NZ) 48.38; 11. Stepanka Mertova (Czech) 48.26; 12. Vivianne Bergh (Swe)
43.94.

1964 (21. Q-F 19 Oct): Press became only the 2nd woman in Olympic history to win the
SP/DT double (although the former was instituted in the Games only in '48). This was a
tougher victory to claim than the shot as Lotz set an OR 57.20 in round 1, a distance Press
could not overcome until round 5 when she reached an OR 57.26. Manoliu regained her bronze
medal some 10 feet behind.

1. Tamara Press (SU)   57.26   187-10 OR (f   55.38 50.58 55.22 57.26 56.08)
2. Ingrid Lotz (EG)   57.20   187-8   (57.20 f   55.40 f   54.58 54.74)
3. Lia Manoliu (Rum)   56.96   186-10   (55.90 f   f   56.08 56.96 f)
4. Virginia Mikhailova (Bul) 56.70   186-0   (47.38 56.56 52.18 56.70 55.76 55.54)
5. Yevgenia Kuznyetsova (SU) 55.16   181-0   (55.16 53.58 f   f   f   53.80)
6. Jolan Kleiber (Hun)   54.86   180-0   (54.46 53.04 53.50 53.14 54.86 51.68)
    7. Kriemhild Limberg (WG) 53.80; 8. Olimpia Catarama (Rum) 53.08; 9. Jirina Nemcova
(Czech) 52.80; 10. Judit Stugner (Hun) 52.52; 11. Nina Ponomaryeva (SU) 52.48; 12. Olga
Connolly (US) 51.58; 13. Val Young (NZ) 49.58; 14. Doris Lorenz (EG) 45.62.
(Kuznyetsova 55.16 OR; Manoliu 55.90 OR; Lotz 57.20 OR)

1968 (16. F 18 Oct): All the placings were decided in the 1st round, save Westermann's in the
2nd stanza. Super-veteran Manoliu hurt her elbow after her 2nd throw but her opening 58.28
was enough. Rain hampered, and delayed the competition several times.

1. Lia Manoliu (Rum)   58.28   191-2 OR (58.28 f   p   f   46.82 f)
2. Liesel Westermann (WG)   57.76   189-6   (54.02 57.76 f   55.78 f   f)
3. Jolan Kleiber (Hun)   54.90   180-1   (54.90 54.24 f   f   f   f)
4. Anita Otto (EG)   54.40   178-6   (54.40 54.10 53.88 f   51.16 52.34)

5. Antonina Popova (SU)   53.42   175-3   (53.42 53.12 51.40 52.60 52.86 f)
6. Olga Connolly (US)   52.96   173-9   (f   52.96 50.74 f   f   50.40)
   7. Christine Speilberg (EG) 52.86; 8. Brigitte Berendonk (WG) 52.80; 9. Lyudmila
Muravyova (SU) 52.26; 10. Karin Illgen (EG) 52.18; 11. Judit Stugner (Hun) 52.08; 12.
Namjilmaa Dashzeveg (Mon) 50.76; 13. Olimpia Catarama (Run) 50.20; 14. Carol Moseke (US)
48.28; 15. Josephine de la Vina (Phil) 46.56; 16. Jean Roberts (Aus) 46.26.

1972 (17. Q 9 Sept; F 10 Sept): World record holder Myelnik took care of arch-rival Menis in
the 4th round, just missing her own best by 14cm.

1. Faina Myelnik (SU)   66.62   218-7 OR   (60.56 61.32 57.96 66.62 62.76 f)
2. Argentina Menis (Rum)   65.06   213-5   (64.28 59.82 60.88 65.06 63.78 64.90)
3. Vassilka Stoyeva (Bul)   64.34   211-1   (61.08 f   64.20 62.24 64.34 62.10)
4. Tamara Danilova (SU)   62.86   206-3   (62.64 58.14 62.86 61.14 f   f)
5. Liesel Westermann (WG)   62.18   204-0   (f   57.04 62.18 61.66 f   f)
6. Gabrielle Hinzmann (EG)   61.72   202-6   (57.52 59.14 60.12 61.08 61.72 60.22)
   7. Carmen Ionescu (Rum) 60.42; 8. Lyudmila Muravyova (SU) 59.00; 9. Lia Manoliu (Rum)
58.50; 10. Svetla Boshkova (Bul) 56.72; 11. Brigitte Berendonk (WG) 56.58; 12. Rosemary
Payne (GB) 56.50.
(Menis 61.28 OR Q; Danilova 62.64 OR; Menis 64.28 OR, 65.06 OR)

1976 (15. Q 28 July; F 29 July): Myelnik was rated as the surest favorite of the whole Games.
She held the silver overnight, but a protested 5th-round throw was taken away and she slipped
to 4th. Only 20, Schlaak was the youngest individual women's winner of the Games.

1. Evelyn Schlaak (EG)   69.00   226-4 OR   (69.00 66.80 66.12 f   61.24 64.80)
2. Maria Vergova (Bul)   67.30   220-9   (62.22 67.30 60.44 59.86 62.70 f)
3. Gabrielle Hinzmann (EG)   66.84   219-3   (66.68 66.10 66.84 66.24 66.32 f)
4. Faina Myelnik (SU)   66.40   217-10   (64.48 65.42 62.76 66.40 f   64.20)
5. Sabine Engel (EG)   65.88   216-2   (f   61.18 65.46 65.88 64.92 61.18)
6. Argentina Menis (Rum)   65.38   214-6   (62.82 62.50 63.70 64.14 65.38 63.48)
   7. Maria Betancourt (Cuba) 63.86; 8. Natalia Gorbachova (SU) 63.46; 9. Carmen Romero
(Cuba) 61.18; 10. Olga Andrianova (SU) 60.80; 11. Jane Haist (Can) 58.74; 12. Rita Pfister
(Switz) 57.24; 13. Lucette Moreau (Can) 55.88;. . . dnc—Danuta Rosani (Pol).
(Hinzmann 66.68 OR)

JAVELIN

1896—1928 (not contested).

1932 (8. F 31 July): The legendary Didrikson showed her versatility with an OR victory 4 days
before she won the 80m hurdles. But her mark was well off the 46.76 (153-4) WR.

1. Mildred Didrikson (US)   43.86   143-4 OR 4. Masako Shimpo (Japan)   39.06 128-2
2. Ellen Braumuller (Ger)   43.48   142-8   5. Nan Gindele (US)   37.94 124-6
3. Tilly Fleischer (Ger)   43.00   141-1   6. Gloria Russell (US)   36.72 120-6
   7. Maria Uribe Jasso (Mex) 33.66; 8. Mitsue Ishizu (Japan) 30.82.

1936 (14. F 2 Aug): Fleischer gave Germany both throwing titles with her OR victory ahead of
teammate Kruger.

1. Tilly Fleischer (Ger)   45.18   148-3 OR 4. Herma Bauma (Aut)   41.66 136-8
2. Luise Kruger (Ger)   43.28   142-8   5. Sadako Yamamoto (Japan) 41.44 135-11
3. Maria Kwasniewska (Pol)   41.80   137-2   6. Lydia Eberhardt (Ger)   41.36 135-8
   7. Gertrude Wilhelmsen (US) 37.34; 8. Gerda de Kock (Hol) 36.92; 9. Martha Worst (US)
36.68; 10. Irja Lipasti (Fin) 33.68.
(Fleischer 44.68 OR)

1948 (15. F 31 July): Bauma turned in the only women's field event OR of the first post-war Games with her 45.56.

1. Herma Bauma (Aut)   45.56   149-6 OR   4. Dorothy Dodson (US)   41.96 137-8
2. Kaisa Parviainen (Fin) 43.78   143-8   5. Johanna Waalboer (Hol)   40.92 134-3
3. Lily Kelsby* (Den)   42.08   138-1   6. Johanne Koning (Hol)   40.32 132-3

7. Dana Zatopkova* (Czech) 39.64; 8. Elly Dammers (Hol) 38.22; 9. Gerda Schilling (Aut) 38.00; 10. Ingrid Almqvist (Swe) 37.26; 11. M. Sinoracka (Pol) 35.74; 12. Theresa Manuel (US) 33.82; 13. N. Saeys (Bel) 31.78; 14. M. Long (GB) 30.28; 15. G. Clarke (GB) 29.58.

1952 (19. Q-F 24 July): In a wonderful day for the Zatopek family, Zatopkova edged LJ runner-up Chudina with an OR 165-7. The story was completed later in the day when the winner's husband (with whom she also coincidentally shared the same birthday) won the 5000.

1. Dana Zatopkova (Czech)   50.46   165-7 OR   (50.46 41.34 46.28 43.44 45.62 47.62)
2. Aleksandra Chudina (SU)   50.00   164-0   (46.70 45.20 47.52 f   49.60 50.00)
3. Yelena Gorchakova (SU)   49.76   163-3   (46.66 49.76 48.26 45.28 43.10 43.28)
4. Galina Zybina (SU)   48.34   158-7   (44.86 48.34 47.24 47.94 47.80 45.94)
5. Lily Kelsby (Den)   46.22   151-8   (46.22 40.90 45.52 42.38 44.82 44.76)
6. Marlies Muller (WG)   44.36   145-6   (f   44.36 f   43.20 f   43.08)

7. Marysza Csiach (Pol) 44.30; 8. Jutta Kruger (WG) 44.30; 9. Herma Bauma (Aut) 42.54; 10. Estrella Puente (Urg) 41.44; 11. A. Turci (It) 41.20; 12. I. Bausenwein (WG) 41.16; 13. Marjorie Larney (US) 40.58; 14. Anni Rattya (Fin) 40.56; 15. Diana Coates (GB) 40.16; 16. K. Parviainen (Fin) 39.82; 17. Elsa Torikka (Fin) 39.58.
(Chudina 46.70 OR)

1956 (19. Q-F 28 Nov): Jaunzeme triumphed over more-heralded teammate Konyayeva (WR holder at 55.48/182-0) with an OR by nearly 3m. Ahrens won the only Olympic track medal ever by a Chilean woman.

1. Inese Jaunzeme (SU)   53.86   176-8 OR   4. Dana Zatopkova (Czech)   49.82 163-5
2. Marlene Ahrens (Chile)   50.38   165-3   5. Ingrid Almqvist (Swe)   49.74 163-2
3. Nadyezhda Konyayeva (SU)50.28   164-11   6. Urszula Figwer (Pol)   48.16 158-0

7. Erszebeth Vigh (Hun) 48.06; 8. Karen Oldham* (US) 48.00; 9. Anna Wojtaszek (Pol) 46.92; 10. Erika Raue (EG) 45.84; 11. Marjorie Larney (US) 45.26; 12. Yoriko Shida (Japan) 44.96; 13. Almut Brommel (WG) 44.66; 14. Amelia Wershoven (US) 44.28.
(Jaunzeme 51.62 OR, 53.40 OR)

1960 (20. Q-F 1 Sept): World record holder Ozolina killed the opposition with her first throw, an OR 55.98. Super-veteran Zatopkova, '52 champion, won her second medal and her family's 7th. Britain's Platt got a throw out in the silver medal range, but was so excited watching the flight, she stepped over the scratch line for a foul.

1. Elvira Ozolina (SU)   55.98   183-8 OR   (55.98 f   51.54 54.78 f   f)
2. Dana Zatopkova (Czech)   53.78   176-5   (49.84 50.34 53.78 51.00 46.12 50.70)
3. Birute Kalediene (SU)   53.44   175-4   (50.16 49.80 53.44 50.86 49.58 f)
4. Vlasta Peskova (Czech)   52.56   172-5   (50.92 f   51.28 52.56 49.00 48.82)
5. Urszula Figwer (Pol)   52.32   171-8   (52.32 f   47.90 50.14 46.54 p)
6. Anna Pazera (Aus)   51.14   167-9   (51.14 47.04 f   42.74 47.34 f)

7. Sue Platt (GB) 51.00; 8. Alevtina Shastitko (SU) 50.90; 9. Marta Rudas* (Hun) 50.25; 10. Maria Diti (Rum) 49.56; 11. Anneliese Gerhards (WG) 49.26; 12. Marlene Ahrens (Chile) 47.52; 13. Karen Oldham (US) 46.52.

1964 (16. Q-F 16 Oct): Rumania's 17-year-old Penes killed the opposition with her opening throw of 60.54. Surprising to many, surely, since Soviet Gorchakova had rifled a WR 62.40 in the qualifying round and defending champ Ozolina had the 2nd-longest distance (Penes was only 6th among the qualifiers and she reached the qualifying distance with on her final toss). But the Soviets were far off their qualifying efforts, Gorchakova managing 3rd and Ozolina only 6th.

1. Mihaela Penes (Rum)   60.54   198-7   (60.54 52.76 f   50.72 51.44 53.76)
2. Marta Rudas (Hun)   58.26   191-2   (53.20 58.26 f   54.16 50.24 f)
3. Yelena Gorchakova (SU) 57.06   187-2   (56.42 49.20 53.10 57.06 55.22 f)
4. Birute Kalediene (SU)   56.30   184-8   (53.78 f   54.12 56.30 54.68 f)
5. Elvira Ozolina (SU)   54.80   179-9   (54.68 54.80 f   f   f   f)
6. Maria Diaconescu (Rum) 53.70   176-2   (f   53.70 50.48 51.20 51.34 52.00)
7. Hiroko Sato (Japan) 52.48; 8. Anneliese Gerhards (WG) 52.36; 9. Sue Platt (GB) 48.60; 10. Michele Demys (Fr) 47.24; 11. Misako Katayama (Japan) 46.86; 12. Rosemarie Schubert (EG) 46.50.
(Gorchakova 62.40 WR, OR Q)

1968 (16. F 14 Oct): Defending champ Penes got her best throw in the first round, while Nemeth succeeded her in the next stanza. A close tussle for the bronze saw Rudas hold 3rd until the final round when Janko slipped ahead and Rudas could not reply with her final effort.

1. Angela Nemeth (Hun)   60.36   198-0   (57.66 60.36 55.56 57.54 f   53.30)
2. Mihaela Penes (Rum)   59.92   196-7   (59.92 54.68 f   51.40 58.36 f)
3. Eva Janko (Aut)   58.04   190-5   (54.60 f   f   46.44 46.24 58.04)
4. Marta Rudas (Hun)   56.38   185-0   (56.38 f   f   51.60 f   52.68)
5. Daniela Jaworska (Pol)   56.06   183-11   (55.78 56.06 52.34 51.88 f   53.20)
6. Natasha Urbancic (Yug)   55.42   181-10   (53.80 f   55.42 f   f   p)
7. Ameli Koloska (WG) 55.20; 8. Kaisa Launela (Fin) 53.96; 9. Barbara Friedrich (US) 53.44; 10. Lidia Tsymozh (SU) 53.40; 11. Ranae Bair (US) 53.14; 12. Lucyna Krawcewicz (Pol) 51.54; 13. Jay Dahlgren (Can) 51.34; 14. Valentina Evert (SU) 51.16; 15. Sue Platt (GB) 48.52;... nm—Erika Strasser (Aut).

1972 (19. Q 31 Aug; F 1 Sept): New world holder Fuchs was in control almost all the way, taking the lead in Round 2 and improving on throws 4 and 5. That penultimate throw, 63.88, rated as history's No. 2 performance. The old guard was completely shut out of the medals as Hein and Schmidt, a pair of 18-year-olds, took silver and bronze.

1. Ruth Fuchs (EG)   63.88   209-7 OR (57.44 60.20 50.20 61.16 63.88 59.16)
2. Jacqueline Hein* (EG)   62.54   205-2   (f   55.44 57.18 59.70 56.92 62.54)
3. Kate Schmidt (US)   59.94   196-8   (59.94 58.32 59.84 f   48.80 56.10)
4. Lutvian Mollova (Bul)   59.36   194-9   (56.46 59.36 55.10 f   56.00 58.44)
5. Natasha Urbancic (Yug)   59.06   193-9   (f   f   56.48 56.38 59.06 f)
6. Eva Janko (Aut)   58.56   192-1   (f   58.50 f   f   58.56 52.06)
7. Ewa Gryziecka (Pol) 57.00; 8. Svyetlana Korolyova (SU) 56.36; 9. Anneliese Gerhards (WG) 55.84; 10. Maria Kucserka (Hun) 54.40; 11. Magda Paulanyi (Hun) 52.36;... nm—Eva Zorgo (Rum).

1976 (14. Q 23 July; F 24 July): Fuchs's opener was enough as US hope Schmidt never materialized. Schmidt, in fact, had to pull out a couple of clutch throws to score at all. Fuchs became the first repeat javelin winner.

1. Ruth Fuchs (EG)   65.94   216-4 OR (65.94 59.58 65.06 54.48 58.82 58.44)
2. Marion Becker (WG)   64.70   212-3   (60.66 60.52 64.70 f   f   f)
3. Kate Schmidt (US)   63.96   209-10   (f   f   59.70 57.90 f   63.96)
4. Jacqueline Hein (EG)   63.84   209-5   (58.30 61.88 60.90 55.16 f   63.84)
5. Sabine Sebrowski (EG)   63.08   206-11   (57.02 59.10 63.08 56.46 54.34 51.72)
6. Svyetlana Babich (SU)   59.42   194-11   (f   49.24 59.42 f   f   f)
7. Nadyezhda Yakubovich (SU) 59.16; 8. Karin Smith (US) 57.50; 9. Eva Janko (Aut) 57.20; 10. Tessa Sanderson (GB) 57.00; 11. Eva Zorgo (Rum) 55.60; 12. Yordanka Peeva (Bul) 52.24.
(Becker 65.14 OR Q)

PENTATHLON

1896–1960 (not contested).

80mH/100mH, SP, HJ, LJ, 200m (80mH replaced by 100mH in 1972; in 1980, 200m will be replaced by 800m).

1964 (20, 16-17 Oct): Irina Press started the Soviet sisters' impressive performances with a WR 5246 total. She was never worse than 5th in any one event, lead one and co-lead another to best LJ winner Rand by more than 200 points. Her shot effort would have placed her 5th in the regular SP, a place higher than she took 4 days later.

1. Irina Press (SU)	(10.7	17.16	1.63	6.24	24.7)	5245 WR
2. Mary Rand (GB)	(10.9	11.05	1.72	6.55	24.2)	5035
3. Galina Bystrova (SU)	(10.7	14.47	1.60	6.11	25.2)	4956
4. Mary Peters (GB)	(11.0	14.48	1.60	5.60	25.4)	4797
5. Draga Stamejcic (Yug)	(10.9	12.73	1.54	6.19	25.2)	4790
6. Helga Hoffmann (WG)	(11.2	10.67	1.60	6.44	25.0)	4737

7. Pat Winslow (US) 4724; 8. Ingrid Mickler* (WG) 4717; 9. Nina Hansen (Den) 4611; 10. Maria Siziakova (SU) 4580; 11. Helen Frith (Aus) 4557; 12. Denise Guenard (Fr) 4548. 20 finishers.

1968 (33. 15 Oct): Pre-Games favorite Heide Rosendahl was injured warming up and withdrew. Prokop led after the first day from Tikhomorova, with Becker 4th. A 6.43/21-1¾ long jump put Mickler within 25 points of Prokop with 1 event left and her fine 23.5 put it away. Prokop held on to the silver by 10 points as Toth's good 200 gave her 3rd ahead of Tikhomirova.

1. Ingrid Mickler* (WG)	(10.9	11.48	1.71	6.43	23.5)	5098
2. Liese Prokop (Aut)	(11.2	14.61	1.68	5.97	25.1)	4966
3. Annamaria Toth (Hun)	(10.9	12.68	1.59	6.12	23.8)	4959
4. Valentina Tikhomirova (SU)	(11.2	14.12	1.65	5.99	24.9)	4927
5. Manon Bornholdt (WG)	(11.0	12.37	1.59	6.42	24.8)	4890
6. Pat Winslow (US)	(11.4	13.33	1.65	5.97	24.5)	4877

7. Inge Bauer (EG) 4849; 8. Meta Antenen (Switz) 4848; 9. Mary Peters (GB) 4803; 10. Sue Scott (GB) 4786; 11. Jenny Meldrum (Can) 4774; 12. Marijana Lubej (Yug) 4764. 31 finishers.

1972 (30. 2-3 Sept): Again Rosendahl was the favorite, but a victory was not to be, as her spectacular second day couldn't overcome the big 301-point bulge Peters had forged through 3 events. Peters, now 33, had scored PRs in the hurdles and HJ and scored a pentathlon best in the SP. Rosendahl came back with a vengeance, her 6.83, although windy, was just 1cm off her world record. Her brilliant 22.96 gave her history's best score, but only momentarily, as Peters scored another PR to eke out a 10-point win. Pollak, the former world record holder at 4741, also bettered the old mark in 3rd.

1. Mary Peters (GB)	(13.29	16.20	1.82	5.98	24.08)	4801 WR
2. Heide Rosendahl (WG)	(13.34	13.86	1.65	6.83	22.96)	4791
3. Burglinde Pollak (EG)	(13.53	16.04	1.76	6.21	23.93)	4768
4. Christine Laser* (EG)	(13.25	12.51	1.76	6.40	23.66)	4671
5. Valentina Tikhomirova (SU)	(13.77	14.64	1.74	6.15	24.25)	4597
6. Nadyalka Angelova (Bul)	(13.84	13.96	1.68	6.32	24.58)	4496

7. Karen Mack (WG) 4449; 8. Ilona Bruzsenyak (Hun) 4419; 9. Nadyezhda Tkachenko (SU) 4370; 10 Diane Jones (Can) 4349; 11. Djurdja Focic (Yug) 4332; 12. Margot Eppinger (WG) 4313;. . . 19. Gale Fitzgerald (US) 4206;. . . 21. Jane Frederick (US) 4167.

1976 (20. 25-26 July): It couldn't have been closer, with the 200 providing a barn-burning finish. After 4 events, the order was 1. Tkachenko, 2. Popovskaya, 3. Pollak, 4. Jones, 5. Laser, 6. Siegl. The 3 East Germans swept home in the 200 and the rush to the scorebooks began.

Yearly-leader Siegl got the nod by taking Laser (the only one to score a PR) 3 events to 2. It was only the second sweep ever in women's events.

1. Sigrun Siegl (EG)	(13.31	12.92	1.74	6.49	23.09)	4745
2. Christine Laser (EG)	(13.55	14.29	1.78	6.27	23.48)	4745
3. Burglinde Pollak (EG)	(13.30	16.25	1.64	6.30	23.64)	4740
4. Lyudmila Popovskaya (SU)	(13.33	15.02	1.74	6.19	24.10)	4700
5. Nadyezhda Tkachenko (SU)	(13.41	14.90	1.80	6.08	24.61)	4669
6. Diane Jones (Can)	(13.79	14.58	1.80	6.29	25.33)	4582

7. Jane Frederick (US) 4566; 8. Margit Papp (Hun) 4535; 9. Penka Sokolova (Bul) 4394; 10. Margot Eppinger (WG) 4352; 11. Djurdja Focic (Yug) 4314; 12. Sue Longden (GB) 4276; 13. Gale Fitzgerald (US) 4263;. . . 17. Marilyn King (US) 4165. 19 finishers.

WOMEN WHO COMPETED UNDER TWO DIFFERENT NAMES

As noted in the introduction to the women's events, we have listed women under one name only. If they competed in an earlier Games under their maiden name, we listed them with their married name and an asterisk. An alphabetical guide to the asterisks:

Married Name	Maiden Name	Married Name	Maiden Name
Ackermann	Witschas	Marcinkiewicz	Wajsowna
Birkemeyer	Kohler	Maslakova	Zharkhova
Boy	Garisch	Mickler	Becker
Brown	Mason	Mracnova	Faithova
Ciepla	Wieczorek	Oldham	Anderson
Connolly	Fikotova	Pensberger	Landheim
de la Hunty	Strickland	Ponomaryeva	Romashkova
Elder	Bernard	Popa	Popescu
Gorecka	Richter	Pursiainen	Strandvall
Gummel	Hemboldt	Rand	Bignal
Haggman	Wilmi	Rudas	Antal
Hein	Todten	Ryan	Kilborn
Hasenjager	Robb	Schulze	Ruger
Hubner	Luttge	Sherwood	Parkin
Hubnerova	Rezkova	Stefanescu	Bufanu
Ilyina	Kolyesnikova	Streidt	Stropahl
Kelsby	Carlstedt	Szewinska	Kirszenstein
Koleva	Zlateva	Tyler	Odam
Krachevskaya	Dolzhyenko	Wellmann	Tittel
Laser	Bodner	Wilden	Jahn
Limberg	Hausmann	Young	Sloper
Lindholm	Ecklund	Zatopkova	Ingrova

Discontinued Events

Listed here are the medal winners in the discontinued events. Some of "discontinued" events were actually just forerunners of events contested today and have been melded in with the regular results (e.g., the 10,000 Walk into the 20,000 Walk, the 80m hurdles into the 100m hurdles). No women's events have been discontinued.

The tug-of-war, which was contested under the aegis of track and field in the Games of 1900 through 1920, is not considered here.

60 METERS
1900
1. Alvin Kraenzlein (US)   7.0 WR
2. Walter Tewksbury (US)   7.1
3. Stanley Rowley (Aus)   7.2
1904
1. Archie Hahn (US)   7.0=OR
2. William Hogenson (US)   7.2
3. Fay Moulton (US)   7.2

5 MILES
1908
1. Emil Voigt (GB)   25:11.2
2. Edward Owen (GB)   25:24.0
3. John Svanberg (Swe)   25:37.2

200m HURDLES
1900
1. Alvin Kraenzlein (US)   25.4
2. Norman Pritchard (Ind)   26.6
3. Walter Tewksbury
1904
1. Harry Hillman (US)   24.6 OR
2. Frank Castleman (US)   24.9
3. George Poage (US)

3000m TEAM RACE (3 members)
1912
1. United States   9
2. Sweden   13
3. Great Britain   23
1920
1. United States   10
2. Great Britain   20
3. Sweden   24
1924
1. Finland   8
2. Great Britain   14
3. United States   25

3M TEAM RACE (3 members)
1908
1. Great Britain   6

2. United States   19
3. France   32

5000m TEAM RACE (5 members)
1900
1. Great Britain   26
2. France   29

INDIVIDUAL CROSS COUNTRY
1912 (c12,000m)
1. Hannes Kohlemainen (Fin)   45:11.6
2. Hjalmar Andersson (Swe)   45:44.8
3. John Eke (Swe)   46:37.6
1920 (c8000m)
1. Paavo Nurmi (Fin)   27:15.0
2. Erik Backman (Swe)   27:17.6
3. Heikki Liimatainen (Fin)   27:37.4
1924 (c10,000m)
1. Paavo Nurmi (Fin)   32:54.8
2. Ville Ritola (Fin)   34:19.4
3. Earl Johnson (US)   35:21.0

TEAM CROSS COUNTRY
1904 (5 members, c4M)
1. New York AC (US)   21:17.8
2. Chicago AA (US)
1912 (3 members, c12,000m)
1. Sweden   10
2. Finland   11
3. Great Britain   49
1920 (3 members, c8000m)
1. Finland   10
2. Great Britain   21
3. Sweden   23
1924 (3 members, c10,000m)
1. Finland   11
2. United States   14
3. France   20

3000m WALK
1920
1. Ugo Frigerio (It)   13:14.2

2. George Parker (Aus)
3. Richard Remer (US)

3500m WALK
1908
1. George Larner (GB)	14:55.0	
2. Ernest Webb (GB)	15:07.4	
3. Harry Kerr (NZ)	15:43.4	

STANDING HIGH JUMP
1900
1. Ray Ewry (US)	1.65	5-5¼ WR
2. Irving Baxter (US)	1.52	5-0
3. Lewis Sheldon (US)	1.50	4-11
1904
1. Ray Ewry (US)	1.50	5-11
2. James Stadler (US)	1.45	4-9
3. Lawson Robertson (US)	1.45	4-9
1908
1. Ray Ewry (US)	1.57	5-2
2. Konst. Tsiklitiras (Gr)	1.55	5-1
3. John Biller (US)	1.55	5-1
1912
1. Platt Adams (US)	1.63	5-4¼
2. Benjamin Adams (US)	1.60	5-3
3. Konst. Tsiklitiras (Gr)	1.55	5-1

STANDING LONG JUMP
1900
1. Ray Ewry (US)	3.21	10-6½
2. Irving Baxter (US)	3.13	10-3¼
3. Emile Torchebouef (Fr)	3.03	9-11¼
1904
1. Ray Ewry (US)	3.47	11-4¾ WR
2. Charles King (US)	3.28	10-9¼
3. John Biller (US)	3.26	10-8¼
1908
1. Ray Ewry (US)	3.33	10-11¼
2. Konst. Tsiklitiras (Gr)	3.23	10-7¼
3. Martin Sheridan (US)	3.22	10-7
1912
1. Konst. Tsiklitiras (Gr)	3.37	11-¾
2. Platt Adams (US)	3.36	11-¼
3. Benjamin Adams (US)	3.28	10-9¼

STANDING TRIPLE JUMP
1900
1. Ray Ewry (US)	10.58	34-8½
2. Irving Baxter (US)	9.95	32-7¾
3. Robert Garrett (US)	9.50	31-2
1904
1. Ray Ewry (US)	10.55	34-7½
2. Charles King (US)	10.16	33-4
3. James Stadler (US)	9.53	31-3¼

BOTH HANDS SHOT PUT (total)
1912
1. Ralph Rose (US)	27.70	90-10½
2. Patrick McDonald (US)	27.53	90-4
3. Elmer Niklander (Fin)	27.14	89-½

BOTH HANDS DISCUS
1912
1. Armas Taipale (Fin)	82.86	271-10
2. Elmer Niklander (Fin)	77.96	255-9
3. Emil Magnusson (Swe)	77.36	253-10

ANCIENT STYLE DISCUS
1908
1. Martin Sheridan (US)	38.00	124-8
2. Marquis Horr (US)	37.32	122-5
3. Werner Jarvinen (Fin)	36.48	119-8

BOTH HANDS JAVELIN
1912
1. Julius Saaristo (Fin)	109.42	358-11
(right hand 61.00 [200-1] WR)		
2. Vaino Siikaniemi (Fin)	101.13	331-9
3. Urho Peltonen (Fin)	100.24	328-10

FREESTYLE JAVELIN
1908
1. Erik Lemming (Swe)	54.44	178-7
2. Michel Dorizas (Gr)	51.36	168-6
3. Arne Halse (Nor)	49.73	163-1

56 POUND WEIGHT
1904
1. Etienne Desmarteau (Can)	10.46	34-4
2. John Flanagan (US)	10.16	33-4
3. James Mitchell (US)	10.13	33-3
1920
1. Patrick McDonald (US)	11.26	36-11½
2. Patrick Ryan(US)	10.96	35-11¾
3. Carl Johan Lind (Swe)	10.25	33-7½

PENTATHLON (LJ, JT, 200, DT, 1500)
1912
—disq. Jim Thorpe (US) [1st]
1. Ferdinand Bie (Nor)	16
2. James Donahue (US)	24
3. Frank Lukeman (Can)	24
1920
1. Eero Lehtonen (Fin)	14
2. Everett Bradley (US)	24
3. Hugo Lahtinen (Fin)	26
1924
1. Eero Lehtonen (Fin)	14
2. Elemer Somfay (Hun)	16
3. Robert LeGendre (US)	18
(LJ 7.76 [25-5½] WR)	

Individual Medals

The preceding pages have told you exactly where a thousand-odd Olympic medals have gone. At this point, we'll extrapolate some of the interesting facts buried within that mountain of results. Who has the most medals? The most golds, etc?

Just about any way you look at it, Paavo Nurmi is the king of the medal departments, with 9 individual medals (8 golds, 1 silver) and 3 team medals (all gold).

(As in the women's results section, all those who won medals under 2 names are listed with their married name only—unless they actually went with a hyphenated name—and an identifying †. See. p. 159 for the key to these names.)

WINNERS OF THREE OR MORE MEDALS

*=Three or more medals in same event.

Men

Erik Backman (Sweden) 5000 20-3; 3000 team 20-3; c.c. ind. 20-2, team 20-3.
Thane Baker (US) 100 56-2; 200 52-2, 56-2; 400R 56-1.
James Ball (Canada) 400 28-2; 1600R 28-3, 32-3.
Irving Baxter (US) HJ 00-1; PV 00-1; SHJ 00-2; SLJ 00-2; STJ 00-2.
Charles Bennett (Great Britain) 1500 00-1; 5000 00-1; 4000St 00-2.
Valeriy Borzov (SU) 100 72-1, 76-3; 200 72-1; 400R 72-2, 76-3.
Ralph Boston* (US) LJ 60-1, 64-2, 68-3.
Hanns Braun (Germany) 400 12-3; 800 08-3; 1600 MedR 08-2.
Guy Butler (Great Britain) 400 20-2, 24-3; 1600R 20-1, 24-3.
Nate Cartmell (US) 100 04-2; 200 04-2, 08-3; 1600 MedR 08-1.
James Connolly (US) HJ 96-2; LJ 96-3; TJ 96-1, 00-2.
Ludvik Danek* (Czechoslovakia) DT 64-2, 68-3, 72-1.
Glenn Davis (US) 400H 56-1, 60-1; 1600R 60-1.
Harrison Dillard (US) 100 48-1; 110H 52-1; 400R 48-1, 52-1.
Phil Edwards (Canada) 800 32-3, 36-3; 1500 32-3; 1600R 28-3, 32-3.
Ray Ewry* (US) SHJ 00-1, 04-1, 08-1; SLJ 00-1, 04-1, 08-1; STJ 00-1, 04-1 (+ 1906, SHJ-1, SLJ-1).
John Flanagan* (US) HT 00-1, 04-1, 08-1; 56 lb WT 04-2.
Ugo Frigerio (Italy) 3000W 20-1; 10,000W 20-1, 24-1; 50,000W 32-3.
Mohamed Gamoudi (Tunisia) 5000 68-1, 72-2; 10,000 64-2, 68-3.
Robert Garrett (US) HJ 96-3; LJ 96-2; SP 96-1, 00-3; DT 96-1; STJ 00-3.
Vladimir Golubnichiy* (SU) 20,000W 60-1, 64-3, 68-1, 72-2.
Archie Hahn (US) 60 04-1; 100 04-1; 200 04-1 (+ 1906 100-1).

Dave Hemery (Great Britain) 400H 68-1, 72-3; 1600R 72-2.
Albert Hill (Great Britain) 800 20-1; 1500 20-1; 3000 team 20-2.
Harry Hillman (US) 400 04-1; 200H 04-1; 400 04-1; 08-2.
Bill Hogenson (Great Britain) 60 04-2; 100 04-3; 200 04-3.
Bud Houser (US) DT 24-1, 28-1; SP 24-1.
Volmari Iso-Hollo (Finland) ST 32-1, 36-1; 10,000 32-2, 36-3.
Kip Keino (Kenya) 1500 68-1, 72-2; St 72-1; 5000 68-2.
Hannes Kolehmainen (Finland) 5000 12-1; 10,000 12-1; marathon 20-1; c.c. indiv.
    12-1; c.c. team 12-2.
Helmut Kornig (Germany) 200 28-3; 400R 28-2, 32-2.
Alvin Kraenzlein (US) 60 00-1; 110H 00-1, 200H 00-1; LJ 00-1.
Gergely Kulcsar* (Hungary) JT 60-3, 64-2, 68-3.
Erik Lemming (Sweden) JT 08-1, 12-1; freestyle JT 08-1 (+ 1906 JT-1, SP-3
    pentathlon-3).
James Lightbody (US) 800 04-1; 1500 04-1; 2500St 04-1; c.c. team 04-2
    (+ 1906 800-2, 1500-1).
Heikki Liimatainen (Finland) c.c. indiv. 20-3; c.c. team 20-1, 24-1.
John Ljunggren* (Sweden) 50,000W 48-1, 56-3, 60-2.
Janis Lusis* (SU) JT 64-3, 68-1, 72-2.
Pat McDonald (US) SP 12-1; SP both hands 12-2; WT 20-1.
Matt McGrath* (US) HT 08-2, 12-1, 24-2.
Herb McKenley (Jamaica) 100 52-2; 400 48-2, 52-2; 1600R 52-1.
Ralph Metcalfe (US) 100 32-2, 36-2; 200 32-3; 400R 36-1.
Alain Mimoun (France) 5000 52-2; 10,000 48-2, 52-2; marathon 56-1.
Bobby Morrow (US) 100 56-1; 200 56-1; 400R 56-1.
Arthur Newton (US) 2500St 04-3; marathon 04-3; c.c. team 04-1.
Elmer Niklander (Finland) SP 20-1; DT 20-1; SP both hands 12-3; DT both hands
    12-2.
Paavo Nurmi* (Finland) 1500 24-1; St 28-2; 5000 20-2, 24-1, 28-2; 10,000 20-1,
    28-1; c.c. indiv. 20-1, 24-1; c.c. team 20-1, 24-1; 3000 team 24-1.
Parry O'Brien* (US) SP 52-1, 56-1, 60-2.
Al Oerter* (US) DT 56-1, 60-1, 64-1, 68-1.
Jesse Owens (US) 100 36-1, 200 36-1, LJ 36-1; 400R 36-1.
Charley Paddock (US) 100 20-1; 200 20-2, 24-2; 400R 20-1.
Myer Prinstein (US) LJ 00-2, 04-1; TJ 00-1, 04-1 (+ LJ 06-1)
Walter Rangeley (Great Britain) 200 28-2; 400R 24-2, 28-3.
Bob Richards* (US) PV 48-3, 52-1, 56-1.
Ville Ritola (Finland) Steeple 24-1; 5000 24-2, 28-1; 10,000 24-1, 28-2; c.c. indiv.
    24-2; c.c. team 24-1; 3000 team 24-1.
Sidney Robinson (Great Britain) 2500St 00-2; 4000St 00-3; 5000 team 00-1.
Ralph Rose* (US) SP 04-1, 08-1, 12-2; DT 04-2; HT 04-3; 2 hand-SP 12-1.
Stanley Rowley (Australia) 60 00-3; 100 00-3; 200 00-3; 5000 team 00-1.
    (representing Great Britain).
Bevil Rudd (South Africa) 400 20-1; 800 20-3; 1600R 20-2.
Viktor Saneyev* (SU) TJ 68-1, 72-1, 76-1.
Jackson Scholz (US) 100 24-2; 200 24-1; 400R 20-1.
Mel Sheppard (US) 800 08-1, 12-2; 1500 08-1; 1600 Medley R 08-1, 1600R 12-1.

Martin Sheridan (US) DT 04-1, 08-1; classic DT 08-1; SLJ 08-3 (+ 1906 DT-1, SP-1, WT-2, SHJ-2, SLJ-2).
Peter Snell (New Zealand) 800 60-1, 64-1; 1500 64-1.
Andy Stanfield (US) 200 52-1, 56-2; 400R 52-1.
Albin Stenroos (Finland) 10,000 12-3; marathon 24-1; c.c. team 12-2.
Armas Taipale (Finland) DT 12-1, 20-2; 2 hand DT 12-1.
F. Morgan Taylor* (US) 400H 24-1, 28-3, 32-3.
Walter Tewksbury (US) 60 00-2; 100 00-2; 200 00-1; 200H 00-3; 400H 00-1.
Konstantin Tsiklitiras (Greece) SHJ 08-2, 12-3; SLJ 08-2, 12-1.
Vilho Tuulos* (Finland) TJ 20-1, 24-3, 28-3.
Lasse Viren (Finland) 5000 72-1, 76-1; 10,000 72-1, 76-1.
Ernest Webb (Great Britain) 3500W 08-2; 10,000W 12-2; 10 mileW 08-2.
Mal Whitfield (US) 400 48-3; 800 48-1, 52-1; 1600R 48-1, 52-2.
Edvin Wide (Sweden) 5000 24-3, 28-3; 10,000 24-2, 28-3.
Alex Wilson (Canada) 400 32-3; 800 32-2; 1600R 28-3, 32-3.
Arthur Wint (Jamaica) 400 48-1; 800 48-2, 52-2 (+ 1600R 52-1).
Mamo Wolde (Ethiopia) 10,000 68-2; marathon 68-1, 72-3.
Frank Wykoff* (US) 400R 28-1, 32-1, 36-1.
Emil Zatopek (Czechoslovakia) 5000 48-2, 52-1; 10,000 48-1, 52-1; marathon 52-1)
Gyula Zsivotzky* (Hungary) HT 60-2, 64-2, 68-1.

Women

Fanny Blankers-Koen (Holland) 100 48-1; 200 48-1; 80H 48-1; 400R 48-1.
Raelene Boyle (Australia) 100 72-2; 200 68-2, 72-2.
Nadyezhda Chizova* (SU) SP 68-3, 72-1, 76-2.
Aleksandra Chudina (SU) HJ 52-3; LJ 52-2; JT 52-2
†Tereza Ciepla (Poland) 80H 64-2; 400R 60-3, 64-1.
Betty Cuthbert (Australia) 100 56-1; 200 56-1; 400 64-1; 400R 56-1.
†Shirley de la Hunty* (Australia) 100 48-3, 52-3; 80H 48-3, 52-1, 56-1; 400R 48-2, 56-1.
Babe Didrikson (US) 80H 32-1; HJ 32-2; JT 32-1.
Gunhild Hoffmeister (East Germany) 800 72-3; 1500 72-2, 76-2.
Dorothy Hyman (Great Britain) 100 60-2; 200 60-3; 400R 64-3.
Lia Manoliu* (Rumania) DT 60-3, 64-3, 68-1.
Micheline Ostermeyer (France) HJ 48-3; SP 48-1; DT 48-1.
†Nina Ponomaryeva* (SU) DT 52-1, 56-3, 60-1.
Tamara Press (SU) SP 60-1, 64-1; DT 60-2, 64-1.
Mary Rand (Great Britain) LJ 64-1; Pent 64-2; 400R 64-3.
Annegret Richter (West Germany) 100 76-1; 200 76-2; 400R 72-1, 76-2.
Elizabeth Robinson (US) 100 28-1; 400R 28-2, 36-1.
Heide Rosendahl (West Germany) LJ 72-1; Pent 72-2; 400R 72-1.
Wilma Rudolph (US) 100 60-1; 200 60-1; 400R 56-3, 60-1.
Renate Stecher (East Germany) 100 72-1, 76-2; 200 72-1, 76-3; 400R 72-2, 76-1.
†Irena Szewinska* (Poland) 100 68-3; 200 64-2, 68-1 72-3; 400 76-1; LJ 64-2; 400R 64-1.
Wyomia Tyus (US) 100 64-1, 68-1; 400R 64-2, 68-1.
Galina Zybina* (SU) SP 52-1, 56-2, 64-3.

MOST MEDALS–INDIVIDUAL AND TEAM

Men

12	Nurmi
8	Ewry, Ritola
6	Garrett, Rose
5	Baxter, Borzov, Edwards, Kolehmainen, Prinstein, Sheppard, Tewksbury, Whitfield, Zatopek
4	Backman, Baker, Butler, Cartmell, Connolly, Dillard, Flanagan, Frigerio, Gamoudi, Garrett, Golubnichiy, Hillman, Iso-Hollo, Keino, Kraenzlein, Lightbody, McKenley, Metcalfe, Mimoun, Oerter, Owens, Paddock, Prinstein, Rowley, Sheridan, Tsiklitiras, Viren, Wide, Wilson, Wint

Women

7	†de la Hunty, †Szewinska
6	Stecher
4	Blankers-Koen, Cuthbert, Press, Rudolph, Tyus
3	Boyle, Chizova, Chudina, †Ciepla, Didrikson, Hoffmeister, Hyman, Manoliu, Ostermeyer, †Ponomaryeva, Rand, Richter, Robinson, Zybina

MOST MEDALS–INDIVIDUAL

Men

9	Nurmi
8	Ewry
6	Garrett, Ritola, Rose
5	Baxter, Tewksbury, Zatopek
4	Connolly, Flanagan, Frigerio, Gamoudi, Golubnichiy, Hillman, Iso-Hollo, Keino, Kolehmainen, Kraenzlein, Mimoun, Niklander, Oerter, Prinstein, Sheridan, Tsiklitiras, Viren, Wide
3	Baker, Bennett, Borzov, Boston, Cartmell, Danek, Edwards, Hahn, Hogenson, Houser, Kulcsar, Lemming, Lightbody, Ljunggren, Lusis, McDonald, McGrath, McKenley, Metcalfe, O'Brien, Owens, Paddock, Richards, Rowley, Saneyev, Sheppard, Snell, Taipale, Taylor, Tuulos, Webb, Whitfield, Wint, Wolde, Zsivotzky.

Women

6	†Szewinska
5	†de la Hunty
4	Press, Stecher
3	Blankers-Koen, Boyle, Chizova, Chudina, Cuthbert, Didrikson, Hoffmeister, Manoliu, Ostermeyer, †Ponomaryeva, Zybina

MOST MEDALS—TEAM

Men

3 Nurmi, Wykoff

Women

2 By many

MOST GOLD MEDALS—INDIVIDUAL AND TEAM

Men

9 Nurmi
8 Ewry
5 Ritola
4 Dillard, Kolehmainen, Kraenzlein, Oerter, Owens, Sheppard, Viren, Zatopek
3 Davis, Flanagan, Frigerio, Hahn, Hillman, Houser, Lemming, Morrow, Prinstein, Rose, Saneyev, Sheridan, Snell, Whitfield, Wykoff

Women

4 Blankers-Koen, Cuthbert
3 †de la Hunty, Press, Rudolph, Stecher, †Szewinska, Tyus

MOST GOLD MEDALS—INDIVIDUAL

Men

8 Ewry
6 Nurmi
4 Kolehmainen, Kraenzlein, Oerter, Viren, Zatopek
3 Flanagan, Frigerio, Hahn, Hillman, Houser, Lemming, Lightbody, Owens, Prinstein, Ritola, Rose, Saneyev, Sheridan, Snell

Women

3 Blankers-Koen, Cuthbert, Press

MOST GOLD MEDALS—TEAM

Men

3 Nurmi, Wykoff

Women

2 Annette Rogers (US) 400R, 32-36.

MOST MEDALS IN SAME EVENT

Men

4   Golubnichiy, Oerter

Women

3   Chizova, †de la Hunty, Manoliu, †Ponomaryeva, †Szewinska, Zybina.

MOST MEDALS IN ONE OLYMPICS—INDIVIDUAL AND TEAM

Men

6   Ritola 24
5   Baxter 00, Tewksbury 00, Nurmi 24
4   Backman 20, Garrett 96, Kraenzlein 00, Lightbody 04, Kolehmainen 12, Nurmi 20, Owens 36, Rowley 00
3   Backer 52, Bennett 00, Connolly 96, Ewry 00, Ewry 04, Hahn 04, Hill 20, Hillman 04, Hogenson 04, Morrow 56, Newton 04, Nurmi 28, Robinson 00, Rose 04, Rudd 20, Sheppard 08, Sheridan 08, Wilson 32, Zatopek 52

Women

3   Cuthbert 56; †de la Hunty 48; Didrikson 32, Ostermeyer 48, Rand 64, Richter 76, Rosendahl 72, Rudolph 60, Stecher 72-76, †Szewinska 64.

MOST MEDALS IN ONE OLYMPICS—INDIVIDUAL

Men

5   Baxter 00, Tewksbury 00
4   Garrett 96, Kraenzlein 00, Ritola 24, Rowley 00
3   Backman 20, Bennett 00, Connolly 96, Ewry 00-04, Hahn 04, Hillman 04, Hogenson 04, Kolehmainen 12, Lightbody 04, Nurmi 20-24-28, Owens 04, Rose 04, Sheridan 08, Zatopek 52.

Women

3   Blankers-Koen 48, Didrikson 32, Ostermeyer 48

MOST MEDALS IN ONE OLYMPICS—TEAM

Men

2   Nurmi, Ritola

Women

1   By 156.

MOST GOLD MEDALS IN ONE OLYMPICS—INDIVIDUAL AND TEAM

Men

5   Nurmi 24
4   Kraenzlein 00, Owens 36, Ritola 24
3   Ewry 00-04, Hahn 04, Hillman 04, Kolehmainen 12, Lightbody 04, Morrow 56, Sheppard 08, Zatopek 52

Women

4   Blankers-Koen 48
3   Cuthbert 56, Rudolph 60

MOST GOLD MEDALS IN ONE OLYMPICS—INDIVIDUAL

Men

4   Kraenzlein 00
3   Ewry 00-04, Hahn 04, Hillman 04, Kolehmainen 12, Lightbody 04, Nurmi 24, Owens 36, Zatopek 52

Women

3   Blankers-Koen 48

MOST GOLD MEDALS IN ONE OLYMPICS—TEAM

Men

2   Nurmi 24, Ritola 24

Women

1   By 52.

GOLD MEDALS WON IN THE MOST EVENTS

Men

6   Nurmi (1500, Steeple, 5000, 10,000, 3000 team, cross country)
7   Ritola (Steeple, 5000, 10,000 , 3000 team, cross country)
4   Kraenzlein (60, 110H, 200H, LJ)
     Kolehmainen (5000, 10,000, marathon, cross country)
     Owens (100, 200, LJ, 400R)

Women

4   Blankers-Koen (100, 200, 80H, 400R)
     Cuthbert (100, 200, 400, 400R)
3   Rudolph (100, 200, 400R)
     Stecher (100, 200, 400R)
     †Szewinska (200, 400, 400R)

MEDALS WON IN MOST EVENTS

Men

7   Nurmi (1500, steeple, 5000, 10,000, c.c. indiv., c.c. team, 3000 team)
6   Ritola (steeple, 5000, 10,000, c.c. indiv., c.c. team, 3000 team)
5   Baxter (HJ, PV, SHJ, SLJ, STJ)
     Garrett (HJ, LJ, SP, DT, STJ)
     Tewksbury (60, 100, 200, 200H, 400H)
     Kolehmainen (5000, 10,000, marathon, c.c. indiv., c.c. team)

Women

5   †Szewinska (100, 200, 400, LJ, 400R)
4   Blankers-Koen (100, 200, 80H, 400R)
     Cuthbert (100, 200, 400, 400R)
3   Chudina (HJ, LJ, JT)
     †de la Hunty (100, 80M, 400R)
     Didrikson (80H, HJ, JT)
     Hyman (100, 200, 400R)
     Ostermeyer (HJ, SP, DT)
     Rand (LJ, Pent, 400R)
     Richter (100, 200, 400R)
     Rosendahl (LJ, Pent, 400R)
     Rudolph (100, 200, 400R)
     Stecher (100, 200, 400R)

MOST SILVER MEDALS WON

Men

3   Baker, Baxter, Mimoun, McKenley, Nurmi, Ritola, Webb.

Women

3   Boyle

MOST BRONZE MEDALS WON

Men

5   Edwards
3   Backman, Garrett, Rowley, Wide, Wilson

Women

3   †de la Hunty

WINNERS OF SET OF MEDALS—GOLD, SILVER, BRONZE

Men

Baker, Borzov, Boston, Butler, Cartmell, Connolly, Danek, Gamoudi, Garrett, Golubnichiy, Hemery, Iso-Hollo, Ljunggren, Lusis, Metcalfe, Niklander, Robinson, Rose, Rudd, Stenroos, Tewksbury, Whitfield, Wolde.

Women

†Ciepla, Chizova, †de la Hunty, Rand, Stecher, †Szewinska (2), Zybina.

WINNERS OF SET MEDALS IN SINGLE EVENT

Men

Boston, Danek, Ljunggren, Lusis

Women

Chizova, †Szewinska, Zybina

WINNERS OF SET OF MEDALS IN SAME OLYMPICS

Men

Baker 56, Connolly 96, Garrett 96, Robinson 00, Rose 04, Rudd 20, Tewksbury 00.

Women

Rand 64, Stecher 76

MOST YEARS BETWEEN GOLD MEDALS

Men

12   Oerter (56-68)
8   Ewry (00-08), Flanagan (00-08), Golubnichiy (60-68), Kolehmainen (12-20),

Nurmi (20-28), Rose (04-12), Saneyev (68-76), Wykoff (28-36)

Women

12 †Szewinska (64-76)
8   Cuthbert (56-64)

MOST YEARS BETWEEN MEDALS

Men

16 McGrath (08-24)
12 Frigerio (20-32), Golubnichiy (60-72), Oerter (56-68), Porhola (20-32), Stenroos (12-24)
8   Boston (60-68), Danek (64-72), Davenport (68-76), Ewry (00-08), Flanagan (00-08), Gamoudi (64-72), Kolehmainen (12-20), Kulcsar (60-68). Lusis (64-72), McDonald (12-20), Mimoun (48-56), Niklander (12-20), Nurmi (20-28), O'Brien (52-60), Richards (48-56), Rose (04-12), Saneyev (68-76), Taipale (12-20), Taylor (24-32), Tuulos (20-28), Wykoff (28-36), Zsivotzky (60-68).

Women

12 †Szewinska (64-76), Zybina (52-64)
8   Chizova (68-76), Cuthbert (56-64), †de la Hunty (48-56), Manoliu (60-68), Robinson (28-36), †Ponomaryeva (52-60).

MOST YEARS WON MEDALS

Men

4   Golubnichiy, Oerter
3   Boston, Danek, Ewry, Flanagan, Frigerio, Gamoudi, Kulcsar, Lusis, McGrath, Mimoun, Nurmi, O'Brien, Richards, Rose, Saneyev, Taylor, Tuulos, Wykoff, Zsivotzky

Women

4   †Szewinska
3   Chizova, †de la Hunty, Manoliu, †Ponomaryeva

SWEEPS ARE HARD TO COME BY

Only three times since 1960 have all three medals in an event gone to the same country. That was in 1968 when the United States ran 1-2-3 in the 400 meters and in 1976 when the Soviet Union hammer throwers and the East German pentathletes

took all the medals.

But a sweep was pretty common through 1960. For the men it has happened 56 times in all and in every event except the 5000. Finland has done it four times, Sweden three and the Soviet Union twice. All the other men's sweeps belong to the US.

Men

100–1904, 1912.
200–1904, 1932, 1952, 1956.
400–1904, 1968.
800–1904, 1912.
1500–1904.
steeple–1928 (Finland), 1948 (Sweden).
10,000–1936 (Finland).
20kW–1956 (SU).
110HH–1900, 1904, 1908, 1912, 1948,
    1952, 1956, 1960.
400H–1904, 1920, 1956, 1960.

HJ–1896, 1936.
PV–1904, 1912, 1924, 1928.
LJ–1896, 1904.
TJ–1900, 1904, 1912 (Sweden).
SP–1900, 1904, 1912, 1924, 1948,
    1952, 1960.
DT–1908, 1956, 1960.
HT–1904, 1908, 1976 (SU).
JT–1920 (Finland), 1932 (Finland).
Dec–1912 (Sweden), 1936, 1952

Discontinued events saw 10 sweeps: 4000 steeplechase-1900 (GB); 60H–1904; 200H-1904; 10 mile walk–1908 (GB); SHJ–1900, 1904; SLJ–1904; STJ–1900. 1904; right-left javelin–1912 (Finland).

Women

    Only twice have all the medals in one event gone to the same country, the Soviet discus throwers pulling it off in 1952 and the East German pentathletes in 1976.

WINNERS OF DIFFERENT EVENTS IN DIFFERENT GAMES

Men

Myer Prinstein (US), TJ (00), LJ & TJ (04)
Pat McDonald (US), SP (12), WT (20)
Hannes Kolehmainen (Fin) 5000 & 10,000 (12), marathon (20)
Paavo Nurmi (Fin) 10,000 & c.c. (20), 1500 & 5000 & c.c. (24), 10,000 (28)
Jackson Scholz (US) 400R (20), 200 (24)
Ville Ritola (Fin) 3000 St & 10,000 (24), 5000 (28)
Bud Houser (US), SP & DT (24), DT (28)
Emil Zatopek (Czech) 10,000 (48), 5000, 10,000 & marathon (52)
Harrison Dillard (US) 100 & 400R (48), 110H & 400R (52)
Ralph Rose (US), SP (04, 08), 2 Hand SP (12)
Peter Snell (NZ) 800 (60), 800 & 1500 (64)
Kip Keino (Kenya) 1500 (68), St (72)

Women

Betty Cuthbert (Aus) 100, 200, 400R (56), 400 (64)
Elizabeth Robinson (US) 100 (28), 400R (36)
Renate Stecher (EG) 100, 200 (72), 400R (76)
†Irena Szewinska (Pol) 400R (64), 200 (68), 400 (76)

REPEAT WINNERS, SAME EVENT

Men

Thirty-four men have won gold medals in the same event in two or more Olympics. Only Ewry did it in three events and only Ewry, Nurmi and Viren in two events. Nurmi and Golubnichiy are the only repeaters whose wins were not consecutive.

Four-Time Winner (1)
DT   Al Oerter (US) 56, 60, 64, 68
Three-Time Winners (3)
HT   John Flanagan (US) 00, 04, 08
400R Frank Wykoff (US) 28, 32, 36
TJ   Viktor Saneyev (SU) 68, 72, 76
Two-Time Winners (26)
800   Douglas Lowe (GB) 24, 28
       Mal Whitfield (US) 48, 52
       Peter Snell (NZ) 60, 64
Steeple
       Volmari Iso-Hollo (Fin) 32, 36
5000
       Lasse Viren (Fin) 72, 76
10,000
       Paavo Nurmi (Fin) 20, 28
       Emil Zatopek (Czech) 48, 52
       Lasse Viren (Fin) 72, 76
Mar   Abebe Bikila (Eth) 60, 64
20kW
       Vladimir Golubnichiy (SU) 60, 68
          (3rd 64, 2nd 72)
110H
       Lee Calhoun (US) 56, 60
400H
       Glenn Davis (US) 56, 60

400R
       Loren Murchison (US) 20, 24
       Harrison Dillard (US) 48, 52
PV   Bob Richards (US) 52, 56 (3rd 48)
TJ   Myer Prinstein (US) 00, 04
       Adhemar da Silva (Brz) 52, 56
       Jozef Schmidt (Pol) 60, 64
SP   Ralph Rose (US) 04, 08 (2nd 12)
       Parry O'Brien (US) 52, 56
          (2nd 60, 4th 64)
DT   Martin Sheridan (US) 04, 08
       Bud Houser (US) 24, 28
HT   Patrick O'Callaghan (Eire) 28, 32
JT   Erik Lemming (Swe) 08, 12
       Jonni Myyra (Fin) 20, 24
Dec   Bob Mathias (US) 48, 52

Women

100   Wyomia Tyus (US) 64, 68
80H   †Shirley de la Hunty (Aus) 52,56
400R Annette Rogers (US) 32, 36
HJ   Iolanda Balas (Rum) 60, 64
SP   Tamara Press (SU) 60, 64
JT   Ruth Fuchs (EG) 72, 76

REPEAT WINNERS—DISCONTINUED EVENTS

Men Only

10kW Ugo Frigerio (It) 20, 24   Pent Eero Oehtonen (Fin) 20, 24
    John Mikaelsson (Swe) 48, 52   SHJ Ray Ewry (US) 00, 04, 08
C.C. Paavo Nurmi (Fin) 20, 24   SLJ Ray Ewry (US) 00, 04, 08
C.C. team Heikki Liimatainen (Fin) 20, 24 STJ Ray Ewry (US) 00, 04

BEST RECORDS IN EVENTS WHICH HAVE
HAD NO TWO-TIME WINNERS

Men

100   Ralph Metcalfe (US) 2nd (32), 2nd (36); Valeriy Borzov (SU) 1st (72), 3rd (76)
200   Andy Stanfield (US) 1st (52), 2nd (56)
400   Herb McKenley (Jam) 2nd (48), 2nd (52)
1500 Kip Keino (Kenya) 1st (68), 2nd (72)
5000 Paavo Nurmi (Fin) 2nd (20), 1st (24), 2nd (28)
50KW John Ljunggren (Swe) 1st (48), 3rd (56), 2nd (60)
HJ   Valeriy Brumel (SU) 2nd (60), 1st (64)
LJ   Ralph Boston (US) 1st (60), 2nd (64), 3rd (68)
1600R
    G. L. Rampling (GB) 2nd (32), 1st (36); Mal Whitfield (US) 1st (48), 2nd (52)

Women

200   †Irena Szewinska (Poland) 2nd (64), 1st (68), 3rd (72)
400   No one in final twice.
800   Ilena Silai (Rum) 2nd (68), 6th (72)
1500 Gunhild Hoffmeister (EG) 2nd (72), 2nd (76)
LJ   Elzbieta Krzesinska (Pol) 1st (56), 2nd (60)
DT   Lia Manoliu (Rum) 3rd (60), 3rd (64), 1st (68)
Pent Mary Peters (GB) 4th (64), 1st (72)
1600R
    †Nadyezhda Ilyina 8th (72), 3rd (76)

GOLD MEDAL WINNERS IN INDIVIDUAL EVENTS AND RELAY

Men

All but two of the 25 men who have won individual events and have been on a winning relay team the same year are Americans. Only Harrison Dillard has done it twice.

400 Relay

1920	Charley Paddock (100)
1936	Jesse Owens (100, 200, LJ)
1948	Harrison Dillard (100)
	Mel Patton (200)
1952	Lindy Remigino (100)
	Andy Stanfield (200)
	Harrison Dillard (HH)
1956	Bobby Morrow (100, 200)
1960	Armin Hary (WG) (100)
1964	Bob Hayes (100)
1968	Jim Hines (100)

1600 Medley Relay

| 1908 | Mel Sheppard (800, 1500) |

1600 Relay

1912	Charles Reidpath (400)
	Ted Meredith (800)
1928	Ray Barbuti (400)
1932	Bill Carr (400)
1948	Mal Whitfield (800)
	Roy Cochran (400H)

1952	George Rhoden (Jam) (400)
1956	Charles Jenkins (400)
	Tom Courtney (800)
1960	Otis Davis (400)
	Glenn Davis (400H)
1964	Mike Larrabee (400)
	Henry Carr (200)
1968	Lee Evans (400)

Women

400 Relay

1936	Helen Stephens (US) (100)
1948	Fanny Blankers-Koen (Hol)
	(100,200,80H)
1956	Betty Cuthbert (Aus) (100,200)
	Shirley de la Hunty (Aus) (80H)
1960	Wilma Rudolph (US) (100,200)
1968	Wyomia Tyus (US) (100)
1972	Heide Rosendahl (WG) (LJ)
1976	Barbel Eckert (EG) (200)

1600 Relay

| 1972 | Monika Zehrt (EG) (400) |

SHIRLEY STRICKLAND-DE LA HUNTY—EIGHT OLYMPIC RECORDS

No less than 22 Olympians each have broken or tied five or more Olympic records. Included are heats and all throws or jumps in the competition, thus permitting a record to be broken more than once in a single event in a single Games.

Women: (10)

†Shirley de la Hunty (Aus) 8
Babe Didrikson (US) 6
Barbara Ferrell (US) 6
Marjorie Jackson (Aus) 6
Iolanda Balas (Rum) 5
Galina Zybina (SU) 5
Tamara Press (SU) 5
Wyomia Tyus (US) 5
Betty Cuthbert (Aus) 5
Fanny Blankers-Koen (Hol) 5

Men: (12)

Wolfgang Nordwig (EG) 7
Al Oerter (US) 6
Gennadiy Bliznyetsov (SU) 6
Claus Schiprowski (WG) 6
Jesse Owens (US) 5
Harry Babcock (US) 5
Frank Wykoff (US) 5 (all relay)
Valeriy Brumel (SU) 5
Gyula Zsivotzky (Hun) 5
Parry O'Brien (US) 5
Fred Hansen (US) 5
Ralph Rose (US) 5

MEDALISTS COMPETING IN THE MOST GAMES

Rumanian discus thrower Lia Manoliu competed in 6 Games, starting in 1952, making the final each time. Three times she won medals. Her record: 52 (6), 56 (9), 60 (3), 60 (3), 64 (3), 72 (9).

Topping the men are walkers Abdon Pamich (Italy) and Vladimir Golubnichiy (SU). Pamich competed in the 50k in 56-72 (winning in 64), while Golubnichiy was in the 20k 60-76 (winning in 60 and 68).

Medalists who competed in 4 Olympics include George Young (US, steeple and 5000) 60-72; John Ljunggren (Sweden, 50kW) 48-64; Adhemar da Silva (Brazil, TJ) 48-60; Parry O'Brien (US, SP) 52-64; Adolfo Consolini (Italy, DT) 48-60; Al Oerter (US, DT) 56-68; Matt McGrath (US, HT) 08-24; Hal Connolly (US, HT) 56-68; Gyula Zsivotzky (Hungary, HT) 60-72; Gergely Kulcsar (Hungary, JT) 60-72; Janusz Sidlo (Poland, JT) 56-68; Ville Porhola (Finland) SP 20-24, HT 32-36.

Parry O'Brien:

medals in 3 of his 4 Games.

This is Helsinki 1952—

gold No. 1.

Medals By Nation

This section contains various compilations concerning the distribution of Olympic medals among the nations. Medals in team events (such as relays) count as 1 medal per nation, not the number of members on the team. See p. 18 for disparities in medals awarded.

Nations' Medals By Year

Which countries won medals in each Olympics. Columns (l-r): gold, silver, bronze, total medals. "Total Nations" indicate how many different countries won each kind of medal.

1896

USA	9	6	1	16
Australia	2	—	—	2
Greece	1	3	5	9
Hungary	—	1	2	3
France	—	1	1	2
Germany	—	1	1	2
Great Britain	—	1	—	1
Total Nations	3	6	5	7

1900

USA	16	13	10	39
Great Britain	4	3	2	9
France	1	4	2	7
Canada	1	—	1	2
Hungary	1	—	1	2
India	—	2	—	2
Bohemia	—	1	—	1
Australia	—	—	3	3
Denmark	—	—	1	1
Norway	—	—	1	1
Sweden	—	—	1	1
Total Nations	5	5	9	11

1904

USA	22	22	19	63
Canada	1	—	—	1
Great Britain	—	1	1	2
Germany	—	—	1	1
Greece	—	—	1	1
Total Nations	2	2	4	5

1908

USA	16	9	10	35
Great Britain	7	7	3	17
Sweden	2	—	3	5
Canada	1	1	3	5
South Africa	1	1	—	2
Greece	—	3	—	3
Norway	—	1	2	3
France	—	1	1	2
Germany	—	1	1	2
Hungary	—	1	1	2
Italy	—	1	—	1
Finland	—	—	1	1
New Zealand	—	—	1	1
Total Nations	5	10	10	13

1912

USA	14	14	11	39
Finland	6	4	3	13
Sweden	4	5	5	14
Great Britain	2	1	5	8
Canada	1	2	1	4
South Africa	1	1	—	2
Greece	1	—	1	2
Norway	1	—	—	1
France	—	2	—	2
Germany	—	2	—	2
Hungary	—	—	1	1
Italy	—	—	1	1
Total Nations	8	8	8	12

1920

USA	9	12	8	29
Finland	9	4	3	16
Great Britain	4	4	4	12
Italy	2	—	2	4
Sweden	1	3	10	14
France	1	2	1	4
South Africa	1	1	1	3
Canada	1	—	—	1
Norway	1	—	—	1
Australia	—	1	—	1
Denmark	—	1	—	1
Estonia	—	1	—	1
Total Nations	9	9	7	12

1924

USA	12	10	10	32
Finland	10	5	2	17
Great Britain	3	3	5	11
Italy	1	1	—	2
Australia	1	—	—	1
Sweden	—	3	2	5
Switzerland	—	2	—	2
South Africa	—	1	1	2
Argentina	—	1	—	1
Hungary	—	1	—	1
France	—	—	3	3
Estonia	—	—	1	1
Holland	—	—	1	1
New Zealand	—	—	1	1
Norway	—	—	1	1
Total Nations	5	9	10	15

1928

USA	8	6	7	21
Finland	5	5	4	14
Great Britain	2	2	1	5
Canada	2	1	1	4
Sweden	1	2	2	5
France	1	1	1	3
Eire	1	—	—	1
Japan	1	—	—	1
South Africa	1	—	—	1
Germany	—	2	5	7
Chile	—	1	—	1
Haiti	—	1	—	1
Hungary	—	1	—	1
Norway	—	—	1	1
Total Nations	9	10	8	14

1932

USA	11	10	5	26
Finland	3	4	4	11
Great Britain	2	4	1	7
Eire	2	—	—	2
Canada	1	1	4	6
Japan	1	1	2	4
Italy	1	—	2	3
Argentina	1	—	—	1
Poland	1	—	—	1

	G	S	B	T
Germany	—	1	2	3
Latvia	—	1	—	1
Sweden	—	1	—	1
Czechoslovakia	—	—	1	1
France	—	—	1	1
Philippines	—	—	1	1
Total Nations	9	8	10	15

1936

USA	12	7	4	23
Finland	3	5	2	10
Germany	3	2	4	9
Japan	2	2	3	7
Great Britain	2	3	—	5
New Zealand	1	—	—	1
Italy	—	2	2	4
Canada	—	1	1	2
Switzerland	—	1	—	1
Holland	—	—	2	2
Sweden	—	—	2	2
Australia	—	—	1	1
Latvia	—	—	1	1
Philippines	—	—	1	1
Total Nations	6	8	11	14

1948

USA	11	5	9	25
Sweden	5	4	4	13
Australia	1	2	—	3
Jamaica	1	2	—	3
Italy	1	1	1	3
Czechoslovakia	1	1	—	2
Finland	1	1	—	2
Belgium	1	—	1	2
Hungary	1	—	1	2
Argentina	1	—	—	1
France	—	3	1	4
Great Britain	—	2	1	3
Switzerland	—	1	1	2
Sri Lanka	—	1	—	1
Yugoslavia	—	1	—	1
Holland	—	—	2	2
Panama	—	—	2	2
Turkey	—	—	1	1
Total Nations	10	12	11	18

1952

USA	14	10	6	30
Czechoslovakia	3	1	—	4
Jamaica	2	3	—	5
Italy	1	1	—	2
Hungary	1	—	4	5
Sweden	1	—	2	3
Brazil	1	—	1	2
Luxembourg	1	—	—	1
USSR	—	4	2	6
France	—	2	—	2
West Germany	—	1	4	5
Argentina	—	1	—	1

Switzerland	—	1	—	1
Great Britain	—	—	2	2
Finland	—	—	1	1
New Zealand	—	—	1	1
Venezuela	—	—	1	1
Total Nations	8	9	10	17

1956

USA	15	9	4	28
USSR	3	4	7	14
Great Britain	1	2	2	5
Norway	1	—	2	3
Brazil	1	—	—	1
Eire	1	—	—	1
France	1	—	—	1
New Zealand	1	—	—	1
Australia	—	2	3	5
Hungary	—	2	—	2
West Germany	—	1	1	2
East Germany	—	1	—	1
Iceland	—	1	—	1
Poland	—	1	—	1
Yugoslavia	—	1	—	1
Finland	—	—	3	3
Czechoslovakia	—	—	1	1
Greece	—	—	1	1
Sweden	—	—	1	1
Total Nations	8	10	10	73

1960

USA	9	8	5	22
USSR	5	4	4	13
West Germany	2	2	—	4
Poland	2	—	2	4
New Zealand	2	—	1	3
Great Britain	1	—	3	4
Australia	1	1	1	3
Italy	1	—	1	2
Ethiopia	1	—	—	1
East Germany	—	3	—	3
Hungary	—	1	2	3
France	—	1	1	2
Belgium	—	1	—	1
Morocco	—	1	—	1
Sweden	—	1	—	1
Taiwan	—	1	—	1
Jamaica	—	—	2	2
Finland	—	—	1	1
South Africa	—	—	1	1
Total Nations	9	11	12	19

1964

USA	12	5	3	20
Great Britain	2	5	—	7
USSR	2	2	6	10
New Zealand	2	—	1	3
West Germany	1	2	3	6
Poland	1	1	1	3
Italy	1	—	1	2
Belgium	1	—	—	1

Ethiopia	1	—	—	1
Finland	1	—	—	1
Hungary	—	2	1	3
Czechoslovakia	—	2	—	2
Trinidad	—	1	2	3
Canada	—	1	1	2
Cuba	—	1	—	1
East Germany	—	1	—	1
Tunisia	—	1	—	1
Australia	—	—	1	1
France	—	—	1	1
Japan	—	—	1	1
Kenya	—	—	1	1
Sweden	—	—	1	1
Total Nations	10	12	14	22

1968

USA	12	5	7	24
Kenya	3	4	1	8
USSR	3	1	3	7
East Germany	1	2	1	4
Hungary	1	1	2	4
Australia	1	1	—	2
Ethiopia	1	1	—	2
Great Britain	1	—	1	2
Tunisia	1	—	1	2
West Germany	—	3	3	6
Brazil	—	1	—	1
Cuba	—	1	—	1
Finland	—	1	—	1
Jamaica	—	1	—	1
Japan	—	1	—	1
Mexico	—	1	—	1
Italy	—	—	2	2
Czechoslovakia	—	—	1	1
France	—	—	1	1
New Zealand	—	—	1	1
Total Nations	9	14	12	20

1972

USA	6	7	6	19
USSR	6	6	1	13
Finland	3	—	1	4
East Germany	2	3	2	7
Kenya	2	2	2	6
West Germany	2	1	1	4
Poland	1	—	1	2
Czechoslovakia	1	—	—	1
Uganda	1	—	—	1
Belgium	—	2	—	2
Great Britain	—	1	2	3
France	—	1	1	2
Tunisia	—	1	—	1
Ethiopia	—	—	2	2
Brazil	—	—	1	1
Italy	—	—	1	1
Jamaica	—	—	1	1
New Zealand	—	—	1	1
Sweden	—	—	1	1

Total Nations	9	9	15	19	Cuba	2	1	–	3	Belgium	–	2	1	3
					Jamaica	1	1	–	2	West Germany	–	1	3	4
1976					New Zealand	1	1	–	2	Canada	–	1	–	1
USA	6	6	7	19	France	1	–	–	1	Portugal	–	1	–	1
USSR	2	2	6	10	Hungary	1	–	–	1	Brazil	–	–	1	1
East Germany	2	3	3	8	Mexico	1	–	–	1	Great Britain	–	–	1	1
Finland	2	2	–	4	Sweden	1	–	–	1	Rumania	–	–	1	1
Poland	2	2	–	4	Trinidad	1	–	–	1	Total Nations	13	12	8	20

WOMEN

1928					USSR	2	4	5	11	Total Nations	7	7	6	10
Canada	2	1	1	4	Great Britain	1	2	3	6					
USA	1	2	1	4	South Africa	1	1	–	2	**1968**				
Germany	1	–	1	2	Czechoslovakia	1	–	–	1	USA	3	1	–	4
Poland	1	–	–	1	New Zealand	1	–	–	1	Rumania	2	2	–	4
Holland	–	1	–	1	USA	1	–	–	1	Australia	1	2	1	4
Japan	–	1	–	1	West Germany	–	2	1	3	East Germany	1	1	–	2
Sweden	–	–	2	2	Holland	–	1	–	1	West Germany	1	1	–	2
Total Nations	4	4	4	7	Total Nations	7	5	4	9	Hungary	1	–	2	3
										Poland	1	–	1	2
1932					**1956**					Czechoslovakia	1	–	–	1
USA	5	3	1	9	Australia	4	–	3	7	France	1	–	–	1
Poland	1	–	1	2	USSR	2	3	3	8	USSR	–	1	5	6
Canada	–	2	1	3	USA	1	1	1	3	Great Britain	–	2	–	2
Germany	–	1	1	2	Czechoslovakia	1	–	–	1	Australia	–	1	1	2
Great Britain	–	–	1	1	Poland	1	–	–	1	Cuba	–	1	–	1
South Africa	–	–	1	1	East Germany	–	3	–	3	Holland	–	–	1	1
Total Nations	2	3	6	6	Great Britain	–	2	–	2	Taiwan	–	–	1	1
1936					Chile	–	1	–	1	Total Nations	9	9	7	15
Germany	2	2	3	7	West Germany	–	–	1	1					
USA	2	–	–	2	Total Nations	5	5	4	9	**1972**				
Hungary	1	–	–	1						East Germany	6	4	3	13
Italy	1	–	–	1	**1960**					West Germany	4	2	1	7
Poland	–	2	1	3	USSR	6	1	1	8	USSR	3	1	–	4
Great Britain	–	2	–	2	USA	3	–	1	4	Great Britain	1	–	–	1
Canada	–	–	2	2	Rumania	1	–	1	2	Bulgaria	–	2	2	4
Total Nations	4	3	3	7	Great Britain	–	3	1	4	Australia	–	2	–	2
					Poland	–	2	1	3	Rumania	–	2	–	2
1948					West Germany	–	2	–	2	USA	–	1	2	3
Holland	4	–	–	4	East Germany	–	1	3	4	Cuba	–	–	2	2
France	2	–	2	4	Australia	–	1	–	1	Austria	–	–	1	1
Austria	1	–	1	2	Czechoslovakia	–	1	–	1	Czechoslovakia	–	–	1	1
USA	1	–	1	2	Italy	–	–	1	1	Italy	–	–	1	1
Hungary	1	–	–	1	Total Nations	3	7	7	10	Poland	–	–	1	1
Great Britain	–	4	–	4						Total Nations	4	7	9	13
Italy	–	2	–	2	**1964**									
Australia	–	1	2	3	USSR	3	–	5	8	**1976**				
Argentina	–	1	–	1	Great Britain	2	2	1	5	East Germany	9	4	6	19
Finland	–	1	–	1	USA	2	2	–	4	USSR	2	2	4	8
Canada	–	–	1	1	Rumania	2	–	1	3	West Germany	1	3	1	5
Denmark	–	–	1	1	Poland	1	3	1	5	Bulgaria	1	2	1	4
Sweden	–	–	1	1	East Germany	1	2	–	3	Poland	1	–	–	1
Total Nations	5	5	7	13	Australia	1	1	3	5	USA	–	2	1	3
					France	–	1	–	1	Italy	–	1	–	1
1952					Hungary	–	1	–	1	Czechoslovakia	–	–	1	1
Australia	3	–	1	4	New Zealand	–	–	1	1	Total Nations	5	6	6	8

Nations' Medals By Event

The number in parentheses after the event indicates the number of Games in which the event has been contested. The 4 columns indicate (l-r) gold medals, silver medals, bronze medals, total medals. As explained in the introduction on p. 18, there are odd instances of there being more/less than 3 medals in a given year. The numbers after "total nations" indicate the number of different countries which have won each type of medal (or a medal at all).

MEN

The U.S. has won more men's medals than any other country except in the steeplechase (3rd), 5000 (=4th), 10,000 (=6th), 20kWalk (=8th), 50kWalk (=4th) and JT (=3rd). Finland leads the 5000, 10,000 and JT, Great Britain the steeple and 50k Walk, the USSR the 20kWalk (and a co-lead with the U.S. in the TJ).

The U.S. is the only country to have won a medal in each event, and has golds in everything but the 2 walks; silvers in everything but the 4 x 100 and 50kW; and bronzes in everything but the 2 relays, the 20kW and 10,000.

Events with most countries winning medals: 20, 800 & marathon; 19, 1500 & TJ. Least countries (excluding the walks): 9, 110H; 10, SP & DT. Most winners: 10, 1500 & marathon; 9. TJ. Least winners: 3, 4 x 100, PV & LJ.

100 METERS (18)

United States	12	12	2	26
Great Britain	1	1	4	6
Canada	1	—	2	3
USSR	1	—	1	2
South Africa	1	—	—	1
West Germany	1	—	—	1
Trinidad	1	—	—	1
Jamaica	—	3	1	4
Germany	—	1	2	3
Cuba	—	1	—	1
Australia	—	—	2	2
Hungary	—	—	1	1
New Zealand	—	—	1	1
Holland	—	—	1	1
Panama	—	—	1	1
Total Nations	7	5	11	15

200 METERS (17)

United States	12	14	7	33
Canada	2	—	—	2
Italy	1	—	1	2
USSR	1	—	—	1
Jamaica	1	—	—	1
Great Britain	—	1	3	4
Australia	—	1	1	2
India	—	1	—	1
Germany	—	—	1	1
Holland	—	—	1	1
Panama	—	—	1	1

France | — | — | 1 | 1
Trinidad | — | — | 1 | 1
Total Nations | 5 | 4 | 9 | 13

400 METERS (18)

United States	12	8	7	27
Great Britain	2	2	1	5
Jamaica	2	2	—	4
South Africa	1	—	1	2
Cuba	1	—	—	1
West Germany	—	2	—	2
Germany	—	1	2	3
Canada	—	1	1	2
Trinidad	—	1	—	1
Denmark	—	—	1	1
Sweden	—	—	1	1
Finland	—	—	1	1
USSR	—	—	1	1
Poland	—	—	1	1
Kenya	—	—	1	1
Total Nations	5	7	11	15

800 METERS (18)

United States	8	4	6	18
Great Britain	5	1	—	6
Australia	2	—	—	2
New Zealand	2	—	—	2
Cuba	1	—	—	1
Canada	—	2	2	4
Jamaica	—	2	1	3

Italy | — | 2 | — | 2
Belgium | — | 2 | — | 2
Kenya | — | 1 | 2 | 3
Hungary | — | 1 | — | 1
Switzerland | — | 1 | — | 1
Sweden | — | 1 | — | 1
USSR | — | 1 | — | 1
Germany | — | — | 2 | 2
West Germany | — | — | 1 | 1
France | — | — | 1 | 1
Greece | — | — | 1 | 1
South Africa | — | — | 1 | 1
Norway | — | — | 1 | 1
Total Nations | 5 | 11 | 10 | 20

1500 METERS (18)

Great Britain	3	3	2	8
New Zealand	3	—	2	5
Finland	3	—	1	4
United States	2	6	4	12
Australia	2	—	1	3
Sweden	1	1	—	2
Kenya	1	1	—	2
Italy	1	—	1	2
Luxemburg	1	—	—	1
Eire	1	—	—	1
France	—	3	1	4
Switzerland	—	1	—	1
East Germany	—	1	—	1
Czechoslovakia	—	1	—	1

Belgium	—	1	—	1
West Germany	—	—	3	3
Canada	—	—	1	1
Holland	—	—	1	1
Hungary	—	—	1	1
Total Nations	10	9	11	19

STEEPLECHASE (17)

Great Britain	4	6	2	12
Finland	4	3	2	9
Kenya	2	2	—	4
United States	2	1	4	7
Sweden	2	1	1	4
Poland	1	1	—	2
Canada	1	—	—	1
Belgium	1	—	—	1
USSR	—	2	2	4
Hungary	—	1	—	1
France	—	—	2	2
Germany	—	—	1	1
Italy	—	—	1	1
Norway	—	—	1	1
East Germany	—	—	1	1
Total Nations	8	8	10	15

5000 METERS (14)

Finland	7	4	1	12
France	1	2	—	3
United States	1	1	1	3
Czechoslovakia	1	1	—	2
Tunisia	1	1	—	2
New Zealand	1	1	—	2
Belgium	1	—	—	1
USSR	1	—	—	1
Great Britain	—	1	3	4
West Germany	—	1	2	3
Kenya	—	1	1	2
East Germany	—	1	—	1
Sweden	—	—	4	4
Holland	—	—	1	1
Poland	—	—	1	1
Total Nations	8	10	8	15

10,000 METERS (14)

Finland	7	3	4	14
USSR	2	—	1	3
Czechoslovakia	2	—	—	2
United States	1	1	—	2
Poland	1	—	—	1
Kenya	1	—	—	1
France	—	3	—	3
Sweden	—	1	2	3
Tunisia	—	1	1	2
Ethiopia	—	1	1	2
Hungary	—	1	—	1
Belgium	—	1	—	1
East Germany	—	1	—	1
Portugal	—	1	—	1
Australia	—	—	3	3

Great Britain	—	—	2	2
Total Nations	6	10	7	16

MARATHON (18)

United States	3	2	4	9
France	3	1	—	4
Ethiopia	3	—	1	4
Argentina	2	1	—	3
Finland	2	—	3	5
South Africa	1	2	—	3
Japan	1	1	2	4
Greece	1	1	—	2
Czechoslovakia	1	—	—	1
East Germany	1	—	—	1
Great Britain	—	4	—	4
Belgium	—	1	2	3
Italy	—	1	1	2
Estonia	—	1	—	1
Chile	—	1	—	1
Yugoslavia	—	1	—	1
Morocco	—	1	—	1
Sweden	—	—	2	2
New Zealand	—	—	2	2
Hungary	—	—	1	1
Total Nations	10	13	9	20

10M/10-20K WALK (12)

USSR	3	2	4	9
Great Britain	2	3	3	8
Sweden	2	1	—	3
Italy	2	—	1	3
East Germany	1	2	2	5
Mexico	1	1	—	2
Canada	1	—	—	1
Switzerland	—	1	1	2
United States	—	1	—	1
Australia	—	1	—	1
South Africa	—	—	1	1
Total Nations	7	8	6	11

50-KILO WALK (9)

Great Britain	3	1	1	5
Italy	2	—	2	4
Sweden	1	1	2	4
New Zealand	1	—	—	1
East Germany	1	—	—	1
West Germany	1	—	—	1
Switzerland	—	2	—	2
USSR	—	2	—	2
Latvia	—	1	1	2
Hungary	—	1	1	2
Czechoslovakia	—	1	—	1
United States	—	—	2	2
Total Nations	6	7	6	12

110M HURDLES (18)

United States	15	13	13	41
South Africa	1	1	—	2
Great Britain	—	2	1	3

Canada	1	—	—	1
France	1	1	—	2
Cuba	—	1	—	1
Sweden	—	—	1	1
USSR	—	—	1	1
Italy	—	—	1	1
Total Nations	4	5	5	9

400M HURDLES (16)

United States	12	9	7	28
Great Britain	2	1	3	6
Eire	1	—	—	1
Uganda	1	—	—	1
Canada	—	1	1	2
USSR	—	1	1	2
France	—	1	—	1
Finland	—	1	—	1
Sri Lanka	—	1	—	1
West Germany	—	1	—	1
Philippines	—	—	1	1
Sweden	—	—	1	1
New Zealand	—	—	1	1
Italy	—	—	1	1
Total Nations	4	8	8	14

4x100 RELAY (14)

United States	12	—	—	12
Great Britain	1	2	2	5
West Germany	1	—	2	3
USSR	—	4	1	5
Germany	—	2	1	3
France	—	1	2	3
Italy	—	1	2	3
Sweden	—	1	1	2
Poland	—	1	—	1
Cuba	—	1	—	1
East Germany	—	1	—	1
Holland	—	—	1	1
Hungary	—	—	1	1
Total Nations	3	9	9	13

4x400 RELAY (14)

United States	10	2	—	12
Great Britain	2	3	3	8
Kenya	1	1	—	2
Jamaica	1	—	1	2
France	—	2	2	4
West Germany	—	1	3	4
Sweden	—	1	1	2
Germany	—	1	1	2
South Africa	—	1	—	1
Australia	—	1	—	1
Poland	—	1	—	1
Canada	—	—	2	2
Trinidad	—	—	1	1
Total Nations	4	10	8	13

HIGH JUMP (18)

United States	12	11	7	30

USSR	3	1	2	6
Australia	1	1	—	2
Canada	1	1	—	2
Poland	1	—	—	1
Great Britain	—	2	—	2
Germany	—	1	1	2
Norway	—	1	—	1
East Germany	—	1	—	1
Hungary	—	1	1	2
France	—	1	2	3
Sweden	—	—	1	1
Philippines	—	—	1	1
Brazil	—	—	1	1
Total Nations	5	10	8	13

POLE VAULT (18)

United States	17	11	9	37
East Germany	1	—	1	2
Poland	1	—	—	1
Japan	—	2	1	3
West Germany	—	2	1	3
Finland	—	2	1	3
Denmark	—	1	—	1
Greece	—	—	2	2
Norway	—	—	1	1
Canada	—	—	1	1
Sweden	—	—	1	1
Total Nations	3	5	9	11

LONG JUMP (18)

United States	16	12	6	34
Sweden	1	—	2	3
Great Britain	1	—	1	2
Canada	—	1	1	2
East Germany	—	1	1	2
Haiti	—	1	—	1
Germany	—	1	—	1
Australia	—	1	—	1
West Germany	—	1	—	1
USSR	—	—	2	2
Japan	—	—	2	2
Norway	—	—	1	1
Hungary	—	—	1	1
Finland	—	—	1	1
Total Nations	3	7	10	14

TRIPLE JUMP (18)

United States	3	4	2	9
USSR	3	3	3	9
Japan	3	1	1	5
Sweden	2	3	2	7
Brazil	2	1	2	5
Poland	2	—	—	2
Australia	1	1	1	3

Finland	1	—	2	3
Great Britain	1	—	—	1
France	—	1	—	1
Canada	—	1	—	1
Argentina	—	1	—	1
Iceland	—	1	—	1
East Germany	—	1	—	1
Greece	—	—	1	1
Norway	—	—	1	1
Turkey	—	—	1	1
Venezuela	—	—	1	1
Italy	—	—	1	1
Total Nations	9	11	12	19

SHOT (18)

United States	14	13	9	36
Finland	1	2	—	3
Germany	1	—	2	3
East Germany	1	—	1	2
Poland	1	—	—	1
USSR	—	1	2	3
Greece	—	1	1	2
Great Britain	—	1	—	1
Czechoslovakia	—	—	2	2
Hungary	—	—	1	1
Total Nations	5	5	7	10

DISCUS (18)

United States	13	8	12	33
Finland	2	3	—	5
Italy	1	2	1	4
Czechoslovakia	1	1	1	3
Hungary	1	—	—	1
East Germany	—	2	—	2
Greece	—	1	2	3
Bohemia	—	1	—	1
France	—	—	1	1
Sweden	—	—	1	1
Total Nations	5	7	6	10

HAMMER (17)

United States	7	4	8	19
USSR	4	3	3	10
Hungary	3	2	2	7
Eire	2	—	—	2
Germany	1	1	—	2
Sweden	—	2	1	3
West Germany	—	1	1	2
Canada	—	1	—	1
Finland	—	1	—	1
Yugoslavia	—	1	—	1
East Germany	—	1	—	1

Great Britain	—	—	1	1
Poland	—	—	1	1
Total Nations	5	10	7	13

JAVELIN (15)

Finland	5	6	4	15
Sweden	3	1	1	5
USSR	2	1	2	5
Hungary	1	2	4	7
United States	1	2	2	5
Norway	1	1	1	3
Germany	1	—	—	1
West Germany	1	—	—	1
Poland	—	1	—	1
East Germany	—	1	—	1
Rumania	—	—	1	1
Total Nations	8	8	7	11

DECATHLON (14)

United States	9	5	4	18
USSR	1	2	3	6
West Germany	1	2	2	5
Finland	1	2	—	3
Norway	1	—	—	1
Sweden	1	1	2	4
France	—	1	—	1
Taiwan	—	1	—	1
Estonia	—	—	1	1
Germany	—	—	1	1
Poland	—	—	1	1
Total Nations	6	7	7	11

DISCONTINUED TRACK (18)

United States	8	6	6	20
Finland	6	2	—	8
Great Britain	4	5	2	11
Sweden	1	3	5	9
France	—	1	2	3
India	—	1	—	1
Germany	—	1	—	1
Australia	—	1	1	2
Italy	1	—	—	1
Hungary	—	—	1	1
New Zealand	—	—	1	1
Total Nations	5	8	7	11

DISCONTINUED FIELD (20)

United States	12	14	10	36
Finland	4	2	4	10
Greece	1	3	1	5
Sweden	1	—	2	3
Canada	1	—	1	2
Norway	1	—	1	2
Hungary	—	1	—	1
France	—	—	1	1
Total Nations	6	4	7	8

WOMEN

The USSR leads (or co-leads) the medal tally in 6 events, East Germany in 5. The U.S. has 4, Australia 2 and Great Britain 1. East Germany is the only nation to have won a medal in every event, while the USSR is missing the 100 and the U.S. is missing the 1500 and pentathlon.

Most countries winning medals: 18, HJ; 14, 800 and hurdles. Most countries having winners: 8, HJ, LJ, DT, HT. (Due to the "recent" introduction of many events, leasts are irrelevant.)

100 METERS (11)

United States	5	2	1	8
Australia	2	1	3	6
Poland	1	1	2	4
East Germany	1	2	—	3
West Germany	1	—	1	2
Holland	1	—	—	1
Canada	—	2	1	3
Great Britain	—	2	—	2
South Africa	—	1	—	1
Germany	—	—	1	1
Italy	—	—	1	1
Cuba	—	—	1	1
Total Nations	6	7	8	12

200 METERS (8)

Australia	2	2	3	7
East Germany	2	1	1	4
United States	2	—	1	3
Poland	1	1	1	3
Holland	1	1	—	2
West Germany	—	2	—	2
Great Britain	—	1	1	2
USSR	—	—	1	1
Total Nations	5	6	6	8

400 METERS (4)

East Germany	1	1	1	3
Australia	1	—	1	2
France	1	—	—	1
Poland	1	—	—	1
Great Britain	—	2	—	2
West Germany	—	1	—	1
USSR	—	—	1	1
United States	—	—	1	1
Total Nations	4	3	4	8

800 METERS (6)

USSR	2	1	—	3
Germany	1	—	—	1
Great Britain	1	—	—	1
United States	1	—	—	1
West Germany	1	—	—	1
Japan	—	1	—	1
Australia	—	1	—	1
France	—	1	—	1
Rumania	—	1	—	1
Bulgaria	—	1	—	1
East Germany	—	—	3	3
Sweden	—	—	1	1

1500 METERS (2)

New Zealand	—	—	1	1
Holland	—	—	1	1
Total Nations	5	6	4	14

USSR	2	—	—	2
East Germany	—	2	1	3
Italy	—	—	1	1
Total Nations	1	1	2	3

HURDLES (10)

Australia	3	1	3	7
East Germany	3	1	2	6
USSR	1	2	1	4
United States	1	1	—	2
Italy	1	—	—	1
Holland	1	—	—	1
Great Britain	—	2	—	2
Germany	—	1	—	1
Poland	—	1	—	1
Rumania	—	1	—	1
South Africa	—	—	1	1
Canada	—	—	1	1
West Germany	—	—	1	1
Taiwan	—	—	1	1
Total Nations	6	8	7	14

4x100 RELAY (11)

United States	5	2	1	8
Canada	1	1	2	4
West Germany	1	3	—	4
Australia	1	1	—	2
East Germany	1	1	—	2
Poland	1	—	1	2
Holland	1	—	—	1
Great Britain	—	2	3	5
Cuba	—	1	1	2
Germany	—	—	1	1
USSR	—	—	2	2
Total Nations	7	7	7	11

4x400 RELAY (2)

East Germany	2	—	—	2
United States	—	2	—	2
West Germany	—	—	1	1
USSR	—	—	1	1
Total Nations	1	1	2	4

HIGH JUMP (11)

United States	3	1	1	5
Rumania	2	—	—	2
Canada	1	—	1	2
Hungary	1	—	—	1
South Africa	1	—	—	1
Czechoslovakia	1	—	—	1
West Germany	1	—	—	1
East Germany	1	—	—	1
Great Britain	—	5	—	5
USSR	—	2	3	5
Bulgaria	—	1	1	2
Holland	—	1	—	1
Poland	—	1	—	1
Australia	—	1	—	1
Italy	—	1	—	1
Germany	—	—	1	1
France	—	—	1	1
Austria	—	—	1	1
Total Nations	8	8	7	18

LONG JUMP (8)

Poland	1	2	—	3
USSR	1	1	4	6
Great Britain	1	1	1	3
East Germany	1	—	1	2
Hungary	1	—	—	1
New Zealand	1	—	—	1
Rumania	1	—	—	1
West Germany	1	—	—	1
United States	—	2	—	2
Argentina	—	1	—	1
Bulgaria	—	1	—	1
Sweden	—	—	1	1
Czechoslovakia	—	—	1	1
Total Nations	8	8	7	13

SHOT (8)

USSR	5	2	3	10
East Germany	1	4	—	5
Bulgaria	1	—	1	2
France	1	—	—	1
West Germany	—	1	1	2
Italy	—	1	—	1
Austria	—	—	1	1
United States	—	—	1	1
Czechoslovakia	—	—	1	1
Total Nations	4	4	6	9

DISCUS (11)

USSR	4	3	2	9
United States	1	2	—	3

Rumania	1	1	2	4
East Germany	1	1	1	3
Poland	1	1	1	3
Germany	1	–	1	2
France	1	–	1	2
Czechoslovakia	1	–	–	1
Italy	–	1	–	1
West Germany	–	1	–	1
Sweden	–	–	1	1
Hungary	–	–	1	1
Bulgaria	–	1	1	2
Total Nations	8	8	9	13

JAVELIN (10)

USSR	2	1	4	7
East Germany	2	1	–	3
Germany	1	2	1	4
Czechoslovakia	1	1	–	2
Rumania	1	1	–	2
Hungary	1	1	–	2
United States	1	–	2	3
Austria	1	–	1	2
Finland	–	1	–	1
Chile	–	1	–	1
West Germany	–	1	–	1
Poland	–	–	1	1
Denmark	–	–	1	1
Total Nations	8	9	6	13

PENTATHLON (4)

East Germany	1	1	2	4
Great Britain	1	1	–	2
West Germany	1	1	–	2
USSR	1	–	1	2
Austria	–	1	–	1
Hungary	–	–	1	1
Total Nations				

Nations Ranked By Medals

In order of rank based on 3 points for gold, 2 for silver, 1 for bronze. First line shows rank, country, points. Second line, gold, silver, bronze, total medals. DR = discontinued running events; DF = discontinued field events.

MEN

1. UNITED STATES — 1102

Total	214	164	132	510
100	12	12	2	26
200	12	14	7	33
400	12	8	7	27
800	8	4	6	18
1500	2	6	4	12
St	2	1	4	7
5000	1	1	1	3
10,000	1	1	–	2
Mar	3	2	4	9
Walks	–	1	2	3
HH	15	13	13	41
IH	12	9	7	28
400R	12	–	–	12
1600R	10	2	–	12
HJ	12	11	7	30
PV	17*	11	9	37
LJ	16	12	6	34
TJ	3	4	2	9
SP	14	13	9	36
DT	13	8	12	33
HT	7	4	8	19
JT	1	2	2	5
Dec	9	5	4	18
DR	8	6	6	20
DF	12	14	10	36

*tie, 1908, 2 medals

2. FINLAND — 215

Total	43	31	24	98
400	–	–	1	1
1500	3	–	1	4
St	4	3	2	9
5000	7	4	1	12
10,000	7	3	4	14
Mar	2	–	3	5
IH	–	1	–	1
PV	–	2	1	3
LJ	–	–	1	1
TJ	1	–	2	3
SP	1	2	–	3
DT	2	3	–	5
HT	–	1	–	1
JT	5	6	4	15
Dec	1	2	–	3
DR	6	2	–	8
DF	4	2	4	10

3. GREAT BRITAIN — 205

Total	31	39	34	104
100	1	1	4	6
200	–	1	3	4
400	2	2	1	5
800	5	1	–	6
1500	3	3	2	8
St	4	6	2	12
5000	–	1	3	4
10,000	–	–	2	2
Mar	–	4	–	4
Walks	5	4	4	13
HH	–	2	1	3
IH	2	1	3	6
400R	1	2	2	5
1600R	2	3	3	8
HJ	–	2	–	2
LJ	1	–	1	2
TJ	1	–	–	1
SP	–	1	–	1
HT	–	–	1	1
DR	3	4	2	9

4. U.S.S.R. — 138

Total	21	23	29	73
100	1	–	1	2
200	1	–	–	1
400	–	–	1	1
800	–	1	–	1
St	–	2	2	4
5000	1	–	–	1
10,000	2	–	1	3
Walks	3	4	4	11
HH	–	–	1	1
IH	–	1	1	2
400R	–	4	1	5
HJ	3	1	2	6
LJ	–	–	2	2
TJ	3	3	3	9
SP	–	1	2	3
HT	4	3	3	10
JT	2	1	2	5
Dec	1	2	3	6

5. SWEDEN — 118

Total	15	19	35	69
400	–	–	1	1
800	–	1	–	1
1500	1	1	–	2
St	2	1	1	4
5000	–	–	4	4
10,000	–	1	2	3
Mar	–	–	2	2
Walks	3	2	2	7
HH	–	–	1	1
IH	–	–	1	1
400R	–	1	1	2
1600R	–	1	1	2
HJ	–	1	1	2

PV	–	–	2	2
LJ	1	–	2	3
TJ	2	3	2	7
DT	–	–	1	1
HT	–	2	1	3
JT	3	1	1	5
Dec	1	1	2	4
DR	1	3	5	9
DF	1	–	2	3

6. FRANCE — 66

Total	5	18	15	38
200	–	–	1	1
800	–	–	1	1
1500	–	3	1	4
St	–	–	2	2
5000	1	2	–	3
10,000	–	3	–	3
Mar	3	1	–	4
HH	1	1	–	2
IH	–	1	–	1
400R	–	1	2	3
1600R	–	2	2	4
HJ	–	1	2	3
TJ	–	1	–	1
DT	–	–	1	1
Dec	–	1	–	1
DR	–	1	2	3
DF	–	–	1	1

7= WEST GERMANY — 52

Total	5	11	15	31
100	1	–	–	1
400	–	2	–	2
800	–	–	1	1
1500	–	–	3	3
5000	–	1	2	3
Walks	1	–	–	1
IH	–	1	–	1
400R	1	–	2	3
1600R	–	1	3	4
PV	–	2	1	3
LJ	–	1	–	1
HT	–	1	1	2
JT	1	–	–	1
Dec	1	2	2	5

7= CANADA — 52

Total	8	8	12	28
100	1	–	2	3
200	2	–	–	2
400	–	1	1	2
800	–	2	2	4
1500	–	–	1	1
St	1	–	–	1
Walks	1	–	–	1
HH	1	–	–	1
IH	–	1	1	2
400R	–	–	2	2
HJ	1	1	–	2
PV	–	–	1	1
LJ	–	1	–	2
TJ	–	1	–	1
HT	–	1	–	1
DF	1	–	1	2

9. HUNGARY — 50

Total	5	10	15	30
100	–	–	1	1
800	–	1	–	1
1500	–	–	1	1
St	–	1	–	1
10,000	–	1	–	1

Mar	–	–	1	1
Walks	–	1	1	2
400R	–	–	1	1
HJ	–	1	1	2
LJ	–	–	1	1
SP	–	–	1	1
DT	1	–	-	1
HT	3	2	2	7
JT	1	2	4	7
DR	–	–	1	1
DF	–	1	–	1

10. EAST GERMANY — 47

Total	5	13	6	24
1500	–	1	–	1
St	–	–	1	1
5000	–	1	–	1
10,000	–	1	–	1
Mar	1	–	–	1
Walks	2	2	2	6
400R	–	1	–	1
HJ	–	1	–	1
PV	1	–	1	2
LJ	–	1	1	2
TJ	–	1	–	1
SP	1	–	1	2
DT	–	2	–	2
HT	–	1	–	1
JT	–	1	–	1

11= AUSTRALIA — 41

Total	6	7	9	22
100	–	–	2	2
200	–	1	1	2
800	2	–	–	2
1500	2	–	1	3
10,000	–	–	3	3
Walks	–	1	–	1
1600R	–	1	–	1
HJ	1	1	–	2
LJ	–	1	–	1
TJ	1	1	1	3
DR	–	1	1	2

11= GERMANY — 41

Total	3	9	14	26
100	–	1	2	3
200	–	–	1	1
400	–	1	2	3
800	–	–	2	2
St	–	–	1	1
400R	–	2	1	3
1600R	–	1	1	2
HJ	–	1	1	2
LJ	–	1	–	1
SP	1	–	2	3
HT	1	1	–	2
JT	1	–	–	1
Dec	–	–	1	1
DR	–	1	–	1

11= ITALY — 41

Total	7	4	12	23
200	1	–	1	2
800	–	2	–	2
1500	–	–	1	2
St	–	–	1	1
Mar	–	1	1	2
Walks	4	·	3	7
HH	–	–	1	1
IH	–	–	1	1
400R	–	1	2	3
TJ	–	–	1	1

DR	1	2	1	4

14. POLAND — 33

Total	7	4	4	15
400	–	–	1	1
St	1	1	–	2
5000	–	–	1	1
10,000	1	–	–	1
1600R	–	1	–	1
400R	–	1	–	1
HJ	1	–	–	1
PV	1	–	–	1
TJ	2	–	–	2
SP	1	–	–	1
HT	–	–	1	1
JT	–	1	–	1
DR	–	–	1	1

15. KENYA — 31

Total	5	6	4	15
400	–	–	1	1
800	–	1	2	3
1500	1	1	–	2
St	2	2	–	4
5000	–	1	1	2
10,000	1	–	–	1
1600R	1	1	–	2

16. NEW ZEALAND — 30

Total	7	1	7	15
100	–	–	1	1
800	2	–	–	2
St	3	–	2	5
5000	1	1	–	2
Mar	–	–	2	2
Walks	1	–	–	1
IH	–	1	1	2
DR	–	1	1	2

17. JAMAICA — 29

Total	4	7	3	14
100	–	3	1	4
200	1	–	–	1
400	2	2	–	4
800	–	2	1	3
1600R	1	–	1	2

18. CZECHOSLOVAKIA — 28

Total	5	5	3	13
1500	–	1	–	1
5000	1	1	–	2
10,000	2	–	–	2
Mar	1	–	–	1
Walks	–	1	–	1
TJ	–	–	2	2
DT	1	2	1	4

19= GREECE — 26

Total	2	6	8	16
800	–	–	1	1
Mar	1	1	–	2
PV	–	–	2	2
TJ	–	–	1	1
SP	–	1	1	2
DT	–	1	2	3
DF	1	3	1	5

19= JAPAN — 26

Total	4	4	6	14
Mar	1	1	2	4
PV	–	2	1	3
LJ	–	–	2	2
TJ	3	1	1	5

21. SOUTH AFRICA				23
Total	4	4	3	11
100	1	–	–	1
400	1	–	1	2
800	–	–	1	1
Mar	1	2	–	3
Walks	–	–	1	1
HH	1	1	–	2
1600R	–	1	–	1

22= BELGIUM				18
Total	2	5	2	9
800	–	2	–	2
1500	–	1	–	1
St	1	–	–	1
5000	1	–	–	1
10,000	--	1	–	1
Mar	–	1	2	3

22= Norway				18
Total	3	1	7	11
800	–	–	1	1
St	–	–	1	1
PV	–	–	1	1
LJ	–	–	1	1
TJ	–	–	1	1
JT	1	1	1	3
DR	1	–	–	1
DF	1	–	1	2

24. ETHIOPIA				13
Total	3	1	2	6
10,000	–	1	1	2
Mar	3	–	1	4

25= CUBA				12
Total	2	3	–	5
100	–	1	–	1
400	1	–	–	1
800	1	–	–	1
HH	–	1	–	1
400R	–	1	–	1

25= EIRE				12
Total	4	–	–	4
1500	1	–	–	1
IH	1	–	–	1
HT	2	–	–	2

27= BRAZIL				11
Total	2	1	3	6
HJ	–	–	1	1
TJ	2	1	2	5

27= SWITZERLAND				11
Total	–	5	1	6
800	–	1	–	1
1500	–	1	–	1
Walks	–	3	1	4

29. ARGENTINA				10
Total	2	2	–	4
Mar	2	1	–	3
TJ	–	1	–	1

30. TUNISIA				8
Total	1	2	1	4
5000	1	1	–	2
10,000	–	1	1	2

31. TRINIDAD-TOBAGO				7
Total	1	1	2	4
100	1	–	–	1
200	–	–	1	1
400	–	1	–	1
1600R	–	–	1	1

32= HOLLAND				5
Total	–	–	5	5
100	–	–	1	1
200	–	–	1	1
1500	–	–	1	1
5000	–	–	1	1
400R	–	–	1	1

32= MEXICO				5
Total	1	1	–	2
Walks	1	1	–	2

34= INDIA				4
200	–	1	–	1
DR	–	1	–	1

34= YUGOSLAVIA				4
Mar	–	1	–	1
HT	–	1	–	1

36= DENMARK				3
400	–	–	1	1
PV	–	1	–	1

36= ESTONIA				3
Mar	–	1	–	1
Dec	–	–	1	1

36= LATVIA				3
Walks	–	1	1	2

36= LUXEMBOURG				3
1500	1	–	–	1

36= UGANDA				3
400H	1	–	–	1

41= BOHEMIA				2
DT	–	1	–	1

41= SRI LANKA				2
IH	–	1		1

41= CHILE				2
Mar	–	1		1

41= HAITI				2
LJ	–	1	–	1

41= ICELAND				2
TJ	–	1	–	1

41= MOROCCO				2
Mar	–	1	–	1

41= PANAMA				2
100	–	–	1	1
200	–	–	1	1

41= PORTUGAL				2
10,000	–	1	–	1

41= PHILIPPINES				2
IH	–	–	1	1
HJ	–	–	1	1

41= TAIWAN				2
Dec	–	1	–	1

51= RUMANIA				1
JT	–	–	1	1

51= TURKEY				1
TJ	–	–	1	1

51= VENEZUELA				1
TJ	–	–	1	1

WOMEN

1. U.S.S.R.				101
Total	18	12	23	53
200	--	–	1	1
400	–	–	1	1
800	2	1	–	3
1500	2	–	–	2
H	1	2	1	4
400R	–	–	2	2
1600R	–	–	1	1
HJ	–	2	3	5
LJ	1	1	4	6
SP	5	2	3	10
DT	4	3	2	9
JT	2	1	4	7
Pen	1	--	1	2

2. EAST GERMANY				93
Total	17	15	12	44
100	1	2	--	3
200	2	1	1	4
400	1	1	1	3
800	–	–	3	3
1500	–	2	1	3
H	3	1	2	6
400R	1	1	–	2
1600R	2	–	–	2
HJ	1	–	–	1
LJ	1	–	1	2
SP	1	4	–	5
DT	1	1	1	3
JT	2	1	–	3
Pen	1	1	2	4

3. UNITED STATES				89
Total	19	12	8	39
100	5	2	1	8
200	2	–	1	3
400	–	–	1	1
800	1	–	–	1
H	1	1	–	2
400R	5	2	1	8
1600R	–	2	–	2
HJ	3	1	1	5
LJ	–	2	–	2
SP	–	–	1	1
DT	1	2	–	3
JT	1	–	2	3

4. AUSTRALIA   51

Total	9	7	10	26
100	2	1	3	6
200	2	2	3	7
400	1	--	1	2
800	–	1	–	1
H	3	1	3	7
400R	1	1	–	2
HJ	–	1	–	1

5. GREAT BRITAIN   46

Total	3	16	5	24
100	–	2	–	2
200	...	1	1	2
400	–	2	–	2
800	1	–	–	1
H	–	2	–	2
400R	–	2	3	5
HJ	--	5	–	5
LJ	1	1	1	3
Pen	1	1	..	2

6. WEST GERMANY   42

Total	6	10	4	20
100	1	--	1	2
200	--	2	–	2
400	–	1	–	1
800	1	--	–	1
H	–	–	1	1
400R	1	3	–	4
1600R	–	–	1	1
HJ	1	--.	–	1
LJ	1	--	..	1
SP	–	1	1	2
DT	–	1	–	1
JT	–	1	--	1
Pen	1	1	–	2

7. POLAND   38

Total	6	7	6	19
100	1	1	2	4
200	1	1	1	3
400	1	–	–	1
H	–	1	–	1
400R	1	–	1	2
HJ	–	1	–	1
LJ	1	2	..	3
DT	1	1	1	3
JT	–	–	1	1

8. RUMANIA   25

Total	5	4	2	11
800	–	1	–	1
H	--	1	–	1
HJ	2	–	–	2
LJ	1	–	–	1
DT	1	1	2	4
JT	1	1	–	2

9. GERMANY   20

Total	3	3	5	11
100	–	–	1	1
800	1	–	--	1
H	–	1	–	1
400R	–	–	1	1
HJ	–	–	1	1
DT	1	–	1	2
JT	1	2	1	4

10= CANADA   17

Total	2	3	5	10
100	–	2	1	3
H	--	–	1	1
400R	1	1	2	4
HJ	1	–	1	2

10= HOLLAND   17

Total	4	2	1	7
100	1	–	–	1
200	1	1	–	2
800	–	–	1	1
H	1	–	--	1
400R	1	–	–	1
HJ	–	1	–	1

12. BULGARIA   14

Total	1	4	3	8
800	–	1	–	1
HJ	–	1	1	2
LJ	--	1	–	1
SP	1	–	1	2
DT	–	1	1	2

13= CZECHOSLOVAKIA   13

Total	3	1	2	6
HJ	1	–	--	1
LJ	--	–	1	1
SP	–	–	1	1
DT	1	–	–	1
JT	1	1	–	2

13= FRANCE   13

Total	3	1	2	6
400	1	--	–	1
800	–	1	–	1
HJ	–	–	1	1
SP	1	–	–	1
DT	1	–	1	2

13= HUNGARY   13

Total	3	1	2	6
HJ	1	–	–	1
LJ	1	–	–	1
DT	–	–	1	1
JT	1	1	–	2
Pen	–	–	1	1

16. ITALY   11

Total	1	3	2	6
100	–	–	1	1
1500	..	–	1	1
H	1	--	–	1
HJ	–	1	–	1
SP	--	1	–	1
DT	–	1	–	1

17. AUSTRIA   8

Total	1	1	3	5
HJ	–	–	1	1
SP	–	–	1	1
JT	1	–	1	2
Pen	–	1	–	1

18. SOUTH AFRICA   6

Total	1	1	1	3
100	–	1	–	1
H	–	–	1	1
HJ	1	–	–	1

19= CUBA   4

Total	–	1	2	3
100	–	–	1	1
400R	–	1	1	2

19= NEW ZEALAND   4

Total	1	–	1	2
800	–	–	1	1
LJ	1	–	–	1

19= SWEDEN   3

Total	–	–	3	3
800	–	–	1	1
LJ	–	–	1	1
DT	–	–	1	1

22= ARGENTINA   2

LJ	–	1	–	1

22= CHILE   2

JT	–	1	–	1

22= FINLAND   2

JT	–	1	--	1

22= JAPAN   2

800	–	1	--	1

26= DENMARK   1

JT	–	–	1	1

26= TAIWAN   1

H	–	–	1	1

Miscellany: Finland has won 99 men's medals, but only one women's. Rumania has just 1 medal won by men, but 11 by women, including 5 golds. Countries strong in men's track but stronger in women's include East Germany (24 and 44 medals), Australia (22 and 26) and Poland (15 and 19).

Combining the men's and women's point totals in the preceding compilation: 1. United States 1191; 2. Great Britain 251; 3. USSR 239; 4. Finland 218; 5. East Germany 140.

U.S. Medals & Places

MEN

	1st	2nd	3rd	4th	5th	6th	Medals	Places
1896	9	6	1	1	—	—	16	17
1900	16	13	10	5	1	4	39	49
1904	22	22	19	20	12	13	63	108
1908	16	9	10	8	6	7	35	56
1912	14	14	11	13	14	6	39	72
1920	9	12	8	10	8	7	29	54
1924	12	10	10	6	9	7	32	54
1928	8	6	7	6	6	7	21	40
1932	11	10	5	7	6	5	26	44
1936	12	7	4	5	6	5	23	39
1948	11	5	9	6	2	5	25	38
1952	14	10	6	3	—	1	30	34
1956	15	9	4	6	1	1	28	36
1960	9	8	5	1	2	6	22	31
1964	12	5	3	3	5	4	20	32
1968	12	5	7	4	4	5	24	37
1972	6	7	6	7	5	1	19	32
1976	6	6	7	4	3	4	19	30
Totals	214	164	132	115	90	87	510	802

WOMEN

	1st	2nd	3rd	4th	5th	6th	Medals	Places
1928	1	2	1	1	—	1	4	6
1932	5	3	1	1	1	3	9	14
1936	2	—	—	—	1	1	2	4
1948	1	—	1	1	—	—	2	3
1952	1	—	—	—	—	1	1	2
1956	1	1	1	2	—	1	3	6
1960	3	—	1	–	—	1	4	5
1964	2	2	—	—	—	—	4	4
1968	3	1	—	2	1	4	4	11
1972	—	1	2	2	1	—	3	6
1976	—	2	1	—	3	2	3	8
Totals	19	12	8	9	7	14	39	69
Gr. Total	233	176	140	124	97	101	549	871

Olympic Trivia

Biggest winner on record in the ancient Olympics was Leonidas. He picked up 12 gold medals in 164-152 BC. Other big winners: Hermogenos (8 golds), 81-89 AD; Astylos (7) 488-480 BC; Chionis (6) 664-656 BC; Gorgos (6) dates unknown. . .

Jim Thorpe competed in 5 events in the 1912 Olympics. He won the decathlon and pentathlon, was 5th in the HJ and 7th in the LJ. His fifth event, ironically, was baseball (in an exhibition performance), the sport in which his semi-pro activities brought about his later disqualification. . .

World Records set in the Olympics in discontinued events: Alvin Kraenzlein in the 60m (1900); Ray Ewry in the standing HJ (1900) and standing LJ (1904); George Larner in the 10M Walk (1908); George Goulding in the 10,000m Walk (1912); Hannes Kolehmainen in the 3000m during the 3000m team race (1912). . .

No Olympic record now dates back farther than 1968. . . The first black to win a medal was George Poage (US), 3rd in the 200H and 400H in 1904. . .

Ever wonder why we have tie-breaking rules? 11 men tied for 6th in the 1936 PV. . .

Probably the closest finishes in the Games have been the men's 100s of 1932 and 1952. . . Only 2 countries have competed in every Olympics in both the men's and women's events—Australia and the United States. Greece and Great Britain have been in all the men's competitions and Canada and Poland in all the women's.

The youngest gold medalist is Bob Mathias, with his 1948 decathlon victory as a recent high school graduate aged 17. Five other high schoolers (US) have won golds. Ted Meredith took a pair in 1912 (800 and 1600R), plus a 4th in the 400; Lee Barnes won the 1928 PV, while Frank Hussey (1924), Frank Wykoff (1928) and Johnny Jones (1976) were on the 400R squad.

Other American preps competing in the Games: Howard Drew (1912) 100, injured, did not compete in final; Sid Bowman (1928) TJ, =9th; Cornelius Johnson (1932) HJ, 4th; Billy Brown (1936) TJ, didn't make final; Milt Campbell (1952) Dec, 2nd; Gerry Lindgren (1964) 10,000, 9th; Jim Ryun (1964) 1500, 9th in semi; Rey Brown (1968) HJ, 5th; Casey Carrigan (1968) PV, didn't make final; Dwayne Evans (1976) 200, 3rd. Houston McTear (1976) 100, made the team but didn't actually compete, injuring himself in the Trials. . .

The ancient-style discus, contested in 1908, was thrown from a standing position off a pedestal, 6" high and 28" x 32". . . The regulation that countries could enter only 3 in an event was adopted in 1932. The number varied before that, and it should be noted that in 1904 (in St. Louis) the U.S. took the first 6 places in 5 events. . .

Ray Ewry (SHJ, SLJ, STJ), Paavo Nurmi (5000, 10,000, cross country) and Shirley de la Hunty (100, 80H, 400R) are the only athletes to win 2 or more medals in each of 3 events.

World Records In The Olympics

Only 2 men's events, the HJ and the DT, have managed to go through their Olympic history without producing a World Record. Every women's event has seen a record. Records in the marathon and walks were made on the road, so are not official World Records, but we have listed those which were at the time the best ever. h=heat; sf=semifinal; q=qualifying round.

MEN

100
Frank Jarvis (US) 10.8=, 00 (h)
Walter Tewksbury (US) 10.8=, 00 (sf)
Donald Lippincott (US) 10.6, 12 (h)
Eddie Tolan (US) 10.3=, 32
Ralph Metcalfe (US) 10.3=, 32
Bob Hayes (US) 10.0=, 64
Jim Hines (US) 9.95, 68
200
Livio Berruti (It) 20.5=, 60 (sf)
Livio Berruti (It) 20.5=, 60
Tommie Smith (US) 19.83, 68
400
Bill Carr (US) 46.2, 32
Otis Davis (US) 44.9, 60
Carl Kaufmann (WG) 44.9=, 60
Lee Evans (US) 43.86, 68
800
Mel Sheppard (US) 1:52.8, 08
Ted Meredith (US) 1:51.9, 12
Tom Hampson (GB) 1:49.7, 32
Ralph Doubell (Aus) 1:44.3=, 68
Alberto Juantorena (Cuba) 1:43.5, 76
1500
Charles Bennett (GB) 4:06.2, 00
James Lightbody (US) 4:05.4, 04
Jack Lovelock (NZ) 3:47.8, 36
Herb Elliott (Aus) 3:35.6, 60
Steeple
Horace Ashenfelter (US) 8:45.4, 52
Anders Garderud (Swe) 8:08.0, 76
5000
Hannes Kolehmainen (Fin) 14:36.6, 12
10,000
Ville Ritola (Fin) 30:23.2, 24
Lasse Viren (Fin) 27:38.4, 72
Marathon
Hannes Kolehmainen (Fin) 2:32:36, 20
Abebe Bikila (Eth) 2:12:12, 64
20k Walk
Daniel Bautista (Mex) 1:24:41, 76
110 Hurdles
Forrest Smithson (US) 15.0, 08
Earl Thomson (Can) 14.8, 20
George Weightman-Smith (S Afr) 14.6, 28 (sf)
George Saling (US) 14.4=, 32 (sf)

Forrest Towns (US) 14.1=, 36 (sf)
Rod Milburn (US) 13.24, 72
400 Hurdles
Charlie Bacon (US) 57.0, 08 (h)
Harry Hillman (US) 56.4, 08 (sf)
Charlie Bacon (US) 55.0, 08
Frank Loomis (US) 54.0, 20
Glenn Hardin (US) 51.9, 32
Dave Hemery (GB) 48.12, 68
John Akii-Bua (Uga) 47.82, 72
Edwin Moses (US) 47.64, 76
4 x 100
United States 43.7, 12 (h)
Sweden 43.6, 12 (h)
Germany 43.6=, 12 (h)
Great Britain 43.4, 12 (sf)
Sweden 42.5, 12 (sf)
Germany 42.3, 12 (sf)
United States 42.2, 20
Great Britain 42.0, 24 (h)
Holland 42.0=, 24 (h)
United States 41.2, 24 (h)
United States 41.0, 24 (sf)
United States 41.0=, 24
United States 41.0=, 28
United States 40.6, 32 (h)
United States 40.0, 32
United States 40.0=, 36 (h)
United States 39.8, 36
United States 39.5, 56
West Germany 39.5=, 60 (h)
West Germany 39.5=, 60
United States 39.0, 64
Jamaica 38.6=, 68 (h)
Jamaica 38.3, 68 (sf)
United States 38.23, 68
United States 38.19, 72
4 x 400
United States 3:16.6, 12
United States 3:16.0, 24
United States 3:14.2, 28
United States 3:11.8, 32 (h)
United States 3:08.2, 32
United States 3:02.2, 60
United States 3:00.7, 64
United States 2:56.1, 68
PV
Frank Foss (US) 4.09 (13-5), 20

LJ
Robert LeGendre (US) 7.76 (25-5¾), 24
Bob Beamon (US) 8.90 (29-2½), 68
TJ
Anthony Winter (Aus) 15.52 (50-11), 24
Chuhei Nambu (Japan) 15.72 (51-7), 32
Naoto Tajima (Japan) 16.00 (52-6), 36
Adhemar da Silva (Brz) 16.22 (53-2½), 52
Giuseppe Gentile (It) 17.10 (56-1¼), 68 (q)
Giuseppe Gentile (It) 17.22 (56-6), 68
Viktor Saneyev (SU) 17.23 (56-6¼), 68
Nelson Prudencio (Brz) 17.27 (56-8), 68
Viktor Saneyev (SU) 17.39 (57-¾), 68
SP
Ralph Rose (US) 14.81 (48-7), 04
John Kuck (US) 15.87 (52-¾), 28
HT
Jozsef Csermak (Hun) 60.34 (197-11), 52
JT
Erik Lemming (Swe) 54.82 (179-10), 08
Erik Lemming (Swe) 60.64 (198-11), 12
Juho Saaristo (Fin) 61.00 (200-1), 12
Egil Danielsen (Nor) 85.70 (281-2), 56
Decathlon
Jim Thorpe (US) 8412 (6756—62), 12
Harold Osborn (US) 7710 (6668—62), 24
Paavo Yrjola (Fin) 8053 (6774—62), 28
Jim Bausch (US) 8462 (6896—62), 32
Glenn Morris (US) 7900 (7421—62), 36
Bob Mathias (US) 7887 (7731—62), 52
Nikolay Avilov (SU) 8456a, 72
Bruce Jenner (US) 8617a, 76

WOMEN

100
Elizabeth Robinson (US) 12.2, 28
Stella Walsh (Pol) 11.9, 32
Marjorie Jackson (Aus) 11.5=, 52
Wilma Rudolph (US) 11.3=, 60 (sf)
Wyomia Tyus (US) 11.2=, 64 (qf)
Irena Szewinska (Pol) 11.1=, 68 (sf)
Wyomia Tyus (US) 11.0, 68
Renate Stecher (EG) 11.07, 72
Annegret Richter (WG) 11.01, 76 (sf)
200
Marjorie Jackson (Aus) 23.6=, 52 (h)
Marjorie Jackson (Aus) 23.4, 52 (qf)
Irena Szewinska (Pol) 22.5, 68
Renate Stecher (EG) 22.40, 72
400
Irena Szewinska (Pol) 49.29, 76
800
Lina Radke (Ger) 2:16.8, 28

Lyudmila Shevtsova (SU) 2:04.3=, 60
Ann Packer (GB) 2:01.1, 64
Tatyana Kazankina (SU) 1:54.9, 76
1500
Lyudmila Bragina (SU) 4:06.5, 72 (h)
Lyudmila Bragina (SU) 4:05.1, 72 (sf)
Lyudmila Bragina (SU) 4:01.4, 72
Hurdles
Mildred Didrikson (US) 11.8=, 32 (h)
Mildred Didrikson (US) 11.7, 32
Evelyne Hall (US) 11.7=, 32
Shirley de la Hunty (Aus) 11.0=, 52 (h)
Shirley de la Hunty (Aus) 10.9, 52
Annelie Ehrhardt (EG) 12.59, 72
4 x 100
Canada 49.3, 28 (h)
Canada 48.4, 28
United States 47.0, 32
Germany 46.4, 36 (h)
Australia 46.1, 52 (h)
United States 45.9, 52
Australia 44.9, 56 (h)
Germany 44.9=, 56 (h)
Australia 44.5, 56
United States 44.4, 60 (h)
Poland 43.6, 64
United States 43.4, 68 (h)
Holland 43.4=, 68 (h)
United States 42.8, 68
West Germany 42.81, 72
4 x 400
East Germany 3:28.5, 72 (h)
East Germany 3:23.0, 72
East Germany 3:19.2, 76
HJ
Ethel Catherwood (Can) 1.59 (5-2½), 28
Jean Shiley (US) 1.65 (5-5), 32
Mildred McDaniel (US) 1.76 (5-9¼), 56
Ulrike Meyfarth (WG) 1.92= (6-3½), 72
LJ
Elzbieta Krzesinska (Pol) 6.35= (20-10), 56
Mary Rand (GB) 6.76 (22-2¼), 64
Viorica Viscopoleanu (Rum) 6.82 (22-4½), 68
SP
Galina Zybina (SU) 15.28 (50-1½), 52
Margitta Gummel (EG) 19.61 (64-4), 68
Nadyezhda Chizova (SU) 21.03 (69-0), 72
DT
Halina Konopacka (Pol) 39.62 (130-0), 28
JT
Yelena Gorchakova (SU) 62.40 (204-8), 64 (q)
Pentathlon
Irena Press (SU) 5246, 64
Mary Peters (GB) 4801, 72

Note: LeGendre's LJ record came in the pentathlon competition... Saaristo's JT record was made in the javelin thrown with each hand competition... 1928 and 1932 decathlon runner-up Akilles Jarvinen had "record" scores of 6815 and 7038 (better than the winners) on the current tables.

1980 Olympic Qualifying Marks

Each nation is allowed to enter one competitor in each event, and one relay team. Two more entries per event may be made if the athletes have made Olympic Qualifying Standard (the walks and marathon have no standards, just a 3-entry limit). To qualify for the 1980 Games, competitors must meet these standards in an outdoor meet between May 31, 1979 and July 6, 1980. Events through 400 meters have qualifying standards for both hand (in parentheses) and automatic timing.

MEN

100	10.44 (10.2)	HJ	2.18	7-2
200	21.04 (20.8)	PV	5.25	17-2¾
400	46.54 (46.4)	LJ	7.80	25-7
800	1:47.4	TJ	16.45	53-11¾
1500	3:40.0	SP	19.40	63-7¾
St	8:30.0	DT	60.00	196-10
5000	13:35.0	HT	70.00	229-8
10,000	28:30.0	JT	81.00	265-9
110HH	14.04 (13.8)	Dec	7550	
400H	50.54 (50.4)		(7650h)	

WOMEN

100	11.54 (11.3)	
200	23.64 (23.4)	
400	52.74 (52.6)	
800	2:02.8	
1500	4:10.0	
100H	13.64 (13.4)	
HJ	1.86	6-1¼
LJ	6.40	21-0
SP	16.60	54-5½
DT	56.00	183-9
JT	55.00	180-5
Pent	4260	(4300h)

Men's Olympic Records

100	9.95	Jim Hines (US) '68	4 x 400	2:56.1		United States '68
200	19.83	Tommie Smith (US) '68	HJ	2.25	7-4½	Jacek Wszola (Pol) '76
400	43.86	Lee Evans (US) '68	PV	5.50	18-½	Wolfgang Nordwig (EG) '72
800	1:43.5	Alberto Juantorena (Cu) '76				Tadeusz Slusarski (Pol) '76
1500	3:34.9	Kip Keino (Ken) '68				Antti Kalliomaki (Fin) '76
St	8:08.0	Anders Garderud (Swe) '76				Dave Roberts (US) '76
5000	13:20.3	Brendan Foster (GB) '76	LJ	8.90	29-2½	Bob Beamon (US) '68
10,000	27:38.4	Lasse Viren (Fin) '72	TJ	17.39	57-¾	Viktor Saneyev (SU) '68
Mar	2:09:55	Waldemar Cierpinski (EG) '76	SP	21.32	69-11½	Alek. Barishnikov (SU) '76
20kWk	1:24:41	Daniel Bautista (Mex) '76	DT	68.28	224-0	Mac Wilkins (US) '76
50kWk	3:56:12	Bernd Kannenberg (WG) '72	HT	77.52	254-4	Yuriy Syedikh (SU) '76
110HH	13.24	Rod Milburn (US) '72	JT	94.58	310-4	Miklos Nemeth (Hun) '76
400H	47.64	Edwin Moses (US) '76	Dec	8617		Bruce Jenner (US) '76
4 x 100	38.19	United States '72				

Women's Olympic Records

100	11.01	Annegret Richter (WG) '76	4 x 400	3:19.2		East Germany '76
200	22.37	Barbel Eckert (EG) '76	HJ	1.93	6-4	Rosem. Ackermann (EG) '7
400	49.29	Irena Szewinska (Pol) '76	LJ	6.82	22-4½	Vior. Viscopoleanu (Rum) '
800	1:54.9	Tatyana Kazankina (SU) '76	SP	21.16	69-5	Ivanka Khristova (Bul) '76
1500	4:01.4	Lyudmila Bragina (SU) '72	DT	69.00	226-4	Evelin Schlaak (EG) '76
100H	12.59	Annelie Ehrhardt (EG) '72	JT	65.94	216-4	Ruth Fuchs (EG) '76
4 x 100	42.55	East Germany '76	Pent	4801		Mary Peters (GB) '72